Dr. Ray m. Frank

An Historical S
of the Old Testament

D0020092

An
Historical Survey
of the
Old Testament

Second Edition

Eugene H. Merrill

BAKER BOOK HOUSE
Grand Rapids, Michigan 49516

Copyright 1991 by
Baker Book House Company

Printed in the United States of America

Library of Congress Cataloging-in-Publication Data

Eugene H. Merrill
An historical survey of the Old Testament/Eugene H. Merrill.—2nd ed.
        p.   cm.
Includes bibliographical references and indexes.
ISBN 0-8010-6283-7
        1. Bible.—O.T.—History of Biblical events. I. Title.
BS1197.M44   1991
221.9'5—dc20

91-31821
CIP

THE AUTHOR

Eugene H. Merrill is Professor of Old Testament Studies at Dallas Theological Seminary, a position he has held since 1975. He is a graduate of Bob Jones University and holds the M.A. in Hebrew Studies from New York University and the M.Phil. and Ph.D. from Columbia University. In addition to the present work, a complete revision of the original publication of 1966, the author's major published works include *Qumran and Predestination: A Theological Study of the Thanksgiving Hymns* (Leiden: Brill, 1975); *Kingdom of Priests: A History of Old Testament Israel* (Grand Rapids: Baker, 1987); *1, 2 Chronicles*, Bible Study Commentary (Grand Rapids: Zondervan, 1988); and *Haggai, Zechariah, Malachi*, Wycliffe Exegetical Commentary (Chicago: Moody, 1992).

Professors who wish to order the test bank for this book should contact Baker Book House, P.O. Box 6287, Grand Rapids, Michigan 49516.

Contents

10. Return and Renewal   279
    The Babylonia-Persia Contest
    The Age of the Captivity
    The Persian Empire
    The First Return from Babylonia
    Subsequent Returns from Babylonia
    Intertestamental History

Preface

The passing of twenty-five years has not essentially altered the premises and concerns that underlay the initial publication of *An Historical Survey of the Old Testament* in 1966. That it passed through fifteen printings over the years also testifies to the ongoing need for a work like this, one that adheres uncompromisingly to the Old Testament as inerrant Scripture and yet, in a clear and fair manner, addresses the difficult issues raised by contemporary biblical scholarship.

Neither time nor knowledge has stood still in a quarter of a century, however, so the time has come for a complete revision of the original work. Former students, colleagues, and the publisher have insisted that the project be undertaken, especially since the fundamental need of undergraduate teachers and their students remains the same as ever: an up-to-date, scholarly, and clearly written exposition and defense of the Old Testament as an historical record of the Word of God. The basic approach in this revision is identical to that of the original edition, but certain sections are rewritten in light of fresh discovery and new insights. Issues dominant in 1966 seem now not so important, but new ones have arisen, issues that could scarely have been anticipated then. Hence, the present work eliminates some old material and adds some new, making the volume familiar to earlier readers but renewed in its credibility and usefulness by virtue of its contemporaneity.

The author expresses special gratitude to friends and family for their continued encouragement to set about this task. His wife, Janet, prepared the test bank. He stands deeply in debt to Mrs. Linda Worrell, who with unbounded patience and enthusiasm undertook the word processing as if it were her own project. In particular, he dedicates the final result to the finest model of collegiality he has ever experienced, the faculty of Old Testament studies of Dallas Theological Seminary: Dick Averbeck, Bob Chisholm, Don Glenn, Mark Rooker, and Rick Taylor.

Preface to the First Edition

Having taught beginning Old Testament courses for a number of years, the author has felt the need for some time for a text that would meet some needs that were not being met by other books in the field. Being firmly committed to the conservative school of thought, he has had to forgo works that, because of their critical historical and theological biases, were deemed inappropriate for the conservative freshman or sophomore student who is in the rudimentary stages of his Old Testament study. And yet many of the conservative books either have not had the depth of scholarship necessary for a college approach or have gone beyond the ability of the beginning student in their details and presuppositions. Moreover, many of them are restricted to too narrow an approach, such as an emphasis on content, historical background, doctrine, or other specific areas.

Since this study approaches the Old Testament as an historical record of God's revelation to the world through Israel, the historical structure of the Old Testament has been the basic framework. To this has been added information from the ancient Near Eastern world in which biblical history took place, including discussions of geographical, historical, and archaeological matters that illuminate the biblical story. Because of current criticisms of the reliability of the Old Testament in its scientific statements, special attention has been paid to this aspect of the record.

Every effort has been made to eliminate paraphrases of the narrative sections of the Old Testament, but naturally some retelling has been necessary in order to maintain coherence and smoothness. In those areas of the Scripture where the account does not speak so clearly of itself the present work provides special attention. It is hoped that the student will study this volume as an ancillary to the Word of God, an aid to its better understanding.

The author hereby expresses much-deserved recognition to those who have contributed long hours in seeing this most enjoyable project to completion. First, to his wife, Janet, who typed the entire final draft and offered unending encouragement and inspiration, a special thanks is due. And warm appreciation is gladly given to Miss Pené Cansler of the Bob Jones University English department who offered invaluable suggestions concerning mechanics and style.

Finally, the generous help and support of many of his students, particularly Mr. William Alford, must not go unrecognized. It is with a sincere prayer that this effort may create a love for the Old Testament as the inspired Word of God that this book is made available.

1

Foundations for Study
of the Old Testament

The fullest understanding of any book depends in part on knowledge of its author, purpose, and overall theme. It helps to have this knowledge before reading a book in its entirety.

This is particularly true of the Old Testament, for the uniqueness of its authorship and contents renders it especially vulnerable to misunderstanding. Many of the literary criteria applied to other works are simply not sufficient to make plain the true nature of this most important composition. For example, how many books consist in turn of thirty-nine separate books, written over a period of one thousand years by perhaps forty writers? How many claim dogmatically to be special revelation from God? How many speak of a people whose entire complex history is interwoven with miraculous, divine intervention, a history whose fundamental purpose is to provide not mere information but truth? In short, any book that has survived for well over two thousand years and has, more than any other literature, revolutionized the course of human history must be approached with more than usual care. It must be addressed with full consideration of its importance as literature, to say nothing of its character as the Word of God. Thus, the study of the Old Testament must be preceded by a review of the introductory materials essential to an intelligent and thorough appreciation of its nature and content.

TABLE 1

The Books of the Old Testament

Hebrew Arrangement	Protestant Arrangement
Torah	*Pentateuch*
Genesis	Genesis
Exodus	Exodus
Leviticus	Leviticus
Numbers	Numbers
Deuteronomy	Deuteronomy
Nebi'im	*History*
Joshua	Joshua
Judges (and Ruth)	Judges
Samuel	Ruth
Kings	1 Samuel
Isaiah	2 Samuel
Jeremiah (and Lamentations)	1 Kings
Ezekiel	2 Kings
The Twelve	1 Chronicles
	2 Chronicles
	Ezra
	Nehemiah
Kethubim	*Poetry*
Psalms	Job
Job	Psalms
Proverbs	Proverbs
Ruth (if not with Judges)	Song of Songs
Song of Songs	Ecclesiastes
Ecclesiastes	
Lamentations (if not with Jeremiah)	
Esther	
Daniel	
Ezra-Nehemiah	
Chronicles	
	Major Prophets
	Isaiah
	Jeremiah
	Lamentations
	Ezekiel
	Daniel

Hebrew Arrangement	Protestant Arrangement
	Minor Prophets
	Hosea
	Joel
	Amos
	Obadiah
	Jonah
	Micah
	Nahum
	Habakkuk
	Zephaniah
	Haggai
	Zechariah
	Malachi

The Book Itself

The Contents of the Old Testament

The Old Testament is that collection of sacred writings that, virtually since the time of their composition, have been considered by the Jews to be Scripture. The Christian church of the first century recognized the Old Testament Scriptures as its source of doctrine and ethics, and when its own literature, the New Testament, was composed, it was added to the Old Testament; both together became accepted as God's Word written. From these earliest times, the two together have been known as the Bible (Greek *biblion* or "book"). Even before the Christian era, the Jews recognized a threefold division in the Old Testament: the Law (*Torah*), the Prophets (*Nebi'im*), and the Writings (*Kethubim*).[1] In the process of translation from the original Hebrew to the various vernaculars, the Jewish division of the Old Testament has basically been followed, though the order of the books has varied, but it has become customary among Protestants to speak of a fivefold rather than threefold division in the English versions. They designate the first section Pentateuch (Greek *Pentateuchos*, or "five scrolls"), which corresponds to the Hebrew division Torah. These are the five books ascribed to Moses. The second division is that of History, twelve books of generally anonymous authorship included in the Hebrew division known as the Prophets, or, more specifically, Former Prophets, because they were thought to have been written by early

1. Prologue to Ecclesiasticus; Luke 24:44; Flavius Josephus *Contra Apionem* 1:8, in *Josephus' Complete Works*, trans. William Whiston (Peabody, Mass.: Hendrickson, 1987).

(pre-ninth-century) men who were prophets or at least had the prophetic gift. The third section, Poetry, consists of five books characterized by literature of a poetic or philosophical nature. David and Solomon were their authors for the most part, though some were composed by lesser known or anonymous individuals. The fourth division is the Major Prophets, so called because they are lengthy and were the product of well-known prophets or men with the prophetic gift. These consist of five books, two written by the same man (Jeremiah). Finally, there is the collection of twelve books known as the Minor Prophets, or, in the Hebrew Bible, simply "The Twelve." These are not designated minor because they are relatively less important than the major but because they are generally much shorter. For example, Isaiah contains sixty-six chapters, and Obadiah, one.

There is a numerical pattern in the total books of each of the sections: five Law, twelve History, five Poetry, five Major Prophets, and twelve Minor Prophets, a total of thirty-nine in all. The Hebrew Old Testament contains only twenty-two books (or twenty-four, if Ruth and Lamentations are counted separately), but in many cases these books consist of two or more of the books in the English versions. For example, the twelve books of the Minor Prophets in English are included in only one book in the Hebrew, which reduces the Hebrew total by at least eleven. And the books of Samuel, Kings, and Chronicles are not broken up, a factor that reduces the Hebrew total by three more.

The names of the various sections should not lead one to conclude that the sections embrace only materials suggested by the names. Just because the first part is called "The Law" does not mean that it contains nothing but laws or rules or ritual. Law per se makes up only a part of the Pentateuch; there are also history, poetry, and prophecy. Likewise, there are law, poetry, and prophecy in the historical books; law, history, and prophecy in the poetic books, and so on. The names assigned to the sections indicate that the major themes or emphases of the sections are of one kind or another.

The historical period embraced by the Pentateuch is from the creation (date unknown) to the beginning of the conquest of Canaan by the Israelites at the end of the fifteenth century B.C. The historical books continue the history from ca. 1400 to ca. 420 B.C., the time of the composition of Chronicles. The poetic books follow no particular historical order but reflect practically every age of Israel's history from the beginning to the end. It is not incorrect to say, however, that Hebrew poetry and wisdom literature flourished at the time of the United Kingdom under David and Solomon, because well over half of the poetic writings were compiled by these two men alone. The major prophets lived and ministered in the period from ca. 740 to 540 B.C., and the minor prophets occupied a longer span, from ca. 800 to 450 B.C. It is clear, then, that many of the prophets were contemporaries and in some instances probably were close friends.

The Composition of the Old Testament

The question must inevitably arise as to the process of selection of the various books that make up the Old Testament. This is especially true in light of the fact that there were other documents written in the historical period of the Old Testament, some possibly by the biblical writers themselves.[2] How did the early Hebrews know which of these should be included in their Scriptures and which should not? How can one be sure that the books now in the Old Testament should be there? What would happen if archaeologists should suddenly discover another book written by Jeremiah, for example, and subsequently lost? Would it find its way into the Bible or should it be rejected, though other writings of Jeremiah are accepted? These and similar questions indicate some of the problems involved in the area of biblical study known as the *canonicity* of the Scriptures. Of the entire collection of ancient documents, which should be and are in truth the very Word of God?

The word *canon* comes from the Hebrew *qaneh*, which means "reed" or "rod." The *qaneh* was the reedy plant that grew beside marshy waters, the stalk of which was often used by the ancients as a measuring stick because of its length and straightness. It was a criterion by which the short could be distinguished from the long, or the crooked from the straight. In time it signified any standard by which anything could be measured, specifically, the standard by which the authenticity or spuriousness of a literary document could be evaluated. When applied to the Scriptures, a book was canonical or not depending on its adherence to certain well-defined principles. Most of these were more or less arbitrary, but are nevertheless valid when considered together.

Jewish scholars, some even before the time of Christ, agreed that for any document to be canonical it must have been written before 400 B.C. or thereabouts.[3] This, of course, is one of the reasons why Jews of the first century A.D. rejected the New Testament as Scripture. Also, they held that a document, to be Scripture, must have been written by a prophet or an individual who at least had the prophetic gift. Moses, the first writer,

---

2. Cf. Num. 21:44; Josh. 10:13; 2 Sam. 1:18; 1 Kings 11:41; 16:27; 22:45.

3. 4 Esdras 14:45–46; *Baba Bathra* 14b–15a. For all these arguments see William Henry Green, *Old Testament Canon and Philology* (Princeton, N.J.: The Princeton Press, 1889), 3–37. See also Roger T. Beckwith, *The Old Testament Canon of the New Testament Church and Its Background in Early Judaism* (Grand Rapids: Eerdmans, 1985); Robert I. Vasholz, *The Old Testament Canon in the Old Testament Church: The Internal Rationale for Old Testament Canonicity* (Lewiston, N.Y.: Edwin Mellen, 1990).

was a prophet, and, it was maintained, no prophet ever arose after Malachi, the writer of the latest book of the Old Testament.[4] Therefore, until God should see fit to raise up a new prophet, there could be no new additions to the Scriptures. Moreover, for a writing to be canonical, it had to be extant. This meant that even if a prophet had written other documents than those included in the Old Testament, if those writings had been lost and never recovered before the "close" of the canon (ca. 400 B.C.), they could not have been Scripture. The reasoning was that it was not believable that God should inspire a man to write Holy Writ and then not be able or care to preserve it. Once a Scripture was written, it was for the benefit of every subsequent age, not just the age in which it was written. If it could meet only the immediate needs of the generation in which it was compiled, it must not be Scripture; it lacked the timelessness that is a characteristic of true Scripture.

Perhaps the most important canonical criterion, however, was inspiration.[5] Any literature not written under the supernatural influence of the Spirit of God was automatically excluded from consideration in the canon, even if it met all the other qualifications. This was much more nebulous than the other standards, but it was at the same time the most important. There came to be a very early and universal consensus among Jewish religious leaders in regard to this matter of inspiration, and though the ways and means by which they ascertained the existence or nonexistence of inspiration cannot be determined today, nobody who accepts the supernatural character of the Old Testament would seriously question their opinions and conclusions in the matter. Further attention will be paid to this crucial question in the next section.

Apparently, the books of the Old Testament were canonized as soon as they were written, or very shortly after.[6] For instance, Joshua, the immediate successor to Moses, recognized not only that his predecessor wrote the Pentateuch but also that it was the authoritative Word of God (Josh. 1:7–8; 22:5, 9). In effect, Joshua and his generation canonized the books of Moses. Similarly, the other books of the Old Testament were accorded recognition as Scripture in following generations, though their recognition as such may not have been as immediately forthcoming as in the case of the Pentateuch. It seems reasonably clear, however, that by the time of the third century B.C., at the latest, all of the books now recognized as Old

4. R. Laird Harris, *Inspiration and Canonicity of the Bible: An Historical and Exegetical Study* (Grand Rapids: Zondervan, 1957), 170–79.

5. Ibid., 178.

6. Herbert Edward Ryle, *The Canon of the Old Testament: An Essay on the Gradual Growth and Formation of the Hebrew Canon of Scripture* (London: Macmillan and Company, 1892), 183.

Testament Scripture were in the canon. There is no convincing basis to the commonly held argument that the development of the canon was a very slow and uncertain matter, not achieving its final form until the end of the first century A.D. or later.[7]

The Nature of the Old Testament

The most honest evaluation of the Old Testament that can be made, on the basis of both internal and external evidence, is that it is the inspired Word of God. Up to the present day, critics have taken issue with this conclusion, but its truthfulness has never been successfully assailed. Since its inception, the Old Testament has been subjected to attacks of all kinds, and reams of apologetic materials have been written to defend the Book in the face of all this criticism. The essential and inescapable question that critics and traditionalists alike must settle is simply this: Is the Old Testament the verbally inspired Word of God, or is it not?

Sincere and honest men of all generations have taken pen in hand to prove that the Bible teaches its own inspiration, and their labors are commendable, but this approach is assailed, and rightly, as a form of theological circular reasoning in the contemporary conflict. The basic issue today is not so much whether the Bible claims to be inspired, for even its most radical critics admit this, but whether the Bible can be believed when it teaches such a doctrine concerning itself. If the Bible is inspired, then any statement that it makes even with regard to its own inspiration must be believed; if, however, the Bible is not inspired, then every statement it makes, including any about its inspiration, is suspect. An uninspired Bible certainly cannot make authoritative statements about its own nature. Even if the words of Jesus and the apostles teach that the Old Testament is inspired (which they certainly do),[8] how can one be sure that Jesus and the apostles actually said such things unless he first of all believes that the Old and New Testaments are inspired? In short, one must first believe a priori, on the basis of faith, that the Bible is inspired, and only then can he believe with confidence what it says about its inspiration as well as matters other than its inspiration. This should not be disturbing to the believer. In the final analysis, all the great truths of Christian theology rest on a foundation of faith. It is no more irrational to accept the doctrine of inspiration by faith than it is to accept any of the other doctrines of the Christian mes-

---

7. Robert Henry Pfeiffer, *Introduction to the Old Testament* (New York: Harper and Brothers, 1941), 50–70; Curt Kuhl, *The Old Testament: Its Origins and Composition*, trans. C. T. M. Herriott (Richmond: John Knox, 1961), 27–33; J. Alberto Soggin, *Introduction to the Old Testament, from Its Origins to the Closing of the Alexandrian Canon*, rev. ed. (Philadelphia: Westminster, 1980), 18.

8. John 10:35; Matt. 5:18; 2 Tim. 3:16–17; 2 Pet. 1:20–21.

sage, all of which must be taken on that basis alone. In fact, what essential truth of any area of life is not couched in a framework of faith?

Argument must not be wasted then on whether the Bible teaches its own inspiration, for assuredly it does. Instead, we must focus on what inspiration means to the believer who has accepted this basic premise by faith. The answers are found in two key passages in the New Testament: 2 Timothy 3:16 and 2 Peter 1:20–21. Here it is possible to see both the source of the Old Testament and the means by which it was transmitted to the ancient writers. In the former passage, Paul argues that "every scrip-ture" (the Old Testament) is "God-breathed" (*theopneustos*) and is prof-itable. The qualifying adjective *all* or *every* (as it may be translated), com-bined with the passive participle, indicates that every part of the Old Testament originated with God apart from any human assistance or inventiveness.[9] In other words, God is the ultimate author of the entire Old Testament. This, however, does not explain how the revelation of the Old Testament came from God, through man, to the written parchment or papyrus. Peter does explain this process of revelation. He writes that "prophecy" (or Scripture) in "old time" (Old Testament period) was not a product of human ingenuity, thus agreeing with Paul, but that "holy men of God spoke as they were carried along (*pheromenoi*) by the Holy Spirit." This means that they spoke, but that what they spoke was somehow not their message but that of God himself.

These two passages are sufficient to indicate both the origin of Scripture and its mode of transmission; they should satisfy the inquisitiveness of any honest seeker concerning the essential nature of the Word of God. However, there still remain unanswered questions, matters that can be solved only by a certain amount of reconstruction and evaluation based on the available data. There are problems such as the great variety of styles and vocabularies employed by the Old Testament writers. If the writers were only recipients of revelation and were, in a sense, passive while being spoken through, how can one account for this variety? Is it likely that God himself would write in such a number of ways to express the one basic rev-elation of the Old Testament? Were the human writers nothing but automata, robots impervious to human sensibility and will? Such questions are valid and deserve answers, even though many of these answers must be sought in a largely inductive consideration of all the evidence.

It is important to note, first of all, that passivity as implied by Peter involves nothing more than the limitation placed on the "holy men of

9. B. B. Warfield, *The Inspiration and Authority of the Bible* (Philadelphia: Presbyterian and Reformed, 1948), 296.

God" as regards the origin of their messages; it has nothing to do with their expression of that message except to render that expression inerrant. They were not permitted to invent their message, but they were permitted to express it within the bounds of their own intellectual and cultural resources, at the same time being divinely shielded from error of content. On the one hand, a comparatively uneducated, roughhewn Amos was given a divine message, but he was not expected to express it in a style and with words beyond his experience. On the other hand, a refined, cultured, poetic Isaiah was entrusted with revelation and permitted to express it in the inimical manner so much admired in his writings. All the time, both men were preserved from error of fact or judgment of any kind.

Paul suggests, in 2 Timothy 3:16, that the Old Testament is verbally inspired; that is, that every word is the Word of God as God intended it to be. This is also a matter of concern, especially in light of the preceding argument regarding individuality of style and vocabulary on the part of the several writers. How is it possible for men to express revealed truth in their own ways and yet for the result to be considered the Word of God to the very smallest particle? If the writers were permitted to express themselves in their own ways, how could the product be considered the words of God's choice? Perhaps the best explanation may be derived analogically.

When a businessman wishes to communicate with an associate or a potential customer, he usually leaves the actual composition and expression of the communication in the hands of his secretary. Perhaps on leaving the office in the middle of the morning he informs her that he wishes to send a letter to Mr. A and he wishes to express ideas 1, 2, 3, and 4. He further notifies her that he will return in the afternoon to check the letter before it is mailed. She goes to work on the letter and, employing her own mode of expression and vocabulary, eventually produces a letter that she feels will be satisfactory. That afternoon the employer returns, examines the letter, and says reassuringly, "That is exactly what I wanted you to say, sentence by sentence, word by word, and even punctuation mark by punctuation mark. If I had written it with my own hand I would not have said anything different in any respect." The secretary has expressed the intentions of her employer to the point of exactness, but she has done so in her own manner.

Bearing in mind the deficiencies in any such parallel, one may still gather from this the essential idea of inspiration. Through some inexplicable means God revealed his intentions to the biblical writers, who in turn recorded them in writing while retaining their own individuality and God's purposes at the same time. One essential point, of course, is that the writers were not mere stenographers. In his omniscience, God had prepared them from before their creation to write what he wanted and in the manner of his choice.

It might be well to point out the differences between inspiration and other concepts that sometimes are confused with it. First of all, inspiration is not tantamount to dictation, except in the sense already described. Perhaps it may be safe to say that inspiration is dictated revelation, if a mechanical dictation is not meant. If the term *dictation* can be stretched to include a qualifiedly controlled mediation of divine truth to man, the use of the term may be legitimate. If it is associated with the idea of Athenagoras that the Scripture writers were nothing but musical instruments on whom God played and that they lost contact with reality,[10] then *dictation* must be rejected as a descriptive term.

Too, one should not interchange the ideas of inspiration and special (or biblical) revelation. The latter is the corpus of truth or information that originates in God and can be made known to man only by divine self-disclosure. Inspiration is the process by which this impartation of revelation took place in inscripturated form. Revelation is the truth; inspiration is the means God used to bring that revelation into human experience via the written page.

Another term frequently misunderstood is *illumination*. This has to do with enlightening of the mind of the believer by the Holy Spirit so that he might understand the Word of God. Paul says that this may be the gift of every believer, not just an esoteric few (1 Cor. 2:9–16). The complete relationship, then, is as follows: God's truth, or revelation, is made available to his servants, the writers of Scripture, by inspiration, and the understanding of that truth in written form is possible through the Spirit's ministry of illumination, a blessing possible to all in whom he dwells.

The Languages of the Old Testament

The greatest part of the Old Testament, by far, was written in Hebrew, a branch of the larger family of languages known as Semitic. In its written form, this was a vowelless, alphabetic tongue that apparently was the official vernacular of the Israelites at least as early as the time of Moses (fifteenth century B.C.). A few sections, notably in Daniel (2:4–7:28), Ezra (4:8–6:18; 7:12–26), and Jeremiah (10:11), were written in a language known as Aramaic, also a Semitic language and closely related to Hebrew. By New Testament times, Aramaic had replaced Hebrew completely as the lingua franca among the Jews, and it is most likely that Jesus himself spoke this language except in synagogue discourses, when he may have

10. Eugene H. Merrill, "Name Terms of the Old Testament Prophet of God," *Journal of the Evangelical Theological Society* 14 (1971): 246.

used Hebrew. Following the completion of the Hebrew canon, the Old Testament was translated into various languages, like Greek (the Septuagint version of ca. 250 B.C.), Syriac, and Latin.

Texts of the Old Testament

As the years passed following the composition of the original manuscripts by the prophets and other Old Testament writers, scribes copied these originals many times, and the originals eventually disappeared. It is likely that they were written on perishable materials like papyrus and parchments, which, because of the rigors of Palestine's climate, could not long survive. However, before these originals were destroyed, every precaution was taken to make absolutely certain that they were exactly preserved in copies. An excellent example of the meticulous care involved in the successful transmitting of the sacred Scriptures may be seen in Jeremiah 36, where the prophet commanded his scribe, Baruch, to duplicate exactly the copy of the book he had written and King Jehoiakim had destroyed in the fire. This reverence for the Word of God written did not diminish with the passing of years; if anything, it increased with every generation. Hundreds of years after the books were composed, scribes devised most ingenious means of guaranteeing the accurate copying of the scrolls. For example, they would count the number of words in a chapter or even a book and then check it by the number of words in their copy. If there was a difference, they would check the entire copy until they located the error, and they would correct it without hesitation. There is even evidence that they would determine the middle word or letter of a book and then check their copy to see that its middle word or letter corresponded with that of the original.[11]

As more and more copies were made and a multitude of translations were produced, it is easy to understand that slight differences in the texts began to appear, especially when the copying and translating were done by individuals who did not ensure carefully enough against copying errors. As a result, the manuscripts that have survived down to the present day, representing many Hebrew text traditions as well as numerous ancient translations and versions, do not agree in every single point. Yet, it is remarkable to note that even those that vary most do so in matters of very little importance, and certainly it is safe to say that their differences are of no theological or doctrinal moment whatsoever. Furthermore, those Hebrew texts that differ most from the Hebrew textus receptus (received

11. Ernst Würthwein, *The Text of the Old Testament*, trans. Peter R. Ackroyd (New York: Macmillan, 1957), 15.

text) are not regarded by scholars as possessing much independent authority on the whole, so the differences are even more minimized.[12]

Until forty-five years ago, the oldest major Hebrew manuscripts dated
from the tenth century A.D., and there were several others from a little
later. The present Hebrew Bible is based mostly on these medieval texts,
and although conservatives at least always believed they were essentially
the same as the Old Testament originals, there was no way to demonstrate
this. Then, in 1947, a revolutionary discovery was made at Wadi Qumran,
on the northwest shore of the Dead Sea. There, in a cave, a shepherd lad
found the first of over forty thousand fragments representing hundreds of
scrolls, including parts of every book of the Old Testament except Esther.
With great anticipation these scrolls were unrolled and translated over a
period of years. The excitement of the find was due to the soon-estab-
lished fact that they came in some cases from a period at least 150 years
before Christ. Here was a chance to see how the modern Hebrew texts
compared with some written over a thousand years earlier than the ones
that had previously been considered most ancient. And to the delight of
those who had all along maintained the integrity of the modern Hebrew
text, those of Qumran were, in the majority of the cases, essentially the
same. The major differences (mostly in Samuel and Kings) can be
accounted for by recognizing that in some cases the scribes at Qumran had
preferred the Septuagint, or Greek, version over the Hebrew, but this by
no means proves that the Septuagint was the more accurate reflection of
the originals as written by the Bible writers.[13]

In short, it is safe to say without hesitation that the originals exist inso-
far as they were faithfully preserved by godly and exacting scribes down
through the ages. It is not overstating the case to say that one can hold in
his hands the Old Testament of the prophets. This is only as it must be,
for it is theologically inconceivable that God, after inspiring the original
manuscripts, would permit them to lose their value as inerrant revelation
by failing to preserve them. The very inspiration of the Old Testament
assures its faithful textual preservation.

Modern Critical Theories

Within the past two centuries, scholars have developed various theories
purporting to explain the biblical phenomena. These postulates reject the
explanation of the origin and development of biblical truth as found in

12. D. Winton Thomas, "The Textual Criticism of the Old Testament," in *The Old Testament and
Modern Study: A Generation of Discovery and Research*, ed. H. H. Rowley (Oxford: Clarendon, 1951),
244–45.
13. F. F. Bruce, *Second Thoughts on the Dead Sea Scrolls* (Grand Rapids: Eerdmans, 1964), 96.

the Bible itself and insist that the Bible must be judged according to certain literary, historical, and philosophical criteria. This entire process of evaluating the Bible with the end in view of ascertaining its "real nature" is known most commonly as higher criticism (not to be confused with lower or textual criticism, a perfectly legitimate science having to do with matters of text composition and collation).

Higher criticism first began to command widespread attention by Old Testament scholars in the middle of the nineteenth century, following the era of German rationalism and the French Enlightenment. Without question, one specific impetus was the revolution in the biological world occasioned by the publication of Charles Darwin's *The Origin of Species* in 1862. As Julian Huxley states, it was not long until every part of the intellectual world was permeated by this philosophy of gradual development, and everything including religion became explicable only in relation to it.[14] Through the work of men like Julius Wellhausen and Abraham Kuenen, the Old Testament was reinterpreted in line with the presuppositions of evolutionary theological and historical development. The Pentateuch was no longer considered a work of Moses, because it allegedly presupposed a much higher theological development than Moses, assuming that he actually lived (which many came to doubt), could have expressed. In fact, the Pentateuch could no longer be considered a unity, because some of its teachings seemed to express later theological and historical concepts than others.[15] The critics assigned the remaining books of the Old Testament to various dates and authors, depending on their internal adherence to the literary and historical canons that became increasingly accepted among critical scholars.

This modern reconstruction of the Old Testament was based on an earlier and widely held view that the Old Testament, and especially the Pentateuch, was made up of a multitude of documents eventually woven together skillfully by editors (redactors). In many cases, it is held, the names of well-known individuals in Israel's history, such as Moses, were attached by these editors to the documents or the finished compositions to lend them the authority they could not possibly obtain otherwise. This "documentary hypothesis" originated with Jean Astruc, a French physician of the eighteenth century, who observed that the Book of Genesis employs the name *Elohim* for God in some chapters and verses and the name *Yahweh* (Jehovah) in others. He concluded that Moses must have used documents written by two different men, one who preferred one name for God, and one who preferred the other. Moses, Astruc main-

14. Henry M. Morris, *The Twilight of Evolution* (Grand Rapids: Baker, 1963), 14–15.
15. Pfeiffer, *Introduction*, 50–70.

tained, blended these two ancient documents that he had at his disposal and produced an edited form today called Genesis. It is interesting to observe, however, that Astruc did not deny Mosaic authorship; he merely felt that Moses used existing documentary sources in his composition.[16]

As time passed, Astruc's thesis led to the inevitable conclusion, espoused by more and more scholars, that not only were literally dozens of various documents employed, but also Moses, after all, had nothing to do even with the composition of the Pentateuch, to say nothing of its authorship. Eventually this piecing together of the Pentateuch from a multitude of alleged sources developed the whole idea into a reductio ad absurdum, for it became clear that every verse, and even parts of verses, could have come from different hands if the principles of the critics were to be rigorously applied.

By the time Wellhausen appeared on the scene (1877), the opinion prevailed in critical circles that there were at least four primary sources for the Pentateuch, and these were indicated by the abbreviations J, E, D, and P. The historical-critical school maintained that J represented the document composed by the school of writers who preferred the divine name *Jehovah*, E the writers preferring *Elohim*, D the writer of the Book of Deuteronomy, and P the writer of those sections of the Pentateuch having to do especially with priestly liturgy, sacrifice, and genealogy and chronology. Some included the Book of Joshua in this reconstruction and labeled the whole production the Hexateuch.[17]

Without attempting to break the Pentateuch down into its various "sources" (which is difficult because the critics by no means agree on the content of each), it might be helpful to illustrate at least one of the most common examples. In Genesis 1:1–2:4a, the creation account, the name *Elohim* appears exclusively as the name for God. Beginning in 2:4b, which is also an account of creation, the name *Yahweh* appears, though usually in connection with *Elohim*. This led the critics to assume that there were two original stories of creation and that these were edited and placed side by side in the Pentateuch. In this case, however, the critics do not believe that E wrote the first chapter of Genesis, but rather P, because they feel that the cosmogony and history there are later than E on the whole and that only P lived late enough in history to be aware of knowledge presupposed in this creation account. The second account is assigned to J, however, because it employs the name *Jehovah* so freely.

16. Edward J. Young, *An Introduction to the Old Testament*, rev. ed. (Grand Rapids: Eerdmans, 1964), 128–30.

17. Walter J. Harrelson, *Interpreting the Old Testament* (New York: Holt, Rinehart and Winston, 1964), 30ff.

In general, critical scholarship taught that the documents originated no earlier than the ninth century B.C., though it was usually admitted that some of the basic ideas may have come in oral form from as early as the time of Moses. The consensus was that J was composed first (850 B.C.), followed shortly by E (750 B.C.), then D (early seventh century B.C.), and finally by P (after 586 B.C.). There were also thought to be certain geographical frameworks discernible in the documents. For example, it seemed that J represented the viewpoint of the Southern Kingdom and was, therefore, most likely written in Judah or at least by a pro-Judah circle. But E, it was supposed, was biased to a northern position, and probably had Israelite orientation. The geographical disposition of D is not quite so clear, though the weight of opinion was that it was eventually Judahite, having originated in northern Levitical circles, and, of course, P, being exilic, was heavily in favor of Judah, though it pretended to be much more ancient than either Israel or Judah and, therefore, more neutral.[18]

The present situation as regards the documentary hypothesis is basically the same as it has been for one hundred years or more, though the evolutionary hypotheses of Wellhausen have been largely abandoned.[19] The tendency today is to hold to the essential concept of four documents but to allow them a much more ancient substructure than was formerly admitted. It is now felt that many of the written sources of the documents are hundreds of years older than previously thought and that some may actually have originated with Moses himself. The Scandinavian school, in particular, advocates a Mosaic origin for the basic themes of the Pentateuch, though at the same time it stresses that these themes were transmitted only orally until they were finally written by later scribes.[20] The most current opinion is that J, representing one tradition of law and history, was written about 950 B.C. in the Southern Kingdom. About 850 B.C., E was written in the Northern Kingdom, expressing a slightly different viewpoint. About 650 B.C., some unknown scribes wrote D (Deuteronomy) to combat certain religious tendencies in both kingdoms (though Israel had already fallen), and for some reason this document was lost, not to be found until 622 B.C., when King Josiah of Judah found it in the temple and made of it the core for the great spiritual revival that took place under his reign. P was not written until late in the Babylonian captivity and was

18. Bernhard W. Anderson, *Understanding the Old Testament*, 4th ed. (Englewood Cliffs, N.J.: Prentice-Hall, 1986), 451–52.

19. John Bright, "Modern Study of Old Testament Literature," in *The Bible and the Ancient Near East*, ed. G. Ernest Wright (Garden City, N.Y.: Doubleday, 1961), 16ff.

20. C. R. North, "Pentateuchal Criticism," in *The Old Testament and Modern Study*, ed. Rowley, 70.

incorporated by the priests into the JED document that had slowly taken shape by previous editing by many hands.[21]

As far as the rest of the Old Testament is concerned, it is quite widely held, with Martin Noth, that the books of Joshua through Kings are a part of the corpus of an anonymous compiler known as the "Deuteronomist," mainly because these books allegedly express the same religious and historical philosophy as Deuteronomy.[22] The poetical books are assigned mostly to anonymous authors and are dated anywhere from David's time to 150 B.C. The books of Chronicles, Ezra, and Nehemiah were allegedly written by the "Chronicler" about 400 B.C. The prophets for the most part are thought to have written the books that bear their names, though there are notable exceptions, such as Daniel and Isaiah 40–66. These last, because of their remarkable predictive prophecies, are dated after the events they prophesy, because otherwise their perfect fulfillment cannot be understood. The remainder of the books not included in this résumé are considered to be anonymous and are dated on purely internal literary evidence.

The mass of "evidence" accumulated by critical scholarship over the years might lead some to think that its reconstruction of the Old Testament is unassailable, but this is far from true. Without answering each point in detail, which is neither desirable nor necessary here, it is sufficient to say simply that the entire process rests on the most tenuous, subjective evidence, all of which is based on the assumption that only religious developmentalism can account for the present shape of the Old Testament phenomena. What the Bible says about itself in these areas, and what Christ, the apostles, and every tradition have averred, is completely rejected in favor of supposed irrefutable internal evidence, no matter how subjective that evidence might be. In other words, the Old Testament has been made to fit a prearranged philosophical and historical framework, even though on every page it cries out against such an artificial and untenable reconstruction.[23]

The Credibility of the Old Testament

The foregoing presentation of the critical approach to the Old Testament leads to some vital questions that should at least be cursorily considered. It is mandatory to know whether the Old Testament is what it claims to be, the works of Moses and the prophets, or whether it is a collection of docu-

---

21. Anderson, *Understanding the Old Testament*, 22.

22. Martin Noth, *A History of Pentateuchal Traditions* (Englewood Cliffs, N.J.: Prentice-Hall, 1972).

23. O. T. Allis, *The Five Books of Moses* (Philadelphia: Presbyterian and Reformed, 1943), 261.

ments by anonymous individuals who tried to give their compositions sanction by appending the names of Moses and the prophets to them.

There are two major lines of evidence to establish the credibility of the Old Testament, internal and external, and these will be considered in that order. First, the Pentateuch claims to have been written by Moses (Exod. 17:14; Num. 33:1–2; Deut. 31:22), and other books of the Old Testament concur without dissent (Judg. 3:4; 2 Kings 21:8; Mal. 4:4). Moreover, intertestamental Jewish literature like the Apocrypha and Pseudepigrapha bear similar testimony (Bar. 2:2; 2 Macc. 7:30). Also of great weight is the fact that the New Testament writers and speakers, including Jesus and the apostles, mention Mosaic authorship of the Pentateuch many times (e.g., Matt. 19:8; Rom. 10:5; Acts 3:22; John 7:19). It is impossible to overcome such testimony, especially in the case of the Lord, for it must be held either that he did not know that Moses did not write the Pentateuch, which calls into question his divine omniscience, or that he "accommodated himself to the ignorance of the people of his time," which constitutes an assault on his integrity. In all accuracy, one can conclude that anyone who denies Mosaic authorship of the Pentateuch therefore denies to Christ the divine attributes. And the evidence for the remainder of the Old Testament is equally clear and convincing. Jesus believed in the historicity of Daniel (Matt. 24:15) and Jonah (Matt. 12:39–40), for example, and also maintained by implication that Isaiah wrote the entire book bearing his name (Matt. 12:17–21). This knowledge was shared by the Jews themselves, the apostles, and universal church tradition.

The external evidence is varied and interesting. For present purposes, it is divided into three areas: archaeological and historical correspondence, scientific accuracy, and fulfilled prophecy. It should be stressed again at the outset that the character of the Old Testament as the Word of God is demonstrated not by mere external proofs that can be adduced to support the claim but by its own claim to be Scripture, a testimony accepted by faith. On the other hand, external support is welcome whenever it is available, and it is reasonable to expect the Old Testament, if it is the inspired Word of God, to be accurate in all historical and scientific matters with which it deals. Yet (and this is vitally important) it is crucial to bear in mind that the Old Testament does not always profess to speak in twentieth-century scientific terms but often employs the prescientific language of the day in which it was written. This has no bearing on the question of verbal inspiration unless the passage in question indicates clearly that it is revealing timeless scientific truth, and that is often difficult to tell. When that clearly is its purpose, it speaks with scientific precision. Moreover, in matters of history, one must recognize that the Old

Testament purpose was not to outline historical data chronologically, though it does this in a great many places, but to emphasize God's dealings in history. It was not written as a modern historian might write it, but rather as a progressive disclosure of theological truth. This does not mean that it is historically unreliable, but only that it may be chronologically out of order and incomplete in places where there was no particular reason for relating historical information that might ordinarily have been included. In any event, where the Old Testament does speak historically, it has yet to be proven in error. In fact, it very often has shed light on extremely complicated historical problems that otherwise would have remained enigmatic to historians.

The Old Testament and History

Both Jewish and Christian traditions universally considered the Old Testament historical record to be completely reliable in all points. With the advent of modern rationalism and naturalism, however, the Old Testament was subjected to a massive attack on its historicity. Higher criticism, it was felt, had completely demolished the integrity of the Scriptures in this respect, for all kinds of alleged unhistorical or nonhistorical biblical references had been uncovered. Historians "demonstrated," for example, that because there was no record of a Hittite people in ancient extrabiblical history, there must be a mistake in the Old Testament where references to the Hittites are made (Gen. 15:20; 25:9; etc.). Similarly, Isaiah mentions an Assyrian king Sargon who, according to the prophet, must have lived near the end of the eighth century B.C. (Isa. 20:1). Yet, there were no Assyrian records of such a king, so Isaiah must have had false historical information. Another favorite target was Belshazzar, who, according to the Book of Daniel, was on the throne of the Neo-Babylonian Empire when Cyrus the Great overthrew that empire (Dan. 5:30). Because extrabiblical historical records failed to mention such a name, Daniel must have made a serious blunder.

One can easily imagine the embarrassment of the critical scholars when it was later discovered that not only were there Hittite peoples, but also these peoples constituted one of the most powerful empires in the Near East in the eighteenth through twelfth centuries. Excavations at Khorsabad in Iraq also uncovered the ruins of one of the most magnificent palaces of all time, ruins dating from the eighth century B.C. Amazingly, the walls of this palace were covered with the name of Sargon the Great (Sargon II) as well as extensive annals and murals relating the magnificence of his kingdom and power. It is well known today that there were few kings of Assyria about whom more is known than Sargon; certainly he was a far cry from some figment of Isaiah's imagination. The Babylonian Chronicles, also uncovered and published in modern times, describe the history of the Mesopotamian world in the seventh and sixth centuries; interestingly, they point out that while King Nabonidus of Babylonia was out on campaigns or treasure seeking (for he was a lover of antiquities), his son Belshazzar was left in the city of Babylon to administer affairs in the capital. During his tenure in Babylon, the Medo-Persians under Darius the Mede entered Babylon without resistance and summarily put Belshazzar to death. Just prior to this, Daniel, who was captive in Babylon and had predicted the collapse of Babylon, had been appointed to a position as "third ruler of the kingdom" (Dan. 5:29). This statement had always puzzled Bible readers, for if Belshazzar was first ruler, who was second? With astounding accuracy the Book of Daniel had implied that there were two kings in Babylonia at once, but until recent times historians did not realize that Nabonidus had a son named Belshazzar and that both were reigning in the period in question. The Old Testament proved itself not only reliable, but much more reliable and informative than had been imagined even by conservatives!

The results of modern archaeological and historical research have been even more amazing for pre-monarchial Hebrew history (before ca. 1000 B.C.). The most skeptical scholars had maintained that Old Testament history beginning with David was, at least in its main points, quite reliable. They declared that anything earlier than that, however, was outside the realm of true history. The figures of the judges, Joshua, Moses, and especially the patriarchs were nothing but shadowy and idealized representations conceived by Israel to give its history and covenantal claims some kind of romantic and meaningful origin. Anyone or anything pre-Abrahamic was immediately consigned to the legendary, if not fictitious, domains of prehistory.

Now, however, all this estimation is rapidly being reexamined and rejected, even by skeptics who just recently held to these opinions most doggedly. Those who taught a century ago that Moses could not have written the Pentateuch because writing was not developed as an art until after his time have been completely confounded. Not that the skeptics have accepted Mosaic authorship; they have not. But now the concession is that Moses *could* have written the Pentateuch so far as the ability to write itself is concerned. Furthermore, many generally concede that the entire historical situation in Canaan and Egypt in the time of Moses and Joshua was exactly what the Bible describes it to have been. Though these critics still do not usually admit that the persons in Genesis named Abraham, Isaac,

Jacob, and Joseph are historical, some scholars freely suggest that what the Old Testament says about these patriarchs fits in perfectly with what is known about life in the Near East in the period from 2000–1660 B.C.[24] Cuneiform tablets from such places as Nuzi, Mari, Alalakh, and Ebla provide fascinating accounts of civil, social, business, and political life from this period or a little later, and the accounts given in the Old Testament from the patriarchal age fit harmoniously into the entire historical and cultural context. In other words, according to much modern historical criticism, though the persons and events of patriarchal times probably are not truly historical, they could be from the standpoint of their adherence to what is now known about the historical milieu of these ancient times. This constitutes something akin to admission that the Old Testament, at least from patriarchal times, is essentially historical. Just a few decades ago, no reputable critical scholar would have made such an admission. Thus are the vicissitudes of those who refuse to take God's Word for what it professes to be: an historical unfolding of God's revelation.

The foregoing is not intended to suggest that all Bible scholars are now completely convinced of the absolute historical accuracy and reliability of the Old Testament. Unfortunately, this is far from true. Yet there is no question that it has come to be appreciated as a record of revelation that fits marvelously into an actual historical background, one that can be demonstrably verified by all the skills of modern historical research. This, however, leads to another approach to Old Testament study, an approach that sees in the Old Testament not so much a chronological history based on historical data as a "sacred history," or, to use the popular German term, *Heilsgeschichte* ("history of salvation").[25]

This "salvation history" is not a history in terms ordinarily applied to the discipline. It is an interpretive history that expresses Israel's faith in Yahweh and his mighty acts on their behalf. That is, the Old Testament is a witness to Israel's faith, and though it has a historical background, its special and individual events may not be history in the commonly conceived sense. For example, the exodus is a biblical event that fits in nicely with the historical milieu of Egypt and Canaan during this period but, because of its supernatural character, obviously cannot be considered factual history. Something happened in time and space by which Israel was delivered from Egyptian bondage, and it was interpreted by Israel's

---

24. W. F. Albright, *From the Stone Age to Christianity* (Garden City, N.Y.: Doubleday, 1957), 241–43.

25. Gerhard von Rad, *Old Testament Theology*, 2 vols. (Edinburgh: Oliver and Boyd, 1962), 1:50–51; for a good exposition of this concept, see James Barr, "Revelation Through History in the Old Testament and in Modern Theology," *Interpretation* 17 (1963): 193–205.

prophets as an act of God. In retelling the event over centuries, "spiritual accretions" were added that, though not absolutely factually accurate, nonetheless became history as expressed in creedal recitations and, therefore, legitimate salvation history as defined by its own canons.

The reason for such a reinterpretation of Old Testament history should be obvious. When the critics realized that they could no longer discount the essential historical reliability of the Scriptures, they were faced with the difficult task of explaining the miracles and other supernatural content. The only feasible thing to do was to admit that the framework of Old Testament history was valid but insist that the miraculous events were merely prophetic interpretations of history in terms of what the prophets believed God did. Even prophets who recorded the events did not believe that they happened exactly as they recorded them, but they "read into" the events their own theological judgments of the meanings of the events. This, in effect, strips the Old Testament of its miraculous content without denying it the essential historicity that it has been proved to possess.

The conservative response is that one cannot reasonably postulate a dichotomy between types of histories without robbing the term *history* of its accepted definitions. How can it be said, indeed, that there is more than one kind of history, that which describes the sum total of the past? Anything less than this is less than history and must be relegated to the realm of myth or legend. Of course, and not surprisingly, modern Old Testament scholarship does speak of these supernatural occurrences as "myth," intending by this term to convey the idea of religious myth as opposed to what is strictly fictitious.[26] Nonetheless, any attempt to philosophize or semanticize history into at least two compartments seems to destroy any recognizable standard of what constitutes history. How a matter can be myth and history at the same time remains an insoluble problem.

Conservative Old Testament students generally hold, then, that the Old Testament is a collection of absolutely reliable historical documents. Efforts made by some critics to rationalize the miraculous elements by cloaking them in the guise of mythical history or straining to interpret them as pious inventions calculated to express only spiritual truth become in themselves arguments for its historicity. Specific cases of the miraculous in history will be discussed in the outline of Israel's covenant and national history to be considered later.

26. Artur Weiser, *The Old Testament: Its Formation and Development*, trans. Dorothea M. Barton (New York: Association, 1961), 57–59.

The Old Testament and Science

The advent of modern scientism, primarily in the nineteenth century, has brought an assault on the scientific accuracy or reliability of the Old Testament. The same rationalistic spirit that attempted to undermine the authority of the Word of God in matters historical is also the genius behind the "Bible-science" conflict. This should come as no surprise, for if the Old Testament can be proven invalid in one of these areas, there is every likelihood that it will be proven so in the others as well.

It will be helpful to approach this discussion with a brief definition of terms. It is not strictly proper for one to speak of a conflict between science and the Bible; rather, one should speak in terms of a "Bible-scientism" antithesis. Science, by definition, is "a branch of study concerned with observation and classification of facts," and, therefore, has to do with natural laws and processes.[27] If one assumes that God is the author of the Old Testament as well as the author of all law, including natural law, it becomes axiomatic that there cannot be conflict. God cannot contradict himself. However, scientism (the term was coined recently to denote the modern philosophy of science) can and does clash with the Scriptures. The problem should be apparent; science truly known and correctly interpreted is biblical; scientism as an expression of man's interpretation of his environment is usually unbiblical. It would not even be incorrect to say that it is anti-biblical.[28]

As pointed out earlier, it is unreasonable to expect the Old Testament to speak scientifically when its intention is to speak poetically or in ordinary popular discourse, for this is placing restrictions on it that would not be placed on any other book or speaker. For example, when the Scriptures speak of the "four corners of the earth" or the "rising of the sun," one should not condemn them for speaking unscientifically, for these are obvious colloquialisms. Who would telephone the television weatherman after the news broadcast to inform him that he is speaking unscientifically when he says the same things? Ordinary fairness to the Bible will permit it to use the speech of the workaday world.

Furthermore, it is inappropriate to judge the Bible unscientific when it speaks of miraculous events that seem to contradict the "rules" of natural science. The basic question is what is really scientific—what is observed and declared to be in conformity with present scientific law, or what reacts according to divine law? This is a vital point, for it raises the issue of

27. *Webster's New Collegiate Dictionary*, 2d ed. (Springfield, Mass.: G. and C. Merriam, 1953).
28. Robert L. Reymond, *A Christian View of Modern Science* (Philadelphia: Presbyterian and Reformed, 1964), 17.

whether God himself is subject to so-called natural law, or whether, as the Creator of all things, including these laws, he transcends them. It seems obvious that only the latter can be correct, so from one perspective any miracles recorded in the Bible must be interpreted as temporary suspensions of natural law. One could even say, at the risk of being misunderstood, that there is no such thing as real miracle, but only relative miracle, and that what appears to be natural law may be only a restriction placed on the universe by God for some specific purpose or other. Paul suggests that the whole world is currently out of joint (Rom. 8:22). Practically all the eschatological passages of the Bible speak of a time when "miracles" will be the rule rather than the exception (Isa. 65:25; Amos 9:13; Joel 2:28–32). Science, when it rejects the miraculous, is only rejecting something that it cannot explain on the basis of known causes and effects. Many of the phenomena today taken for granted would have seemed nothing less than miraculous to even relatively modern generations, for the laws that control or permit these things were unknown or misunderstood until recently. Given a supranatural set of laws, what could possibly be "the natural order" is impossible to imagine, though the Bible bears eloquent testimonies to marvelous occurrences both past and future that might offer suggestions.

In brief, the basic conflict between the Bible and science is one of philosophies. The alternatives are to accept by faith the record of the Bible regarding creation, the flood, and other miraculous acts of God, or to accept by faith the reconstruction of all these events by ungodly scientism. The evidence is there for all to see; the responsibility of the individual is to properly evaluate and interpret the evidence. If one proceeds from the concept of an ontological sovereign Deity, he has no difficulty accepting the biblical account; if he takes as his premise a no-God thesis, he must explain the evidence as best he can. The only truly satisfying approach in supporting the scientific claims of the Bible is not to defend it point by point in its scientific pronouncements, though it is defensible, but to accept it as the Word of God with the implicit corollary of its scientific accuracy.

Two or three examples of the scientific accuracy of the Old Testament in a "prescientific" age will suffice, though they by no means exhaust the possibilities. One of the best-known statements is that of Isaiah, who spoke of God as he who "sits enthroned above the circle of the earth" (40:22). Though the fact that the earth is round may always have been believed by a few, there is no question that until comparatively modern times the consensus was that it is flat. For Isaiah in the eighth century B.C. to contradict the prevailing scientific opinion presupposes either a "lucky guess" or a highly advanced scientific notion known to him only by revelation. The same applies to the statement in Leviticus 17:11 with regard to the "life of the flesh consisting of the blood." Only a little over three centuries ago, William Harvey discovered the full meaning of the blood's relationship to life. When Job said that God "suspended the earth over nothing" (Job 26:7) was he only speaking poetically? It does not seem likely, for though the Book of Job is numbered among the poetic books of the Old Testament, this need not imply that every statement in it is poetic. Indeed, the context in this case argues that Job is speaking earnestly and scientifically, using information that could have come only through revelation.

It is true that the Bible was not written as a science textbook, but it is equally true that it cannot be disproved in its scientific claims and that it bespeaks a scientific knowledge far in advance of its own time.

The Old Testament and Prophecy

Fulfilled prophecy has given great concern to modern criticism. If the prophets could accurately predict the future even in a broad sense, to say nothing of specific details, then one must automatically yield to the Old Testament a certain amount of supernatural character. If they actually could not, then either their prophecies must be dated after the events they prophesied, or the fulfillment must be regarded as a fortuitous accident and only one of several possible interpretations of the prophecy. Both of these "solutions" have been applied by many scholars, with the result that some entire prophetic books (Daniel especially) and great parts of others (Isa. 40–66) have been completely redated to allow for prediction to follow fulfillment. This obviously nullifies the prediction and makes it, instead, history. As for fulfillments that materialized after Old Testament times and could not, therefore, have occurred before the prediction in the Old Testament books, these are usually described as fulfillments only in the sense that they have been "shaped" or interpreted by later writers as having some correspondence to an Old Testament prophecy. For example, when Matthew states (Matt. 1:23) that the virgin birth of Jesus Christ was in fulfillment of Isaiah's prophecy (Isa. 7:14), he merely intends to suggest that, of all the passages of the Old Testament, this one most closely approximates what was really involved in the birth of Christ. This was not to say that Jesus was really born of a virgin, but that Matthew, as a Christian apologete, was interested in validating the uniqueness of Jesus' birth, and, therefore, used the "virgin birth symbol" suggested to him by Isaiah.[29] By employing such tactics, the critics can remove every possible Old Testament fulfillment in the New, but

29. Morton Scott Enslin, *The Literature of the Christian Movement* (New York: Harper and Brothers, 1938), 397–98.

not without impugning the integrity and intelligence of every New Testament writer or speaker, including Jesus himself.

The problem of Old Testament prophecies fulfilled later in the Old Testament is not nearly so difficult to the critic, but it is still fraught with all kinds of problems relative to the evaluation by Jesus and the apostles of the books and prophecies involved. The usual procedure, as already suggested, is to assign to the book a date late enough to prevent its having been written earlier than the fulfillment. The Book of Daniel, for example, alleges to have been written by Daniel no later than 530 B.C. Yet, it contains most remarkably accurate descriptions of the affairs of individuals and nations that did not even exist until hundreds of years after Daniel's time. The solution is to date Daniel at ca. 165 B.C., thus reducing his prophecies to an outline of history and current events. The same thing is done to the Book of Isaiah, though in this case only a part of the book is redated. The first thirty-nine chapters are admittedly ascribed to Isaiah of Jerusalem, but chapters 40 through 66 are attributed to an anonymous prophet (or prophets) who lived not until after the Babylonian captivity (ca. 540 B.C.).[30] Why? Because these last twenty-seven chapters contain such notes of comfort and hope, and because they speak with such amazing predictive accuracy regarding events and persons who do not appear until after the death of Isaiah of Jerusalem (ca. 685 B.C.). It has always remained a puzzle to the critics that this Second Isaiah who, they admit, wrote the most glorious prophetic work of all should remain anonymous, though other prophets with shorter and much less polished works should be remembered. All efforts to account for this disparity have failed, because there is no proof to support such a writer in history or the Bible. Jesus quotes from these last chapters of Isaiah on several occasions, and the Gospel writers invariably assign them to the prophet (Matt. 3:3; 8:17; Luke 3:4–5; John 12:38–39). Jesus does the same with Daniel (Matt. 24:15) and other disputed books. Once again, the integrity of the Lord is in question if these books were not written by the men and in the times to which they bear internal witness. The effectiveness of fulfilled prophecy as an evidence of the supernatural character of the Old Testament is amply demonstrated by the machinations to which the critics must resort in order to try to disprove it.

The People of the Old Testament

The history revealed in the Old Testament is the history of a special people. This people, from earliest times known as the Hebrews and later as Israelites and Jews, constitute the human theme of the book. Naturally,

30. Anderson, *Understanding the Old Testament*, 472–75.

their origin in a general sense is to be traced back to the very beginning, the creation of mankind; their existence as a special people, however, commenced with Abraham, to whom the ethnic covenant was given, along with Jacob (or Israel), through whom it became nationalized, and Moses, through whom it became fully historicized. The reason for the need of a special people through whom God could reveal his redemptive purposes to all the world is fairly obvious; why Israel was selected to be that people, however, is not quite so plain. In the final analysis, all that can be said is that God loved them (Deut. 7:8) and made them a special object of his grace.

Throughout the Old Testament may be seen the continually unfolding vicissitudes of this people or nation in both history and prophecy. What they failed to accomplish in Old Testament times was apparently reserved for them to accomplish in the eschatological plan of God, both in conjunction with and independent of the church of all the ages. Theirs is a spiritual and a temporal kingdom, one that existed in both space and time, but ultimately restricted to neither.

There are other peoples and nations mentioned throughout the Old Testament, but these are only ancillary to the nation Israel and to God's acts and messages of revelation through that one nation. Though Egypt, Assyria, and Babylonia do not act outside God's overall purposes, for he is the God of all the world, their main function still is understood only in connection with Israel. To understand the Old Testament, then, is to understand Israel in all its historical and geographical contexts; any failure to properly appreciate these must inevitably result in an inability to correctly interpret Israel's faith and its role as the channel of God's redemptive grace. Because of the extreme complexity of these considerations and because they actually do constitute the substratum of the Old Testament story, further remarks will be deferred until they can be used in unfolding that story throughout this book.

The History of the Old Testament Period

The complete story of God's people in the Old Testament covers a period of many thousands of years, but within this span various epochs or eras become quite plainly discernible; these epochs, in fact, constitute the main outline of this study. It is necessary merely to outline these periods at this point, indicating their dates (approximate in some cases) and the sections of the Old Testament that discuss them.[31] The terms employed will become clear to students as they proceed to study each of these periods in its own historical order. Table 2 indicates briefly the ground to be covered.

31. For a detailed account of the history of Israel see Eugene H. Merrill, *Kingdom of Priests: A History of Old Testament Israel* (Grand Rapids: Baker, 1987).

TABLE 2

Pre-patriarchal period	(ca. 10,000–2100 B.C.)	Genesis 1:1–11:26
Patriarchal period	(2100–1800)	Genesis 11:27–50:26
Egyptian and exodus period	(1800–1406)	Exodus 1:1–Deuteronomy 34:12
Conquest and judges period	(1406–1050)	Joshua 1:1–1 Samuel 10:1
United monarchy period	(1050–931)	1 Samuel 10:1–1 Kings 12:15
Divided monarchy period to Jehu	(931–841)	1 Kings 12:15–2 Kings 9:27
Divided monarchy period to fall of Israel	(841–722)	2 Kings 9:27–16:6
Kingdom of Judah period to fall of Judah	(722–586)	2 Kings 16:6–25:26
Babylonian exile, captivity period, and postexilic period	(586–420)	2 Kings 25:26–30; Ezra; Nehemiah

Other books, such as Ruth, Esther, and Lamentations, shed valuable light on historical conditions during some of these periods, and, of course, the prophetic books contain long historical sections. In addition, the books of Chronicles consist of a parallel history of the entire period from Saul to Cyrus (1050–530 B.C.), written from a slightly different viewpoint, and also they contain helpful genealogical and chronological data that have a direct bearing on the history. Even the poetic books share in an understanding of Israel's history, for they reflect the philosophical, cultural, and theological conditions of the times in which they were written.

The Land of the Old Testament

Because the Old Testament is an historical book, there must be some attention paid to its geography, for the stage on which the drama of Israel's life is portrayed is essential to its role as God's chosen people. People live and act within a geographical environment that shapes to a measurable degree the fortunes of the people who live within it. This was true of Israel; in fact, it could be said that the influence of Palestine's geography on the nation Israel was all out of proportion to what ordinarily might be expected. The basic reasons for this may be found through a careful examination of the physical, geological, and climatic features that made up Palestine.[32]

The land itself is only a tiny fraction of the great land mass known as the Near East, but its location within that mass more than compensated for its small area. From most ancient times the world's population was centered in an area bounded by the Indus Valley on the east, the Caspian and Black seas on the north, Anatolia and the Mediterranean Sea on the west, and Egypt and the Arabian Peninsula to the southwest and south, respectively. The two major centers of civilization within the greater part of Old Testament history were in Mesopotamia to the north and east and in Egypt to the south and west, with Palestine right between them. Ancient historical records from both Babylonia-Assyria and Egypt reveal that thousands of years before the time of Christ extensive trade was conducted between these two population centers, and because Palestine was located between the Mediterranean Sea and the impassable deserts of the Arabian Peninsula, it became the highway for virtually all of this traffic. This entire land area, stretching from the Euphrates to the Nile Valley, has become known as the Fertile Crescent. It soon became clear that Palestine was to be the "bridge of the Fertile Crescent."

Israel's location seemed to make it ideally situated to absorb the cultures and material benefits of all the nations that passed through its territory in the process of conducting merchandise; in some respects this is exactly what Israel did, as did all the indigenous populations of Palestine before Israel. However, the peculiarly fractured topography of the land was conducive to provincialism and insularity. The various chains of hills and mountains, crisscrossed by streams and precipitous valleys, made of Palestine a heterogeneous collection of enclaves that tended to produce within themselves independent cultures having a variety of forms. A look at these geographical structures will illustrate these remarks.

Palestine is basically divided into north-south regions, though there are some east-west features. Stretching normally no more than two hundred miles from north to south and at approximately 31–30 degrees latitude north, the land consists, first of all, of a coastal littoral varying in width from a few hundred yards north of Carmel to over thirty miles in the extreme south. This coastal plain was lined at the edge of the sea by high sand dunes and ledges that prevented the streams from flowing into the

---

32. See Denis Baly, *The Geography of the Bible: A Study in Historical Geography*, rev. ed. (New York: Harper and Brothers, 1974).

sea from the central hills, thus reducing a great part of the plain to a swamp in the rainy season. Besides this, the coastline is so straight and unbroken that there were few or no opportunities for any maritime industry. These two factors combined to limit settlement of the plain except in the south, where the Philistines managed to maintain a pentapolis of cities—Gaza, Ashkelon, Ashdod, Ekron, and Gath. Historically, the Israelites never settled in this area, both because of the agricultural difficulties and because the Philistines and other native peoples were successful in maintaining their possessions there.

The coastal plain gradually rises in elevation until it blends with the central hills of Palestine toward the east. These hills, from north to south, were known as the Galilean Hills, Mount Ephraim, and the Hills of Judaea. The first two of these mountainous regions are bisected by the Valley of Jezreel and the second two by the valleys of Sorek and Aijalon. Though none of these hills is very high, and scarcely any deserves to be called a mountain, they are quite rugged and steep, forming natural frontiers throughout the whole length of the country. The Israelites found these hills largely abandoned by an indigenous population at the time of the conquest, so most of the important cities they built or rebuilt were located in the hills and valleys of Palestine. These include such places as Hazor, Shechem, Samaria, Bethel, Shiloh, Gezer, Lachish, Gibeon, Jerusalem, Bethlehem, and Hebron.

East of the mountains is one of the most interesting and unusual geographical phenomena on the face of the earth—the Great Rift. Beginning in south-central Asia, a long, continuous geological fault ranges over a distance of several thousand miles, eventually culminating in the great lakes of southeast Africa. This fault produced a deep cleft in the crust of the earth that reaches its greatest depth in Palestine. The rift enters the Near Eastern world in northern Syria, passes between the Lebanon and Anti-Lebanon mountains, and reaches sea level at a point between Lake Huleh and the Sea of Galilee. From there it drops below sea level, reaching a depth of –650 feet at the surface of the Sea of Galilee. The Jordan River, which flows down the rift from Galilee, winds and meanders over two hundred miles until it reaches its end at the Dead Sea. Here the rift dips to the astounding depth of 1292 feet below sea level at the surface of the Dead Sea (about 2500 feet below at the Dead Sea's deepest point), making the area of the Dead Sea the lowest point on earth, more than 1000 feet lower than Death Valley in California. From the Dead Sea the rift rises to about 600 feet above sea level in the arid waste south of the Dead Sea known as the Arabah. From this elevation it drops once again until it reaches sea level at the Gulf of Aqaba.

The rift, with the River Jordan, experienced the greatest differences in vegetation imaginable in so small an area because of the vast differences in elevation. In the north, plants of the Galilean region most frequently abound, but at Jericho, near the Dead Sea, a luxuriant tropical life usually found only in equatorial regions thrives. There is evidence that in biblical times tropical animals frequented this area. This whole system also provided a great barrier to travel from east to west, so that peoples on either side of the river had very little contact with each other. The primary crossing places were at Jericho in the south, near the Jabbok River in the central region, and near Beth-shean, just south of the Sea of Galilee, and even these places could not be forded except at certain times of the year.

The easternmost section of Palestine was known as the Eastern Plateau or Transjordan. This region consists of a high plateau to the north that gradually lowers in the middle and then rises to several thousand feet in the south. At one time this plateau, like the central hills of Palestine, was covered with a dense forest growth, and its pastures became proverbial for their ability to sustain great herds and flocks. Now both of these regions have been denuded of their vegetation, and only in limited areas is there much growth. In ancient times the Eastern Plateau was inhabited by quite highly advanced peoples including the Ammonites, Moabites, Edomites, and various groups of the Amorites. Eventually, this land was conquered and settled by Israel, particularly by the tribes of Reuben, Gad, and a part of Manasseh.

Two other major geographical features deserve mention. First, the Valley of Jezreel is an essential part of the land, for it provided the richest agricultural territory of all. Furthermore, through it passed over 90 percent of the commercial and military traffic of Palestine. The plain stretches from the Carmel Hills along the Mediterranean to the Jordan Valley, forming a triangle whose apex is to the west. One arm of the triangle runs to the east, where it enters the Jordan Valley at Beth-shean, and the other to the northeast, where it leads to the Sea of Galilee. The principal trade route, the Via Maris, led from Egypt along the Mediterranean coastal plain and, a few miles north of the Plain of Sharon, went inland through a mountain pass and entered the Valley of Jezreel. It crossed the valley and passed near Mount Tabor, heading toward the fords to the south or north of the Sea of Galilee and ending up in Damascus and even beyond, in Mesopotamia. Another principal route, that from Asia Minor, also crossed the Valley of Jezreel and, on its way to Egypt, led through the same cut in the mountains as did the Via Maris. From most ancient times it became apparent that he who controlled this mountain pass could become powerful and wealthy. The city of Megiddo was built there, and, along with several other fortresses, it became the key to the possession of this strategic and productive valley.

The final geographic area is known as the Shephelah or Lowlands. This extends from the coastal plain, in its southern reaches, east to the central hills, and down into the South (the Negev) until it blends with the undulating hills of the Sinai Desert. This land was very dry, at least in the extreme south, and was used primarily for pasturage. In the more northern part of the Shephelah, the territory between Philistia and Judah, many wars between the Philistines and Israelites were waged, and, in a sense, the whole region was a kind of buffer zone or no man's land.

The climate of Palestine has had a profound effect on the geographical and even historical affairs of Old Testament peoples. There are only two real seasons there, the rainy and the dry. True to the Mediterranean pattern, the rains begin to fall in the month of October, maintain themselves to varying degrees throughout the winter months, and then increase for one last time in April. In the Old Testament these rainy periods are called, respectively, the "former rains" and the "latter rains." From April through September, precipitation is rarely or never experienced in most of the country.

The rain pattern is from west to east and from north to south; that is, the coastal plain generally receives the greatest amounts, and Galilee experiences more than the Shephelah and Negev. The amounts range anywhere from forty inches or more per annum in the extreme north coast to less than two inches in parts of the most southern deserts. The central hills catch most of the moisture that does not fall on the plain, and what manages to cross the mountains falls on the Transjordanian Plateau, leaving the rift with virtually no rainfall except in the area just east of the Valley of Jezreel. All this means that Galilee receives abundant rain and is, therefore, a good farming area, as are the Valley of Jezreel, the western slopes of the central hills, and most of Transjordan. If the soil were not so rocky and were otherwise more conducive to agriculture, the productivity of Palestine would be much greater than it already is, except in the south, where lack of moisture prohibits any kind of agriculture without the most ingenious irrigation.

Rainfall is the most important climatic factor, but temperature is also worth considering because of its variety in this small land. In the summer, the entire country is quite hot, with temperatures in the rift and the Negev reaching as high as 125 degrees F. This, combined with the humidity, uncomfortable except in the higher hills and in the deserts, produces almost unbearable conditions at times. In the winter, temperatures are quite raw because of the rains and infrequent snows. The major exception is the lower areas of the rift, commonly resorted to today as winter havens.

Finally, the rivers and streams must receive at least brief notice. Besides the Jordan, which is by far the most important, there are its tributaries, the Yarmuk and the Jabbok, which flow into it from the Transjordanian Plateau. Farther south there are two principal streams flowing into the Dead Sea, also from the east—the Arnon and the Zered. There is one main tributary flowing from the west, the Jalud, which empties the Valley of Jezreel. The only two rivers of any importance at all that empty into the Mediterranean Sea are the Kishon, north of Mount Carmel, and the Yarkon, near the modern city of Tel Aviv. These are normally nothing more than mere creeks except in the rainy season when they may extensively overflow their banks. One feature of Palestine is the presence of wadis or "dry streams." These are brooks that flow only in the winter and, perhaps, only for a few days in the deserts. They are treacherous, however, and have been known to fill their banks so rapidly after a violent rainstorm that everything in their path, including men and vehicles, has been swept to destruction. Unless the water of these wadis could be harnessed and controlled, as sometimes it was, it merely flowed out into the sea or was absorbed by the porous soil, serving little or no useful purpose to agriculture. This very soil, largely of limestone, retained ground water on a more or less permanent basis and was tapped by the ancients, as it still is, for wells and springs so necessary in the long dry months of summer.

The book, the history, the people, the land—a knowledge of all these in their interrelationships is essential for students of the Bible to grasp the intended meaning of the Old Testament successfully. With all this background in mind, it is time to turn now to a closer examination of the Old Testament story itself, by God's grace learning from it the mysteries of his redemptive revelation that point, like a schoolmaster, to Christ (Gal. 3:24–25).

2

In the Beginning

The Ancient Near Eastern World

The pre-patriarchal period of biblical history embraces more than the affairs of any single nation; indeed, it may properly be called the period of universal dealings, for at this ancient time God made himself known indiscriminately to individuals and nations alike. A knowledge of the historical background in which this original revelation took place is almost indispensable to its complete understanding.

Aside from certain "prehistoric" remains that are variously dated as early as 60,000 B.C., the first genuine evidence of village occupation in the Near East is from the so-called Neolithic Age (ca. 8000–4500 B.C.). This civilization centered on the Tigris-Euphrates river system and a few other spots like Jericho and Ugarit in the Levant.[1] There seems to be no doubt that Mesopotamia was the cradle of civilization, for the earliest remains in Egypt, long held to be the oldest, are now known to be a great deal later, and those elsewhere are also from a later age. There is little information about this earliest time, except that, with some surprising anomalies, fairly primitive conditions are generally reflected. It appears that man was pri-

---

1. Adam Falkenstein, "The Prehistory and Protohistory of Western Asia," in *The Near East: The Early Civilizations*, ed. Jean Bottéro, Elena Cassin, Jean Vercoutter (New York: Delacorte, 1967), 10–31.

marily a community dweller and practiced various forms of agriculture and herding.

Beginning with the Chalcolithic Age (4500–3000), various cultures began to use copper extensively in the Fertile Crescent and made the first efforts discernible archaeologically to dwell in cities. Sometime during this period, great city-states developed and occasionally became fairly powerful and widespread in their influence. The racial characteristics of these Mesopotamians are uncertain, though it is clear that sometime during this era there was an incursion of peoples identified as the Sumerians. These people developed the first true and independently observable culture and concentrated it on the Persian Gulf at the mouths of the Tigris and Euphrates rivers. Their neighbors, and perhaps their predecessors, appear to have been various Semitic or proto-Semitic mixtures, for the Sumerian gods, clothing, and certain other features seem to be Semitic in form and style and probably were borrowed from peoples with whom they came in contact in Mesopotamia. Without doubt, by 2500 B.C. there was a highly advanced Sumerian culture that could name among its accomplishments great skill in ceramics, art, and literature.[2]

Meanwhile, a civilization was slowly evolving in the Nile Valley; certainly by 4000 B.C. there were city-states (known to classical authors as nomes) maintaining themselves up and down the valley. These remained independent of each other for at least a millennium, but by 3000 B.C. they were united under a common head, the founder of the First Dynasty. The culture of the Nile seemed crude in comparison with that of Mesopotamia, at least at first, but very quickly these populations made great strides, so that, by the beginning of the third millennium, the level may have been about equal in both areas. The situation was similar in the Jordan Valley, though advancement there was much inferior as a whole.

The history of Egypt from 3000–2000 consisted of organization and centralization of power in the First and Second dynasties (3000–2800), a tremendous peak of building, including the age of the pyramids, in the Third through Fifth dynasties, or Old Kingdom (2800–2600), and a decline featuring civil wars and internal disintegration throughout most of the Sixth through Eleventh dynasties (2600–2000). Though there were problems of various kinds, the civilization of Egypt through this long period was remarkably stable and homogeneous and had considerable contact with the outside world.[3]

2. Samuel Noah Kramer, *The Sumerians: Their History, Culture, and Character* (Chicago: University of Chicago Press, 1963), 33–43.

3. William W. Hallo and William Kelly Simpson, *The Ancient Near East* (New York: Harcourt Brace Jovanovich, 1971), 188–90.

The situation in Mesopotamia was much more complex. There, city-state after city-state gained ascendancy only to be toppled and replaced. The Sumerians maintained only a tenuous grip on their lands, though their culture continued to dominate and even to spread widely. Very little is known from the period following 3000 B.C. until near the end of that millennium, except that there was an utter lack of stability and centralization in the land between the rivers. Eventually, however, a man with sufficient power and leadership rose at Akkad, a city-state on the Euphrates, and began to establish the first world empire, the Akkadian. This figure, Sargon the Great (ca. 2360–2305),[4] expanded his influence in all directions, even reaching to the northwest as far as Anatolia and the Mediterranean Sea. His dynasty maintained Mesopotamian control until about 2180, when a people known as the Gutians moved in from the mountains and dominated for about one hundred years, only to be replaced themselves by a new city-state dynasty, Sumerian in character, at the city of Ur. This so-called Third Dynasty of Ur remained in power until about 1950 B.C., or well into the patriarchal period of the Old Testament.

Palestine during this thousand-year period was passing through the epoch known as the Early Bronze Age (ca. 3000–2000 B.C.), a period from which there is a paucity of historical information, though material remains from the area are quite impressive. It appears that cultures there were advancing, especially in the Jordan Valley, throughout most of this age, but for some reason as yet undetermined the civilization came almost to a standstill under the influence of thousands of seminomads from the north and east. For most of the later part of the Early Bronze Age, Palestinian culture passed through this "dark age," not to emerge from it until the turn of the Middle Bronze Age (ca. 2000–1800 B.C.), when a cultural rise again becomes quite evident.[5]

The ancient Near East prior to 2000 presents a picture that only in its last millennium becomes quite understandable; even then there are gaps that make any complete interpretation an impossibility. Several points of importance do emerge, however. Civilization throughout the entire region was much more complicated and refined than was thought true only a few years ago. Moreover, there were great movements of people everywhere except in Egypt, though even there these occurred sporadically in earliest times. Finally, the historical context suggested by Genesis 1–11 is consis-

4. The dates here are those of the "low chronology" of W. F. Albright; cf. Edward F. Campbell, Jr., "The Ancient Near East: Chronological Bibliography and Charts," in *The Bible and the Ancient Near East*, ed. by G. Ernest Wright (Garden City, N.Y.: Doubleday, 1961), 288–93.

5. Kathleen M. Kenyon, *Amorites and Canaanites* (London: Oxford University Press for the British Academy, 1966), 8–35.

tent with the knowledge of this age gained from extrabiblical literature and archaeological excavation. These will be discussed in more detail as they bear on the biblical record.

Views of Creation

At no point are the Bible and modern scientism more in conflict than in their cosmogonies. There are, on the one hand, the simple, unsophisticated, yet majestic account of Genesis, and, on the other hand, the complex evolutionary hypothesis of scientism. The biblical account makes God the Creator; scientism explains creation as a fortuitous combination of original gases, whose origin, in turn, defies explanation. Genesis allows for a period of only several thousand years from creation to the present; scientism maintains that billions of years are necessary to allow for the slowly developing evolutionary process. The Bible states categorically that creation was a once-and-for-all event, a completed act; scientism holds that there is continuous creation and that this creation can lead only to higher and more complex results.[6]

Scientism rests on two main assumptions in its effort to explain the origin and maintenance of the universe.[7] First, the unproven and unprovable theory of evolution provides the key to understanding the present. Things are as they are because they have come through a long process. It is inconceivable to the evolutionist that the complex organisms of today were not originally only one-celled, and he asserts that, even before that, they somehow became alive, though they originated in inorganic matter. The second assumption is uniformitarianism, a term that suggests that the present is the key to the past. That is, the rates of change, whether positive or negative, that are observable today and can be calculated, have always been the same in the past. If a mountain erodes today at one millimeter per century, and it appears to have eroded 100 meters, that mountain must, according to the uniformitarian, be at least 100,000 centuries, or ten million years, old. The whole argument is based on the undemonstrable assumption that the rate of erosion has always been constant. If some unknown factor in the past had either speeded up or retarded the rate of erosion, there would be absolutely no way to determine the age of the mountain in question.

In support of the great age theory of the universe, many dating mechanisms have been developed. Besides the erosion technique described

6. Colin A. Ronan, *Changing Views of the Universe* (New York: Macmillan, 1961), 180–81.
7. John C. Whitcomb and Henry M. Morris, *The Genesis Flood: The Biblical Record and Its Scientific Implications* (Philadelphia: Presbyterian and Reformed, 1963), 130–32.

above, there are more scientific explanations, like the potassium-argon and uranium 235-lead methods. In addition, there is the carbon 14 method, which is applied to organic materials. These all work on basically the same principle: certain materials under certain conditions tend to decay and change into other materials.[8] For example, potassium deteriorates into argon at a consistent rate. If a given deposit of potassium and argon is found, the ratio of the two amounts found should indicate how long the process has gone on in that particular deposit. In most cases this will appear to be measured in hundreds of millions of years, if not billions. The fallacy of the entire procedure becomes obvious in light of two or three factors. First, it must be proved that the original deposit containing the potassium had no lead whatsoever; or, at least, the original ratio must be known. Obviously, neither of these is possible, because no scientist observed the initial formation. Second, one must assume that there has been no leakage of the deposit, that no lead has percolated into the deposit, or that no potassium has leaked out, or both. Unless and until this can be firmly demonstrated, the process is unreliable and therefore unscientific. Third, if there had been some means whereby the present potassium-argon ratio could have arisen quickly, what appears to be millions of years old might be only thousands. There has as yet been no scientific means of dating the age of inorganic materials without a great deal of groundless assumption lying at its foundation.[9]

Similarly, there is no way to date organic remains conclusively, for even the carbon 14 method has gradually been discredited as a certain means of dating materials any more than a very few thousand years old. The variables are so great that as eminent an archaeologist as G. Ernest Wright said that he felt no confidence in using this means for very ancient materials.[10] Yet, as they do with the other methods just mentioned, many scientists continue to use the carbon 14 method and to base allegedly sound conclusions on it, knowing full well that only assumed premises justify it.

Scientism teaches that the earth is the product of aeons of evolutionary development because, apart from the Scriptures, it has absolutely no alternatives. The universe must be old because it looks old and because nothing but great age can account for its development. It assumes evolution and uniformitarianism, and it forces the phenomena to conform to them;

8. Donald Collier, "New Radiocarbon Method for Dating the Past," in *The Biblical Archaeologist Reader*, vol. 1, ed. G. Ernest Wright and David Noel Freedman (Garden City, N.Y.: Doubleday, Anchor Books, 1961), 330–37.

9. Frank Hole and Robert Heizer, *An Introduction to Prehistoric Archaeology* (New York: Holt, Rinehart, and Winston, 1965), 151.

10. Lecture at Hebrew Union College, Jerusalem, July 21, 1965.

anything less, to scientism, is unscientific. In so reconstructing the origin
and development of the universe, scientism acts on faith in the infallibil-
ity of its postulates. What, then, makes the Christian position any less
tenable? It, too, operates by faith, but the object of its faith is the God of
creation who has revealed himself as Creator and Redeemer in the Old
and New Testaments. If true scientific principle demands an observer and
recorder of phenomena, only the Genesis account can be considered scientific, for only it dares to claim that there was an Observer present—the
Triune God.[11]

The Act of Creation (Genesis 1–2)

The Cosmological Approach (1:1–2:3)

Critics have long maintained that there are two separate strands of tradition regarding the creation and that these appear in Genesis in parallel
passages, Genesis 1:1–2:4a and 2:4b–7. This erroneous view rests on the
use of the divine names in the passages, Elohim and Yahweh (Jehovah),
respectively. It overlooks that it might have been the writer's purpose to
discuss creation from two different viewpoints. The name *Elohim* suggests
the power and majesty of the transcendent God of creation, so it is only
natural to expect that, when the creation of the universe is in view, that
name should be employed. Yahweh is the personal name of God whereby
he reveals himself to man; it is the covenant name of him who is imma-
nent and who deigns to have close relations with man (Exod. 3:13–15;
6:1–4).[12] In Genesis 2, where the creation of man is the key point, one
would expect the very name that is used.

The first act mentioned in Genesis is the creation of the original mass
of "heaven and earth" (Gen. 1–2). This was "in the beginning," an
expression that, to the practical, nonspeculative Hebrew mind, simply
meant the absolute beginning: in this case, the beginning of everything
but God. The verb used to describe the creative act, *bārāʾ* is what suggests
"creation from nothing" (*creatio ex nihilo*), and it is used, furthermore, only
with Deity.[13] The scientific implication is clear. The mass, the totality of
all that is, came purely and simply from nothing by divine fiat. This is
indeed a refreshing distinction from scientism, which says in so many

11. For an important treatment of the philosophical nature of humanistic scientism see R. J.
Rushdoony, *The Mythology of Science* (Nutley, N.J.: Craig, 1967).

12. Geerhardus Vos, *Biblical Theology: Old and New Testaments* (Grand Rapids: Eerdmans, 1948),
77, 129.

13. Francis Brown, S. R. Driver, and Charles Briggs, *A Hebrew and English Lexicon of the Old
Testament* (London: Oxford University Press, 1962), 135.

words that everything that exists must, in some form, have existed always. This is tantamount to dualism, the concept of eternal matter, a point of view that is unscriptural and irrational.

Exactly what this primeval mass consisted of cannot be known. All that is certain is that everything in the universe consisted of this original material. The process by which God shaped it is related in the immediately following verses.

Without a break, the account goes on to describe the next event of the first day of creation: the appearance of light (vv. 3–5). Verse 2 had indicated that the earth was "without form and void" (tōhû wāvōhû) and that darkness enveloped the face of the entire watery surface of the earth. Now the darkness was dispelled, and light from some unnamed source began to break forth on the unfinished scene. This light in turn was separated from the darkness, which apparently was on the opposite side of the globe, and day and night became distinguished. The entire process thus far completed was performed on "day one," an expression highly suggestive of a twenty-four-hour period of time. Certain scholars attempt to interpret these days as geologic ages; they feel that this permits a reconciliation of the biblical statements with the scientific evidence of vast periods of time before man's appearance. Besides the literary objection of the expression *day one*, however, there is the problem of the delicate balance of nature that depends on the co-existence of animals and plants. Yet, according to verses 11–20, there was one day, or "era," between the appearance of plants and the creation of animals. The difficulty of answering these objections is greater than that of accepting these as literal days.[14]

On the second day the "firmament" was created (vv. 6–8). This Elizabethan term translates a Hebrew word meaning "something hammered out." To the ancient observer, the sky appeared to be a bowl-like covering for the earth through which the heavenly bodies shone. The actual meaning is that of space, expanse, or even atmosphere. The idea is that God created an atmosphere that, among its other functions, was to "divide the waters from the waters." This strange language can only suggest that, in the earliest period of earth's history, there was a body of water above the earth as well as the seas on the earth. Exactly what form this super-terrestrial water took is a mystery, but the most reasonable assumption is that it consisted of a kind of canopy of vapor, translucent enough to let in the light of the sun, but opaque enough to prevent many agents

14. For good arguments for the twenty-four hour day see Edward J. Young, *Studies in Genesis One* (Philadelphia: Presbyterian and Reformed, 1964), 103–5. Young himself does not reach any conclusion as to the length of the days. See also Henry M. Morris, *Studies in Science and the Bible* (Philadelphia: Presbyterian and Reformed, 1966), 33–38.

in outer space from entering the lower atmosphere. The atmosphere is called heaven, meaning in this context not the dwelling place of God but simply any height above the surface of the earth itself.

On the third day, the waters were gathered together into one place and the dry land appeared (vv. 9–10). Thus is described the formation of the continent or continents. As soon as this was accomplished, plants began to shoot up from the earth, each plant and tree so created that it would bring forth only according to its own kind (*min*). This is a direct assault on the evolutionary hypothesis that not only allows but necessitates a violation of this principle. Evolution cannot take place, according to its own canons, without development from one kind to another, an idea flatly contradicted here.

The fourth day witnessed the positioning of "light holders" in the heavens to be the source of light from that day forth (vv. 14–19). The light that up to that point had emanated from some other unnamed source now originated from the sun, the moon, and the stars.

The verb *bārā'* is used once again in verse 21 to describe the beginning of animal life (vv. 20–25). Obviously, the verb is used here in connection with every kind of animal but man, for it is repeated later in connection with the creation of man as a separate act. The implication is that there are three distinct acts of creation and, therefore, that these three must be qualitatively different. The first was the original mass; the second was the animals; and the third (vv. 26–30) was man. The evolutionist who suggests that man evolved from a lower form must face squarely this differentiation in Genesis. For just as *bārā'* implies making something from nothing in a material sense, it also, and here specifically, implies making something that had never existed before.[15] Man is so different from the animals that preceded him that he must be a special object of God's creative power, just as those animals were different from the plants that had been created before them. Animals, like plants, are to reproduce after their kind. It will be the law of nature that they do so, a fact precisely contrary to the law of evolution that one species must come from another.

Finally, on the sixth day, man himself was created (*bārā'*; vv. 26–28). The nature of man is implied. He was in the image (*ṣelem*) and likeness (*dᵉmût*) of God and his function is clearly spelled out: he was to multiply, fill the earth, and dominate all things. All that is intended here is the mere mention of the fact and purpose of man's creation. Chapter 2 enlarges on both a great deal.

15. Gordon J. Wenham, *Genesis 1–15*, Word Biblical Commentary (Waco: Word, 1987), 14, 24.

TABLE 3

The Days of Creation[16]

First Day — The heaven, earth, and light (1:1–5)
Second Day — The expanse (1:6–8)
Third Day — The dry land and plants (1:9–13)
Fourth Day — The sun, moon, and stars (1:14–19)
Fifth Day — Water and air animals (1:20–23)
Sixth Day — Land animals and man (1:24–31)
Seventh Day — Cessation from creation (2:1–3)

Because of the great emphasis on man's having dominion over all nature, at least in the animal world, and its attestation in subsequent history until the flood, it appears that this was a most essential point. To what extent this domination was possible is uncertain, but it surely involved much more than is commonly thought. It is very likely that the remarkable conditions described by the prophets with regard to millennial life were the common, ordinary features of man's life in his innocence (Isa. 11:6–9; 65:25; Hos. 2:18). "The lion and the lamb shall lie down together, and a little child shall lead them" may not be poetic after all, for the evidence clearly supports the possibility that man at one time could do this very thing. All this fortifies the earlier contention that natural law, after all, may be neither more nor less than restrictive measures placed on man as a result of sin. What might man do apart from this curse? The innocent Adam and the sinless Christ, with their domination of nature, answer that question eloquently (Matt. 17:20; Mark 4:39–41; 6:48–50; Luke 19:30–35).[17]

Finally, God told man what he might eat, a diet consisting only of vegetables, both for him and for all animals (1:29–31). Only after the flood did men and animals become carnivorous, an indication of the deteriorating relationship between them, a deterioration that permeated the entire earth as a result of sin (Rom. 8:19–23).

The seventh day was set apart as a day of rest, for within six days God had created all things, and now he rested (2:1–3). The thought is not that God was weary and needed respite, but merely that he ceased from cre-

16. For an excellent discussion of the days of Gen. 1 as a thematic rather than chronological construct, see Wenham, *Genesis 1–15*, 6–7.
17. See Eugene H. Merrill, "Covenant and the Kingdom: Genesis 1–3 as Foundation for Biblical Theology," *Criswell Theological Review* 1 (1987): 298–302.

ative work. His was now a task of maintenance, not creating. So the seventh day was set apart by God; from that time man was to commemorate the creation on the sabbath day as a monument to God's power and glory.

God's resting from creation flies in the face of evolution, which requires some form of eternal creationism. It is more scientific than scientism, which claims that creation is an ongoing process, for one of the cardinal principles of true science is that matter can be neither created nor destroyed; it can only be converted nonreversibly to heat energy.

The Anthropological Approach (2:4–25)

The parallel account of creation in Genesis 2 deals almost exclusively with man. The passage begins by describing the purposelessness of a creation without a subregent acting on God's behalf in nature (2:4–7). The stage is set, the scene is drawn, but there is no prime actor to give it all life and meaning. Then the creation of this actor is described in profoundly simple terms. The verbs employed here are of great interest, for they relate the steps involved in the creative act. Genesis 1:27 records that man was created (*bārā᾽*), meaning that the concept of a man first came into existence. Now man is made (*ʿāsāh*, 1:26) and formed (*yāṣar*). *ʿĀsāh* refers to the assembling of anything, *yāṣar* to the perfecting of what is made. All together they suggest the tender and loving care that God lavished on his chief created object.

Of paramount importance is the expression *image and likeness* in 1:26 as it relates to the creation process of 2:7. The formation of the body itself poses no particularly difficult problems comparatively, but the concept of man as a living soul (*nepeš ḥayyîm*) is a little more obscure. Genesis 1:30 states that even the animals possess a "soulishness" (*nepeš*), so man's uniqueness lies not in the mere soul itself. His difference from the animals must be explained in the light of "image and likeness" and in the process by which the *nepeš* is granted. The only realistic interpretation is that man's soul was breathed into his body by God and that as a result of the relationship of this act to the body itself, man became a *nepeš* in God's image and likeness. The animals apparently were created, body and soul, by a spoken word of God; man was created through a process of inbreathing that transmitted to him in a peculiar and unique manner the characteristics constituting God's image and likeness. Such attributes as personality, sensibility, will, and reason separate man from the animal world and show him to be a creature related in some wonderful way to God. Moreover, man is not so much "in the image" of God as he is that very image itself. The Hebrew preposition translated "in" can just as readily speak of equivalence. Man thus is God's very image, that is, his represen-tative on the earth.[18]

"Theistic" or "threshold" evolution teaches that the spiritual nature of man was immediately created but that his physical makeup was the result of a long process of evolution. When *homo sapiens* had sufficiently advanced beyond the higher primates, he was given a soul by God, and this is what is meant by the divine inbreathing.[19] This is clearly nothing more than ordinary evolution except that the uniqueness of man, accord-ing to this view, resulted from an instantaneous creative act. The hypoth-esis rests on the basic assumptions of atheistic evolution; the two stand or fall together. Surely the evidence for subhuman societies can be explained in some way other than saying that they represent a stage in human evo-lution, perhaps the stage before man finally evolved into the image of God. From the scanty bone fragments and material remains that exist, lit-tle can actually be proved about the periods from which they supposedly come. What is demonstrable may suggest only that some human beings advanced more quickly than others, or that certain hereditary or environ-mental factors contributed to aberration in physical and mental growth patterns. The existence of pygmies in Africa in the neighborhood of giants indicates that people can have vastly different skull sizes and bodily shapes and yet be from the same period and virtually the same place.[20]

The next matter of import in the account of man's creation is the loca-tion of his original home (2:8–17), a place called Eden ("delight"), whose location is highly speculative. It is true that four rivers are named in connection with it, two of which, the Tigris and Euphrates, are known from extrabiblical sources. If the flood was universal and as destructive as the account implies, there would be no means of locating pre-flood geo-graphical places, however, for the beds of rivers and other geographical features would certainly have been tremendously altered. The most out-standing fact about the garden of Eden concerns the two trees in its midst, the tree of life and the tree of knowledge of good and evil. That these trees had no inherent ability to produce either life or knowledge should be clear from even a superficial understanding of Old Testament theology, which is markedly free of the superstition that such an assumption would require. Rather, the trees were symbolic or sacramental; that is, eating or refraining from eating of them would express faith and obedience in the

18. Gerhard von Rad, *Genesis* (London: SCM, 1961), 55–59.

19. Ernest Charles Messenger, *Evolution and Theology: The Problem of Man's Origin* (New York: Macmillan, 1932), 144.

20. W. E. LeGros Clark, *The Antecedents of Man* (reprint ed.; New York: Harper and Row, 1963), 23.

God who issued the command. Whatever they imparted, they imparted only as vehicles of God's gracious bestowal.[21]

The existence of the tree of life in the garden indicates that man was not created with life in its fullest realization. He was created as an immortal candidate for eternal life, but the conferment of this life depended entirely on his reaction to the divine prohibition to eat of the tree of knowledge of good and evil. Genesis 3 shows that he did not overcome the satanic temptation to eat of this tree, so he was automatically barred from the tree of life (3:22–24). One can only assume that had he obeyed God fully, he would have eaten of the tree of life and immediately received the life of the highest order represented by the tree. God pointed out to man that if he did eat of the tree of knowledge of good and evil, he would thenceforth become a creature subject to death, one to whom physical death would be a necessity, though another way would be provided to guarantee him eternal life in response to faith.

The last part of Genesis 2 records that man was given a companion who was "meet" or "fit" for him (vv. 18–25). Adam certainly had observed that all animals had their mates, but when he gathered them all before him and gave them their names, he found not one among them suitable to his particular needs. God therefore extracted from Adam one of his ribs, from which he fashioned a woman. Adam said that she should be called woman (ʾiššāh) because she came from man (ʾiš), stating that from that day it would be part of the divine purpose for man and woman to be joined together as one flesh. The last statement, that they were naked and were not ashamed, proleptically speaks of the tragedy of sin that was to ensue so early in their experience together.

The Fall of Man (Genesis 3)

The story of man's original sin hangs like a black shadow over the beauty of everything that has transpired so far. In some unexplained way, sin was hatched in the heart of Satan, who now, in the form of a serpent in the garden, tempted man successfully to follow him in his rebellion against the Almighty.[22] Because the serpent was naturally more subtle than any other creature, Satan took advantage of it to accomplish his end by becoming incarnate in it. Through a series of questions and doubts, he finally convinced the woman that the only reason God had prohibited the

21. Vos, *Biblical Theology*, 37–43.
22. Isaiah 14 and Ezekiel 28 may indirectly allude to Satan's fall, though the context in each case shows the immediate concern to be judgment on the rulers of Babylon and Tyre respectively. See Walther Eichrodt, *Theology of the Old Testament*, 2 vols. (Philadelphia: Westminster, 1967), 2:205–9.

eating of the tree of knowledge was that God was jealous for his own sovereignty and that his sovereignty would be jeopardized by man's acquisition of knowledge. If the woman had only reasoned carefully, she would have realized how preposterous the whole satanic proposition was, for if God were so terrified that man would be equal to him in knowledge, why would God create the very means of man's acquiring that knowledge? But woman, who had already misconstrued the prohibition of God in her debate with Satan (3:2–3), was unable to let her reason rule over her emotions. When she realized the desirability of the tree, she partook of it, sharing it with her husband, who ate with her. Immediately their spiritual eyes were opened, and they recognized all too late the enormity of their transgression, for their nakedness became a source of embarrassment to them for the first time, an indication of their deeper and more serious spiritual nakedness.

The knowledge of good and evil was not merely the ability to distinguish between the two but the complete understanding of all that they involved.[23] This knowledge could be gained in either of two ways. Presumably, if the temptation had been resisted, man would have gained this knowledge by divine revelation, without having experienced evil. Because he did not, however, he became aware of the nature of good and evil by experiencing the evil, marking its infinite contrast to the good that had made up the totality of his experience before he sinned. He now had the knowledge he wanted, but at the cost of his own physical and spiritual existence. All that could possibly avail now was an act of divine saving grace.

When they recognized that they were physically and spiritually naked, man and woman hid themselves from God, who nonetheless found them and elicited from them a confession of sin. God then proceeded to speak prophetic curses to all three, Satan, woman, and man. To Satan he promised immediate retaliation, as represented in the perpetual crawling of the serpent and its ultimate destruction by the seed of the woman. This reference to the seed (singular) of the woman (not the man, as would ordinarily be the case) is the first messianic promise in the Old Testament (3:15; cf. Isa. 7:14). This Seed, which can only be Christ, the virgin-born Son of God, would eventually destroy Satan and sin forever. God predicted that the woman would experience pain in childbirth and subservience to her husband, both of which were to remind her henceforth of her part in tempting her husband (1 Tim. 2:12–15). Finally, the man was

---

23. The combination *good and evil* is a figure of speech known as a merismus. It suggests totality by expressing opposites. See von Rad, *Genesis*, 79.

told that the ground would be cursed and that, as he expended his energy and very life in an effort to produce from it the food of life, he would weary himself in agonizing toil even to the point of death, eventually returning as dust to that very soil. Then, as though to palliate the awfulness of the curse on man and woman, God slew an innocent animal and made from the victim garments of skins to cover them. The fig leaves of their own invention were insufficient, for what was actually needed was spiritual covering (atonement), something that would be accomplished only by faith in shed blood (Heb. 9:22).

Man was then barred from the tree of life. The possibility of a sinful human being eating of the tree reserved for the innocent and thereby achieving eternal life was reprehensible to God. Man might be saved, but, having forfeited the way of the tree of life by his disobedience, he must now cast himself on the mercy of God and, through faith in the divinely ordained system of sacrifice, receive what could have been his without the shedding of blood.

The Genealogy of Adam and Eve (Genesis 4–5)

The Family of Cain (4:1–24)

Sometime after man's sin, children were born to Adam and Eve. The first was named Cain ("gotten"), for it is likely that in him Eve saw the fulfillment of the promised seed of Genesis 3:15. She felt that this one whom she had gotten by God's grace might be the one who could crush Satan once and for all. Eventually a second son, Abel, was born. In the course of time both sons took up their own occupations, Cain as a tiller of the ground and Abel as a keeper of sheep.

On a certain occasion, they appeared before God bearing their offerings. Abel and his offering were accepted, while Cain and his offering were rejected by God, apparently because of Cain's improper attitude or lack of true faith (Heb. 11:4; John 3:12). God gave Cain an opportunity to repent and warned him what would happen if he did not. But the enraged Cain slew Abel one day in the open field. God called him to account and, finding Cain yet unrepentant, sentenced him to the life of a vagabond, perhaps to be understood as a nomadic life. Yet, he graciously shielded him with divine protection lest any human being kill him in revenge.

The first murderer was then sent out into the land of Nod, where he and his wife, who no doubt was one of his sisters, founded a civilization at a city named Enoch. Several generations probably had passed by this time, and Cain likely had produced hundreds of descendants, though a city by

Old Testament standards was certainly not necessarily very large. This perhaps was no more than a cluster of bedouin tents where a type of simple life was practiced. In the fifth generation after Cain, Lamech appears in the genealogy, receiving special recognition. This man, the first bigamist, produced three sons: Jubal, Jabal, and Tubal-cain, each of whom became proficient in an art or skill, presupposing rather high cultural development these many thousands of years before Christ. Lamech furthermore sang the first recorded poetry, a verse of boasting arrogance against God and society. The trend of the Cainite civilization had become unquestionably clear and the outlook for world history extremely pessimistic.

The Family of Seth (4:25–5:32)

Following Abel's death, a son was born to take his place, appropriately named Seth ("appointed"). He in turn sired a son named Enos ("weak man"), a clue that illustrates the true condition of fallen man as recognized by the godly Seth. At that time, however, men began to call on the name of Yahweh. It is surely possible that the Sethites recognized that the God of heaven had revealed himself through them as a witness against the unrighteous Cainites.

Genesis 5 is essentially a genealogy of Seth, tracing his posterity through to Noah and his three sons. Immediately striking are the references to the extremely long lives of these pre-deluge patriarchs. Many scholars have tried unsuccessfully to discredit the literalism of these lifespans.[24] The years mentioned cannot be based on a lunar calendar rather than solar, as some suggest, making a year only one-twelfth as long as these appear, for in the case of Enoch, for example, this breaks down completely. It is as great a miracle for Enoch to beget Methuselah at the age of five as it is for Adam to live for 930 years! John C. Whitcomb and Henry M. Morris suggest that, before the flood, the vapor canopy in the heavens filtered out cosmic rays that contribute to aging, and men simply did not age so quickly.[25] Certainly, for an immediate realization of God's command for man to be fruitful and multiply and fill the earth, man must have been able to produce children much more prolifically than now. Extension of his productive years would have facilitated this greatly. The Sumerian King List, which purports to list all the ancient kings both before and after the flood, is also of great importance in the argument. These kings allegedly lived

24. John Skinner, A Critical and Exegetical Commentary on Genesis (New York: Charles Scribner's Sons, 1910), 129.
25. Whitcomb and Morris, The Genesis Flood, 399–405.

not just hundreds but many thousands of years. A few, in fact, reigned as many as forty thousand years![26] These figures are greatly exaggerated, but they testify that man's memory could recall a time when people lived much longer than now. The Old Testament and these traditions both refer to a common reality, the longevity of these persons, but the latter, over the course of thousands of years of oral (and possibly written) transmission, have completely corrupted the original facts. The biblical figures, having come from either divinely preserved historical records or by immediate revelation to Moses, reflect the actual case, as the evidence makes clear.

Two figures of this godly race stand out more vividly than the rest: Enoch for his godliness, and Methuselah for his great age, 969 years. The former "patterned his life after God" and so was excepted from the principle that "it is appointed unto man once to die" (Heb. 9:27). In simple majesty the account states that "he was not, for God took him" (Gen. 5:24).

The Flood (Genesis 6–9)

The parallel races of humanity described in Genesis 4 and 5, those of the Cainites and Sethites, continued to multiply through many generations. As long as there was separation between them, the knowledge of the true God could be maintained even in the face of increasing wickedness on earth. The time finally came, however, when that division was no longer preserved, for Genesis 6:1–2 relates that intermarriage took place between the two, resulting in absorption of the covenant race. Only Noah and his family retained their faith. Some would suggest that the "sons of God" in this passage were angels, while the "daughters of men" were human beings, and that there was, therefore, marriage between angels and men.[27] Though this interpretation appears to have some support, especially from Job (1:6), Peter (2 Pet. 2:4), and Jude (6, 7), the overall arguments against it seem to outweigh it. Jesus described the angels as sexless (Mark 12:25). Moreover, the purpose for carefully outlining the fortunes of the Cainites and Sethites in Genesis 4 and 5 is meaningless apart from assuming that Cainites and Sethites are intended in Genesis 6 and that their intermarriage was the occasion of God's judging man by the flood.

Regardless of the identification, the narrator observes that the world was a place in which none followed after God. God decided to alter his

26. Thorkild Jacobsen, *The Sumerian King List* (Chicago: University of Chicago Press, 1939), 71–73.
27. Franz Delitzsch, *A New Commentary on Genesis* (Edinburgh: T. and T. Clark, 1899), 225–26.

procedure (which is the meaning here of "repent") and to destroy man from off the earth within a period of 120 more years (6:3). One man alone found grace in his eyes. Noah, whose name means "comfort" or "rest," was chosen to be saved from the flood and to be the means of reestablishing the human race in a post-deluge world. He, like Enoch, patterned his life after God (compare 5:24 with 6:9), but the reason for his selection by God still must rest ultimately in his being an object of God's special sovereign grace (6:8).

Because it was God's intention to destroy mankind alone, only those animals that could not survive flood waters needed to be saved along with Noah and his family. Following divine specifications, Noah built a vessel large enough to accomplish the task of preserving at least two of every species, except, of course, creatures that would survive even better apart from an ark. The dimensions, following the eighteen-inch cubit, were 450 x 75 x 45 feet. The craft was divided into three decks, each with an area of about 33,750 square feet, so the entire capacity was roughly 1.5 million cubic feet.

This is an important fact, for one of the most prevalent arguments against the universality of the flood is that the boat could not have accommodated all the animals and food necessary if two of every kind were preserved. Modern taxonomy estimates that there are about one million different species, over 95 percent of which, however, could conceivably have existed outside the ark.[28] This means that there were no more than fifty thousand animals in all, though Whitcomb and Morris believe the figure should be no higher than thirty-five thousand[29] and the average size of these would be about equivalent to that of a sheep. Simple calculation leads to the conclusion that all of the animals could have been accommodated on one deck by itself, leaving the other two for food storage and other purposes. Of course, there was no water problem, for it is likely that rain fell throughout most of the duration of the flood.

After the long period of preparation was completed, during which Noah served God as a preacher of righteousness warning and urging the people to repent (2 Pet. 2:5; Heb. 11:7), God instructed him to enter the ark with two of every unclean animal and seven of every clean (6:19; 7:2). The seventh of each was no doubt for sacrifice following the deliverance, and more of them were taken also to ensure their continued existence. Having shut the door of the ark, God opened the "floodgates of the heavens" and, for forty days, the rains fell, apparently never having done so before. If the

28. Whitcomb and Morris, *The Genesis Flood*, 68.
29. Ibid., 69.

concept of the "canopy" is correct, it could easily have been the source of this deluge and, depending on its thickness, could have deposited literally hundreds of feet of water on the earth. In addition, the "fountains of the great deep" were broken open, and water from subterranean reservoirs began to gush forth with unrestrained fury, rising perhaps thousands of feet, sweeping all before it and destroying all nonaquatic creatures. In addition, it is likely that the continents dropped considerably, causing even more extensive flooding. The waters covered all land, even the highest mountains, by the 150th day. God's purpose was achieved.

After 150 days, the water began to recede, most of it returning to its underground sources and filling the greatly deepened ocean beds. Probably the continents also rose, thrusting up great mountain peaks in the wake of phenomenal tectonic pressures (Ps. 104:6–9). Finally, after sending out birds to determine the state of the earth, Noah disembarked, setting foot on dry ground for the first time in over a year. All about him was chaos, for the civilization that presumably had reached such a peak of development before the flood had been reduced to oblivion. Yet in the midst of all this, Noah set out to offer sacrifices of thanksgiving and praise to his Creator and Redeemer, sacrifices that God accepted, promising never again to destroy the earth with the waters of a flood (9:8–17).

Arguments for a Universal Flood

One of the most critical and debated problems involved with the flood story has to do with its extent. Was it local in scope, covering only the Mesopotamian area, or was it universal? If it was universal, was it only anthropologically universal, or was it also geographically universal? The biblical narrative itself almost certainly implies a universal flood, one covering the face of the whole earth and destroying every creature on its surface. The only way that this can be circumvented is to believe that the writer, or Noah himself, was using the language of appearance: the flood appeared to be universal because it covered everything within man's immediate scope of observation.[30]

Whitcomb and Morris again have some telling arguments that the interested reader should consult, among which are the following:[31]

1. The depth of the flood (Gen. 7:19–20). If the flood was only in a restricted area, it is difficult to comprehend the fact that it cov-

30. Bernard L. Ramm, *The Christian View of Science and Scripture* (Grand Rapids: Eerdmans, 1954), 240.

31. Whitcomb and Morris, *The Genesis Flood*, 1–35.

ered the highest mountains, even in a small area, without overflowing to other areas. The fact that water seeks its own level seems to be decisively against a local flood.

2. The duration of the flood. It appears that the flood lasted for over one year in all from the time Noah entered the ark until he left it. During most of that time, the water was on the earth. No local flood in history ever lasted that long. Any flood that endured for such a long period would, therefore, have to be universal.

3. The size of the ark. Why would Noah build a vessel large enough to accommodate all the land species on earth when all he needed was one large enough to save the species that lived only in Mesopotamia, of which there must have been very few?

4. The need for an ark at all. More fatal to the local flood is the utter lack of any need for an ark in such an event, for Noah could easily have walked from the scene of the impending disaster, taking with him any animals in danger of drowning. Why spend 120 years building a boat for which there was no real need?

5. The testimony of Peter. Peter argues (2 Pet. 3:3–7) that, at the end of this age, God will destroy the world with a fiery judgment. He bases his argument for the extensiveness of this judgment on the analogy of the destruction by water in Noah's time. If Peter is trying to teach a universal devastation by fire, which he assuredly is, why should he compare it to a merely local flood of Noah's time?

Other Basic Questions

The extent of the flood raises related problems, especially if the waters covered the whole earth. One of the most intriguing of these is the source of the flood waters and their disposition following the deluge. It has already been suggested that the canopy of water above the earth, coupled with the "fountains of the great deep," could easily account for the water's source, particularly if the land masses were not as high as they presently are and therefore required less water to be submerged. As the waters rose to greater and greater heights, their tremendous weight began to cause the earth's crust to sink in some places and to be folded higher in others. The result was that, during or right after the flood, the ocean beds deepened considerably and the land masses shrank, though probably they increased in height.[32] Psalm 104:6–9, which speaks of the primeval chaos and emergence of dry land from water, contains the same language as the flood nar-

32. For the same idea from a different perspective, see von Rad, *Genesis*, 124.

rative, especially in verse 8, which says literally, "the mountains ascend, the valleys descend." The continental shelves, which ring the continents of the world at a distance of several hundred miles in some cases and are several thousand feet below the ocean's surface, indicate either that at one time the oceans were very much smaller or that the continents have sunk. The former, it seems, is just as easy to prove as the latter, and the flood would provide the very factors needed.

Another interesting speculation has to do with fossils and rock strata. Scientists commonly use these as indications of age, but only at the risk of circular reasoning. For example, they allege that the age of a rock can be determined by the nature of the imbedded fossils and that the age of those fossils is indicated by the level of rock in which they are found.[33] But this ignores the question, How can one account for rock stratification and fossil indices in the first place? The scientist is hard put to explain both of these phenomena, usually resorting to uniformitarian hypotheses that are completely unsatisfying to the unprejudiced mind. What current process now at work in nature could ever, even in billions of years, produce the Grand Canyon? How can whole beds of millions of fossils be deposited by the ordinary processes of erosion and deposition presupposed by the evolutionary theory? Yet a catastrophic occurrence like the flood could account for both. As billions of tons of materials were swept up and suspended by the flood waters, they were eventually deposited, and in a generally predictable order. Heavy and light materials or materials with varying viscosity would be laid down in discernible layers, exactly as they appear today. Fossils of animals caught in the flood, too, would naturally follow a general pattern of deposition, both because of the animals' varying shapes and sizes and because of their varying abilities to escape the flood waters. The less complex the organism, the less is its adaptability to danger and the earlier is its burial in water and mud. Simple marine creatures would be deposited first, and this is what we find in the fossil index. The more complex the organism, the higher it would climb away from the encroaching waters and the later it would be entombed. The highest orders of all, the more intelligent mammals, would drown last. One would expect to find them on the top strata, and that is precisely where they usually are found. Exceptions to the index are common, but some are explainable by later overthrusts and faulting.[34] However, in a sudden catastrophe, in some cases even large mammals would be trapped at the outset. Local circumstances and the reworking of deposits during the flood would also affect the location of fossils.

33. William Charles Putnam, *Geology* (New York: Oxford University Press, 1964), 440–41.
34. Whitcomb and Morris, *The Genesis Flood*, 271–75.

The problem of the formation of canyons is also germane. Under no uniformitarian set of principles can they be understood, for the conditions requisite for their original state and formation could not exist under these assumptions. But the waters of a flood several hundred feet deep, returning to their beds in the oceans with the eroding force presupposed by as brief a period of return as that described in the Bible, could cut their way through the freshly deposited materials of the flood in a few years, while the uniformitarian assumption would require millions of years. In other words, given soft soils and tremendous amounts of swiftly moving water, both of which are a tacit concomitant of a universal flood, the problem of the canyons disappears.

Finally, it is helpful to consider briefly the great glaciers, tropical fossils in the polar regions, and woolly mammoths. Scientists generally agree today that at one time the earth enjoyed a tropical climate throughout and that tropical plants were to be found everywhere. As a matter of fact, fossils of these plants have been found as far north as the Arctic Circle. Moreover, hunters and other people have found in the Siberian tundra the frozen carcasses of woolly mammoths so well preserved that their meat was still edible![35] When they were cut open, tropical plants were found still undigested, perfectly intact, in their stomachs. Scientism has a very difficult time accounting for all of this, but the universal flood presents some solutions that are worthy of consideration. The canopy of water no doubt provided a greenhouse effect that rendered the climate of the earth equally warm throughout. When this canopy disappeared as rain, rapid climatic changes ensued, and the polar zones became frozen. Anything living there also froze, becoming trapped in the mud and rock laid down by the flood. If the process of drowning, entombment, and freezing occurred quickly enough, thousands of animals could be preserved indefinitely. Uniformitarianism has no adequate solution to these problems, but the flood, rightly understood, is quite satisfactory.[36] By allowing for a proper "stretching" of the biblical chronology, a proposal to be advanced later, the date of the flood could be between 10,000 and 6000 B.C. The usual scientific dating for the last Ice Age is about 10,000 B.C., which ties in nicely with this reconstruction. After the flood, the polar areas froze, the climate made even more subsequent changes, and eventually the frozen area receded to the polar regions. The Ice Age was over, leaving

35. Charles Schuchert, *Outlines of Historical Geology* (New York: John Wiley and Sons, 1947), 37.
36. Needless to say, the "Whitcomb and Morris hypothesis" is only one of many valid approaches to the scientific aspects of the flood. For an alternative that takes strong exception to that hypothesis and understands creation and flood geology in a radically different way, see Davis A. Young, *Creation and the Flood: An Alternative to Flood Geology and Theistic Evolution* (Grand Rapids: Baker, 1977).

the scarred remains so evident in the northeastern part of the United States and other places.

A great deal of attention has been devoted to the narratives of the creation and the flood because they are of paramount importance, forming as they do the foundations for all that ensues in Old Testament history. The reliability of that history depends largely on the reliability of these accounts properly interpreted. It is not mere naiveté to say that they stand or fall together.

The Noahic Covenant (Genesis 9)

The first act of God following the flood was the acceptance of the sacrificial offering made to him by Noah. This was followed by his promise never again to destroy the earth by a flood. Catastrophism was not to be the rule from that time forward, except at the end of the world (9:9–11). Nature was to continue an orderly course, or was to be "uniform," manifesting its stability in the regularity of the seasonal cycles and by unending alternation of day and night.

God continued his promise to mankind by outlining the basic features of the covenant he was about to make with Noah, the covenant that formed the real basis for God's having spared man from extinction in the first place. In virtually the same words as those of the Adamic covenant, God informed this second father of the human race that he was to be fruitful and multiply and to replenish the earth (9:1–7). However, there is now a decisive difference. Mankind must continue to have dominion over all things, but this dominion will take the form of forced subservience rather than the docile, voluntary acquiescence demonstrated by nature before the flood. Evidently the environment was now hostile in a way that was not apparent before. The whole universe was out of joint, as Paul was later to imply (Rom. 8:19–22). The best that the human race could expect was to control the environment by sheer strength and ingenuity. This control by force was to issue in the slaughter of animals for food, an occurrence not noted before. In fact, it seems almost certain that such a thing was actually prohibited before the flood. At the same time, man was to be very careful concerning the shedding and eating of blood, for in some peculiar sense blood was sacrosanct. It was to be poured out on the ground and not consumed, for it represented life. Feeding on what was so sacred would be inconsistent with the high premium God placed on life, even that of an animal. This explains the later Mosaic stipulations concerning the meticulous use or nonuse of blood (Lev. 17).

In line with this divine equivalence of life with blood, God states that the shedding of human blood to the point of death was punishable by the death of the one who had shed the blood, whether man or beast (9:5–6). This by no means implies merely human, individual revenge, but rather the prerogative of organized mankind, or government, to assume this function of reprisal. The basic reason for such a harsh punishment is that life is sacred, especially because the human being bears the image of God. To slay the bearer of God's image is to assault the very God whom the image represents, just as the desecration of the national flag constitutes an attack on the nation for which it stands.

The covenant is outlined further beginning in verse 8, where God again enunciated the promise that he would never again destroy the earth by a flood, though this by no means ruled out the possibility of destruction through some other agency (2 Pet. 3:1–17). Then, as though visibly to guarantee to mankind the inviolability of the covenant and also to be consistent with such covenant arrangements, God set in the heavens a rainbow as a sign of the promise. Whoever viewed the bow from that day hence was to take heart in the realization that God, who had made the covenant, would be faithful to its stipulations.

Following the declaration of the Noahic covenant is a narrative about the immediately following course of human history (9:18–28), a tragically sordid beginning to the new human civilization. Noah had no sooner received the promises of God in the covenant than he showed dramatically the utter inability of mankind to measure up to his covenant responsibility. He planted a vineyard, drank from the wine that it produced, and lay in a drunken, naked stupor within his tent. His son Ham found him there and, with none of the common filial regard expected of a son, refused to cover his father and keep from his brothers the awful details of his father's shame; in fact, there is every likelihood that he acted with a positive assertion of the latent immorality that seemed to characterize him, or certainly his son Canaan.[37] Upon awakening, Noah issued a prophetic statement of cursing and blessing on the three sons, expressing in capsule form the affairs of the three great branches of mankind as they would develop in history. These were not racial divisions, as is apparent from Genesis 10 and 11. They seem rather to be constituted along spiritual lines. Canaan, the son of Ham, was cursed in his father's place, the curse manifesting itself primarily in Canaan's servitude to his brethren (Josh. 9:22–27). Shem, the meaning of whose name is "name," was to be Canaan's master. Japheth was to be enlarged and to dwell in the tents of Shem and be dominant over Canaan.

---

37. For various possibilities, see Allen P. Ross, *Creation and Blessing: A Guide to the Study and Exposition of the Book of Genesis* (Grand Rapids: Baker, 1988), 214–15.

It is important to note that there is no basis here for assigning the black race to bondage because of any divine curse. The Hamites, from whom the negroid peoples undoubtedly sprang, were not objects of the curse. Only Canaan, a tiny part of that great group of humanity, was involved. Moreover, Canaan by no stretch of the imagination can be considered negroid, for the Canaanites settled primarily on the eastern Mediterranean, and any mention of them in the Old Testament seems to suggest that they were not racially distinct from the Hebrews or any other peoples with whom they come in contact. The subjugation of Canaan was fulfilled in its defeat at the hands of the Hebrews under Joshua and, later, the conquests of the Phoenicians (who were related to the Canaanites) by Babylonia and Persia and of the Carthaginians (Phoenician colonists) by Rome in the Punic Wars.

The exaltation of Shem was bound up in the fact that God would reveal his saving name to the world through Shem. Shem was to be the vehicle of divine revelation and salvation, a concept amply illustrated in Abraham, Isaac, Jacob, David, and the whole messianic line down to and including Christ, all of whom were Shemites (Semites). The idea of Japheth's dwelling in the tents of Shem may include both the occupation of the Near East by Gentile nations throughout history and the extension of the gospel message to the non-Jewish world, the latter being far more likely.

The Dispersion of the Nations (Genesis 10–11)

One of the stated objectives of the Noahic covenant was for man to scatter abroad on the face of the whole earth so that he could exercise rule over every part of the creation. The events described immediately after the flood indicate, however, that the descendants of Noah were slow to carry out this obligation. This is especially noticeable when the events of Genesis 10 and 11 appear in their proper chronological order and perspective. The first description of post-deluge humanity occurs in Genesis 11:1–2, where it is clear that everyone on earth spoke a common language, presupposing a common civilization and culture and, therefore, certain geographic cohesion. This is in antithesis to the covenant, which stipulated that the human race was to overspread the whole earth; indeed, the expression of that antithesis is found in 11:4 in the remark by the builders of Babel to the effect that they wished to countermand God's will by remaining where they were, a cohesive and unified community.

The listing of the nations in Genesis 10, then, must be anticipatory of the dispersion of man by God disclosed in 11:8–9. The latter passage explains how and why the nations were divided, the former, where they settled.

The genealogy of Noah in chapter 10 is an account of the origin of the nations and their earliest ethnic characteristics, for verse 32 states that of Noah and his sons "were the nations divided in the earth after the flood." It is plain that the descendants of Japheth settled basically in south-central Asia and Europe (10:2–5). The early Hamites were located primarily in Africa, with the notable exception of Canaan (10:6–20). The Shemites lived in the Mesopotamian and Iranian region of the Near East (10:21–31; 11:21–32). These are not hard-and-fast distinctions, for there are too many exceptions and overlaps and too much subsequent migration from place to place to make the division constant. Furthermore, there is no hint of reference here to races or colors. Such differences must have developed later, probably after the Tower of Babel incident.

One or two points of special interest in chapter 10 must suffice. First, Nimrod the Cushite moved eastward to found the kingdoms of the Plain of Shinar (10:8–10). This is a good example of a Hamite who moved into Semitic territory to establish a culture, a situation described also in extra-biblical literature.[38] Also, verse 25 points out that a certain Semite by the name of Peleg ("division") lived on the earth at the time of its division. There is only one account of such a division in the Bible, and that is in connection with the dispersion of man after Babel. The mention of Peleg in the Semitic genealogy, therefore, provides valuable information in approximating the date of Babel.

Genesis 11 begins with the story of Nimrod (at least he best fits the situation) and his migration to Mesopotamia (not "from the east" as in many versions). When he and his colleagues settled, they decided to build a city and a tower, the purpose of the latter being to provide a visible monument to the desire of mankind for homogeneity in the face of God's clear commands to disperse. There is no suggestion here that the tower had any religious connotations, though such towers in later Babylonian history did serve as temple towers or shrines in some sense.[39] Rather, there is a definite anti-religious or at least anti-God spirit. Mankind was not attempting to reach heaven; to the contrary, the struggle was one of man against God in the interests of human independence.

God responded to this flagrant disobedience to the covenant conditions by scattering mankind across the earth, a scattering that seems to follow naturally the confusion of human speech. Because people would not spread

38. Skinner, *A Critical and Exegetical Commentary on Genesis*, 208.
39. C. Leonard Woolley, *The Sumerians* (New York: Norton, 1965), 141–42.

throughout the earth voluntarily, God confounded their language so that they were unable to conduct the most ordinary affairs of life; consequently, they lost a sense of fellowship with every other person. They began to gather into small enclaves, each possessing its own speech, and became widespread from the necessity of being distinguished from others with whom they now had so very little in common. This, then, explains the origins of the various worldwide civilizations, each with different languages and customs, yet all possessing certain common traditions like those of the creation and the flood, traditions based on a common experience in their dim pre-Babel world.[40] Perhaps the beginnings of the races may be found here also, for if it was God's purpose to render humanity incapable of cohesion, its separation into races would compound the difficulties inherent in the confounding of languages. As a result of both, mankind would be up against linguistic and sociological obstacles like none he had ever experienced, difficulties he would never be able to overcome completely, no matter how hard he might try. Indeed, the very efforts of moderns to minimize and even eradicate linguistic and racial differences testify to the nature of the problem created at Babel. God's continuing plan is that humanity should overspread the earth, and modern people react as their ancestors did at Babel. They want to unite as one against God's will. The name of the place, Babel, indicates "confusion" (though etymologically it means "gate of god"), and this term exactly describes the timeless condition of the human race in rebellion against the Creator.

Because the Shemites were selected to bear the covenant promises according to Noah's prophecy, the interest of the narrator from this point on centers on them. The last part of Genesis 11 records the Semitic genealogy from Shem to Abram, the man who was to become the father of a chosen people through whom God would manifest himself to the rest of the world in saving grace. This genealogy is interesting in many respects. It is noteworthy that the ages of the individuals listed are much shorter than those of the pre-deluge patriarchs. This may suggest a change in the environment in which people lived, one detrimental to their health. Or it may simply reflect the increasingly deadly toll of humanity's cursed existence. In addition, by totaling up the years of the various generations, it is possible to arrive at approximate dates for the period between Abraham and the flood, though the probability of gaps in the genealogy and careful interpretation of the data contained therein may well extend the period considerably longer than that reached by a simple addition of

40. John Bright, "Has Archaeology Found Evidence of the Flood?" in *The Biblical Archaeologist Reader*, 1:33.

the figures. Biblical historians now agree that Abraham was born about 2166 B.C.[41] According to a strictly literal exposition of genealogy, the flood must be dated no earlier than 2600 B.C., a figure that is obviously too late. Evidence of thriving and uninterrupted civilizations in both Egypt and Mesopotamia as far back as 4500 B.C. supports this contention. The solution is to attach to the genealogical information certain interpretive criteria that allow the pre-Abrahamic period to be expanded,[42] though such expansion cannot stretch to the tens of thousands of years required by uniformitarian anthropological hypotheses. It may be safe to say, on the basis of both scientific and biblical evidence, that the flood occurred about 8000–7000 B.C. and the Tower of Babel dispersion about 7000–6000 B.C.

The way the genealogy of Genesis 11 proceeds leaves no doubt that the family of Terah of Ur, especially as traced through his son Abram, was to occupy a special place in redemptive history. The whole course of the Genesis historical account swings from national and international considerations to the biographical story of Abram (Abraham) and his family, particularly those of his descendants who were chosen by God to mediate the covenant blessings. To these individuals, known initially as the patriarchs, the story now turns.

41. Eugene H. Merrill, *Kingdom of Priests: A History of Old Testament Israel* (Grand Rapids: Baker, 1987), 25.
42. O. T. Allis, *The Five Books of Moses* (Philadelphia: Presbyterian and Reformed, 1943), 295–98.

3

The Founding Fathers

The Historical Background[1]

In Mesopotamia

At the end of the third millennium, Mesopotamia was for the most part under the domination of the Third Dynasty of Ur, a Sumerian political entity flavored with Semitic influences. In about the middle of the twentieth century B.C., this dynasty was overthrown and supplanted by rival states at Isin and Larsa, both of which maintained at least a tenuous existence until the close of the eighteenth century. Meanwhile, the center of power gradually shifted up the Euphrates to the city of Babylon, where, about 1990 B.C., Shumu-Abum founded the First Dynasty of Babylon. The might of this state increased with the passing of the years; by the time of its famous sixth king, Hammurabi (ca. 1792–1750), it had expanded at least as far as any preceding empire. This level was maintained until ca. 1600, when a violent incursion into the Mesopotamian world by a savage people known as the Kassites ushered in the Babylonian "Dark Ages," a period that was to last, for all practical purposes, until the rise of the Neo-Babylonian Empire in 626 B.C.

1. For an excellent discussion from the standpoint of the "low chronology," see John Bright, A *History of Israel*, 3d ed. (Philadelphia: Westminster, 1981), 47–66.

Other nations were making their impact on this part of the ancient world at this time, notably the Assyrians. Their history before 2000 B.C. is obscure, but by the turn of the millennium they were making their presence felt in a way that indicated the future role they were to play in international affairs. The first monarch of great repute, Shamshi-Adad I (ca. 1813–1781), began to reign in the time of the Hebrew patriarchs and was for a time a contemporary of the great Hammurabi. For some time there was intense rivalry between Assyria and Babylonia, both vying for control of Mesopotamia, until the Kassite invasion of 1600 put Babylonia out of contention and opened the way for a gradual building up of Assyrian strength and influence. It was not until well after the patriarchal period, however, that Assyria was to be reckoned as a first-rate power in Near Eastern diplomacy.

In Egypt

The Eleventh Dynasty of Egypt, which marked the beginning of revival of power in that kingdom, commenced its authority about the beginning of the patriarchal period (ca. 2133 B.C.). It was followed shortly by the Twelfth Dynasty under Amenemhet I (1991–1962), a dynasty that was to become one of the most important in Egyptian history, but one that in turn was followed by a period of disruption hardly paralleled in the life of any other nation, ancient or modern. For about 200 years, the Middle Kingdom (Twelfth Dynasty) made Egypt equal in prestige and power to Mesopotamia in the Near East, and it is now well known that the two cradles of civilization carried on extensive contacts of all kinds.[2] Just as Babylonia had pushed out in many directions in extending its sway over other peoples, Egypt now began to do the same, reaching as far south as the land of Nubia and as far east and north as the Arabian peninsula and southern Syria, including, therefore, Palestine. This imperialism was short-lived, however, for in about the year 1730 Egypt succumbed to a people known in history only as the Hyksos, an apparently seminomadic Semitic race that gradually began to settle near and just within the borders of northeast Egypt and then occupied the whole northern part of the country by military force. The identification of these people has been one of the thorniest of historical problems, for they left few material remains, especially literary, whereby they might be studied. There is no doubt, however, that they made some major contributions to Egypt, including the use of the chariot and a new type of fortification known as the revetment

---

2. William W. Hallo and William Kelly Simpson, *The Ancient Near East* (New York: Harcourt Brace Jovanovich, 1971), 209.

wall.[3] What is most important is that they completely disrupted Egyptian civilization, creating a lacuna in that nation's history that is difficult to fill. They maintained their grip for at least 150 years (ca. 1730–1580) until finally, under Ahmose I of the Eighteenth Dynasty, they were expelled.

In Palestine

The period from 2000 to 1600 B.C. in Palestine was characterized by an almost complete break with the civilization that had existed in the third millennium. Before 2000 there had been many important city-states, the archaeological remains of which suggest that they were strongly fortified and remarkably advanced culturally.[4] Then, almost without intermission, and certainly without explanation as yet, these city-states were overwhelmed in a series of devastations that rendered them completely incapable of continuing their existence. By the end of the Middle Bronze II A period (ca. 1800 B.C.), the process of urbanization recommenced, and once more large and significant towns dotted the Canaanite landscape. Who their builders were is not at all clear, though Amorites and Hyksos are the most likely candidates.[5] Historians now know that there was a tremendous movement of peoples everywhere in the Near East during this chaotic period in history, and the overrunning of Palestine may reflect the results of such mass migration in the Fertile Crescent. Throughout the patriarchal period Palestine seems to have been the home of seminomadic people; not until the middle of the Middle Bronze Age is there much evidence of a sedentary population.

The Old Testament and the Patriarchal Period

The great majority of Old Testament scholars rejects the Old Testament account of the Hebrew patriarchs and their historical background, considering it nothing more than legend or etiology. However, the tremendous wealth of information available today, thanks to systematic excavation in nearly every part of the Near East, has overthrown much of the objective argument against the historicity of the period.[6] Now scholars generally concede that the history depicted in Genesis

3. W. F. Albright, *The Archaeology of Palestine*, rev. ed. (Baltimore: Penguin, 1971), 86. See also John Van Seters, *The Hyksos: A New Investigation* (New Haven, Conn.: Yale University Press, 1966).

4. G. Ernest Wright, "The Archaeology of Palestine," in *The Bible and the Ancient Near East*, ed. G. Ernest Wright (Garden City, N.Y.: Doubleday, 1961), 101.

5. John H. Hayes and J. Maxwell Miller, eds., *Israelite and Judaean History* (Philadelphia: Westminster, 1977), 84–88.

6. W. F. Albright, *The Biblical Period from Abraham to Ezra* (New York: Harper and Row, 1963), 3.

12–50 is reliable, though the figures of Abraham, Isaac, Jacob, and their families are, in their opinion, only retrojections from much later Hebrew history. They are folkloric or etiological, that is, invented by Israelite historians to account for the origin and development of the nation from prehistoric times.[7] Naturally, one presently cannot prove the existence of the patriarchs apart from the text of Scripture, for as yet no archaeological evidence mentioning them has been found. But if one now can establish that the period in which they lived is the same as what Genesis accurately describes, there is no objective reason for dismissing their historicity.

Examples of the reliability of the Old Testament in the light of what is now known extrabiblically about Near East history and culture are not difficult to find in the biblical narrative. The move of Abram from Ur to Haran is consistent with the fact, now recognized, that both cities were centers of moon god worship; it is only logical that Abram, still untaught in his new faith, would seek out a place of residence whose religious practices were familiar to him (Gen. 11:31).[8] The picture in Genesis of Palestine as a land of few or no cities, largely settled by seminomads like what Abram became, is consonant with what is now known for certain about Palestine at this time in history. The story of Abram's migration from the Negev to Egypt at a time of famine (seen again later in the story of Jacob) also is consistent with much Egyptian literature describing the immigration of thousands of Semites into Egypt at this same period and for the same reasons.[9] The selling of Joseph into Egypt with a Midianite caravan and his subsequent elevation to a place of prominence in the Twelfth Dynasty are transactions of a type amply attested in Egyptian sources that, though they do not mention Joseph, do describe similar advancements of Semites in Egyptian government.[10] Joseph's familiarity with the Egyptian customs of his day and Moses' recording of those customs in Genesis are attested to by secular literary material from Egypt that speaks of these same customs.

In addition to the specific instances listed, there is the overall conviction that the patriarchal historical milieu rings authentic. Nothing whatever in the Old Testament, whether in individual statements or in occurrences or in general background, fails to square with the knowledge of the Near East gained in the past one hundred years; as the archaeologist's diligent toil yields more and more information, the historicity of the Genesis

7. Theophile J. Meek, *Hebrew Origins* (New York: Harper, 1960), 2; J. Maxwell Miller and John H. Hayes, *A History of Ancient Israel and Judah* (Philadelphia: Westminster, 1986), 62–63.
8. Merrill F. Unger, *Archaeology and the Old Testament* (Grand Rapids: Zondervan, 1954), 112.
9. Bright, *A History of Israel*, 77–87.
10. Roland de Vaux, *The Early History of Israel* (Philadelphia: Westminster, 1978), 298–99.

account of this patriarchal period becomes more and more firmly supported.

Abraham (Genesis 11:26–25:8)

After the dispersion of mankind at the Tower of Babel, the knowledge of the true God seems to have become even more limited. There is no biblical evidence of any believers at all in the time of Abram, a fact that may account for his having been called by God from idolatrous circumstances in Ur of the Chaldees (the same Ur of the previously discussed Third Dynasty). Still, God maintained his faithfulness to man by singling out an individual in this apostate world condition through whom the covenant promises might be promulgated and realized. This is in line with the principle already discernible that though God's blessings fell on all mankind they were mediated through individuals like Adam, Noah, and now Abram.

Little can be known of Abram's background except that he was a Semite of Mesopotamia whose immediate ancestors were pagan worshipers of the moon god, Sin. The narrator relates that his father Terah migrated from Ur to Haran on the northern curve of the Fertile Crescent and died there when Abram was seventy-five years old. The New Testament adds that Abram had been called by God to leave Ur (Acts 7:2–4), so Terah's move may have been encouraged or even motivated by this call to his son. The circumstances of that initial revelation to Abram are clouded in mystery, but in some way unmistakable to him God called him to set forth in faith to a land that he would show him (Heb. 11:8–12). No doubt these directions were preceded by a divine self-disclosure so plain and so forcefully impressed upon Abram that he immediately forsook his old religious and even geographical environment to embrace the faith of Yahweh, the true and only God. In any event, God made a covenant with Abram, an agreement in which he promised to bless the patriarch immeasurably and to make him and his descendants a blessing to all the world (Gen. 12:1–3).[11]

After leaving Haran, Abram, with his wife Sarai and nephew Lot, traveled south into Canaan, settling first at Shechem (a name given only later to this place), near Bethel, and finally in the Negev. At each of these places he built an altar, a symbol of his new faith and of the awareness of the presence of his God wherever he went (12:4–9). After a time,

---

11. For the nature of this covenant as a royal grant see Moshe Weinfeld, "The Covenant of Grant in the Old Testament and in the Ancient Near East," *Journal of the American Oriental Society* 90 (1970): 184–203.

he moved on into Egypt to escape a famine in Palestine, for though the
Near East might suffer from lack of rain, Egypt, "the gift of the Nile,"
could always rely on the unceasing faithfulness of the great river to overflow its banks annually and provide the necessary topsoil and irrigation.
As he traveled toward Egypt, he revealed his human nature by instructing his wife to explain to the Egyptians that she was his sister and not his
wife, for he feared that, according to custom, the Egyptians might be
attracted to her beauty and kill him in order to make her available to
them legitimately. This half-truth (for she was, indeed, his half-sister) by
so saintly a man is understandable in light of the fact that God had
revealed himself to the patriarch only recently, and then surely in a very
limited way. One cannot expect Abram to measure up to Mosaic truth
when he antedated the giving of that truth by over half a millennium;
yet, he cannot be excused, for even the law codes and culture of his day
advocated standards of truth. The Egyptians did take Sarai, as Abram
feared, but when God began to afflict them for it, they recognized
Abram's deception and, graciously restoring Sarai to him, bade them
leave the country (12:10–20).

Abram and Lot next moved northward to Bethel, where they soon
found that their greatly enlarged herds and flocks were too numerous to be
sustained in the same pastures. To avoid the risk of serious hostility
between them, Abram wisely suggested that Lot select the land he wished
to have, agreeing to take what was left over. Lot, after assessing the situation carefully, chose the well-watered plain of the Jordan, probably south
of the Dead Sea, and "pitched his tent toward Sodom," one of the cities of
the area. God then appeared to Abram and attached geographical
promises to the covenant by assuring him that all the land that he could
see would be his and his descendants' (13).

Genesis 14 is one of the most difficult chapters in the Old Testament
from the standpoint of historical perspective, for though it describes actual
historical persons and events, these cannot be matched with anything yet
known from other than biblical sources. It seems that a coalition of four
Near Eastern kings invaded the plain of Jordan and subjugated the five
city-states there, including Sodom. The kings all bear names that are in
no way anachronistic to the nineteenth century and may even be tenta-
tively identified with monarchs from this period, but no way has yet been
found to equate them with kings known to be contemporaries. It was long
maintained that Amraphel, the king of Shinar, was Hammurabi. Three
basic objections to this are that no other kings with the other names mentioned were contemporary with Hammurabi; Abraham, if the biblical
chronology is to be accepted at face value, antedated Hammurabi by over

three hundred years;[12] and the names *Hammurabi* and *Amraphel* cannot be philologically equated.[13] It is best at present to say that the identifications of these kings are uncertain and to trust that fresh documentary discoveries will clear up the whole matter in time.

For twelve years these eastern kings maintained suzerainty over various parts of Palestine, but then a rebellion took place on a wide scale, the cities of the plain being among the participants. This coup was quashed, the cities were sacked, and various captives, including Lot of Sodom, were carried off to the north. Here another historical difficulty creeps in, for Abram, with 318 servants, set out after these kings and overtook them near Damascus, where he soundly defeated them and rescued Lot and the other prisoners. It is impossible to comprehend that Abram, with such limited forces, could rout four kings and their armies; but on closer scrutiny the problem dissolves. For one thing, the four eastern kings were not necessarily there in person, and there is no evidence that their armies were very substantial. If these were great imperial monarchs, it is likely that they had sent only token forces to campaign in Canaan. Furthermore, what troops they did have were spread over a much larger area than the plain of Jordan alone, so it is only reasonable to conclude that a relative handful were directly involved with the cities of the plain. This being the case, Abram could well have pursued and defeated the small contingent that had defeated Sodom and carried off some of its inhabitants. Besides, Abram undoubtedly had confederates who went with him, and these may have amounted to several hundreds of men (14:13).

Following his victory, Abram returned to Mamre, but on the way he was intercepted by Melchizedek, king of Salem, who appeared bearing bread and wine. As priest of the most high God (El Elyon), he blessed Abram and received from him tithes of all that he possessed. Many scholars maintain that Melchizedek was a Canaanite priest of a tribal deity named El Elyon and that Abram ignorantly confused him with the Hebrew God, or even identified El Elyon with Yahweh.[14] This view is baseless, especially in light of the New Testament. Hebrews 7 deals with Melchizedek, pointing out that he was a mysterious figure who had neither beginning nor end, neither father nor mother, and that he was the prototype of Jesus Christ, the High Priest of the New Testament. It would indeed be strange for the writer of Hebrews to associate Christ with a

12. Eugene H. Merrill, *Kingdom of Priests: A History of Old Testament Israel* (Grand Rapids: Baker, 1987), 37.

13. de Vaux, *The Early History of Israel*, 218.

14. Martin Buber, *Moses* (New York: Harper and Row, 1958), 96–97.

Canaanite priest. Besides, the strange description of Melchizedek, in both
Genesis and Hebrews, leads many interpreters to the conclusion that he
may have been more than a mortal being; indeed, one possibility is to
ascribe Deity to him. Because God did appear many times in the Old
Testament in bodily form (a theophany), it is not incredible that he so
appeared here. One possible objection is that Melchizedek is called the
"king of Salem," and it is difficult to imagine God as the king of this
earthly place (Jerusalem). However, the word salem (šālôm in Hebrew)
means "peace," so one might argue that he is not being called the king of
a place, Jerusalem, but the King of Peace, a term reminiscent of Isaiah's
description of Messiah (Isa. 9:6). Moreover, the name Melchizedek itself
literally means "king of righteousness," another appellation attributed to
God. In summation, some suggest that God appeared to Abram once
again to remind him graciously of his presence and that, in respect of
God's saving power in victory over the kings, Abram offered a tithe of his
possessions.[15]

It is more likely that Melchizedek was a fully human king, probably the
ruler of Jerusalem, who gives evidence of genuine monotheistic faith in
pre-Mosaic times. His name is typical of the era and served the typological
purposes of Old and New Testament messianic theology perfectly. His
major importance lay not only in his name but also in his non-Levitical
priesthood, a priesthood that provided an analogy to that of both David
(2 Sam. 6:12–15; Ps. 110:4) and Jesus (Heb. 7:1–8:6). The reference to his
being without beginning or end and without father and mother means
only that there is no record of such in the Old Testament, a fact that
again sets him in contrast to the descendants of Levi.[16]

The promise of an Abrahamic seed is continued and elaborated in
Genesis 15:1–18:15 in the following way: God appeared in a vision to
Abram and disclosed that, though Abram was old, he would sire a child.
Abram proceeded to argue that the only heir he possessed at present was
Eliezer, his servant, whom he had no doubt adopted as his heir, in line
with the prevailing Near Eastern custom.[17] God corrected Abram by
revealing explicitly that he and Sarai would have a covenant son. The
promise was strengthened by a continuation of the vision in which Abram

15. See, for the view that this is a theophanic disclosure, F. F. Bruce, The Epistle to the Hebrews,
New International Commentary on the New Testament (Grand Rapids: Eerdmans, 1964), 137. Bruce
rejects this view in favor of the more common (and correct) position that Melchizedek is a type of
Christ.

16. Ibid., 133–38.

17. H. J. Cadbury, ed., Annual of the American Schools of Oriental Research, vol. 10 (New Haven,
Conn.: Yale University Press, 1930), Tablet H60.

witnessed a slaughter of animals and their division into two rows.[18] Between them God and Abram passed symbolically, the total effect suggesting the binding of God and Abram together in a blood relationship, the nature of which would lend to the covenant promise a certain unconditional indissolubility. Added to the ceremony was the prophetic declaration of a future four-hundred-year bondage in a strange land (Egypt), followed by a reoccupation of Palestine, the land of the Amorites.   Gen. 15:13

In their desire to realize God's covenant promise, Abram and Sarai, who was barren, decided to have children by Hagar, their Egyptian handmaid (16:1–3). According to the Nuzi tablets, ancient Hurrian cuneiform documents dealing with custom and law of a somewhat later period, the action of Abram and his wife in this respect was perfectly normal.[19] Any children born of this proxy arrangement would be considered legal heirs of the husband unless and until children were born of the wife herself. Hagar conceived but, because of Sarai's jealousy, was banished into the wilderness. There God met her and promised that she, too, would be the mother of a great people (16:10), a people known historically as the Arabs. Ishmael, the son whom she bore, was to be the head of this mighty nation.

Finally, thirteen years later, God appeared once more to Abram, revealing himself this time as the Almighty God (El Shaddai) and promising that though Abram was now ninety-nine years old he would be the father of a nation of kings. As an evidence of God's faithfulness, Abram's name was changed to Abraham. Whereas he had been "great father" (*Abram*), he would be known from now on as the "father of a great people" (*Abraham*). The fulfillment was so imminent and certain that God proceeded to declare to Abraham the sign of the covenant: circumcision. As the rainbow had been the token of the Noahic covenant, the rite of circumcision was to be the token of the Abrahamic covenant, a sign that Abraham immediately put into effect in his own household, circumcising even Ishmael, who had meanwhile returned home. In conjunction with all this, Sarai's name was changed to Sarah ("princess") by virtue of her impending role as mother of the promised race. In spite of this apparent demonstration of faith, both Abraham and Sarah found the promise of a child still too much to accept. They both laughed; consequently God told them that the child would be named Isaac ("laughter").

Soon thereafter, Abraham was outside his tent at Mamre one day when he was approached by three strange visitors whom he, according to cus-

---

18. W. F. Albright, "The Hebrew Expression for 'Making a Covenant' in Pre-Israelite Documents," *Bulletin of the American Schools of Oriental Research* 121 (1951): 21–22.

19. Cadbury, *AASOR* 10, Tablet #80.

tom, began to entertain lavishly. In the course of their conversation, one of the three announced once more to Abraham that he would have a son in the near future, an idea that was so preposterous to the aged Sarah, who was eavesdropping within the tent, that she again laughed to herself. At this the chief visitor, the Angel of Yahweh, rebuked her and, despite her denial, reminded her that the child would surely be named "laughter," a name to remind the patriarch and his wife perpetually of their little faith.

Following the conversation, two of the angelic strangers departed to Sodom to warn the city of its imminent destruction, occasioned by its great wickedness before God. The third, the Angel of Yahweh, remained with Abraham, who began to "bargain" with him concerning Sodom for Lot's sake. After much entreaty, Abraham elicited from the Angel the promise not to destroy the city if even ten righteous inhabitants might be found in it. At the conclusion of the discussion the third stranger, that is, Yahweh, left Abraham. This striking identification of the Angel of Yahweh with Yahweh himself indicates the deity of the Angel and that God could and did reveal himself in bodily form in the Old Testament (cf. Gen. 16:7–13; 18:1–2, 17–22; 22:11, 15–16; Num. 22:23; Judg. 5:23; 6:11; 13:3).

The angels finally reached Sodom and were greeted at the city gate by none other than Lot, who urged them to spend the night with him, though he, like Abraham, did not initially discover their angelic nature. In the night, some perverted men surrounded the house and demanded to "know" Lot's visitors with a carnal knowledge, for the men involved were homosexuals. (The term sodomy derives from this situation of debauchery that seemed so characteristic of the city.) Lot refused to release his visitors to them but offered to send out his unmarried daughters, whom these perverted men could abuse in whatever way they desired. Only by the intercession of the angels was this prevented, and, after God blinded the wicked Sodomites, the heavenly messengers warned Lot of the destruction coming immediately on the city. Lot went to the homes of his married daughters and sons-in-law, desperately trying to warn them to flee the wrath of God, but they were little inclined to listen to one who had reared them in such an atmosphere. In resignation, Lot took only his wife and two unmarried daughters from the city. But his wife, deaf to the angels' warning not to turn back, did so and became a pillar of salt. With a deafening roar, the entire earth erupted, and, perhaps by means of volcanic explosion, fire and brimstone rained from the skies until all that was left of the city was a charred ruin that defies location to this day. Lot and his daughters fled to nearby Zoar and from thence to the mountain caves overlooking the horrible scene. But the sin of Sodom clung to them, for in their utter frustration at having been denied husbands and children, both of which were considered essential to blessing, the daughters of Lot made him drunk, committed incest with him, and bore him two children: Moab, the ancestor of the Moabites, and Ben-Ammi, the father of the Ammonites (19:37–38).

Genesis 20 contains an account that is reminiscent of Abraham's deception of Pharaoh in Genesis 12, but this time, though the situation is similar, the circumstances are not the same throughout. This time Abraham migrated to Gerar, a small Philistine kingdom between Canaan and Egypt, and on the way advised his wife to keep her true relationship to him secret. Abimelech, the king of Gerar, convinced that Sarah was Abraham's sister, took her into his household. God appeared to Abimelech in a dream, however, and disclosed Sarah's true identity, whereupon Abimelech, whose own family had begun to suffer divine retribution for the king's mistake, released Sarah and entreated Abraham, designated here a prophet, to pray for his family's healing. This was done, and without further ado Abraham left for Mamre once again.

Shortly after this escapade, Sarah became with child and bore Isaac, the realization of all their fondest hopes and dreams and the fulfillment of the divine promise of a covenant son. Isaac's birth provoked Hagar and Ishmael to mockery, however, for they now stood to lose the claims of inheritance. For this they were sustained by God's mercy and reminded that they, too, would produce a great nation. At about the same time Abraham and Abimelech made a covenant with each other to respect each other's territorial rights, for their lands were contiguous. They sealed this agreement at a place called Beer-Sheba ("well of the oath") in the Negev.

Only a few years after the birth of Isaac, God demanded that Abraham take this only begotten son and present him as an offering to God. Though Abraham could not reconcile the idea that Isaac had been given as the son of promise with God's request that this son be sacrificed, the patriarch had realized by now the wisdom of acting in obedient faith. Apparently without hesitation, he took Isaac with him to Moriah, to a certain mountain where the act might be performed. While ascending the mountain, Isaac noted that his father had everything necessary but the sacrificial victim itself. When Abraham gave the assurance that God would so provide, Isaac went obediently forward and, even when told the shocking truth that he was to be the sacrifice, acquiesced and voluntarily submitted to the knife. In this moment, vindicating this highest expression of faith by Abraham, God spoke and provided a substitute. Having passed this most severe test of faith, Abraham was comforted by God with the promise that all the blessings of the covenant, so frequently reiterated in the past, would most assuredly be his (22:15–18).

The day finally came when Sarah died, an event that prompted Abraham to acquire a burial place that forever after would be made holy by the bodies of the saint and his family. After negotiations with a certain Ephron, a Hittite, Abraham purchased the burial cave and the field containing it. There the mother of kings was buried. Abraham now saw plainly that his own life must soon end, so he called his faithful servant to him and commissioned him to go to Mesopotamia to seek a wife for his son, Isaac, who as yet had not produced a covenant son of his own. After much seeking of divine guidance, the servant arrived in the city of Nahor, where he met Abraham's kinfolk, and especially the beautiful maiden Rebekah (24:15). Convinced that this was the proper selection for his master, the servant presented Abraham's request to Laban, the girl's brother and guardian. He agreed that, in view of all the circumstances, this must be the will of God. After a parting blessing from her family, Rebekah departed for Canaan, where she married Isaac, bringing to him the comfort he needed following his mother's recent death.

The final years of Abraham are recorded in Genesis 25, which relates that he took a second wife, Keturah, who also bore him a family, including Midian, the father of the Midianite tribes. He eventually bestowed his patriarchal blessings, which consisted of both material and spiritual provisions, on his many sons. Isaac, as covenant son, naturally was most richly favored. Finally, after 175 years of pilgrimage, Abraham died and was buried at Machpelah by his sons Ishmael and Isaac.

Isaac (Genesis 25:9–27:46)

In the chain of patriarchal history, Isaac forms the weakest link. It is almost possible to pass directly from Abraham to Jacob without interruption, and one tends to suppose that Isaac's only significance is that he was the son of Abraham and the father of Jacob. This surely is not a fair view of Isaac, however. The reason for the brevity of the narrative concerning him may not be so much his lack of importance as his conformity to the will of God. His was not a life of bizarre escapades that warranted much discussion. In silent, obedient faith, he pursued the will of God, carefully ordering his life as God's servant.

The first event of importance in Isaac's life following his marriage was the birth of his twin sons, Esau and Jacob (25:21–26). These two, who struggled together even in their mother's womb, bore testimony in this fashion that their lives would be fraught with competition that would result in the subordination of the elder to the younger. Esau, born first, became a hunter and the favorite of his father, whereas Jacob, who pursued the more domesticated life of a nomadic herdsman, was especially favored by Rebekah. This unfortunate family division became the source of grievous trouble in days to come.

The two men's relationship first became clear when Esau, returning hungry from the hunt, begged his brother to give him a bowl of soup, in return for which he would surrender his birthright. It seems likely that Esau never expected Jacob to take him literally and seriously in this lopsided bargain, though such transactions have been recorded elsewhere in Mesopotamian sources.[20] But if so, Esau sorely misread Jacob. Nonetheless, evidently all was done according to due process of law, for Esau never challenged the validity of the transaction, though he regretted it bitterly.

After another famine had come and gone, one in which Isaac had moved to Gerar, where he deceived the king (perhaps Abimelech II or III) about his wife as his father Abraham had done, Isaac returned to Beer-Sheba. There, as his father had also done, he made a covenant with the Philistine king with regard to property rights and trespassing. The brazenness of Isaac in palming off his wife as his sister in this instance is matched only by the extreme naiveté of the king of Gerar in believing him, for their fathers had similarly become involved in their own generation. It seems that just as history repeats itself, human nature remains basically the same.

The main thread of the narrative is taken up once more in Genesis 27. Isaac, an old man by now and blinded by the years, called in Esau, his elder son, and informed him that he was about to bestow on him the patriarchal, covenant blessing pending Esau's preparing for him once more a meal of the venison stew for which he was renowned. While Esau was gone about his father's bidding, Rebekah, who had overheard the plans, suggested to Jacob a way to disguise himself and extort the promised blessing from Isaac. Jacob, in compliance, dressed himself in his brother's clothing, placed on his hands and neck animal skins to resemble the hairy body of Esau, and brought to Isaac a dish of "savory meat." Finally convinced, though with reservation, that this was Esau, Isaac blessed him with the irrevocable patriarchal blessing.[21] This promise, of a spiritual nature as opposed to the purely material provisions of the birthright that

---

20. Cyrus Gordon, "Biblical Customs and the Nuzu Tablets," in *The Biblical Archaeologist Reader*, vol. 2, ed. David Noel Freedman and Edward F. Campbell, Jr. (Garden City, N.Y.: Doubleday, Anchor Books, 1964), 23. It is fully recognized that the Nuzu (or Nuzi) tablets, originating as they do several centuries after patriarchal times, do not offer the compelling comparisons advanced by Gordon and other scholars a generation ago. Yet, many of the customs attested therein are known in the Code of Hammurabi and other earlier texts and still retain at least general value for comparison.

21. Ibid., 27.

Jacob had already obtained from Esau, was neither more nor less than the covenant of Abraham of which Isaac had become the custodian.

Upon his return, Esau persuaded Isaac of his identity, but Isaac had just pronounced the blessing and was unable to retract it, though he had been deceived into giving it to Jacob. Esau recognized the validity even of this transaction and, without appealing for a reversal, merely begged for an additional blessing for himself. Isaac gave him one, but compared to his blessing on Jacob it had little real significance. Esau did envision revenge, however, and planned to slay Jacob after his father's death. Again Rebekah, coming to Jacob's assistance, engineered his escape by convincing Isaac that Jacob should go to Haran, the homeland of their kinfolk, under the pretext that there he might find a wife.

Jacob (Genesis 28:1–38:30)

Jacob ventured to Haran, where he soon located the home and family of his mother. On his way the Lord appeared to him at Bethel in a dream of angels ascending and descending a stairway to heaven, certifying to him that the covenant promises given to his fathers would be his as well (28:10–15). His arrival at Haran, then, was filled with a realization that the future was bright before him. After staying there for a few weeks, he was invited by his uncle Laban to remain indefinitely and work for him for wages. Jacob agreed, with the understanding that his wages for seven years' work should be the hand of Laban's younger daughter, Rachel. One may surmise, in accordance with what has been learned from ancient Near Eastern custom, that Laban actually adopted Jacob, since he at this time appears to have been without sons of his own.[22] This meant that Jacob stood to inherit Laban's estate, provided, of course, that no sons were born to Laban later.

When the seven years had passed, the wedding date was set and the seven-day feast began. At its conclusion, the veiled bride and Jacob were united in marriage and ushered into the darkness of their tent home. In the morning, however, Jacob was infuriated to discover that he had married not Rachel but her sister Leah! Laban hastily explained that the custom of the land was that the elder daughter must be married first. But, apparently not convinced that Jacob's wrath was ameliorated, he agreed to offer Rachel also, if Jacob would labor seven years more. In addition, Laban added to the dowry two handmaidens, one for each of the wives.

The motif of the barren wife (see also Gen. 16:1 [Sarai]; 25:21 [Rebekah]; Judg. 13:2 [the wife of Manoah]; 1 Sam. 1:2 [Hannah]) occurs

22. Ibid., 25.

again in this context, for Rachel, because she was more favored by Jacob than was Leah, was unable to conceive. Leah, by way of divine compensation, was fruitful and soon bore Jacob four sons: Reuben, Simeon, Levi, and Judah. Rachel then attempted to make up for this lack in her own productivity by offering Jacob her maiden, Bilhah, who bore two sons, Dan and Naphtali (cf. Gen. 16:1–3). Leah, who had ceased bearing in the meantime, retaliated now by presenting Zilpah, her servant, to her husband; as a result of this union, two more sons were born to Leah by proxy, Gad and Asher. In an effort to renew the fertility of his mother, Leah, Reuben brought her some mandrake plants, superstitiously believed to be aphrodisiac. Leah refused to offer some of these to her rival, Rachel, and on partaking of them herself was able to produce yet two more sons, Issachar and Zebulun. The plants obviously had no inherent beneficent effects, for the Scripture says plainly that the children were born because "God heard Leah" (30:17). Finally, after much prayer and agony of soul, Rachel was blessed by God, and she gave birth to Joseph, the first of the two sons she was to have.

At least fourteen years had passed by this time, and Jacob decided to return to Canaan. Laban, however, persuaded that the secret of his success lay in Jacob, urged him to remain for any wages he would name. Jacob generously agreed to remain if he would be made owner of all the cattle and sheep of Laban that were not purebred. Immediately upon the consummation of this agreement, and unknown to Jacob, Laban instructed his sons to remove all the inferior animals from the flocks and herds and to pasture them at a site three days' journey from the homestead. When Jacob went to claim his property the next day, he found that it had become nonexistent. But because the contract specified only that he should have all except the purebred, he was in no legal position to do anything but accept the fact that he had been at least temporarily outsmarted. With a mixture of superstition and ingenuity, Jacob devised a means not only of regaining his rightful property but also of punishing Laban for his craftiness. He peeled the bark from certain rods and placed them in the watering troughs near where the cattle customarily bred. When they drank from the water, viewing all the time the striped, spotted, and speckled rods, the offspring they produced later bore the markings of the sticks. By thus ensuring such "marked births," Jacob was soon able to acquire quite a herd, for even the purebred cattle of Laban gave birth to impure progeny.[23] Furthermore, Jacob would not put the rods in the troughs

23. For comment on this "transition from magical to scientific thinking," see Claus Westermann, *Genesis 12–36: A Commentary* (Minneapolis: Augsburg, 1985), 483.

except when the better cattle came to drink, with the result that whatever cattle Laban did retain were of the weaker and less valuable variety. The whole matter smacks of gross superstition, but that the results actually did accrue is clear from the following passage, which states that it was not Jacob's shrewdness but God's grace that caused the miraculous result (31:9).

During all this, Laban had frequently attempted to counter Jacob by changing the conditions of his wages, but all to no avail, for God continued to overrule in Jacob's favor, making the patriarch very wealthy. Finally relations became so strained that Jacob, in line with divine guidance, decided to leave Haran and return to Canaan. His wives supported this decision, for they had seen their father's guile. And, they were angry because Laban's own sons, born since Jacob had come to Haran, now held the rights of primogeniture, leaving Jacob with no inheritance and in possession only of what he had managed to gain despite Laban's connivance. So one day, when Laban had gone to a sheepshearing, Jacob seized the opportunity to make his abrupt departure, taking with him his entire family and all his goods.

When Laban became aware of the move, he pursued the travelers, finally catching them at Gilead, near the border of Canaan and Aram. With hypocritical indignation he scolded Jacob for not having notified him of his plans, assuring him that had he done so he would have been sent off with a blessing. Besides, Laban had not been permitted to bid farewell to his daughters and grandchildren. Finally, and this is most important, Jacob had stolen the household images (teraphim), the possession of which entitled the owner to the inheritance rights of the firstborn, rights that had originally belonged to Jacob as Laban's adopted son. Jacob was unaware that Rachel had, indeed, stolen these images, and he stoutly protested that the person with whom the images were found should be put to death. Rachel had taken the images to her tent and placed them under the camel saddles and blankets on which she was seated when her father came into the tent to search there. Laban, out of respect for his daughter's physical condition, did not insist that she rise, so the teraphim remained hidden.

After Laban had demonstrated that, apart from divine prohibition to the contrary, he would have slain Jacob, the two agreed that further argument was fruitless. Thereupon they agreed to leave one another in peace, but with the specific understanding that neither would ever encroach on the property of the other and that Laban's daughters would always be treated with the care and respect consonant with their position. A ceremony of attestation followed, consisting of the erection of stones of witness whose presence there on the border of the two countries was to be a perpetual reminder of the inviolability of their covenant (31:49). Thereupon Laban returned to his own home.

Jacob was threatened next with the realization that he must now prepare to meet the brother from whom he had fled twenty years before. Somehow Esau had learned of his return, and, in a series of maneuvers, Jacob plotted how to make their encounter as safe for himself as possible. First, he sent messengers to spy out Esau's strength; they returned with the disheartening news that he was accompanied by at least four hundred men. Next he resorted to earnest prayer, in which he both pleaded for God's help and reminded him of the covenant that he now must not break. Then he sent gifts of animals to soothe his brother's ruffled feelings. Having done all that he could think of, Jacob separated himself from his family near the Jabbok brook, where, in a most unusual encounter, he began to wrestle with a strange nocturnal visitor. Whether this was in a vision or in the flesh is unimportant. The main thought is that Jacob persistently refused to release the man from his grip until he had blessed him, an indication that Jacob recognized the heavenly nature of the assailant. As a result he was blessed, indeed, in a most singular fashion. In this hour of great need Jacob was told by the angel that God was with him, a fact that was expressed in the change of Jacob's name to Israel (32:28). He had been "supplanter," but because he had prevailed with God he was to be a "prince of God." Surely no greater word of comfort could have been given Jacob, for as prince he would live to continue the promised line of covenant blessing.

The next day the dreaded meeting took place, but Esau welcomed his brother with inexplicable kindness, even refusing to accept the proffered gifts. Still, Jacob was wary of accepting his brother's invitation to visit him in Edom, so with typical persuasiveness he convinced Esau that he would follow him there at a slower pace, a promise he had no intention of keeping. As soon as Esau was out of sight, Jacob turned due west and, with great haste, crossed the Jordan into Canaan.

After a short time, Jacob and his family settled at Shalem (Shechem) in the central highlands adjacent to a Canaanite community headed by a certain Hamor and his son Shechem. The latter became infatuated with Dinah, Jacob's daughter, and assaulted her, an occurrence that prompted Hamor to negotiate with Jacob over the marriage of the two. Jacob readily agreed to this, but two of Dinah's brothers, Simeon and Levi, were greatly incensed over the whole affair and stipulated that such a marriage could be consummated only if the men of Shalem would agree to join Israel in covenant and express that unity by becoming circumcised. To this all were agreed, but just after the rite had been effected, and while the Shalemites were all therefore physically incapacitated, Simeon and Levi, sword in hand, proceeded to decimate the entire male population (34:25–29). Fearing now that other Canaanite communities would seek to avenge this massacre, Jacob fled from Shalem to Bethel, having first carefully buried the teraphim and other Aramean cultic objects under an oak tree.

At Bethel, the scene of his dream of the ladder twenty years earlier, Jacob once again was reminded of the presence of God and his continued blessing despite the enormous inconsistencies in the patriarch's life. From there he proceeded to Ephrath near Bethlehem, where Rachel died in childbirth and was buried. Finally he reached his destination, Mamre, where he found his father still alive, though extremely feeble. Shortly thereafter the old saint died; in an act of joint respect, his two sons buried him at Machpelah (35:29).

For several years Jacob lived an uneventful life in the Negev. The narrative picks up with the introduction of Joseph at age seventeen. Because he was the son of Rachel, the favorite wife, he was accorded special privileges, among them the right to be clothed in a long, flowing robe of many colors (or pieces), a garment that indicated his genteel position in life. Not only was he the family pet, however, he was also the recipient of dream revelation, a fact that only increased the animosity of his brothers toward him, for they invariably were depicted in the dreams as subordinate to Joseph (37:5–11).

One day Jacob sent his sons to Shechem, his original Canaanite homestead, where they were to feed their flocks on the comparatively richer pastures to be found there. Later the patriarch deployed Joseph to Shechem to learn of their activities, but he failed to find them there. A stranger who had seen the brothers go to Dothan, a town to the northwest that lay on the coastal highway, directed him to go there. As Joseph approached, the brothers observed him and determined to take this opportunity to do away with him. Reuben, no doubt sensing the special responsibility he bore as the eldest son, advocated that they not shed their own brother's blood, but cast him into a pit where he might starve to death. All the time it was Reuben's intention to rescue Joseph later and send him back to Mamre. Meanwhile, and in Reuben's absence, a Midianite caravan bound for Egypt with a rich cargo of spices from Gilead appeared on the horizon. Judah suggested that they rid themselves of Joseph by selling him as a slave to the merchant for twenty pieces of silver, thereby accomplishing simultaneously the removal of their hated brother and a profit. By the time Reuben returned, the transaction had been completed, and the brothers, needing a way to account to Jacob for Joseph's disappearance, soaked the boy's cloak in animal blood. When Jacob later examined this telltale evidence, he could only conclude that Joseph was dead, not knowing that, indeed, his favorite son was even then in the employ of an Egyptian nobleman (37:35–36).

The lengthy account of the selling of Joseph into Egypt can be understood only in light of the hazardous predicament of Israel at this time in history. His descent into Egypt paved the way for the later migration of the entire family of over seventy souls, a migration that eventually would result in the settlement of Israel in Egypt for more than four hundred years. The point has already been made that God's purpose in the Old Testament was to reveal himself through men and nations in his mighty saving power. In order for this revelation to be clear and unimpaired, it was necessary that the vehicles through whom he spoke be preserved from anything that would render them incapable of fulfilling their divine commission. That message of promise had been entrusted to Israel and his sons and families; if they should fail to hold it in trust, the witness to the true and only God would be jeopardized.

It has also been most apparent that the effectiveness of Jacob and his family as the bearers of the covenant to the world had been imperilled. This was clear in the attempted union between Israel and the Shalemites, a union prevented only by the timely action of Simeon and Levi. The influence of the Canaanite immorality is also seen in the incest committed by Reuben against his father's concubine, Bilhah (35:22). But it is in Genesis 38 that the need for the removal of Israel from Canaanite ethical and religious contexts is best discovered. The narrator relates that Judah, son of Jacob, married a Canaanite woman and that, over the course of the years, they had three sons. The eldest of these also married a Canaanite, Tamar by name. This son was thereafter struck dead by God for some unnamed sin, and, after the so-called levirate custom (Deut. 25:5–10), his brother was supposed to marry her to raise up children in his brother's name. The younger brother refused to do so, however, perhaps because of pride or envy of his brother, so Yahweh slew him also. This left only Shelah, the youngest brother, who was yet a child. Judah promised Tamar that, if she would wait, she might marry Shelah when he was grown. Evidently the desire to have a son in this covenant line, or at least the simple desire to be a mother at all, encouraged Tamar to wait these years. When the boy was grown, though, Judah reneged, which meant that Tamar, who no doubt was very unlikely by this time to find another husband, was destined to remain childless. To preclude this possibility, she disguised herself as a prostitute and, meeting Judah on the road to

Timnath, seduced him. Because Judah had no money with which to pay for her favors, he left his staff, bracelets, and personal signet as pledges.

When Tamar became pregnant, Judah indignantly haled her into the presence of witnesses and demanded to know who had committed adultery with her. When she summarily brought forth Judah's personal effects and exhibited them for all to see, the mortified accuser could do nothing but admit his guilt. Though one of the children born of this relationship, Perez, was destined to become an ancestor of David the king and of Christ Jesus himself, an amazing example of God's overruling providence, the whole sorry picture nevertheless demonstrated the urgent need for God's people to be removed from Canaan to a place where they could be socially and spiritually insulated from reoccurrences of such corruption. In all the ancient world, no place satisfied this need better than Egypt; hence, God providentially placed Joseph there.

Joseph (Genesis 39:1–50:26)

The geographical background of the patriarchal narrative now switches to Egypt; for that reason, Joseph must be considered the focal point of the discussion. His life there, and the life of the Israelites in general against the backdrop of Egyptian culture, will be discussed in the following chapter.

Providentially, Joseph was sold into the hands of an Egyptian nobleman, Potiphar, who was also the captain of Pharaoh's guard. Joseph quickly gained the favor of his master and was appointed overseer of all that he had. Unfortunately, he also incurred the attentions of Potiphar's wife, who became enamored of his handsome features, his intelligence, and his overall demeanor. Frequently she attempted to entice him to sin with her, but he stoutly maintained his fidelity to his master as well as to his God. One day she seized him in desperation. In his frantic effort to escape her designs, he left his cloak behind, circumstantial evidence sufficient to have him imprisoned. The fact that Joseph did not suffer capital punishment may suggest that Potiphar's wife had become rather notorious for this sort of thing. One may even conclude that the only reason he was imprisoned at all was because the presence of the cloak implied that Joseph had at least cooperated in the affair.

Immediately upon his imprisonment, Joseph began to be promoted, until finally he became a trustee over all the prison (39:21–23). While in this capacity he later encountered two men, the butler and baker of Pharaoh, who, for some reason, had been thrown into the same prison. They related to him dreams they had had, for he had testified to them that his God was the giver and interpreter of dreams and that as God's servant he could give them the meaning they sought. As it turned out, the butler was restored to his position in Pharaoh's court, exactly as Joseph had interpreted, whereas the baker was hanged and decapitated, in line with Joseph's interpretation of his dream as well. Joseph had requested the butler to make known to Pharaoh his innocence, but it was not until two years later that the ungrateful man remembered Joseph, and then only because another dream, this time Pharaoh's, brought his own dream and its consequences back to the butler's mind.

It seems that Pharaoh had seen in his dreams seven fat cattle followed by seven lean ones that devoured them, and after that seven healthy ears of corn consumed by seven withered ears (41:1–8). When all the sorcerers and magicians of the realm were unable to offer any sensible interpretations, Joseph, summoned at the advice of the butler, without delay made known all the ramifications of the dreams, acknowledging that God had enabled him to see that seven years of bounty were approaching in Egypt, to be followed by seven years of famine. Amazed and convinced by this exhibition of wisdom, Pharaoh, following the counsel of Joseph that a wise administrator be found who could regulate the collection and distribution of food during this time, set Joseph "over all the land of Egypt" (Gen. 41:43), proclaiming that the Semitic wise man was to be second only to him throughout the kingdom.

Commensurate with this position and with Joseph's reputation as a man "in whom the Spirit of God is" (41:38), Pharaoh gave him the daughter of the chief priest of On (Heliopolis) to be his wife. Asenath bore him two sons, Ephraim ("fruitful") and Manasseh ("forgetting"), whose names suggested that Joseph had become prosperous and had forgotten all his miseries. When the years of famine eventually came, Joseph proved the wisdom of Pharaoh's choice, for God used him to save both Egypt and Israel from disaster.

The widespread famine was beginning to take its deadly toll in Canaan, and Jacob was forced to send his sons to Egypt for grain (42:1–2). On their arrival they were presented to Joseph, who recognized them at once. They could not even guess his true identity, however, for the passing of some thirteen years (41:46), coupled with his Egyptian language and dress, precluded recognition. When they had stated their request, Joseph curtly rebuffed them, accused them of being spies, and cast them into prison. This and the following treatment of the brothers by Joseph may be explained as an attempt to teach them a badly needed lesson, an irresistible opportunity to play a practical joke, or a combination of both. Whatever the purpose, Joseph succeeded in frightening them so much that they could not but rue the fact that they were in Egypt before this austere figure.

Finally, Joseph permitted them to return home. He retained Simeon as a hostage, however, and warned them not to come back to Egypt without their youngest brother, Benjamin, who had not accompanied them this first time. On their way home they discovered, to their utter consternation and amazement, that the money they had taken to pay for the grain was still in their possession. They told their father about the whole series of events, but, despite Simeon's arrest in Egypt, he refused to let them return if they had to take Benjamin as well.

When the grain was exhausted, however, Jacob finally relented, and all ten brothers returned once again for supplies. This time Joseph amazed them by inviting them to a feast at his home. To their amazement, he seated them around the table in the order of their ages. When they prepared to return to Canaan once more, Joseph told his servants to put their money in their grain sacks and his silver divining cup in the sack of Benjamin. After the brothers had gone a short distance, they were overtaken and searched by Pharaoh's troops, who found the money and the cup. Fearing now that Benjamin's death would cast their father into such grief that he, too, would die, they fell on their faces before Joseph, begging his mercy—a gesture that Joseph could no longer endure. At once he revealed his identity to them with tears and embraces. Finally convinced that this lord was indeed their long-lost brother, they rejoiced with him, though in bewilderment at this turn of events. Joseph outlined to them the providence of God, who had used the brothers as unwitting accomplices in sending him to Egypt. He declared that God had done so to preserve them through the famine and to remove them from the subtle but more dangerous threat of Canaanite assimilation. He followed this disclosure by entreating the brethren to return to Canaan to fetch their father and families and to live with him in Goshen, the choicest part of Egypt (45:1–15).

Even Jacob was convinced when he saw the gifts sent by Joseph with his sons, so he and all his descendants emigrated from Canaan, the land of promise, to which his family would not return for over four hundred years. On arriving in Egypt, Jacob was presented to Pharaoh, whom he blessed, and was assigned by him a dwelling place in the northeast delta region of the land. For seventeen more years, all during the famine and afterward, Jacob lived in Goshen, his last years of peace contrasting sharply with those tumultuous years that had preceded the entrance into Egypt.

When the day of Jacob's death appeared imminent, he requested that his remains be carried to Machpelah for burial; he blessed the two sons of

Joseph, Ephraim and Manasseh, deliberately giving the inheritance promise to the younger, Ephraim, rather than to Manasseh; and he blessed all twelve of his sons with the beautifully poetic and prophetic patriarchal blessing of Genesis 49. The tenth verse has special interest, for in the words "The scepter shall not depart from Judah, nor a lawgiver from between his feet, until Shiloh come; and unto him shall the gathering of the people be" the covenantal Messianic promise receives clear focus. Later it became abundantly evident that the tribe of Judah, ancestor of David and the Christ, was the object of God's special concern in history.

In accordance with his wishes, Jacob was buried in Hebron with his fathers. After the interment, Joseph and his brothers returned to Egypt to live out their days. Now that Jacob was dead, the brothers expressed fear of retribution, but Joseph assured them that they had nothing to fear from him, for he had forgiven all their misdeeds in recognition of the fact that God had used them to preserve for himself this remnant of witness to the truth. Later, Joseph, at the age of 110 years, lay at death's door with the prophecy on his lips that God would lead his people out of Egypt one day. Moreover, he demanded of his brethren and their descendants the promise that when that day came they would carry his body with them (Josh. 24:32). Though he had lived all but seventeen years in Egypt, he knew in his heart that his real home was the land of promise, the inheritance of Abraham, Isaac, and Jacob.

Egyptian Culture and Life in the Patriarchal Period

The biblical history of the early patriarchal period centered on Mesopotamia very briefly, then shifted to Canaan. There are extensive references in Genesis to Near Eastern customs and traditions, most of which have been remarkably illustrated by such finds as the Nuzi tablets and the documents from such places as Mari, Alalakh, and Ebla.[24] Many of the contemporary Egyptian cultures may also now be studied as a result of archaeology and more advanced historiography, and they shed a great deal of light on the biblical accounts of Jacob and Joseph during the course of this Middle Kingdom period. The following cannot hope to be exhaustive but can at least point out the amazing accuracy of the Genesis account of life in Egypt at this time. This, besides substantiating biblical historicity itself, supports strongly the Mosaic authorship of the book.

24. G. E. Mendenhall, "Mari," in *The Biblical Archaeologist Reader*, vol. 2, ed. David Noel Freedman and Edward F. Campbell, Jr. (Garden City, N.Y.: Doubleday, 1964), 3ff.; Eugene H. Merrill, "Ebla and Biblical Historical Inerrancy," *Bibliotheca Sacra* 140 (1983): 302–21.

Besides the incursions of Abram and Jacob into Egypt for food, which have been illustrated from Egyptian literature that speaks of such movements by Semites on a major scale, there are other matters of importance by way of illustration. For example, the abundance of dreams, the despotism of Pharaoh, famines of seven years' duration, and the elevation of Semites and other foreigners to prominent places in Egypt, all appear in nonbiblical Egyptian documents.[25] In addition, there are matters of custom that are of great interest. For example, when Joseph was summoned out of prison to appear before Pharaoh, he shaved himself and dressed in Egyptian clothing in order not to offend the king by appearing in his Semitic beard and clothing.[26] Also, Joseph advised Pharaoh to retain 20 percent of the food in the seven years of plenty, a custom attested by secular documents. The segregation of the Egyptians and Semites at the meal table is in line with the Egyptian feeling of superiority and religious separation. The "divining cup" of Joseph was a common instrument of wise men of the Middle Kingdom who sought occult wisdom. Joseph's advice to his father and brethren not to reveal their occupation as shepherds accords perfectly with the knowledge that the Egyptians could not countenance sheep and shepherds, for they themselves were cattlemen.[27] One of the most striking examples of all is the description of Egyptian embalming and burial practices. The account states that the embalming of Jacob lasted for forty days and was followed by thirty days of public mourning. The Egyptian Book of the Dead, an extensive collection of miscellaneous data pertaining to death and burial, comes from this period of history and specifies the process outlined in Genesis (50:2–3).[28]

Besides these specific references, nothing in the tenor of the Bible suggests that the account is amiss. Surely, unless one extremely familiar with Egyptian life and customs had written this book, there would be some kind of inconsistency with what is known from ancient Egyptian sources; but there is none. Conversely, the evidence available from these extrabiblical materials has considerably illuminated the Genesis story of the patriarchs in Egypt. Further consideration as to the relationship of the biblical narratives to the historical situation as known from other sources must be reserved for later discussion.

25. J. A. Thompson, *The Bible and Archaeology* (Grand Rapids: Eerdmans, 1982), 43–51.

26. Ira M. Price, *The Monuments and the Old Testament* (Philadelphia: American Baptist Publication Society, 1907), 104.

27. Unger, *Archaeology and the Old Testament*, 133.

28. Samuel A. B. Mercer, *The Religion of Ancient Egypt* (London: Luzac, 1949), 313–17.

Creation of a Nation

Old Testament Chronology

The date of the exodus, the most important historical event in Israel's past, is so crucial to the rest of the story that it is mandatory to give some consideration to the problem of ascertaining that date and as many other important dates as possible. Obviously, there is no reckoning of time in the Old Testament with reference to B.C. or A.D. or any other point fixed and known to the Old Testament authors, so the matter is more complicated than it might ordinarily seem. For years the dates of Archbishop Ussher, a British prelate of the seventeenth century, were accepted almost universally. This scholar added up all the years between the time of Christ and the close of the Old Testament historical record, thus determining the final date of that record. Then he added backward the genealogies and other chronological data in the Old Testament, making allowance for such matters as co-regencies or interregna of the kings, parallel or synchronistic evidences, and passages that tied various parts of the Old Testament together. On the whole, he succeeded well, at least as far back as Abraham, though he placed the patriarch about eighty years too early.[1]

1. See p. 70. Ussher dated Abraham's birth at 2247 B.C.

With the advent of the modern age of archaeological and historical scholarship, Ussher's chronology has become somewhat discredited, though even now his dates are not to be corrected as much as one might think. Certain persons and events known in the Bible became datable because they were mentioned in literary and other material remains discovered in the past century or so. These extrabiblical data provide points of reference that can be dated with absolute certainty. One major breakthrough came with the uncovering of the Assyrian Eponym Lists, which listed all the years from about 892 to 648 B.C., each being named for the *limmu*, or prime minister, of Assyria elected for that year. In addition to the names of these officials, the tablets contained accounts of the most important events of each year. Thus, there is an unbroken series of events embracing almost three centuries of Assyrian history and touching on the histories of other nations as well.[2]

In the year of a *limmu* named Bur-Sagale, the Assyrians noted a complete eclipse of the sun, which, for various religious and scientific reasons, must have impressed them deeply. Modern astronomy has calculated that this eclipse could have occurred only on June 15, 763 B.C., for the mathematical precision of such phenomena permit them to be calculated hundreds of years later with no appreciable margin of error. Ninety years earlier than this eclipse, in the year 853, the most noteworthy event was the Battle of Qarqar, a battle that Shalmaneser III of Assyria claims to have won over a Palestinian-Syrian coalition including Israel and her king Ahab.[3] The internal biblical evidence indicates that this battle must have occurred near the end of the reign of Ahab, for only then was he on friendly enough terms with Syria to ally himself with it in battle (1 Kings 22:1). This point of contact was most important, but it alone was hardly conclusive. More information was forthcoming, however, in the form of the Black Obelisk, a stele erected by Shalmaneser III in honor of his subjugation of his enemies, including King Jehu of Israel. This unhappy king is depicted kneeling in submission to his Assyrian overlord in the eighteenth year of Shalmaneser, an occurrence that, therefore, can be dated, for the dates of Shalmaneser are known from the Eponym Lists. The Black Obelisk date is 841 B.C., apparently in Jehu's first year.[4] The Book of Kings says that there were twelve years between Ahab and Jehu (2 Kings 3:1; cf.

2. For a convenient publication of the Eponym Lists see Edwin R. Thiele, *The Mysterious Numbers of the Hebrew Kings*, 3d ed. (Grand Rapids: Eerdmans, 1983), 221–26.

3. D. Winton Thomas, ed., *Documents from Old Testament Times* (London: Thomas Nelson, 1958), 47.

4. Ibid., 48.

9:24), so the dates 853 and 841 are thereby established in their biblical relationship to Ahab and Jehu.

From this information it is relatively easy to reconstruct the rest of the Old Testament chronology. The lengths of the reigns of each of the kings of Israel and Judah are given, both before and after the time of Ahab and Jehu, and by adding them up one can arrive at the accession years of each and learn the dates of many of the events mentioned in connection with them. The matter must not be oversimplified, however, for there are such factors as co-regencies and interregna to consider; because the two kingdoms of Israel and Judah used different systems of reckoning time at different periods in their histories, diligent study must be made of all the data in order to work out a self-consistent, harmonious reconstruction.[5]

Ahab, who must have died ca. 853/852 B.C., reigned for twenty-two years, so he ascended the throne of Israel in 874 (1 Kings 16:29). His father Omri reigned twelve years, having been crowned in 886 (1 Kings 16:23). Elah, his predecessor, reigned two years, or from 887–886 (1 Kings 16:8). His father, Baasha, maintained a rule of twenty-four years, from 910 to 887 (1 Kings 15:33). Nadab, son of Jeroboam, reigned two years, from 912 to 910 (1 Kings 15:25), while Jeroboam took the kingdom in 931 B.C. and ruled for twenty-two years (1 Kings 14:20). Because Jeroboam seized the throne of the Northern Kingdom on the death of Solomon, and Solomon reigned for forty years, Solomon's dates must be 971–931 (1 Kings 11:42); the dates of his father, David, 1011–971 (1 Kings 2:11); and so on. Working from a different angle, there is a very important statement in 1 Kings 6:1 that flatly states that Solomon began to build his temple in his fourth year (967/66), which was also the 480th year after the exodus. This places the date of the exodus at 1446 B.C. Exodus 12:40 points out that Israel was in Egypt for 430 years; therefore, Jacob's migration there must have been in 1876 B.C. When Jacob had his audience with Pharaoh, he stated that he was then 130 years of age (Gen. 47:9), indicating that he was born in 2006 B.C. His father was sixty when Jacob was born, so Isaac's birth date is 2066 B.C. (Gen. 25:26), while Abraham, one hundred years old when Isaac was born, must have been born in 2166 (Gen. 21:5).[6]

The chronology earlier than that is most uncertain, for, as already pointed out, strong evidence exists that there were gaps in the earlier genealogies, perhaps as many as thousands of years being unaccounted for chronologically. From Jehu on to the time of Christ, however, the dating

5. Thiele, *The Mysterious Numbers of the Hebrew Kings*, 16–38.

6. For other early dates see Eugene H. Merrill, "Fixed Dates in Patriarchal Chronology," *Bibliotheca Sacra* 137 (1980): 241–51.

is almost certain, for the biblical figures, combined with materials such as the Babylonian Chronicles and the various King Lists,[7] spell out in detail the passing of the years. The entire chronological system, especially in later times, is controlled by other factors such as the Canon of Ptolemy from Egypt, the sources available to historians such as Josephus, Herodotus, Tacitus, Berossus, Manetho, and others, and certain other independent witnesses that provide valuable checkpoints and criteria with which to support or correct the Assyrian Eponym data and the Old Testament figures themselves. That the present understanding of the Old Testament chronology, especially from the time of David and later, rests on a scientific and accurate basis is not disputed. Dates earlier than that are subject to reinterpretation by the critics in many instances, but to the objective student the overall framework is consistent and valid.

The Historical Background and Date of the Exodus

The historical milieu of the exodus period can be comprehended only in the context of the several centuries that preceded it, especially in Egypt. The role of Egypt in the Near Eastern scene has already received some attention, but only in very general terms. Now it will be useful to go back and gather up the strands that, when woven together, will provide the setting for the Egyptian-Israelite relationship lying at the very foundation of the exodus movement.

The rise of the Twelfth Dynasty at about 2000 B.C. inaugurated an era of Egyptian power and influence hitherto unmatched. Yet Egypt even in this period was not concerned so much with the outside world as with her own peculiar internal interests. There was, however, an interest in Egypt on the part of outsiders; history records the movement of thousands of people to and from Egypt throughout this time. These peoples seemed to be Semitic primarily. Though most of them were merchants who went to Egypt only temporarily for trading purposes, some remained there to occupy various parts of the country. Sesostris III (1878–1843) was one pharaoh of the dynasty who was interested in expansion. There is evidence that he pressed as far north as Shechem in Canaan. From the period of a predecessor, Amenemhet I (1991–1962), comes the story of Sinuhe, an Egyptian physician, who describes his travels throughout the Mediterranean in an epic known as the Tales of Sinuhe.[8]

---

7. David Noel Freedman, "Old Testament Chronology," in *The Bible and the Ancient Near East*, ed. G. Ernest Wright (Garden City, N.Y.: Doubleday, 1961), 265–81.

8. Miriam Lichtheim, *Ancient Egyptian Literature; A Book of Readings*, vol. 1, *The Old and Middle Kingdoms* (Berkeley: University of California Press, 1975), 222–35.

Near the beginning of the eighteenth century, the Egyptian government collapsed under the influence of the Hyksos, whose domination was gradually achieved, though it consisted first of all of a mere coexistence with the Egyptians. As these "foreign chieftains"[9] moved into the land in great numbers, the Egyptians feared a takeover, but their efforts to remove them or prevent further immigration proved too late. By 1730 B.C. at least, all of Lower Egypt was firmly in Hyksos hands. Unfortunately the Hyksos were not active in producing a material culture in Egypt, so there are comparatively few remains from the period. They were not totally unproductive in these areas, however, as is now attested from their military equipment, indicating the use of the horse and chariot for the first time in Egypt. And there are also abundant literary remains consisting primarily of scarabs containing Hyksos personal names.[10] They moved the capital of Egypt from near Memphis to a site known as Avaris in the northeast delta region. There they maintained rule until they were finally expelled (ca. 1580).

Some Egyptian control was sustained through this Hyksos period, namely, the Thirteenth through Seventeenth dynasties in southern Egypt, but their influence was nil because they themselves were embroiled in internal problems. Out of the last of these dynasties, however, came a figure, Ahmose (ca. 1580–1548), who became the founder of the powerful Eighteenth Dynasty. He united Egypt against the Hyksos oppressors and finally drove the Asiatics from the borders of Egypt up into Palestine and even farther.

At this point it is helpful to consider the biblical record concerning Jacob and Joseph. Abraham visited Egypt during the Eleventh or Twelfth Dynasty, a visit quite consistent with the common practice of those periods. The date of that migration may be around 2090 B.C. The next contact with Egypt concerns Joseph's enslavement there in about 1900. This would be in the reign of Amenemhet II, so it was probably the dream of the next pharaoh, Sesostris II (1894–1878), that he interpreted. This king elevated Joseph to his position of governor, a promotion that certainly cannot be disproved. The argument is sometimes advanced that the migration of Jacob into Egypt at about this time was the same as the Hyksos invasion and takeover, and that this explains how Joseph, a Semite, could reach such heights in Egyptian government.[11] This theory

9. John Van Seters, *The Hyksos: A New Investigation* (New Haven, Conn.: Yale University Press, 1966), 187–88.

10. Ibid., 154–55.

11. So argued Josephus in *Contra Apionem* 1.73; W. F. Albright, *From the Stone Age to Christianity* (Garden City, N.Y.: Doubleday, 1957), 200.

seems to be overthrown by the insistence of Joseph on observing Egyptian customs both before and after his father's arrival. This would be wholly inexplicable if the king in Joseph's time were an anti-Egyptian Hyksos. Moreover, it is not necessary to assume a Hyksos king in order to account for Joseph's elevation, for, as has already been shown, there are other examples of Semitic advancement in the Middle Kingdom.

Jacob must have entered Egypt in the reign of Sesostris III (1878–1841), who not only was an expansionist abroad but also was successful in breaking the power of the local nobility (nomarchs) and confiscating their land for the crown. This would be the time of Joseph's administration, in which he advocated to the king the acquisition of lands during famine in order to be able to dole out foodstuffs as the need arose. Joseph died during the reign of the next king, Amenemhet III, in about 1806 B.C. The Twelfth Dynasty itself came to an end about twenty-five years after that date. For the next two hundred years, the Israelites lived in comparative peace and prosperity in Egypt, the rule of the Hyksos no doubt contributing to this state of affairs in that they, too, were largely Semites. It is interesting to note that the Israelites lived in Goshen (or Raamses) all this time and that this was the location of the Hyksos capital, Avaris. Evidently, though the Hyksos and Hebrews were not one and the same, they had definite similarities and a close relationship.

Exodus 1:8 relates that "a new king, who did not know about Joseph, came to power in Egypt" and that this monarch proceeded to deal harshly with the Israelites lest they defect and join Egypt's enemies (possibly the recently evicted Hyksos). This king, it seems, must have been Ahmose, first king of the Eighteenth Dynasty and enemy of the hated Hyksos, with whom he prejudicially related the Israelites. In this sense he "knew not" Joseph, or had no sympathy with the Hebrew cause. He placed the Israelites in bondage and required them to build public works, including the cities of Pithom and Raamses (Exod. 1:11). The difficulty involved with this assertion will be considered under the arguments concerning the date of the exodus.

Ahmose managed to unite Egypt and drive the Hyksos out of the country and into Canaan, where they eventually intermingled with the native stock and disappeared as an independent people. His successors followed up his brilliant victories by occupying Canaan and other nearby lands and building strong fortifications against the possibility of ever being invaded again by northern hordes. It is very likely that there were still thousands of Semites in Egypt following this defeat of the Hyksos, among whom surely the Hebrews would constitute a large element. Amenhotep I (1548–1528) very likely carried out the oppressive measures of Ahmose against the

Hebrews, and it is entirely possible that he was the pharaoh who made the decree that all the male infants of the Hebrews should be slain (Exod. 1:22). As suggested earlier, the biblical date of the exodus is 1446 B.C., and Moses was eighty years old when he led the people from Egypt (Exod. 7:7). This means that he was born in 1526, a date that fits in nicely with the reign of Amenhotep I if he was indeed the pharaoh who had made the infamous decree.

Thutmose I (1528–1508) led many campaigns into Palestine, even as far as the Euphrates, but he is perhaps best known in history as the father of Hatshepsut (1504–1483). This ambitious woman married her own half-brother, Thutmose II (1508–1504), in order that she might have a legitimate claim to the throne. When he died under rather inexplicable circumstances, she exercised her domination through her stepson, Thutmose III (1504–1448).[12] Only after her death was Thutmose III able to take the throne by himself. It is very tempting to identify Hatshepsut with the daughter of the pharaoh mentioned in Exodus 2:5, for her age at the time would fit the situation perfectly, as would her boldness in rescuing a Hebrew baby and rearing him within the very palace of the king.

Thutmose III occupied himself with at least sixteen campaigns into Palestine and beyond to the north. He also apparently penetrated south for some considerable distance. The chief opposition he faced was from the newly emerging kingdom of the Mitanni, which was located on the upper reaches of the Tigris-Euphrates river system. After Thutmose had reached terms of peace with these new neighbors, the pharaohs frequently married Mitannian princesses from then on to solidify their friendly relationship.[13]

Thutmose III was followed by Amenhotep II (1448–1423), who may have been the pharaoh of the exodus, and he in turn was succeeded by Thutmose IV (1423–1410). Throughout this whole period, Egypt maintained its strength and continued to be active in conquest and trade in all directions. But then a noticeable decline began to occur. Amenhotep III (1410–1377) had his hands full with a rising discontent within Egypt, the turmoil related to the ascendancy of one god or the other. His son Amenhotep IV (1377–1358) settled the matter by originating or refining a monotheistic religion[14] that revolutionized Egyptian theology and also had an indelible political impact. To symbolize his reverence for his new god, Aton, whom he worshiped in the form of the sun disk, Amenhotep

12. I. E. S. Edwards et al., eds., *The Cambridge Ancient History*, 3d ed. (Cambridge: Cambridge University Press, 1973), 2/1:316–17.

13. John Bright, *A History of Israel*, 3d ed. (Philadelphia: Westminster, 1981), 109.

14. There is no basis to the claim that Moses was influenced in his monotheism by Akhnaton. In fact, if the biblical date for the exodus be correct, Moses preceded Akhnaton by nearly one hundred years. It is far more likely that Akhnaton was familiar with Moses' teaching.

changed his name to Akhnaton and moved the capital of Egypt to a new city that he named Akhetaton. Its later name, el Amarna, is found in connection with the Tell el Amarna letters discovered there.

These letters consist of communications from the various kings of city-states, particularly in Canaan, who were under Egyptian hegemony. Because Akhnaton was so consumed with the internal religious problems of his land, he had little time to protect his provinces from outside interference. As a result, these provinces were laid open to attack by all kinds of marauding peoples, including some known as the *Habiru* (or *apiru*). The king of Jerusalem, for example, wrote an urgent appeal to the pharaoh to send even a few troops if at all possible, for the Habiru were overrunning the land. Some scholars argue that there is every probability that these invaders were none other than the Hebrews who had escaped from Egypt some fifty years or more earlier.

Before Egypt collapsed entirely, the eccentric Akhnaton died (perhaps violently) and was followed by his young son-in-law, Tutankhamon (1358–1349), who attempted to restore the worship of Amon. Then, with two more rulers, Ay (1349–1345) and Haremhab (1345–1318), the Eighteenth Dynasty came to a close.

The Nineteenth Dynasty was founded by Rameses I, who reigned for a very brief time (1318–1317) but gave his name to one of the most illustrious families in history, the Ramessides. He was followed by Seti I (1317–1301), who resumed the imperialistic policies of the early kings of the preceding dynasty and passed on to his successor the beginnings of a renewed empire. This successor was the famous Rameses II (1301–1234), the length of whose reign suggests his stability and endurance. Though he no doubt appropriated to himself many glorious feats he never accomplished, he nevertheless was the single means of restoring a great measure of Egypt's prestige in the world. Were it not for the Hittites, who were beginning to assume tremendous proportions in the north and northwest, Egypt under Rameses II might well have achieved its greatest extent and power. The Hittites, though, were his constant problem, and it is likely that, following the disastrous Battle of Kadesh in 1286, he was never able to subdue them.[15] The Nineteenth Dynasty ended with his son, Merneptah (1234–1222), who was also his general in Rameses' later years. Merneptah managed to occupy as far north as Beth-shean in Canaan and, as a matter of fact, left a monument bearing the earliest reference to Israel

15. O. R. Gurney, *The Hittites* (Baltimore: Penguin, 1952), 35.

outside the Bible.[16] After his death, however, the empire collapsed; never again was Egypt to exercise any extensive control outside its own borders.

This discussion of Egyptian history from the end of the Hyksos period through the Nineteenth Dynasty was necessary because of its bearing on the date, route, and interpretation of the exodus and conquest. Now, specific arguments for the biblical dates must be brought to bear with a consideration of the most pertinent historical and archaeological materials available. The point has already been made that 1 Kings 6:1 implies that the exodus must be dated at 1446, but this date is denied by the majority of scholars, who date the exodus in the middle of the thirteenth century.[17] The consensus is that either the text of 1 Kings 6:1 is corrupt, the historian who wrote the words was not in possession of the facts, or the figure 480 must be interpreted. It is urged, for example, that there were twelve generations from Moses to Solomon; if each generation is about twenty-five years in length, there would be only a period of three hundred years from the exodus to the building of the Temple.[18] This would permit the date of the exodus to be no earlier than ca. 1260 B.C., a date generally maintained by the critics.

It is obvious, then, that the validity of the chronological information in 1 Kings 6:1 is at stake; this in turn has a bearing on the whole problem of Old Testament historicity. There is other information within the Bible, however, that may be cited to strengthen the 1446 date. In Judges 11:26, Jephthah reminds the king of Ammon that the Israelites had been in Ammon for three hundred years. Jephthah can be dated no later than 1100 B.C., so the arrival of Israel in Transjordan could be no later than 1400 B.C., a remarkable agreement with 1 Kings 6:1. All that is necessary is for statements such as 1 Kings 6:1 and Judges 11:26 to be accepted at face value, particularly when there is no textual or other internal reason for rejecting them. When other factors are considered and correctly interpreted, the biblical date as indicated by these passages can be absolutely corroborated.

Besides this inherent biblical witness to the exodus date, there are supporting arguments from Egyptian and Near Eastern history and archaeology. For example, the Moses stories fit into the historical milieu of the early Eighteenth Dynasty more easily than into any other period of Egyptian history. The command to purge all Hebrew infants well accords with the period immediately following the Hyksos' expulsion under

16. Thomas, *Documents from Old Testament Times*, 139.

17. H. H. Rowley, *From Joseph to Joshua: Biblical Traditions in the Light of Archaeology* (London: Oxford University Press for the British Academy, 1950), 132–38.

18. Bright, *A History of Israel*, 123.

Ahmose and Amenhotep I. The daughter of Pharaoh could hardly be any other than Hatshepsut, daughter of Thutmose I, for only she of all known Egyptian princesses would have the audacity to rear a Hebrew male child in the very palace of Egypt despite her father's orders. Also, Moses was in Midian for a total of forty years before he could return to Egypt, a stay necessary until the death of the pharaoh from whom he had fled (Acts 7:23; cf. Exod. 7:7). There was only one king of Egypt before Rameses II who reigned over forty years, and that was Thutmose III, a contemporary of Moses. The pharaoh of the exodus, Amenhotep II, had a son who became pharaoh, but it was not his eldest son. What became of the eldest son? Could he have been the son slain by the God of Israel? Moreover, the son who did succeed him was Thutmose IV, the pharaoh who left the famous "Dream Stele" found between the feet of the Great Sphinx of Cheops. On this inscription Thutmose IV records that he had been told by the sphinx in a dream that, though he was not the eldest son of his father, he would nonetheless be the next monarch, a very strange turn of events to say the least.[19]

The Tell el Amarna letters, written in the first quarter of the fourteenth century, recite the appeals for help by the chieftains and princes of the various small city-states and provinces of the Egyptian Empire, especially in Canaan and Syria. These kings were desperate because their cities were being overrun by people called ʿapiru, a term equivalent to Habiru in Akkadian texts and perhaps to Hebrew in the Old Testament.[20] Even if ʿapiru and Hebrew have a common etymology, there is no way they can always be viewed as one and the same people, however. People known as ʿapiru (or, in the Sumerian form, SA GAZ) appear earlier than Abraham and are attested throughout the Near East, while Israel was confined to Egypt. It is best, perhaps, to assume that the terms ʿapiru and Hebrew were close enough linguistically that they were sometimes used interchangeably. One might even say that all Hebrews were ʿapiru, but not all ʿapiru were Hebrews.

In any event, it is not likely that the ʿapiru of the Amarna texts were the Israelites of the conquest narratives, for the conquest under Joshua preceded the earliest of the Amarna letters by twenty-five years. Moreover, the personal names that occur in the biblical and Amarna texts do not agree, suggesting that two different periods are in view. It is best, no doubt, to conclude that the initial conquest was largely completed before the Amarna period and that the Amarna texts refer to struggles

---

19. G. Frederick Owens, *Archaeology and the Bible* (Westwood, N.J.: Revell, 1961), 202–3.

20. W. F. Albright, *The Biblical Period from Abraham to Ezra* (New York: Harper and Row, 1963), 26; Moshe Greenberg, *The Hab/piru* (New Haven, Conn.: American Oriental Society, 1955), 88–96.

that followed Israel's unsuccessful attempts to subjugate and occupy Canaan. In that case, ʿapiru in those texts could refer both to Israel and to other, non-Hebrew, peoples.[21]

The destruction of Jericho was dated, until recent years, at ca. 1400, thanks largely to the work there by John Garstang. When Garstang's work was completed some fifty years ago, there was almost universal agreement that his dates were correct and that the destruction of City D, the stratum in which the walls had fallen outward, was by the Israelites in 1400.[22] W. F. Albright, who generally concurred with this date initially, later modified his opinion and in the light of further evidence, including Kathleen Kenyon's more recent work at Jericho, eventually accepted a date of 1225 or later for Jericho's fall under Israel.[23] Yet Garstang has not been completely discredited, if at all, in the opinion of many scholars.[24]

Very interesting also are inscriptions found in Egypt that mention the name of the tribe Asher. These must be dated in the fourteenth century and would agree most favorably with the biblical date for the exodus and conquest.[25] The critic, by assuming that the tribe of Asher did not participate in the exodus, is able thereby to overcome this evidence, but this begging the question seems to be merely a way to explain away the original unity of Israel and the tribes' composite departure from Egypt under Moses. It is difficult to explain how Asher could be in Canaan a hundred years before the critics date the exodus except by maintaining that Asher was not part of the movement. There is also the Stele of Merneptah, previously mentioned, which speaks of "Israel" as a power in Canaan about 1231 B.C. If the exodus did not take place until 1300 at the earliest, and the period of wandering was another forty years, it is difficult to understand how Israel could be represented as a mighty power as early as 1231, especially if, as the critical view alleges, the formation of Israel into any kind of a confederacy did not take place until hundreds of years after the conquest. These are indeed difficulties in the late date and, though they do not prove the early date, certainly favor it.

In fairness, one must consider the evidence against the early date, for there are certainly arguments in that direction. Exodus 1:11 states that the Israelite slaves in Egypt built the treasure cities Pithom and Rameses.

21. Eugene H. Merrill, *Kingdom of Priests: A History of Old Testament Israel* (Grand Rapids: Baker, 1987), 100–108.

22. John Garstang, *The Foundations of Bible History* (London: Constable and Company, 1931), 61ff.

23. W. F. Albright, *The Archaeology of Palestine* (Baltimore: Penguin, 1960), 108.

24. Bryant G. Wood, "Did the Israelites Conquer Jericho? A New Look at the Archaeological Evidence," *Biblical Archaeology Review* 16:2 (1990): 44–58.

25. Rowley, *From Joseph to Joshua*, 33–35.

These cities have been excavated, and evidence indicates that they were built by the Hyksos originally, perhaps in the eighteenth century. Later they were rebuilt by Rameses II, but this was not until the thirteenth century. In addition, there is evidence of Semitic slave labor having been used in the construction of the cities in Rameses' time.[26] The problem is, how could the Israelites have built these cities in 1290 B.C. when the exodus, according to the biblical dating, occurred 150 years earlier? First, it is by no means certain that the city of Rameses was named after the pharaoh of that name. In fact, Genesis 47:11 states that Jacob and his family settled in the land of Rameses when they entered Egypt in the nineteenth century; unless one postulates an anachronism, for which there is not the slightest proof, he must conclude that there was an area by that name before there was ever a Pharaoh Rameses. It could well be that there had been an ancient Ramesside dynasty long ages before and that the Ramessides of the Nineteenth Dynasty were named for them, the city also having taken this name.[27] In any case, there is no need to assume that the mention of the city of Rameses proves that the exodus must have taken place during the reign of Rameses II. The reconstruction of the cities in the thirteenth century could very well have been done under Rameses II, but the presence of Semitic slaves is not sufficient evidence to prove that the Hebrews of the exodus were the Semites in question.

Nelson Glueck argued years ago that there were no sedentary populations in Edom and Moab between the twentieth and thirteenth centuries B.C. When Moses requested permission for Israel to pass through Edom (Num. 20:14), and when he bypassed Moab to avoid warfare with the Moabites, how could he have expected any interference if there were no people in these countries during the late fifteenth century?[28] The answer is quite obvious from a careful study of the Old Testament record and even a superficial knowledge of biblical geography. The narrative records that Moses wanted to take the Kings' Highway, a route that passed through an extremely narrow mountain pass into and out of the city of Petra (Sela). This pass could easily be defended by only a very few hundred well-trained troops, and they need not be sedentary peoples.[29] Nomads or seminomads could well have occupied the area in numbers sufficient to preclude Israel's passing through their difficult land; yet the

26. Bright, A History of Israel, 123.

27. See Albright's interesting evidence along this line in From the Stone Age to Christianity (Garden City, N.Y.: Doubleday, 1957), 223.

28. Nelson Glueck, The Other Side of the Jordan (New Haven, Conn.: The American Schools of Oriental Research, 1940), 146ff.

29. Denis Baly, The Geography of the Bible: A Study in Historical Geography, rev. ed. (New York: Harper and Brothers, 1974), 245–51.

nature of their existence would explain the lack of any material remains such as permanent structures.[30] Likewise, Moab could have been settled by tribal people who, though not so advantageously situated, were spared by the Israelites because they were akin to them ethnically (Gen. 19:36–37). The absence of remains of a settled people need not militate against the early date of the exodus if the people simply did not leave remains. *Argumentum ad silentium* is not sufficient to overthrow the biblical position.

A further objection to an early exodus and conquest date is that archaeological research has shown rather conclusively, if the evidence has been correctly interpreted (often a moot point), that there was no large-scale destruction in Canaan in the fourteenth century but that there was such devastation in the thirteenth.[31] If Joshua conquered Canaan, and if this did not happen until only after 1250 or so, where is the evidence? Again, the problem results from an incorrect interpretation of the biblical record. The books of Joshua and Judges leave the impression that Joshua's campaign was not wholly successful (Josh. 13:1–6; Judg. 1). In many instances, places had to be taken more than once, which suggests that they were not demolished the first time and perhaps not at all until the time of the judges in the thirteenth century. In fact, it seems to have been Joshua's policy not to destroy the cities of the enemy, but only to defeat them on the field of battle (Josh. 10:28–42).[32] A good example of this policy is seen in Joshua 11, which describes the northern campaign. The battle against the coalition of northern kings centered around Hazor, and only Hazor of all the towns mentioned was destroyed by the Israelites. The others were left "standing on their tells." There is little evidence of violent destruction of Canaanite city-states in the fourteenth century simply because it was not Joshua's intention to destroy them.

Extrabiblical arguments are far from conclusive in support of either position, but there is no question that the Old Testament leans to the early date of 1446 for the exodus and 1406 for the beginning of the conquest. Only by assuming a series of movements by Israelites into Canaan can this evidence be overthrown, and such an assumption rests on the most tenuous support.

30. Glueck admitted that there could have been nomads in Edom and Moab during this period; cf. "The Civilization of the Edomites," in *The Biblical Archaeologist Reader*, vol. 2, ed. David Noel Freedman and Edward F. Campbell, Jr. (Garden City, N.Y.: Doubleday, Anchor Books, 1964), 51–52.

31. Albright, *The Biblical Period from Abraham to Ezra*, 27.

32. Eugene H. Merrill, "Palestinian Archaeology and the Date of the Conquest: Do Tells Tell Tales?" *Grace Theological Journal* 3 (1982): 107–21.

Israel in Egypt (Exodus 1–14)

To return to the biblical narrative, after the expulsion of the Hyksos about 1580 B.C., a native Egyptian monarch, Ahmose I, became pharaoh. It is possible that he is the pharaoh "which knew not Joseph" (Exod. 1:8), in the sense that he was now prejudiced against all Semites because of the Hyksos domination through which Egypt had so recently passed. To prevent Israel from becoming a threat to Egypt's security, he placed them under bondage. Exodus 1:11 relates that they built for the pharaoh store cities including Pithom (Tell er-Retebah) and Rameses (Qantir),[33] but this oppression did not deter the enlargement and strengthening of Israel. Finally, the pharaoh (probably Amenhotep I or Thutmose I) deemed it necessary to slaughter all the Hebrew male infants in an effort to curb the population. It is in this period of genocide that Moses was born of Levite ancestry.

When the child had reached the age of three months, his mother found it impossible to conceal him in the house, so she fashioned a reed basket, which she waterproofed and placed among the rushes in the Nile. The infant Moses was laid in this floating cradle, while his sister Miriam watched nearby to see what would become of him. It just so happened that Pharaoh's daughter, possibly Hatshepsut, coming to bathe near where the basket floated, noticed the ark with its pitiful cargo. Her heart was so touched by the sight that she, forgetting her prejudice and her father's edict, rescued the child, whom she named Moses (Hebrew, "drawn forth"; Egyptian, "son"). She decided to adopt the child and, following the far-sighted advice of Miriam, who witnessed all this, sought out a Hebrew nurse to attend him. This nurse, of course, was Moses' mother, who was able, therefore, to train him in the traditions and customs of her Hebrew heritage at the same time that he was nurtured in all the arts and sciences of Egypt (Heb. 11:23–27).

Little is known of Moses' life in his first forty years except that he became highly favored in the royal household. One day, however, he witnessed the beating of a Hebrew slave by an Egyptian foreman and, in a fit of anger, slew the Egyptian. Fearing reprisal because of his Hebrew background, he fled to Midian, a distant land two hundred miles to the east of Egypt. There he met Jethro (or Reuel), a priest of Midian, and, after marrying his daughter Zipporah, settled down to live with him. For forty long years, all through the reign of Thutmose III, from whom he had fled,

33. For these identifications, see John J. Bimson, *Redating the Exodus and Conquest* (Sheffield: JSOT, University of Sheffield, 1978), 46, 43, respectively.

Moses remained in the Arabian desert tending the flocks—a far cry from his days of luxury in the courts of Heliopolis.

The purpose for his having been driven to the desert was dramatically explained one day when Moses was in the south Sinai peninsula at Horeb tending his father-in-law's sheep. There God appeared to him in a theophany consisting of a bush that burned but was not consumed. For the first time in four hundred years, as far as the biblical record recounts, God revealed himself in an audible way by identifying himself to Moses as the God of Abraham, Isaac, and Jacob. He followed this declaration with the call to Moses to lead Israel, whose prayer and groaning he had heard, from Egypt back to the land of promise, the covenant land. When Moses protested that he was incapable and was unsure of the response he would receive from his people, God reiterated his promise by revealing himself in a new name. Moses had asked what name of God he should use when describing to Israel their call from Egypt, and God replied that he should mention to them that *I AM* had sent him (Exod. 3:14; 6:3). This name, simply the first person singular of the Hebrew verb *hāyāh* ("to be"), would indicate to Israel that God was the one who eternally exists and that he would be more than sufficient to protect, accompany, and bless them every step of the way. The expression of that name in the third person singular gave rise to the name *Yahweh*, "He is." This name of God is usually rendered LORD, though "Jehovah" occurs in the American Standard Version (1901). To be sure, this name had been known to the saints of old, but not in its full meaning. They knew the name, but not its significance for this hour of deliverance. Israel was about to be redeemed, rescued, and reconstituted as a covenant nation, and Yahweh meant all of this. The name, in other words, was to be the name of God in his redemptive, covenant capacity.[34] It was in the power of this Name that Moses was to return and lead his people forth; such power he would need, for Pharaoh would by no means permit them to leave.

After Moses argued further about his own capabilities as a leader, God silenced his objections once and for all by a series of signs: changing his shepherd's rod to a serpent, afflicting him with leprosy and delivering him from it, and promising that his elder brother Aaron would serve as spokesman. Furthermore, as a token of his promise, God revealed to Moses that Israel would worship him at this mountain (Sinai) and then would realize God's covenant faithfulness. Finally Moses agreed to go. After bidding his father-in-law adieu, he took his wife and two sons

---

34. Geerhardus Vos, *Biblical Theology: Old and New Testaments* (Grand Rapids: Eerdmans, 1948), 129–34.

TABLE 4

The Ten Plagues

1. Turning water into blood	(Exod. 7:19–25)
2. Frogs	(Exod. 8:1–15)
3. Lice	(Exod. 8:16–19)
4. Flies	(Exod. 8:20–32)
5. Cattle disease	(Exod. 9:1–7)
6. Boils	(Exod. 9:8–12)
7. Hail	(Exod. 9:13–35)
8. Locusts	(Exod. 10:1–20)
9. Darkness	(Exod. 10:21–29)
10. Death of the firstborn	(Exod. 12:29–30)

toward Egypt. On the way, his wife and he parted over a dispute concerning the circumcision of their elder son; she returned to Midian, not to rejoin him until he later returned to Horeb. Aaron in the meantime had been led by God out of Egypt to meet his brother in the wilderness, and together they returned to Egypt to assume their ponderous responsibilities.

On the initial encounter with Pharaoh, no doubt Amenhotep II, they suffered a setback, for he refused to permit Israel to go and worship Yahweh in the desert of Sinai, as Moses requested (Exod. 5:1–2). In fact, he interpreted Moses' request as reflecting too much leisure, so he punished his insolence by increasing the severity of Israelite slavery. In great discouragement, Moses and Aaron turned to Yahweh, who proceeded to reaffirm his promise, the same promise made to their fathers centuries earlier. He told them, moreover, to return to Pharaoh again, this time to perform mighty works in his name before him. If Pharaoh still refused to permit them to worship in the desert, God would bring on Egypt a series of plagues so severe that Pharaoh would be compelled to grant their request. The second audience was no more successful, and, though Aaron's rod became a serpent and swallowed up the serpents that the Egyptian magicians were able to create by satanic power, the king was adamant. Thereupon God unleashed on the land the plagues, ten in all, which, in spite of temporary indications to the contrary, left Pharaoh unmoved in his determination to resist Israel's demands.

The miracles of the rods, plagues, and so on have always been a source of consternation to the critics, who dismiss them as exaggerated accounts of phenomena of nature, at best. For example, they maintain that the turning of water into blood was simply a darkening of the Nile by some muddy materials that had been carried down the river from Ethiopia and central Africa. The lice were merely sand fleas, which are common today, and they were caused by the stirring up of the dust in which they breed. The total darkness was caused by a tremendous dust storm that blotted out the sun.[35] The objections to such circumventions of the miraculous should be obvious, for they completely fail to explain all of the plagues, and the incredible results that followed are not explicable on the basis of purely natural occurrences. How could it be that only in Goshen, where Israel lived, there were no flies or darkness? Granted even that forces of nature were at work in some cases, how did these forces exclude Israel from their devastating effects? No answer apart from God is sufficient to account for these facts; to say that these stories are only legendary or spiritually interpreted memories of God's mighty acts in nature is begging the question and relegating history to nonsense.

The tenth and final plague, the slaughter of the firstborn of Egypt, was the most horrible and momentous of all. To the Egyptians, it indicated the superiority of Yahweh over their gods of life and death, but to Israel it spoke of his gracious deliverance and salvation. It occasioned the institution of one of the most meaningful services of the Hebrew religious year, the Passover, a rite that forever after would commemorate God's selection of the slave band Israel to be his special people, the proof of that selection being their marvelous deliverance from the tenth plague and exodus from the land of their bondage.

The description of the Passover in Exodus 12 is filled with meaning for both Israel and the church. Every Israelite household must select a lamb on the tenth day of the month Abib (Nisan), the month that from henceforth was to be the first in the religious year. This lamb was to be tethered in the dooryard of the home until the fourteenth day, when it was to be slaughtered "between the evenings," or between the going down of the sun and absolute darkness. The blood from the victim must be applied to the two side posts and the lintel of each house with a sprig of hyssop. The entire roasted flesh of the lamb was then to be eaten with unleavened bread and bitter herbs. During this hurried meal, the family must be in a state of preparation, dressed for a journey. The lamb typified the Lamb of God mentioned by John the Baptist at the baptism of Jesus (John 1:29) and prophesied by Isaiah, particularly in Isaiah 53. The blood spoke of

35. Martin Buber, *Moses: The Revelation and the Covenant* (New York: Harper and Row, 1958), 67–68.

atonement, which in the Hebrew literally means "covering." The application of the blood indicated the faith of the one making the application in the ability of the blood to protect him from the wrath of God, or, as later theology was to express it, to save him from his sin (Lev. 17:11; Heb. 9:22). The roasting by fire conveyed the idea of judgment, which Christ vicariously suffered; the wholeness of the victim's body revealed that "not a bone of his body should be broken" (Ps. 34:20; John 19:36). There are other typical elements as well, but these are sufficient to indicate the spiritual nature of the Passover feast as well as its meaning in the historical context of the exodus.[36]

That fateful night of the fourteenth of Abib finally came; when God's judgment passed over the land of Egypt, only those homes sheltered by the sprinkled blood escaped the awful toll exacted on the firstborn. In sorrow and rage, Pharaoh, who also had lost his firstborn son, commanded the Israelites to leave his land. With the clothing and valuables they had requested from the Egyptians, they left in haste from Rameses in Goshen, fleeing to Succoth near the edge of the Sinai wilderness. The magnitude of the migration staggers the imagination, for over six hundred thousand adults, plus children and animals, entered the sojourn (Exod. 12:37). In fact, the multitude was so great that some scholars account for it by suggesting that the term *thousand* in Hebrew ('elep) should be understood as a military term meaning a certain contingent of troops. If an 'elep contained on the average no more than fifty men, it might mean that only 30,000 adults left (50 x 600). Together with children, the total under this reckoning would amount to no more than 120,000 persons, a much more understandable figure. The line of reasoning just presented is inconsistent, however, with the totals given by tribes later on,[37] where there is no question as to the meaning. As difficult as it must have been to manage and sustain such a crowd in a desert for forty years, one must, in light of present knowledge, accept the biblical account, for the entire exodus event is in the spirit of the miraculous, the miracle of this great host being but one of many examples.

Following the Passover feast, and apparently while in Succoth, Moses was further instructed concerning its significance. For seven days following the feast itself, there was to be a secondary, though related, observance known as the Feast of Unleavened Bread. Leaven, generally a symbol of sin in the Scriptures, was to be removed from the home as a sign of the

36. Willem VanGemeren, *The Progress of Redemption: The Story of Salvation from Creation to the New Jerusalem* (Grand Rapids: Zondervan, Academic Books, 1988), 161–63.
37. George E. Mendenhall, "The Census Lists of Numbers 1 and 26," *Journal of Biblical Literature* 77 (1958): 52–66.

separation of its inhabitant from the sinful elements of his past life. Moreover, because God had graciously spared the firstborn of Israel at the Passover, all firstborn sons were to be dedicated to his service (13:11–15). All firstborn animals, likewise, were to be offered in sacrifice if they were sacrificial animals; otherwise, they were to be substituted for by a sacrificial animal. For example, the ass, because it was a valuable work animal, could be "redeemed" by a lamb that would die in its place. The male children of Israel could likewise be redeemed by a lamb in lieu of service to God.

The journey was resumed from Succoth. Contrary to expectation, God forbade Moses to take the coastal highway from Egypt directly to Canaan, because that way crossed Philistine territory, and God knew that when Israel met the warlike Philistines they would desire to turn back to Egypt. A more southerly route was selected, though its details are irrecoverable because of the present lack of biblical and archaeological information. In any event, they camped near Etham, thought to be at the northern end of the Bitter Lakes, from whence they turned again and encamped before Pihahiroth, "between Migdol and the sea," and near Baal-zephon. These places have never been conclusively identified, so the route at this point is highly speculative.[38] The narrator discloses that they were shut in by the desert and the sea, no exit being available to them but the sea itself. Pharaoh, by this time regretting that he had permitted all these slaves to escape, pursued the Israelites with a select unit of charioteers, finally overtaking them at their encampment near the sea. At this time, however, God intervened and, in a most extraordinary miracle, parted the waters of the sea to permit the entire Israelite host to cross on dry ground. The pursuing Egyptians, attempting to cross in the same path, were overwhelmed by the returning waters that God permitted to flood to their original bed.

This entire miracle, including the place of crossing, demands further investigation in light of the criticisms that have assailed it on nearly every hand. It is generally pointed out, and correctly, that the term describing the sea in the Hebrew, *Yam Suph*, means Reed Sea and not Red Sea,[39] and this is taken to mean that the crossing place was very shallow.[40] However, this same term appears to apply to the entire gulfs of Suez and Aqaba

---

38. For suggestions see Yohanan Aharoni, *The Land of the Bible*, trans. and ed. Anson F. Rainey, rev. and enl. ed. (Philadelphia: Westminster, 1979), 196–97; Herbert G. May, ed., *Oxford Bible Atlas*, 3d ed. (New York: Oxford University Press, 1984), 58–59.

39. Francis Brown, S. R. Driver, and Charles Briggs, *A Hebrew and English Lexicon of the Old Testament* (London: Oxford University Press, 1962), 693.

40. Bernhard W. Anderson, *Understanding the Old Testament*, 4th ed. (Englewood Cliffs, N.J.: Prentice-Hall, 1986), 78–79.

(Exod. 10:19; Josh. 2:10; Deut. 11:4; Num. 21:4). The argument that the Reed Sea must imply a shallow body of water is thus overthrown, for the Gulf of Suez is hardly so. In fact, even the Bitter Lakes, Lake Timsah, and Lake Ballah, are deep enough, or certainly were in ancient times, to demand a miraculous act of God for Israel to pass through and for the Egyptian charioteers and horses to be drowned. It is possible to allow that Israel crossed one of these lakes (the writer's opinion being that it was the southernmost, the Bitter Lakes), and still believe in the full need for a miracle. Such explanations as a blowing back of shallow waters by a strong wind, or the crossing point being merely through a swamp in which the Egyptians became lost and ensnared, are only feeble attempts to skirt the miraculous nature of the exodus.[41] It is not enough to say that a small renegade band fled through shallow water, lost its pursuers in the darkness, and later reinterpreted these events as miraculous, mighty acts of God on their behalf. The massive structure of the Judaeo-Christian faith can hardly be supported by such a shaky foundation. Only a genuine miracle, as recorded here, can account for Israel's memory of this forever after as the greatest historical event in its national experience (Ps. 66:6; 136:10–15; Ezek. 20:5–6; Hos. 11:1; Amos 3:1–2).

Israel in the Sinai (Exodus 15–Numbers 21)

After singing the praises of God in one of the most stirring poems of the Old Testament (Exod. 15:1–18), Moses continued to lead the way to Marah, three days' journey south of the crossing point. If the average day's journey was fifteen miles, a figure comparable to such a journey under such circumstances today, the Bitter Lakes crossing point is somewhat substantiated, any place farther north being too far for three days, and any place farther south not necessitating three days. At Marah the water was too bitter to drink; hence the name mārāh ("bitter"). The water became palatable, however, when Moses cast a certain medicinal plant into it, and it remains pure to this day.[42] From Marah they journeyed on to Elim ("palms"); a month or more after their departure, they moved into the Wilderness of Sin in the southern part of the peninsula. There, possibly in view of Egypt, which lay across the Suez Gulf, they began to long for the old life they had left only recently. They tired of the lack of meat and bread and the arduous existence they had inherited. One familiar with the

41. Lewis Hay, "What Really Happened at the Sea of Reeds?" *Journal of Biblical Literature* 83 (1964): 397–403.
42. According to Manasseh Harel, who was engaged in the Sinai campaign of 1947–48, the waters at Marah are quite palatable. From a lecture in Jerusalem, Israel, July 17, 1965. Harel is professor of geography at Hebrew University.

desert can well sympathize with their plight, for the heat and lack of mois-ture, coupled with the difficulty of traveling, must have been extremely taxing even to these who had been accustomed to the Egyptian slave lash.

To alleviate their hunger, God promised to shower on them quail and bread in such supply that they would never again lack these necessities in all their journey. At the first appearance of manna, they were dumb-founded because of its source and nature; all they could exclaim was *mān nû* ("what is it?"). To memorialize this wonderful event, a supply of the manna was conserved in a pot and later placed in the ark of the covenant (Exod. 16:32–36; Heb. 9:4).

The next stop was at Rephidim, where Moses struck a rock to secure water; it was there also that Israel encountered its first enemy. Swooping down on the Hebrews' rear flank and attacking the elderly and infirm, the Amalekites, a nomadic and fierce tribe of the Sinai interior, struck Israel hard, but not without retaliation. Untrained militarily as Israel presum-ably was, she was not lacking in leadership or resources; as Moses raised his hands in benediction over the Israelite hosts with their captain, Joshua, they prevailed in the power of God over their enemies. At the conclusion of the fracas, Jethro, Moses' father-in-law, arrived at Rephidim with Moses' wife Zipporah and their two sons, Gershom and Eliezer (18:1–6). He had heard rumors to the effect that Yahweh had delivered Israel from Egypt, and he wanted to verify them. Having been assured of their truth, Jethro, as priest of Midian, presented a burnt offering in praise to Yahweh. The question of Jethro's relationship to the faith of Israel is too involved to be considered fully here, but the evidence available would surely indicate that he was intimately familiar with Israel's God.[43] His say-ing that he now knows that Yahweh is superior to the gods of Egypt does not mean that he questioned that up until now; he is simply saying that now he has seen it proved beyond any reasonable doubt. Noticing that Moses was continually troubled by the hordes of people who came to him for advice and judgment in thousands of petty matters, Jethro warned him that he would overtax himself and advised him to set up a court system of minor judges who could settle at least the less significant cases. To this advice Moses gave heed, though apparently the system had only brief use.

Jethro left Rephidim, and, shortly thereafter, Moses did also. Israel's next stop, and its most important, was in the Plain of Sinai before the mountain where Moses had first seen the manifestation of God in the burning bush. Here were to take place some of the most important events in Israel's history, for this place was, in many respects, the cradle of the

43. Bright, *A History of Israel*, 127.

theocracy ("rule of God"). A covenant had been made with Abraham, inherited by Isaac and Jacob, and expressed ethnically in Israel. A remarkable deliverance had been effected by God when this people had fled from four hundred years of bondage in Egypt. And now this rather heterogeneous band, Israel, was at the threshold of a new and vital experience, the giving of the covenant law that would lend their loose federation cohesion, enabling them to know the will of God in government, society, and worship.

Moses, as the mediator between Yahweh and Israel, was summoned by God to the summit of the holy mountain, where God told him that the time for the creation of a nation of believers had come. In unmistakable language, he informed Moses that he was to remind Israel that God had delivered them from Egypt by his mighty power, that he would confirm and enlarge the terms of the ancient covenant with them, that he expected faithful obedience from them, and that on the condition of their obedience he would make of them a kingdom of priests and a holy nation (Exod. 19:4–6). Agreeing to this condition and in solemn oaths, the representatives of Israel prepared themselves for the reception of the details of this covenant. Three days later in a great demonstration of power, God appeared before Moses in fire and thunderings and earthquakes and set the stage for the giving of the Book of the Covenant (Exod. 20–23), the very heart of the theocratic economy.[44]

After the law was announced and spelled out, it was accepted in a ceremony of covenant agreement by a council of elders representing the twelve tribes. The seventy elders gathered about an altar and a circle of twelve pillars especially erected for the occasion; sacrificial offerings were made, and the blood of the sacrifices was sprinkled in turn on the altar and the participants. As in the Abrahamic covenant, the slaughter of animals and the use of the blood as an intermediary agent bound the parties of the contract into an indissoluble relationship. God and Israel had become "blood brothers" in a very real sense. Following this, God summoned Moses up to Sinai once again to give him the Decalogue (Ten Commandments) on the tables of stone as well as instructions concerning a place of worship where he might meet Israel (24:12–18).

44. It is now generally recognized that the covenant made between Yahweh and Israel was patterned, in form and style, after treaty texts well known in the Late Bronze Age, particularly those devised by the Hittite kings and imposed on subject peoples. These documents, referred to technically as "suzerain-vassal" treaties, contained basic elements found in generally the same order as occur in the Book of the Covenant (Exod. 20:1–23:33) and in Deuteronomy. For the fundamental study of the relationship between the suzerain-vassal treaties and the Old Testament texts see George E. Mendenhall, *Law and Covenant in Israel and the Ancient Near East* (Pittsburgh: The Biblical Colloquium, 1955).

The tabernacle and priesthood are discussed in the remainder of the Book of Exodus (25–40). Now that Israel was a nation with a king (God) and a body of laws (Torah), there must be a provision made for Israel to have communion with God. This involved both a place of communion and a means whereby communion might take place, since sin barred direct access to God. The parts of the tabernacle and the acts of the priest have highly symbolic value, so it will be necessary to give them special attention in the next chapter.

The historical narrative is resumed in Exodus 31 with the selection of men who were to oversee the construction of the tabernacle with all its accoutrements. Because of the extreme complexity of all the work involved, it was necessary that men be endowed with the Holy Spirit in order to have the requisite skill and wisdom. The two chief foremen, Bezaleel and Aholiab, were especially singled out as chosen instruments of God, and under their direction the work was carried out successfully.

While Moses was on the summit of Sinai receiving all these aforementioned laws and instructions, the people down in the plains concluded that he was gone forever. In their opinion, Yahweh had forsaken them, and nothing significant was ever to come of the covenant. Bereft of their human leader also, they resorted to making an image of gold that would become to them a tangible object of worship. This image of a bull (not calf) was not of a foreign god but was supposed to represent the pedestal on which Yahweh stood.[45] That the feast that followed was dedicated to Yahweh is sufficient to prove that the sin was not a departure from God but an attempt to represent God materially, at least indirectly. This was clearly prohibited by the second commandment.

In the midst of the orgy of feasting and dancing, in which Aaron apparently took a prominent role, God related to Moses what was transpiring below and threatened to destroy Israel for its sin. On hearing this, Moses urged God to remember his eternal covenant; then he went down from the mountain, carrying the tablets of stone on which God had inscribed the commandments. Almost symbolically, he cast the stones on the ground when he saw the awful picture before his eyes; breaking the stones seemed to depict the terrible breaking of the law so recently given. In rage, Moses took the image, smashed it into pieces, ground it to dust that he threw into the nearby brook, and caused the ringleaders to drink of the water. He then proceeded to excoriate Aaron for his part, though Aaron tried vainly to excuse the act as a miracle beyond his knowledge or control, for he stated that when certain gold objects were cast into a fire, the golden bull appeared as though by magic. The dreadful conclusion came

---

45. Buber, *Moses*, 214.

when Moses commanded the Levites, who by now seemed to exercise a certain religious authority, to slaughter the guilty parties, whereupon at least three thousand men perished. Moses now turned to God and, in some of the most moving and selfless words ever penned, asked God to forgive Israel, offering to give himself for his people if God might see fit (32:30–32). God instead forgave the people and reassured Moses of his continued presence with them.

God then revealed himself to Moses in a magnificent way. Having called him to the temporary tent of meeting outside the camp, he manifested himself to Moses and all the people in a pillar of cloud that rested over the tent. Then he informed Moses that he would permit him to see his "back parts," though not his face, as a testimony to Moses that he would continue to be with him in the days ahead. What Moses saw was no doubt the reflected glory of God, the effulgent radiance of his presence, and nothing physical; for the Father, as a spirit, would not manifest himself otherwise (John 4:24). Moses then was summoned once more to the top of Sinai, where he was given a set of tablets to replace those that had been broken. When he reappeared, the brilliance of God's presence reflected on his face was so intense that Israel could not bear to look on him unless he covered his countenance with a veil (34:29–35; 2 Cor. 3:13).

The construction of the tabernacle, manufacturing of the vessels, garments, and other objects, and anointing of the priests are described in Exodus 35–40. The mass of details in these chapters indicates clearly the precision of the work and that every item had great importance in the eyes of God and is instructive to those who study it carefully.[46] When the tabernacle was finally reared and the furniture placed therein, God filled it with his presence glory.[47] When the cloud appeared by day and the fire by night over this holy shrine, Israel was to know that God was there and that when they moved he was leading them on to new experiences.

Next, the priests were anointed and consecrated according to the divine instruction (Lev. 8), following which they offered their first sacrificial offerings (Lev. 9). Two of Aaron's sons, Nadab and Abihu, presumed to make an offering with "strange fire" and were slain by the Lord as a result (Lev. 10:1–7). The harshness of the punishment would serve as a warning to others that the very technique of offering to God was a sacred procedure laden with meaning that could not be abridged. At about the same time, Moses was commanded to number the people and arrange

46. For a good study of the historical basis for the tabernacle, see Frank M. Cross, "The Priestly Tabernacle," in *The Biblical Archaeologist Reader*, 2:201–28.

47. This is the so-called shekinah glory, a phrase derived from the Hebrew verb šākan, "to dwell."

them in order that they might continue the long journey to Canaan (Num. 1–2). They were to march according to camps, three tribes on each side of the tabernacle and the Levites surrounding it on all sides. Each camp had its own standard and was to position itself in the same order whether marching or settled.

The selection of the tribe of Levi for special service followed (Num. 3), though it was implied even earlier (Exod. 13:11–6). Formerly, the first-born of every house of Israel was to be dedicated to God for perpetual service, but now God selected a whole tribe, Levi, to render this service. Every firstborn could be represented by a Levite according to the law; in the event that there were not enough Levites for each firstborn (as the case actually was), the remaining firstborn were to be redeemed from their service by the sacrifice of five shekels apiece (Num. 3:44–51). The Levites themselves were divided according to families into the Gershonites, Kohathites, and the sons of Merari, these three having been the sons of Levi the patriarch. To each of these groups was given a special responsibility in regard to the services, care, and transportation of the tabernacle and all that pertained to it. Further instructions concerning the selection and consecration of the Levites are given in Numbers 8.

Finally the day came for resuming the journey to the land of promise (Num. 10:11). For over a year, Israel had rested at Sinai while the nation was being formed; now, with a blowing of trumpets, they proceeded to the desert of Paran. Hardly out of sight of Sinai, however, they began to complain again about their condition, the chief grievance being the lack of meat and spicy Egyptian foods. Moses, about at the breaking point from the burden of the people, was given seventy elders filled with the Spirit and delegated to help in his overwhelming tasks of ministering to so great a host (11:24–30). Then God sent an abundance of quail, but the people in their greed began to devour them without offering thanks. At this God slew a great many; in memorial of their lust, the place of their death was called Kibroth–hattaavah ("graves of sinning").

From here they moved to Hazeroth, the place where Miriam and Aaron rose in rebellion against Moses, ostensibly because he had married an Ethiopian woman.[48] The real reason for their attitude was a feeling of envy because they apparently did not share the intimate relationship with God that Moses enjoyed, though they, too, could lay claim to the title *prophet*. In retaliation, God summoned Miriam and Aaron before him;

48. It could be that this was an interracial marriage, though the Hebrew term *Cushite* could refer to natives of the Arabian peninsula; see R. K. Harrison, *Numbers*, The Wycliffe Exegetical Commentary (Chicago: Moody, 1990), 194–95. Harrison suggests that this may refer to Zipporah herself (cf. Exod. 2:21).

possibly because Miriam as the prime instigator had sought to undermine the divinely appointed authority of her younger brother, she was struck by leprosy. Only after earnest intercession by Moses was she healed and permitted back in the camp.

On reaching the desert of Paran, Moses sent spies into Canaan (Num. 13:1–25). Israel had come now nearly to Canaan's southern boundaries; it seems that Moses' purpose was to enter Canaan from the south. Twelve men were appointed to trek throughout the land and report their findings. Forty days later they returned to Kadesh-barnea, where Israel now camped. Ten brought back a pessimistic report of great giants and high-walled cities in Canaan that Israel could in no wise overcome. Only two, Caleb and Joshua, tried to convince Israel to trust God and to move in and occupy the land by his grace. Their arguments were not convincing, however, and in a near rebellion the nation decided to hearken to the majority report, overthrow the leadership of Moses and Aaron, and return to Egypt. God threatened once again to disinherit Israel and to make of Moses a mightier nation yet, but, true to his prophetic calling, Moses interceded for the people as he had done before. God spared them from death but sentenced them to wander for thirty-eight more years, or a total of forty, never to reach Canaan except as represented by their children twenty years of age and under (14:22–24). Only Joshua and Caleb, of all the men of war, would enter that land because of their obedience.

On hearing this, Israel attempted an immediate entry into Canaan from the south but was soundly defeated at Hormah by a Canaanite force. This was only the first of many events in the next thirty-eight-year period, but very few of those are recorded in the account of Moses. Perhaps the most outstanding is the rebellion of Korah, Dathan, and Abiram (Num. 16). These men, with their families and friends, decided that Moses and Aaron were arrogating too much authority to themselves and challenged them to prove the uniqueness of their divine calling as mediators between Israel and God. Moses accepted the challenge, but when these pretenders attempted to offer sacrifice, the earth opened up beneath them and swallowed them, together with their unbelieving families and their tents and possessions. Rather than accepting this as a sign of God's blessing on Moses and Aaron, however, the nation protested; were it not for the intercession of these two faithful men of God, once more God would have destroyed the nation "as in a moment" (16:45). In a final and convincing act, each tribe was to supply a rod that, with Aaron's rod, was to be placed in the tabernacle overnight. The rod that shot forth buds would be the symbol of its owner's call from God. On the next day, the rods were examined, and, of course, Aaron's budded and even brought forth flowers. All arguments being silenced, the rod was placed beside the ark of the covenant, a worthy retirement for an instrument that had been so singularly used of God.

At long last the period of wandering about the oasis of Kadesh-barnea and vicinity was over, and Israel moved into the desert of Zin. There Miriam died at a very advanced age. In the vast desert there was no water, a situation so disheartening that the people complained. In a burst of anger Moses, violating God's command, struck a rock, in an effort to procure water (20:7–11). This cost him the privilege of entering the land of promise, though God assured him that he would see it from a distance. This denial to Moses, who for so many years had unfailingly followed the will of God until this moment of anger, can be understood only in light of the principle that of those to whom God has granted great blessing and responsibility does he at the same time expect unswerving obedience. A lesser man no doubt would have gone virtually unscathed, but a "little" sin in such a spiritual giant loomed larger than the aggregate sin of a whole generation.

When Moses realized the impossibility of penetrating Canaan from the south, he decided to do so from the plains of Moab just across Jordan from Jericho. To reach this area, he must pass through the Kings' Highway if at all possible. This route wended its way north from the Gulf of Aqaba through the Kingdom of Edom, particularly its capital city, Sela (Petra in Greek). The route traversed terrain impassable except through narrow mountain gaps. The result was that caravans or armies were compelled to go almost single file; if the Edomites so wished, they could withstand many thousands of invaders with a few hundred well-trained troops. Moses, therefore, sought permission from the king of Edom to pass through his land, but the king refused (20:17–21). While Moses decided what to do next, his brother Aaron died and was buried at Mount Hor. Then Israel was attacked near there by the Canaanite king of Arad but won the battle (21:1–3).

Moses next turned south, apparently deciding to go east of Edom through the Syro-Arabian Desert, but when the way became too difficult, he had to retrace his steps north and make the effort to venture up through the Arabah and bypass Edom on the west. Somewhere along the way, the people began to murmur once again, and this time they fell victim to serpents that God set on them. Only when they looked in faith on a bronze serpent Moses had made and placed on a pole did they recover from the plague (21:9); even then, many people died.[49] They finally reached the mouth of the Wadi Zered, just to the north of Edom at the southeast coast of the Dead Sea, and, proceeding up the Zered Valley, which formed the

---

49. This may have been at Timnah or Punon, both places being rich sources of copper to this day. See Baly, *The Geography of the Bible*, 212.

border between Edom and Moab, they arrived at the Plains of Moab just south of the Amorite kingdom. There they remained for the most part until they crossed the Jordan under the leadership of Joshua.

Israel in the Plains of Moab (Numbers 22–Deuteronomy 34)

In the course of entering the Plains of Moab and while they were settled there, Israel encountered many obstacles. The first was the battle with the Amorite settlers who occupied the territory north of Moab (21:21–25). Sihon, their king, in response to Moses' request to permit the passage of Israel through their land, refused to comply, whereupon Israel attacked, defeated them, and occupied their holdings. This first of the Israelite possessions was later settled for the most part by the tribe of Gad. As a follow-up, Israel's armies went north of Sihon's realm to the land of Bashan; after a short skirmish they defeated Og, the king of Bashan, and occupied this area that later became the home of half of the tribe of Manasseh (21:33–35). Thus, in two quick assaults, Israel occupied virtually everything east of the Jordan and north of Moab.

The most serious test of all, though not in the form of military action, came in Israel's contacts with the Moabites (Num. 22–25). Moses had refused to force his way through Moab, despite the ease with which this no doubt could have been done, because he recognized the ancient relationship between Israel and Moab. Nevertheless, the king of Moab, Balak, when he saw how Sihon and Og had both been defeated by Israel, feared that his kingdom was next in line to be assimilated by these powerful Hebrew nomads. At the same time, he felt that military strength could not defeat them, so he resorted to supernatural power. He called a certain soothsayer, Balaam by name, to come from Mesopotamia and curse Israel for him, believing that in this way Israel would become immobilized. At first Balaam refused to come, for God had forbidden him. After much persuasion, aided by an offer of substantial financial remuneration, he decided that he could go, but he still insisted that he could speak only what God permitted him to speak. Balaam encountered an angel of God blocking his way to Moab, and when he failed at first to notice the angelic visitor, the beast of burden on which he rode spoke to him.[50] This naturally shocked Balaam, making him realize that God was trying to reveal something further to him: that he must speak only the word of God.

---

50. See C. F. Keil and Franz Delitzsch, *Biblical Commentary on the Old Testament: The Pentateuch*, vol. 3 (reprint ed.; Grand Rapids: Eerdmans, 1948), 173, for an explanation of this strange phenomenon.

As soon as Balaam arrived in Moab, Balak took him to the high places of worship and sacrifice, where, after a series of cultic acts, he proceeded to curse Israel, which he could see spread out in the plains below him. To Balaam's amazement and Balak's chagrin, only a blessing issued forth (23:7–10); Balaam admitted the impossibility of cursing what God had blessed. Twice more Balak urged Balaam to curse Israel, but both times only marvelous prophetic blessings were proclaimed (23:18–24; 24:4–9). Finally, in utter frustration, Balak dismissed his hireling soothsayer, who, nevertheless, was still not finished with his blessing. In an act entirely beyond his control, he spoke one final word, one of the most glorious prophecies in the Old Testament. In somber tones he said, "I see him, but not now; I behold him, but not near. A star will come out of Jacob; a scepter will rise out of Israel. He will crush the foreheads of Moab, the skulls of all the sons of Sheth" (Num. 24:17 NIV). A representation of this same star centuries later would lead wise men from Mesopotamia to seek him who was the subject of this majestic prophecy (Isa. 60:3; Matt. 2:2).

But Balaam's work was not yet finished. He apparently dwelt among the Moabites and somehow became instrumental in causing Israel to go after the Baal of Peor, a Moabite god. What he could not accomplish in a curse he did achieve subtly, for thousands of Israelites, especially from the tribe of Simeon, began to "commit whoredom" with the daughters of Moab. This apostasy from Yahweh was not only spiritual fornication, though it was that to be sure, but also physical. This was the first contact with the immoral fertility cults of Canaan, the very essence of which was sexual aberration of all kinds. The result was death to twenty-four thousand Israelites, for God had plainly declared that all such things were abominations and could not be tolerated if Israel were to survive at all.

At last the days of Moses' ministry came to an end, but before he died he was privileged to glimpse the land to the borders of which he had led his people. Also, there must be one to take his place after his departure; God's choice was Joshua (Deut. 31:14–23). Another matter that came to his attention was the request by the tribes of Reuben, Gad, and half the tribe of Manasseh to settle the lands east of the Jordan, which they had already subjugated and was ideal for pastures and farms. Moses granted the petition on the condition that the fighting men of these tribes cross the Jordan with the other tribes and help them occupy the western portions of Palestine. Then and only then could they return to their families and lands (Num. 32:20–33). Gad took the area formerly known as the Amorite kingdom, Manasseh settled in Bashan, and Reuben eventually occupied parts of Moab. At the same time, Moses outlined the borders of Canaan where the other tribes were soon to settle (Num. 34). In addition, he selected forty-eight cities in which the Levites would live and minister, because Levi as a religious tribe had no inheritance; six of these he designated as cities of refuge, three on each side of the Jordan (Num. 35; Deut. 19:1–13).

After reviewing all the law and making certain necessary additions and modifications thereto, Moses gathered all the people together for preparations for a final assembly (Deut. 27:1).[51] He first commanded them to build an altar at Shechem, between the mountains Ebal and Gerizim, when they entered Canaan (27:2–8). There they were to write the words of the law, presumably the Decalogue, on stones and reaffirm their obedience to the terms of the covenant. Following this, the Levites were to utter a series of curses that would become applicable on the breach of certain points of the covenant, and the people were to accept the justice of these curses by giving their assent at the Shechem assembly (27:11–26). Then Moses pointed out another series of blessings and curses that would follow Israel's obedience or disobedience in the days ahead, and he concluded the list by summoning Israel into covenant once again with God then and there (28–30).

After this great gathering in which he spelled out God's requirements for his people, Moses wrote down all the law (31:9), gave Joshua a final charge (31:23), and recited a song in which he extolled God for his faithfulness to Israel (31:30–32:43). Then he gave his final blessing to the tribes (33), went to the top of Mount Pisgah, where he had his last view of the land of promise, and finally, at the age of 120, died in Moab, where God buried him in an unknown grave (34:1–7). No more fitting epitaph could be given than that at the end of Deuteronomy: "Since then no prophet has risen in Israel like Moses, whom the Lord knew face to face . . ." (Deut. 34:10).

---

51. The entire Book of Deuteronomy is, in effect, the text of a covenant renewal document. See, in support of this, Peter C. Craigie, *The Book of Deuteronomy* (Grand Rapids: Eerdmans, 1976), 24–32.

5

The Theocratic Foundation

Ancient Near Eastern Law

There were law codes in the Near East hundreds of years before the time of Moses. Hammurabi's Code of Laws, most famous of all, came from the eighteenth century B.C., but even it was largely a collection and refinement of Sumerian and ancient Semitic law from many centuries earlier.[1] All of the other nations of the Mediterranean world had their laws, some rather crude, to be sure, but all reflecting a great common tradition of jurisprudence. As Albrecht Alt and others pointed out, Mosaic law is quite similar to many of these, though there are notable exceptions.[2] For example, in Hebrew law there are two types, apodictic and casuistic. The former is best illustrated in the Ten Commandments, which are nearly unique in ancient law in that they contain the simple injunction or prohibition without reference to specific cases.[3] They set forth principles that are always binding and that must always be strictly observed simply because they are right. Casuistic law, as the term suggests, has to do with

1. D. Winton Thomas, ed., *Documents from Old Testament Times* (London: Thomas Nelson, 1958), 27–28.
2. Albrecht Alt, "The Origins of Israelite Law," *Essays on Old Testament History and Religion* (Garden City, N.Y.: Doubleday, 1968), 133–71.
3. The uniqueness of the Hebrew Decalogue in terms of its apodictic form has come under increasing attack. For a survey of contrary evidence see Harry W. Gilmer, *The If-You Form in Israelite Law* (Missoula, Mont.: Scholars, 1975), 14.

specific laws dealing with individual cases that might arise. This is not peculiarly Hebrew, for in Hammurabi's Code, to cite the best known example, there are nearly three hundred statutes dealing with many possible infractions of various kinds. The formula in the casuistic law is usually phrased, "If a man do thus and so . . . then the punishment shall be such and such." There are no specific principles as such, no statements of universal legal obligation.

Beyond the mere form of the laws, that of Moses is definitely superior in moral and spiritual tone and is leavened with a spirit of mercy noticeably absent from other codes. For example, Babylonian law stated that if a physician were performing an operation and the patient died, the physician's hand must be amputated.[4] No such harshness exists in Mosaic law at all, nor is there anything remotely similar. The closest would be the principle of lex talionis (literally, "law of retaliation") embodied in the figure of speech "an eye for an eye and a tooth for a tooth" (Exod. 21:24), and even this was closely and justly regulated by society. Many scholars argue that Hebrew law, like other laws, was based largely on other more ancient law codes.[5] This is true only in the sense that all law codes have a common basis in ordinary human ethics and in established norms of what constitutes right and wrong. No doubt Moses incorporated much such "natural" law into his code under divine inspiration, but the distinctive features such as the religious nature of the law and those having to do with Israel's peculiar relationship to Yahweh can be accounted for only as revelation from God. The theocracy was a unique institution, and the legal framework, both civil and religious, in which it operated was on that account also unique, even though elements within it resembled those found elsewhere. These will be discussed in greater detail when we consider the individual law codes.

Enlargement of the Covenant and Meaning of the Theocracy

The Old Testament clearly teaches that Israel had its origins in a family, that of Abraham, Isaac, and Jacob (Gen. 12:1–3). But it is equally clear that all through its patriarchal history it had no real national existence. It was merely a family or clan in Canaan before the movement to Egypt, and all through its Egyptian sojourn it was nothing more than a

---

4. G. R. Driver and John C. Miles, The Babylonian Laws, 2 vols. (Oxford: Clarendon, 1952–55), 2: 81, law #218.
5. So, for example, Alt, "The Origins of Israelite Law," 124–25. Alt suggests that Israelite law derived directly from Canaanite sources that in turn may go back to Egypt and Mesopotamia.

very loose association of people with a common racial and historical background, an association nonetheless recognizable because of the covenant
that had brought it into being in the first place. Then at Sinai a decisive
event took place: the formation of these people into a nation of tribes that
would be the custodian of the ancient faith of Abraham. This formation
was not a simple matter, for these seminomadic wanderers now had to be
welded together politically, socially, and religiously into a covenant people
who not only could agree among themselves to stay together and keep the
terms of the covenant but also must resist all efforts on the part of others
to destroy this solidarity. On top of all this, they had no land, only the
promise of one to come, and no central government or law. Moreover,
they had no formal statement of their faith or ritual in which to express it.
All this had to be created at Sinai for the metamorphosis of a people into
a nation to occur.

The first part of the legal element of the covenant at Sinai, which was
given to Moses in his first encounter with Yahweh on the mountaintop, is
called the Book of the Covenant (Exod. 20–23). It in turn consists of the
Decalogue ("Ten Words") or Ten Commandments (20:2–17), which in a
sense formed the constitution of the new nation, just as the exodus events
had proclaimed a declaration of independence, plus a series of religious,
civil, and moral statutes calculated to guide Israel in these areas of life.
The code here in Exodus was the earliest expression of the Mosaic
covenant, but not by any means its only expression. Also at Sinai regulations were promulgated concerning the place of worship, the priesthood,
and liturgy. These constitute almost all of the Book of Leviticus, the last
seventeen chapters of Exodus, and the first ten chapters of Numbers. In
addition, there are scattered places throughout the remainder of Numbers
where certain ideas were expanded or repeated in the course of the wilderness journey. Finally, the Book of Deuteronomy, as the name ("second
law") implies, consists largely of slight modifications of the Sinaitic law or
additions thereto given nearly forty years later in the plains of Moab just
prior to Moses' death and the conquest. This repetition of the law is sometimes known as the Deuteronomic covenant, a designation that may be
justified because of the ways in which this covenant differs from the one
delivered at Sinai.[6] Following Moses, however, there were no additional
laws as such, though there were confirmations of the covenant from time

---

6. The entire Book of Deuteronomy is a covenant renewal document, one made necessary by
virtue of the fact that the generation that had sworn to the Sinaitic covenant would not enter the
promised land and their descendants, who would enter, must make a fresh covenant commitment for
themselves. See Meredith G. Kline, *The Structure of Biblical Authority* (Grand Rapids: Eerdmans,
1972), 10–12.

to time all through Israel's history, usually at certain annual festal occasions or in times of spiritual revival (Josh. 24; 2 Kings 23:3; 2 Chron. 15:12; Neh. 9:38).

The name applied to these books of Moses, the Torah ("instruction"), is a singularly appropriate term, for it expresses the real essence of the Sinaitic and Deuteronomic revelation. The people had been called together, joined in a theocratic society, and given a divine commission as partners with God in an eternal covenant. The instruction of Torah, in its social, political, and religious aspects, was to be the means of assuring both understanding of and adherence to the terms of the covenant.

The Mosaic Law

In one respect Mosaic law was divided into three parts—civil, moral, and ceremonial or liturgical. Yet, because the theocratic community was essentially a religious society with no distinction between "church" and "state," such divisions are rather superficial. Every part of every law was religious as well as secular and impinged on every part of the nation. It was a matter of religion to plant one's crops according to the law, and it was a matter of state to offer the sacrifices in the prescribed manner. Yet, for practical purposes some arbitrary outline of the Mosaic legislation must be attempted so that its nature and purpose can be more fully understood.

Civil Law

Attention will first be given to the laws having to do with man and his relationship to his fellows. These are expressed first of all in the Ten Commandments, the last six (Exod. 20:12–17) embodying the basic principles of society: honoring parents, esteeming human life, regarding the sanctity of the neighbor's wife, his property rights, the value of his reputation, and not desiring anything belonging to him. The remainder of the laws interpret these basic commandments or indicate special applications of them.

Many laws have to do with one's parents and family (Exod. 21:17; Lev. 19:3; 20:9; Deut. 21:18–21). It was taken for granted that the father and mother were the heads of the families, and unquestioning obedience was expected from the children. Akin to these rules were laws regarding marriage and sexual relationships. Of special interest in the former case are the laws regulating the marriage of an Israelite to a woman taken as a war prisoner (Deut. 21:10–17) and permitting divorce in the case of adultery alone (Deut. 24:1–5). Certain marriages were considered illicit, such as those within families (Lev. 18; 20:10–21), and, of course, any acts of sexual perversion were severely condemned (Exod. 22:16–17, 19; Lev. 19:20–22; Num. 5:11–31; Deut. 22:22–30). In addition, there were special prohibitions against prostitution, which was an especially dangerous temptation because it formed such an important part of Canaanite religion (Lev. 19:29; Deut. 23:17–18).

Special reverence was shown for old age (Lev. 19:32) and special consideration to widows and orphans (Exod. 22:22–24; Deut. 24:17–18), the poor (Exod. 23:6; Lev. 19:9–10; 23:22; Deut. 24:19–22), and the handicapped (Lev. 19:14). For example, the farmer was not to reap the corners of his fields or rake up the scatterings, so that the poor might come into his fields and take the leftovers. Furthermore, because Israel had been a stranger in Egypt, Israelites were to have particular regard for the strangers among them (Exod. 22:21; 23:9; Lev. 19:33–34). In this connection also there were laws regulating slavery and voluntary servitude. In times of dire need, a Hebrew could sell himself to his neighbor for a certain price, and the money he thus obtained could be used to pay his debts. In turn he must serve his neighbor for a six-year period, but he was to be permitted his freedom in the seventh year. If he chose to remain with his master longer, he could indicate this choice by having his ear bored through with an awl in the presence of witnesses. In this way he expressed his voluntary indenture, a condition not altogether undesirable in many cases, for these servants had every need of life provided without the responsibility that accompanies independence (Exod. 21:1–11; Lev. 25:39–55; Deut. 15:12–18; 24:14–15). Involuntary slavery of aliens was permitted, though clearly not prescribed by God. In any case the slave must be treated with mercy, and the whole institution was subject to stringent regulations (Exod. 21:20–21; Deut. 23:15–16). If a slave's eye or tooth were knocked out by the master, for example, the slave was to be freed as compensation (Exod. 21:26). This naturally ameliorated the harshness of his bondage, for the loss of a slave would be a financial blow to his owner.

The Israelite's relationship to his peers was also covered by the law. Thieves were strictly dealt with (Exod. 22:1–5), as were arsonists (Exod. 22:6), tale-bearers (Exod. 23:1; Lev. 19:16), and rioters (Exod. 23:2). In the case of assault and battery, the principle of *lex talionis* required "an eye for an eye," that is, punishment proportionate to the crime (Exod. 21:18–36; Lev. 24:18–22; Deut. 25:11–12). Manslaughter or unpremeditated murder was punished but not capitally (Num. 35:6–28; Deut. 19:4–10). The slayer under the law must flee to a designated city of refuge, where he was to be protected from revenge until he had a fair trial. If proven innocent, he must remain in the city until the death of the high priest; if proven guilty of murder, he must be put to death. In cases of

known and proven murder, immediate vengeance was taken, and the murderer was punished by death at the hands of the elders or avengers (Exod.
21:12–15; Lev. 24:17; Num. 35:30–34; Deut. 19:11–13; 21:1–9).[7]

The business dealings of the Israelites were included within the compass of
the law. Such matters as lending money (Exod. 22:25–27), charging interest
on loans (Exod. 22:25; Lev. 25:35–37; Deut. 23:19–20), and using fair weights
and measures (Lev. 19:35–37; Deut. 25:13–15) were strictly regulated. They
were also to beware of taking gifts (bribes) because such gifts tended to blind
their eyes to right and wrong, whether in business or otherwise (Exod. 23:8).
If they had been entrusted with the care of their neighbor's goods, they were
to make recompense for any loss of those goods incurred (Exod. 22:7–15)
unless, of course, it was not the fault of the custodian.

Because the land and soil were so important to the nation's economy
and represented stewardship of properties belonging ultimately to Yahweh,
there had to be carefully defined regulations relative to their use. For
example, every seventh year the land was to lie fallow both to commemorate the creation of the universe in six days and to give the land a chance
to be replenished with nutrients (Exod. 23:10–13). In addition, every fiftieth year was to be a year of jubilee in which nothing was to be planted;
therefore, both the forty-ninth and fiftieth years would be years of rest
(Lev. 25:1–24). One interesting law in regard to the crops in the fields
states that one had the privilege of plucking grapes or grain from his
neighbor's fields if he were only passing through. He could not, however,
expect to do so with a sickle in his hand (Deut. 23:24–25).

Other stipulations have to do with the inheritance of property and the
redemption of persons and goods. To prevent the development of a poor
element in society if at all possible, a family's land or real property was to
be retained by the family forever. This land was to be properly marked by
boundary markers that were never to be removed by anyone (Deut.
19:14). In the event the property had to be sold for some reason, it must
in any event be returned to the original owner on the year of jubilee, with
the exception of property within city walls (Lev. 25:25–34). Any Hebrew
who had had to become indebted to another was automatically released of
his debt in the seventh year, the year of release (Deut. 15:1–11). In case of
either selling the family property or personal indebtedness, one may presume that there was the possibility of redemption; this was true of
Hebrews who had sold themselves into indentured service as well. If a

---

7. The avenger would be a member of the family of the deceased and would bear the responsibility
of taking the life of the murderer, though, of course, under the aegis of law and government. See
Roland de Vaux, *Ancient Israel*, 2 vols. (New York: McGraw-Hill, 1961), 1:11–12.

man had sold his property, it could be repurchased for him by his next of kin (Ruth 4:1–8), who would pay the value of the harvests remaining before the next jubilee, this price being computed in the same manner as the original price of the land (Lev. 25:13–17, 25–27). In other words, if land was sold forty years before jubilee, its price would be forty times the value of its annual harvest. If it were redeemed by its seller or his next of kin twenty years later, the redemption price would be twenty (forty minus twenty) times the value of its annual harvest, "because what he is really selling you is the number of crops" (Lev. 25:16 NIV). If no one was able to redeem it or no one cared to, the land would return to the original owner in the year of jubilee without cost to him, because the crops harvested since the sale compensated the purchaser for the price he paid. The same principle of redemption applied to the release of Hebrews who were servants of foreigners living in the land. But they did not go out in the year of release, though they could in the year of jubilee. If at any time in the course of servitude a next of kin desired to purchase the freedom of a servant, he paid a price commensurate with the number of years of servitude left until the year of jubilee and proportionate to the original sale price (Lev. 25:47–55). As a whole, every effort was made to maintain personal independence and to guarantee possession of family property from generation to generation. Special consideration was given to women, who were able to inherit their father's goods if they had no brother who could do so (Num. 27:1–11; 36:1–10; cf. Josh. 17:3–4).

If a man died and left no children, his widow must marry one of his brothers, and any children produced from such a marriage would be considered heirs of the deceased brother (Deut. 25:5–10; cf. Luke 20:27–40). This no doubt presupposes that the second brother did not already have a wife of his own and that not all of the children born of the second marriage would be considered the posterity of the deceased. Otherwise it seems that the law would be sanctioning bigamy on the one hand and a callous disregard for the desire of a man to have his own family on the other. The example of Judah and Tamar, already discussed (Gen. 38), is most helpful in demonstrating the application of this levirate law. Also, there are many allusions to the practice in New Testament literature. The case of Ruth and Boaz suggests that it was permissible for the widow (Ruth) to marry the next of kin outside the immediate family (Boaz) if there were no other males within the family proper.

Even kings and government must be guided by the law, for in the theocracy no one was exempt from its authority (Deut. 17:14–20). This meant that there must be justice in the courts (Deut. 16:18–20; 19:15–21; 24:16; 25:1–3) and that due respect must be had for authority of all kinds (Exod.

22:28; Deut. 17:8–13). One point of special interest in the administration of justice is that anyone hanged must be removed from the gallows before sunset of the execution day (Deut. 21:22–23). This provides the precedent for the removal of the body of Christ from the cross on the same day in which he was crucified (John 19:31). The sense of justice extended even into the realm of warfare, where there were clearly spelled out principles of behavior toward the enemy (Deut. 20; 23:9). There were further regulations regarding the treatment of friendly aliens (Deut. 23:3–8).

In every society there are undesirable elements, and ancient Israel was no exception. These individuals were subject to the law in a drastic manner, however, and persons such as witches (Exod. 22:18; Lev. 19:31; 20:27; Deut. 18:9–14), false prophets (Deut. 13:1–5; 18:20–22), and leaders in heresy (Deut. 13:6–18; 17:2–7) were dealt with harshly. Such matters as transvestism were especially singled out for condemnation (Deut. 22:5).

Finally, there were numerous miscellaneous laws, some partially covered elsewhere, that had to do with the treatment of one's fellow man (Lev. 19:11, 13, 15, 17–18; Deut. 22:1–4, 8; 24:6, 10–13) and even with the kind treatment of animals (Deut. 22:6–7; 25:4). There were few areas of life, indeed, that were not at least touched on by Mosaic civil law. Had they been followed faithfully, Israel would have had a well-managed society, but the ideals embraced were usually badly neglected, especially in Israel's later history.

Ceremonial Law

The remainder of Mosaic law has to do with the more religious or ceremonial aspects of life, including the ritual of the cultus, though this last will be discussed separately because it is so important and also detached from the everyday life of the common people. Chief among such laws are those dealing with the worship of God only and the rejection of idols and false gods (Exod. 20:2–11, 22–23; 22:20; 23:24, 32–33; 34:12–17; Lev. 20:1–6; 26:1; Deut. 4:14–24; 7:25–26; 11:16; 16:21–22). Also important was the stipulation that the proper place of worship was at the tabernacle or (later) the temple (Deut. 12:1–14), though there was also the permission to worship wherever God had "placed his name" (Exod. 20:24–26); presumably that meant that the tabernacle was the central shrine to which all Israel must come for special occasions, but that in Canaan there would be the possibility of worshiping God in other places for ordinary occasions.[8]

---

8. O. T. Allis, *The Five Books of Moses* (Philadelphia: Presbyterian and Reformed, 1943), 178–84. For the view that the central sanctuary was a late development, see H. H. Rowley, *The Growth of the Old Testament* (New York: Harper and Row, 1963), 28.

Besides the sabbath, which must be meticulously observed (Exod. 31:12–17; 34:21; 35:2–3; Lev. 19:30; 26:2), there were certain days of special religious importance. One day of every month was honored by a Feast of the New Moon, this probably being the first day (Num. 28:11–15). There were also three stated feasts of the year necessitating a convocation of at least all the adult males of the land to the tabernacle. These three were the Feast of Unleavened Bread (Exod. 12; 23:15; 34:18–20; Lev. 23:5–8; Num. 9:1–14; Deut. 16:1–8), the Feast of Harvest or Pentecost (Exod. 23:16; 34:22; Lev. 23:15–21; Deut. 16:9–12), which came fifty days later, and the Feast of Tabernacles or Booths, which fell on the fifteenth day of the seventh month (Exod. 23:16; 34:22; Lev. 23:34–44; Deut. 16:13–16). In conjunction with the Feast of Unleavened Bread was the Passover, which actually inaugurated it (Exod. 12); at the time of the Feast of Tabernacles was the Feast of Trumpets on the first day of the seventh month, the Day of Atonement on the tenth day, and the week-long Feast of Ingathering or Tabernacles itself from the fifteenth day through the twenty-first day. There were seven festal observances in all, then, grouped for the most part around the spring Feast of Unleavened Bread and the autumn Feast of Tabernacles. The only exception was the Feast of Weeks in the third month, or summertime.

The purpose of the spring feasts has already been discussed, and the Day of Atonement will be considered later. The Feast of Weeks celebrated the harvesting of the early crops, usually barley. The Feast of Trumpets announced the commencement of the autumnal festal season; the Feast of Tabernacles, the week during which the people dwelt in rude huts in the fields, reminded Israel of the deprivations of their forebears, who had lived in such dwellings in the wilderness; the Feast of Ingathering was to celebrate the final harvest of the year. The critics have tried from time to time, unsuccessfully, to attach pagan Canaanite ideas to the origin of these various feasts. But there is no evidence to prove, for example, that the Feast of Tabernacles was derived from a nature cult that met at that time of year to induce the forces of fertility to fructify the soil for the coming year. Neither can it be established that the feast was only a modified New Year's celebration taken over from the Canaanites and other Near Eastern peoples who usually began their year in the fall.[9] There is no reason to doubt that the feast originated in the manner and served the very purposes outlined in the Old Testament.

9. Geo Widengren, "Early Hebrew Myths and Their Interpretation," in *Myth, Ritual, and Kingship*, ed. S. H. Hooke (Oxford: Clarendon, 1958), 197–98.

The personal lives and habits of the people, though in a sense incorporated within civil law, also had perceptible religious overtones. There were principles of separation designed to remind Israel that it was a chosen people, a nation separate from all others. Even in such matters as plowing with two different kinds of animals or wearing garments of mixed fabric there were strict requirements (Lev. 10:9–11; 11; 19:19; 20:25; Num. 19:1–10; Deut. 14:3–21; 22:9–11). There were also regulations of a hygienic nature that dealt with the purification of women (Lev. 12), detection and cure of disease (Lev. 13–15; Num. 5:1–4; Deut. 24:8), and uncleanness in general (Num 19:11–22; Deut. 23:1–2, 10–14). Eating certain foods besides those considered unclean for sacrifice was subject to legal definition as well (Exod. 22:31; Deut. 12:15).

Many Israelites, particularly the priests and Levites, dedicated themselves to God as lifetime servants, and others, like the Nazirites, would enter into limited periods of service or devotion. For each case there must be definite procedural policies in the undertaking, maintenance, and cessation of such relationships. The priests, all of whom must be descendants of Aaron, were consecrated to their holy office by a very significant ceremony and in accordance with well-defined regulations already discussed (Exod. 29:1–37; Lev. 8). The one high priest and, eventually, it seems, several thousand regular priests in Canaan had to observe ceremonial washings (Exod. 30:17–21), careful instructions in the making of ritual ointments and incenses (Exod. 30:22–38; Lev. 24:1–9), and exacting standards within their family and social lives (Lev. 21:1–22:13; Num. 18:8–19; Deut. 18:3–5).

The Levites were a quasi-clergy whose main function was to assist the priests, maintain the place or places of worship, and look out for the general well-being of the nation's spiritual life. It will be remembered that God had demanded that the firstborn of each family in Israel was to be given to him as a token of gratitude for his having saved the nation from Egypt and from the death of the firstborn there. Later this was modified to permit the tribe of Levi to substitute for the firstborn of the remaining tribes, one Levite for one firstborn (Num. 3:5–36, 40–51; 4:1–33; 8:5–26; 18:20–32; Deut. 18:1–2, 6–8). If there were not enough Levites to match the number of firstborn, the remaining firstborn could be redeemed from service to God through payment of money.

One could become a Nazirite ("separated one") by making a vow to God that he would not shave his hair, touch a dead body, or drink any fruit of the vine or any intoxicating drink (Num. 6:1–21). There was no requirement that one make such a vow, but if one felt a special sense of gratitude or love to God, he or she could voluntarily assume the deprivation associated with being a Nazirite and for any length of time. If the individual violated the terms of the vow, however, he or she was required to begin the period of the vow all over again after he or she had made suitable offerings for cleansing. Samson and Samuel were two of the better-known Nazirites, but their cases are unique in that they were made such through dedication by their mothers.

There were other vows besides the vow of the Nazirite in which objects, lands, and persons could be dedicated to Yahweh for varying lengths of time. When these objects of the vow were released from their obligation, it was only at the price of a redemption payment that varied depending on the object, the age of the individuals, and certain other factors (Lev. 27; Num. 30; Deut. 23:21–23). The firstborn, the tithe on the crops and goods, and any other possessions that belonged to God automatically could not be devoted in a vow, for they were his without such a vow anyway. Again, all such vows were purely voluntary and were made only as expressions of love and gratitude to God. Once undertaken, however, they must be carried through; any failure to do so would constitute an act of sin (Deut. 23:21).

Finally, miscellaneous instructions concerned the use of the land and crops on the arrival of the people in Canaan (Lev. 19:23–25), the payment of a religious tax or "ransom" annually (Exod. 30:11–16), special reverence for the name and person of God (Lev. 19:12), the disfigurement of their bodies in imitation of the heathen, which was prohibited (Lev. 19:27–28; Deut. 14:1–2), and the eating of holy things (Lev. 22:15–16; Deut. 12:17–18, 20–28; 15:19–22). This last law had to do with eating materials offered in sacrifice either deliberately or inadvertently. The only place where such food could be eaten was the place of offering, usually the tabernacle. Later, when the Israelites settled in the land and the tabernacle was too far away to make this practicable, they could eat their portion of the offering at home, provided they did not eat the blood, which was sacred and belonged only to God.

Offerings and Sacrifices

A whole set of laws regulated the procedure of worship in Israel. God and Israel had entered into covenant; a place of worship, the tabernacle, had been built; a priesthood and Levitical order had been established to represent the people before God. Now there had to be a means whereby Israel could express its religious devotion to God in an orderly, ritualistic fashion. This was by offering to God something one owned, the surrender of which would constitute a real sacrifice. The need of man's heart has always been to express his devotion, thanksgiving, and love to God and to find a means whereby his sins might be forgiven so that he might have unbroken fellowship with him. All of this could be accomplished in the Old Testament via the offerings made from a heart full of faith. There was no salvation by the keeping of the law, and no merit in the mere offering of one's goods to God; but when both were done in dependence on God's grace and in a spirit of faith, the worshiper could know the reality of the presence of God in his life.

Gustave Oehler has outlined quite well the content and purpose of Mosaic sacrificial ritual; the following represents for the most part his study of the matter.[10] That offering was integral to Mosaic worship is easily seen in light of all the passages devoted to it (Exod. 22:29–30; 23:18–19; 29:38–42; 30:7–10; 34:25–26; Lev. 17; 19:5–8; 22:17–33; Num. 15:1–31; 28–29; Deut. 14:22–29; 17:1; 26:1–15). It is important now to consider briefly what could or could not be offered, how things were offered, and for what purposes.

To employ Oehler's terminology, there were bloody and bloodless offerings, the former, of course, animal sacrifices, and the latter vegetable or drink. Sometimes the vegetable offerings were made independently, but usually they accompanied the bloody offerings in one way or other. There were strict rules in the selection of materials, both bloody and bloodless, and actually few were qualified to be offered. Animals must be clean to be acceptable for sacrifice (Lev. 27:9, 11). This meant that of the large animals, only those that chewed the cud and had cloven hooves could be used (Lev. 11). Of water animals, only those with both fins and scales were acceptable. Some twenty-two different birds were considered unclean and so could not be offered or eaten (Lev. 11). Only the grasshopper, of the small "animals," was suitable, and none of the so-called crawling animals like the reptiles and amphibians was permitted. In addition, an animal, to be suitable for offering, must be domesticated.[11] It would hardly be a sacrifice in the true sense of the term for an individual to hunt down wild game, which was not his anyway, and present it to God. This meant that a deer, for example, though it had cloven hooves and chewed the cud, could not be an offering. Also, an animal offering must be at least eight days old (Lev. 22:27), for only after eight days would an animal's survival be assured. It would hardly be a sacrifice, again, if one offered a newborn animal that might die shortly anyway. Finally, an offering animal must not be past its prime of life (Lev. 9:3; 12:6; Num. 28:3). Usually this

10. Gustave Oehler, *Theology of the Old Testament* (Grand Rapids: Zondervan, 1883), 261–319. See also Werner H. Schmidt, *The Faith of the Old Testament* (Philadelphia: Westminster, 1983), 112–32.

11. Oehler, *Theology of the Old Testament*, 269.

amounted to about one year of age for a lamb and three for a bull. Besides representing the animal's greatest time of value to the owner, the prime of life would preclude one's sacrificing an animal so old that it would soon die a natural death.

The vegetable offerings could consist of roasted grain, flour, or unleavened cakes or loaves (Lev. 2). These were accompanied without fail by salt and usually also by oil and incense (Lev. 2:13, 15). It was prohibited to offer any kind of leaven or honey, for these materials spoke of corruption. The drink offering, which could be only wine, was also offered in conjunction with other offerings.

The ritual of sacrifice was generally consistent, in its main outlines, at least, no matter which kind of offering was being performed. The vegetable offerings were simple, consisting merely of a presentation of the material at the altar, where it was burned (Lev. 2). Drink offerings were simply poured out on and about the altar. The animal offerings were more complex, however, and took the following form.[12] First the animal was led to the altar by the offerer. Then the offerer laid his hands on the victim's head, transferring himself thereby to the animal in a symbolical way. Next the slaughter itself was accomplished, by the offerer in a private service and by the priest in a public ceremony. This was usually performed by slitting the victim's throat. When the blood had begun to flow, it was caught in a basin and then sprinkled on various places, depending on the kind of offering. Usually some was sprinkled on the altar or its horns, toward the veil, on various pieces of furniture in the tabernacle, or, on the Day of Atonement, on the mercy seat in the Holy of Holies. The reason for the use of blood was that it might serve as an atonement (covering), representatively covering the soul of the one making the offering. Because in the Hebrew mentality blood was essentially equivalent to life, it was the life of the animal that was covering the life of the offerer. The guiltless life substituted for the life of the sinful man who placed his faith in its efficacy for hiding his sin. The removal of sin is seen only in the chasing off of the scapegoat on the Day of Atonement, an event discussed subsequently. After the proper application of blood, the animal was burnt. The rising of the smoke suggested, perhaps, that the real essence of the victim was ascending to the presence of God, who smelled its savor and was satisfied in the act of sacrifice.

The various kinds of offerings should now be considered. The first of these was the simple burnt offering, made twice a day at the tabernacle on behalf of all the people (Lev. 1). It was a sacrifice of devotion to God and

12. Ibid., 274–83.

consisted of a male lamb without blemish. On special occasions such as sabbath, holy days, and feasts, the number would be increased to several lambs in both morning and evening. The second type of offering was the peace or thank offering, which signalled a peaceful relationship between God and the offerer (Lev. 3). It was not made to achieve a harmonious relationship between the two, but to denote that all was well. In times of particular gratitude or special need, one could offer a peace offering to God as an expression of love or as a supplicatory gesture. There was always a sacrificial meal with the peace offering, with a strong possibility that the Hebrew thought of himself feasting at a common table with God. This supports the idea of the covenant relationship, for even in extrabiblical covenant ceremonies the parties involved celebrated their oneness by feasting together. The fat, certain internal organs, and other choice parts of the sacrifice were burnt on the altar as God's portion. The breast and right shoulder were taken by the officiating priest, who waved them hori-zontally and "heaved" them vertically, in both motions indicating the pre-sentation of them to both God and himself. The offerer, his family, the Levites who were present, and any poor who wished then sat down and consumed the remainder of the sacrifice. The priests and God already had been served their portions, that of God consisting of the burning of the choice parts.

The trespass offering was made by one who had been guilty of the infraction of a specific and clearly defined statute, whether this was con-cerned only with his neighbor or with God (Lev. 5). Only a ram could be used; no matter how rich or poor the offender might be, each had to make the same offering. This suggested that in point of law all were equal and all must make equal restitution. The choice parts of the ram were burnt, and the priests consumed the rest. Naturally, one could not partake of the very offering that was atoning for his trespass, so the offerer received none.

The last of the offerings, the sin offering, was made for the establish-ment of a proper moral relationship with God (Lev. 4). Three grades of offerings were possible: one for the high priest on the Day of Atonement and for the consecration of priests, one for the nation on the Day of Atonement and at festivals, and one for the ordinary Israelite whenever he felt the need. In the first-class offering, only a young bullock could be sacrificed. In the second class, the victim was a kid goat. A goat or female lamb sufficed for the third class. The poor who could not afford a goat or lamb could offer a turtle dove or pigeon, and those still poorer could merely offer fine flour. If the offering was low grade, it was consumed by the priests; if first class, it was burned outside the camp, except for the fat, which was burned on the altar.

One of the most important occasions of the year in Israel, and certainly a greatly significant religious event, was the Day of Atonement, on which the entire nation was collectively atoned for (Lev. 16).[13] This ceremony, which formed a part of the autumnal convocation, followed a rather elaborate ritual, the essential features of which are as follows. Early in the morning of the tenth of the month Tishri, the high priest bathed himself completely and dressed in a garment all of white. He then slew a bullock at the great altar of burnt offerings. Next he carried into the Holy of Holies a censer filled with burning coals, the smoke of which spoke of the prayers of the people. He then returned to the outer court to get the blood of the bullock, which he carried into the Holy of Holies and sprinkled before the mercy seat. Following this, he returned once again to the outer court to slay the first of two goats that had been standing near the altar. The blood of this animal was carried into the Holy of Holies and sprinkled on the mercy seat, thus atoning for the nation as the blood of the bullock had atoned for the priest himself. After this, the blood of the two animals was mixed and sprinkled on the two altars and the interior of the tabernacle, signifying the consecration of these sacred precincts for another year. The same blood was applied to the head of the other goat, which, as the scapegoat, was sent off into the wilderness beyond the camp bearing on his head the collective sin of the nation. In this manner the sin was not only covered but also removed completely, at least for another year. Finally the high priest bathed himself completely once again and changed back into his regular vestments.

Mosaic law, then, with all its aspects and categories, still was nothing more than the framework in which Israel expressed the fact that it was a covenant people and that it desired to worship the God who had called it and made of it a nation. The regulations, the statutes, the ritual—all were purposeful expressions of the covenant faith; though meaningless in and of themselves, they were indispensable for that people at that time. They were not inventions of an ancient Semitic mind, but divine revelation from their God.

The Tabernacle[14]

Though the Hebrews early realized that God could not and did not dwell in only one place at a time, they nevertheless came to see that he had chosen certain places above others as places where he might be found in a special way by his worshiping people. At first these places had been

---

13. Ibid., 309–19.
14. For a history and description of the tabernacle, see de Vaux, *Ancient Israel*, 2:294–302.

altars and other simple shrines, later Sinai itself, and now that the covenant had been given, a portable tabernacle that could be carried on their journeys through the wilderness to Canaan. Once there, other arrangements would be made; by the time of Solomon, Yahweh's earthly dwelling place came to be a massive temple in Jerusalem. Eventually even that was done away with, and, as Jesus said to the Samaritan woman, no special place was the proper place of worship (John 4:21–24). All places then became his as men worshiped him in spirit and in truth. But before then, he resided in a building made with hands, the Sinaitic expression of it being a tent made according to exact specifications.

The materials necessary for the construction of the meeting place are listed first (Exod. 25–30); then follows a description of the various pieces of furniture to be housed therein, beginning with the ark of the covenant. This was merely a chest-like box measuring some forty-five by twenty-seven by twenty-seven inches and made of shittim (acacia) wood covered with a layer of gold. Its cover, known as the *kappōret* ("mercy seat"), consisted of a slab of gold on which rested two cherubim ("covering ones") who faced each other and whose wings touched over the ark. In the corners of the ark were rings through which gold-plated staves could be passed, enabling the Levites to carry it on their shoulders. The area directly above the ark and between the cherubim was the immediate place of God's dwelling, the holy spot where settled the shekinah ("presence") glory of God. Within the ark were the pot of manna and the tables of the Decalogue.

The table of showbread, also covered with gold, was thirty-six by eighteen by twenty-seven inches and contained rings in its corners so that it, too, could be carried on staves. The main purpose of the table was to hold the bread, twelve loaves of which were to be baked every day as a symbol of God's abundant provision for Israel's material needs. Certain vessels of gold useful in the worship were also set on the table. A golden candlestick (actually a seven-branched lampstand) held seven oil lamps, one directly in the center and three on either side in a branch-like formation. Joints in the branches were made in the shape of flowers, making the whole object ingeniously artistic. The candlestick served not only to give light but also to remind Israel that God was the source of the light of revelation.

The manufacture of the tabernacle itself is next described. It was to be forty-five by fifteen by fifteen feet and divided into two rooms, the holy place and the Holy of Holies. The former was to contain the table of showbread on the north side and the candlestick on the south side, while the latter housed the ark of the covenant. The dimensions of the Holy of Holies were fifteen by fifteen by fifteen feet, constituting a perfect cube, while the holy place was fifteen by fifteen by thirty feet. The sides and rear of the tabernacle were made of thick planks stood on end and bound together by horizontal bars connecting them. They were secured at the bottom by being driven firmly into sockets of some kind. The top of the structure was covered by layers of various kinds of cloth and animal skins that draped down over the sides and back nearly to the ground. These coverings were interwoven in some cases into beautiful designs, whereas the purpose of others was merely utilitarian—to keep the elements out. The two rooms in the tent (for so it basically was) were separated by a curtain or veil suspended on a row of pillars. This veil was woven from four kinds of cloth, blue, purple, scarlet, and white (fine twined linen), and contained embroidered images of cherubim. No one at all could go behind this veil except the high priest, and he only on the Day of Atonement. The other priests could serve in the holy place. The ordinary Israelite was absolutely forbidden entrance to any part of the tabernacle.

Other pieces of furniture were the altar of burnt offering, the altar of incense, and the laver. The altar of burnt offering was $7^1/2$ x $7^1/2$ x $4^1/2$ feet and was made of wood covered with a bronze grate to prevent it from being set afire. Conspicuous features of this altar were the horns, which extended from every corner, horns like those of a bull and signifying strength and security. Rings in the corners of the altar enabled it to be carried on staves. The altar was placed in front of the tabernacle and was the center of all animal and vegetable sacrifice. The smaller altar of incense was located just in front of the veil in the holy place. It was sheeted over with gold and symbolized prayer. As the smoke of the incense ascended above the veil, Israel would be reminded that God was accepting the prayer and would meet the people's needs. The laver was a basin placed directly in front of the altar of burnt offering. Its function was to contain the waters of purification with which the priests must wash their hands and feet before they could officiate at any of the tabernacle services.

Surrounding the tabernacle was the court, an open area 150 feet long by 75 feet wide. This was encircled by a fence of cloth hangings standing $7^1/2$ feet high. The court had one entrance, an opening covered by a curtain of the same kind of cloth as the veil within the tabernacle. Apparently the ordinary people were permitted in the court, but only in very small numbers because of its limited area.

No doubt the tabernacle and its furniture have great typical meaning, though interpreters sometimes read far more into it than can be justified by sound hermeneutics and biblical theology.[15] For example, the show-

---

15. For a careful and sensible discussion of the tabernacle as typology, see Geerhardus Vos, *Biblical Theology: Old and New Testaments* (Grand Rapids: Eerdmans, 1948), 164–72.

bread does speak of the fact that Jesus is the Bread of Life, and the candle-stick typifies that he is the Light of the world. The altar of burnt offering is a reminder of Calvary, where the Lamb of God died for the sins of the world, and the altar of incense is a type of prayer, even for the Christian. The veil, especially, is a type of the body of the Savior, and it is striking that when his body was impaled on the cross the veil of the temple at Jerusalem was torn in two, from top to bottom. The writer of Hebrews verifies this type when he declares that the veil indeed represented the body of the Lord (Heb. 10:20). To make every aspect typical of something in New Testament faith may be going too far, however, for the very nature of typology demands that it not be considered a type in the Old Testament if there is no evidence of a New Testament counterpart.

The Priesthood

Of the three great institutions of the theocracy, the prophets, the monarchy, and the priesthood, the priesthood arose first. This is under-standable, because before Israel had ever settled in Canaan and become a sedentary people requiring a king, its religion had already become well for-mulated. The prophets for the most part did not become numerous and prominent until the rise of the monarchy, for they seemed to serve often to keep the kings in line. Underlying the whole successive history of Israel was the religious or cultic substratum, an integral part of which was the order of priests.

Attention has already been focused on the ceremony whereby Aaron and his sons were anointed to the priesthood after the giving of the instruction regarding the tabernacle. From that day onward, only those of Aaronic descent could lay claim to the office of priest legally, and the whole institution became hedged about with a great deal of regulation and meaning. The anointing, the dress, the function of the priest all must be strictly according to the law. For example, the principal piece of clothing was an ephod (Exod. 28), an apron-like garment that hung down both in the front and the back and that was joined at the shoulders only by shoul-der pieces. On these shoulder pieces were two precious stones, one on each shoulder, on which were engraved the names of the twelve tribes, six to each stone. This no doubt signified that the priest bore on his shoulders before God the responsibility for his people. On the front of the ephod was a breastplate consisting of a square piece about nine by nine inches. To this were attached twelve precious stones arranged three to a row; they were engraved with the names of the tribes, one on each stone. This may have suggested that the priest bore over his heart the concern for his people. In addition to these twelve stones in the breastplate, there were also two more, the stones of judgment. These were called Urim ("light") and Thummim ("uprightness") and were probably used by the priest as a kind of sacred lots or dice in determining the will of God in any particular matter (1 Sam. 28:6; Ezra 2:63; Neh. 7:65). It seems that with the coming of seers and prophets the use of these stones diminished.

After listing various other pieces of clothing, Exodus 29 goes on to describe the consecration of a priest to his holy office. First, a bullock must be slain as a sin offering on behalf of the candidates, who placed their hands on its head as a symbol of the transference of their sin to the victim. Next, a ram must be sacrificed as an act of consecration. Again the hands of the priests were placed on the head of the animal, which was dedicated vicariously to God on their behalf. The blood of the ram was taken and applied consecutively to the right ear, right thumb, and right toe of the candidates to indicate that they were consecrating their ears to hear the word of God, their hands to perform the will of God, and their feet to walk in the paths of righteousness.

Originally, only Aaron and his four sons were priests; under wilderness conditions this was sufficient, for they had, in addition, the assistance of the Levites, who were, in a sense, lay ministers. Later, however, when Israel became more widely spread in Canaan and the exclusive use of one central sanctuary became impracticable, the number of the priests increased, eventually, perhaps, to hundreds. Only the major services were then conducted at the tabernacle or temple, the lesser observances being regulated by the priests at the local shrines. The command that only the tabernacle was to be the legitimate place of worship was obviously intended for the seminomadic life in Sinai and also for the three chief convocations of the year. Under later conditions, a multiplicity of altars was not only permitted but even authorized, though the precedence of a central place must always be understood.

Conquest and Conflict

The Historical Background of the Period

Next to Israel itself, which is the major focus of this chapter, the nation whose affairs are of only slightly less interest and importance is Canaan.[1] In the same breath we must say that this is not the account of just one nation, but many, for Canaan, especially at this time, was extremely fragmented and occupied by people with widely divergent backgrounds and interests. Most of these are listed in passages such as Joshua 9:1, which speaks of Hittites, Amorites, Canaanites, Perizzites, Hivites (Hurrians), and Jebusites, all living in the same land and in some cases quite intermingled. Yet, they did not form one single nation at any time, though under the threat of the Israelite invasion and other such emergencies they coalesced from time to time.

Following the Hyksos domination of Egypt, these Semitic warriors had retreated from Egypt into Canaan, especially the northern reaches, where at least some were assimilated into the native Canaanite populations. The rest apparently moved even farther north and were gradually lost to history. With the impetus given them by this Hyksos accretion, the Canaanites (to use the general term for all the native population from as

---

1. A. R. Millard, "The Canaanites," in *Peoples of Old Testament Times*, ed. D. J. Wiseman (Oxford: Clarendon, 1973), 29–52.

early as 3000 B.C.) became a greatly strengthened people who no doubt would have exercised larger influence than they did if Egypt had not so rapidly recouped after 1580 B.C. Especially under Ahmose I the Egyptians began to penetrate into the Fertile Crescent until they had annexed Palestine as early as 1560 B.C.[2] The Canaanites, therefore, became Egyptian vassals and remained so, at least theoretically, until the Hebrew monarchy 450 years later. Yet the hegemony of Egypt was exceedingly loose throughout much of this time; it is no surprise that the books of Joshua and Judges record little or nothing of Egypt.

The primary factors contributing to this state of affairs were the reigns of Amenhotep III and, especially, of his successor, Amenhotep IV. These two kings, who lived near the end of the illustrious Eighteenth Dynasty, witnessed the beginning of its demise, largely caused by their own inefficiency. The government of Canaan was in the hands of scores of petty kings who were answerable to Egypt but, it seems, received very little help from Egypt. This is seen especially in the Tell el Amarna letters, to which reference has already been made. When the 'apiru rose up and harassed the Canaanite city-states near the beginning of the fourteenth century, the various vassal kings under attack wrote to both Amenhotep III and Amenhotep IV requesting their aid, but, because other matters occupied their attention, these two kings paid little heed.[3] The former was apparently concerned with his relationships with the Mitanni, a recently friendly and powerful force at the headwaters of the Euphrates, while the latter was experimenting with a monotheistic philosophical concept he had helped to develop.

Another reason that Egypt figures so slightly in the biblical account of the period is that the Canaanite populace under its jurisdiction lived primarily in the plains of Palestine, whereas the Israelites occupied the hills. There was very little contact between Canaanites and Hebrews, except for the initial confrontation recorded in both the Book of Joshua and the Tell el Amarna letters, and that was unaffected by Egyptian interference. By the time the Israelites had encountered the Canaanites again on a large scale, in the time of Deborah, Egypt was safely out of the way because of the Hittite threat from the north. The one time Egypt did regain effective control over parts of Canaan was in the beginning of the reign of Rameses II (1304–1236), but during his long reign the Hittites

2. Margaret S. Drower, "Syria c. 1550–1400 B.C.," *The Cambridge Ancient History*, ed. I. E. S. Edwards et al. (Cambridge: Cambridge University Press, 1973), 2/1:431–32.

3. The most important of these communications can be found in J. B. Pritchard, ed., *Ancient Near Eastern Texts Relating to the Old Testament*, 3d ed. (Princeton, N.J.: Princeton University Press, 1969), 483–90.

drove the Egyptians south or at least contained them in Palestine, where the latter maintained only a shaky rule.

The Mitanni came to prominence in the early fifteenth century B.C., for some time exercising primary control over upper Mesopotamia. In fact, they were such a threat to Egypt that the two nations warred almost continually throughout the fifteenth century. About 1400 B.C., the Hittites began to push eastward and engaged the Mitanni in conflict; the latter were forced to turn to Egypt for help. Relations between the two peoples became so good that Amenhotep III even married a Mitannian princess, but the Hittite menace ended this period of peace. By 1370 the Hittites occupied Mitanni and became neighbors with Egypt in Syria.[4] Both countries were concerned with internal matters for a few years, during which Israel accomplished much of its conquest of Canaan, but finally hostilities broke out again between them. Rameses II, as already noted, tried to restore Egyptian suzerainty over the whole area, but the Hittites proved too much for him. Nevertheless, the Hittites could not occupy or even be concerned much with Canaan either because of their problems with the newly aroused Assyrians or because of the rise of other powers to the north and west. Thus, Palestine lay wide open for Hebrew conquest throughout the fourteenth and thirteenth centuries, a situation accounted for only by God's gracious ordering of the times.

The Hittite Empire collapsed ca. 1200 B.C., in the time of Gideon. The Assyrians, who gained the ascendancy,[5] had been increasing in influence from ca. 1300 B.C., and their overthrow of the Hittites encountered very little resistance from any source. The end of the Nineteenth and all of the Twentieth dynasties in Egypt were powerless to resist Assyria and, in fact, could not even interfere in Canaan. Yet, in its infancy Assyria was unable to press any farther south than northern Syria, so once again, as in the preceding century, Canaan remained aloof from the great powers all through the period from 1200–1100. But another force must be reckoned with, and that is one emphatically described in the Bible. At about 1200 B.C., the eastern Mediterranean coast, especially in the south, was settled by the Philistines, who had recently come from Asia Minor and Egypt but originally from the Aegean.[6] Philistines had been there from much earlier days (Exod. 13:17), but their numbers were now greatly augmented. They threatened Israel in the days of Samson, especially (ca. 1100 B.C.), and later, in Samuel's day, almost extinguished God's people (ca. 1080). Not

4. O. R. Gurney, *The Hittites* (Baltimore: Penguin, 1952), 29.
5. Ibid., 38-39.
6. Sabatino Moscati, *Ancient Semitic Civilizations* (New York: G. P. Putnam's Sons, 1957), 110–11.

until David's reign in Jerusalem was Israel able to overcome them and reduce them to tributaries.

The Babylonians all this time slumbered in their dark ages under the domination of various peoples from the north and east; only sporadically did they show any strength, and then not in a way that affected the settlement of Israel in the land of promise.

With this historical sketch, as limited as it must be, it is possible to see more readily that the stage of the Near Eastern world was set for the momentous event of Israelite conquest and settlement. The great powers, beset by conflicts between themselves and problems within, had little time to be concerned with the migration of a horde of desert peoples into so insignificant a place as was Canaan at the time. The many small city-states within its borders, disunited as they were and confined largely to the plains, could offer little concerted opposition to Joshua's invaders. Only the Philistines, and occasionally the surrounding little nations like the Ammonites, Moabites, and Midianites, whom God raised up for the purpose, could and did provide a means of chastening his people in their hours of unbelief. At no other time before or since could the Hebrew tribes accomplish the divine objective in Canaan.

The Conquest (Joshua 1:1–Judges 3:7)

Preparations (Joshua 1:1–5:15)

Moses died about 1406 B.C., and the conquest of the promised land of Canaan commenced immediately thereafter. Joshua, the newly appointed leader of Israel, must have reflected carefully on the weighty responsibility that was now his, and perhaps he viewed with great trepidation the prospects of what lay ahead. Moses, his mentor and example, was no more; that in itself was sufficient to make Joshua feel inadequate. Yet, the moment for which the nation had hoped for nearly forty years was here, the moment when it would finally occupy in reality the land that had been guaranteed to the forefathers hundreds of years earlier and the promise of which had only recently been reaffirmed to them. Joshua knew what he must do, but would he have the courage and resourcefulness to do it?

God spoke to Joshua in the midst of his dilemma, instructing him to set out for the inheritance, reassuring him that he was with him every step of the way, even as he had been with Moses. To guarantee the continuance of the divine presence, Joshua and Israel must saturate themselves in the law of Moses so recently given to the nation. They knew that God must work extraordinarily at this time, for the command to cross the Jordan and enter the plains of Jericho would otherwise be precluded by the flooding Jordan, this being the spring of the year, the time of barley harvest, when floods from the melting snows of the Lebanons came plunging down the Rift Valley, sweeping all before them (Josh. 3:15). Ordinarily the river at this place could be crossed only in late summer, but the immediacy of the command of God meant that the impossible must be accomplished now as it had been at the Red Sea exactly forty years earlier to the very month.

Apparently Joshua's strategy was well in mind for some time before the attempted crossing, for he sent out spies to Jericho, the city that guarded the pass from the Jordan Valley to the central highlands to the west. He recognized the absolute necessity of subduing this fortress first, both to allow his forces to proceed past it and to prevent any Canaanite threat from the rear after he had moved to the interior of the land. These two spies stealthily mapped out the strengths and weaknesses of the ancient city, but they nearly lost their lives, for their presence was soon detected. Only through the bravery of a certain harlot of the city, Rahab by name, were they able to escape and carry their intelligence back to Joshua at Shittim. This courageous act on her part elicited from the spies a promise that she would be spared the wrath of Israel when the city was sacked (Josh. 2:8–22). Far more rewarding than this, this infamous woman was brought into the covenant family, by God's grace becoming the ancestress of King David and of Messiah himself (Ruth 4:18–22; Matt. 1:5).

Once the spies' report was digested and tactical decisions had been formulated, Joshua commanded the people to form a line of march and make their preparations to cross the river. The priests, bearing the ark of the covenant, were to proceed first, and the nation would follow at a distance. The faith involved in such an action is difficult to imagine, but, perhaps with the memory of the exodus still in their minds, the people stepped forward in ready obedience. When the priests' feet barely touched the edge of the raging flood, it ceased its flow and stood "in a heap" several miles up the river at Zaretan in repetition of the exodus miracle. Some would suggest that an earthquake caused the high limestone cliffs of the Ghor to slide into the Jordan where it narrows at Zaretan, thus causing the waters to be dammed up. Other occurrences of this nature are cited from history.[7] This, of course, is a distinct possibility, but the occurrence of an earthquake at precisely the moment when it was needed is no less a miracle than any other way of stopping the river. Furthermore, the narrative points out, as though deliberately, the priests and people passed over the

7. Samuel Schultz, *The Old Testament Speaks*, 3d ed. (New York: Harper and Row, 1980), 94.

Jordan on dry ground, not through puddles or mud, as one ordinarily would expect so shortly after a natural event like an earthquake.

Once the crossing had been successfully completed, Joshua commanded that twelve stones be taken from the river bottom and piled in a heap on the western side as a memorial of the miraculous passing. Likewise, a heap of stones was placed in the middle of the river as a testimony of God's miraculous power on behalf of his people (Josh. 4:1–9). This crossing, like that of the exodus, was to be a reminder to all generations to come that Israel was a redeemed people, a people with a special redemptive mission. This done, the Israelites were circumcised, the rite having been neglected in the wilderness, and they celebrated the Passover. How fitting that the tokens of both the Abrahamic and Mosaic covenants should be enacted here and now, just as Israel reached its promised destination! And how singularly appropriate that these were followed almost immediately by the appearance of the Captain of the Lord's Host, who reminded Joshua that this new land was holy ground (Josh. 5:15)! The nation then encamped at Gilgal, a site that became its base of operations for several years.

The Central Campaign (Joshua 6:1–10:27)

There is no question that the city of Jericho was strongly fortified and, under ordinary circumstances, could easily withstand a siege of several years. The walls were high and thick, the access to the city was most difficult because of the steepness of the slopes of the ancient mound, and there was a plentiful supply of water within the enclosure. Special means must be undertaken, then, if Joshua was to take the city with a minimum of time and effort. For the second time in a few days, Joshua ordered the people to form a strange line of march. This time they were to prepare to walk around the mound of Jericho once each day for six days and seven times on the sabbath. He commanded the priests to blow their trumpets all this time, and he especially instructed the people to shout with a loud cry once the thirteenth circuit had been made. Following this, they were to annihilate the population of the city, retaining nothing of the material goods, for both population and spoil were accursed. This means that everything and everyone in the city was under God's special wrath because of the people's idolatrous propensities that would occasion Israel's downfall if they were permitted to remain alive. In technical language, Jericho was under the ḥērem ("ban") of God and must be devoted to him in extermination. Israel was waging "holy war."[8]

---

8. See G. Johannes Botterweck and Helmer Ringgren, eds., *Theological Dictionary of the Old Testament,* 10 vols. (Grand Rapids: Eerdmans, 1986), 5:180–99, s.v. *haram,* by N. Lohfink.

The results Joshua anticipated came to pass, for at the shout of the people, the walls fell down "under it," that is, down the slopes of the mound (Josh. 6:20). There is no point in explaining this miracle as another perfectly timed earthquake, or a result of the shock produced by thousands of people marching in precise cadence, or a wall-shattering note from the trumpets of the priests.[9] These are hardly possible from a scientific standpoint unless, as in the case of the crossing of the river, one wants to understand any one of these as the means God used at the necessary moment to carry out his purposes. In this case, the miracle is not diminished one iota. Though the remains of the wall from this period are disputed at present, John Garstang, at least, felt that he had located them, offering fairly convincing proof that these walls, dating from the end of the fifteenth century B.C., did indeed fall outward.[10] This is remarkable in light of the fact that in ordinary warfare one would expect the walls to fall inward beneath the blows of the battering rams and other instruments of war extant in that period. Only one part of the wall was spared, that on which rested the house of Rahab, unless Rahab and her family had been brought out of the city before the walls collapsed, a possibility allowed by the text. Finally, the entire city was burned and everything destroyed according to the commandment of the Lord (6:24).

Tragically, one man presumed to disobey the clear will of God, violating the ḥērem. Achan ben Carmi, in the midst of the tremendous conflagration, saw certain items of value in Jericho that he could not resist. Greedily he took them to his tent, buried them beneath its floor, and kept the whole matter a secret. When Israel attempted to take the city of Ai, however, their sound defeat revealed that someone had incurred divine displeasure. This small city, possibly a military garrison attached to the city of Bethel,[11] was able to repel three thousand Israelite troops and kill about thirty-six. In the wake of the overwhelming victory over Jericho so recently, this reversal was particularly bitter. Joshua fell on his face before God in supplication, asking the reason for the defeat by such inferior forces. God revealed to Joshua the means whereby the guilty party might be exposed. Achan, realizing that all was lost, confessed before Joshua that he had broken the terms of the ḥērem and taken what was rightfully devoted to God alone. Achan and his family, who no doubt were aware of

9. John Garstang, *The Story of Jericho* (London: Hodder and Stoughton, 1940), 137–38.
10. Ibid., 136.
11. Thus L. H. Vincent, cited in Joseph A. Calloway, "Ai (Et-Tell): Problem Site for Biblical Archaeologists," *Archaeology and Biblical Interpretation: Essays in Memory of D. Glenn Rose*, ed. Leo G. Perdue et al. (Atlanta: John Knox, 1987), 89.

what he had done and had collaborated by maintaining silence, were all killed (7:22–26).

Once the matter was cleared up, a second siege against Ai proved successful, thanks largely to a clever system of ambuscades. The city was reduced to a ruin, and the king was hanged. Apparently the elimination of Ai paved the way for an effortless conquest of the central hill country of Canaan, for the story next relates that Israel assembled together at the ancient and sacred site of Shechem.[12] There, between Mount Ebal and Mount Gerizim, Joshua built an altar at the place where Abraham had built one many centuries earlier (Gen. 12:6–7). In obedience to the final instructions of Moses, the nation listened to the law and the blessings and curses associated with their destiny as the chosen people (8:32–35). That Israel met no opposition in the central hills is not to be explained by the fact that there were already tribes related to them who had lived there for many generations and who now gladly welcomed their invasion. Rather, it seems that there were very few people living in this area at all, a point established by the archaeological evidence.[13] The Canaanites, it must be remembered, concentrated along the coastal areas and the plains; in the central hills, especially, one would expect Israel to have very little contact with them.

This was not so for the hills south of Ai, however, for concentrations of peoples known in the Old Testament as Amorites dwelt there. These peoples, when they heard of the success of Israel, banded together to resist the encroachments of these intrusive nomads (9:1–2). One enclave, however, at Gibeon, decided that the odds were on Israel's side and that the only wise course was to join the enemy (9:3–15). This could not be done easily, they realized, because Israel's stated policy was to not make alliances with enemies. With ingenious subtlety, they sent ambassadors to Gilgal, Israel's first permanent settlement in Canaan. The envoys, wearing worn-out clothing and shoes and bearing moldy bread, feigned to be from a distant land and, therefore, not subject to the law against alliance. Joshua and the elders gullibly accepted the story and swore to maintain peace with the strangers. When the plot was divulged three days later, Joshua was helpless to punish the Gibeonites, for the pact was inviolable, but he immediately placed them in bondage. Regrettably, even though in ignorance, Israel

---

12. For the biblical importance of Shechem, see Bernhard W. Anderson, "The Place of Shechem in the Bible," in *The Biblical Archaeologist Reader*, vol. 2, ed. David Noel Freedman and Edward F. Campbell, Jr. (Garden City, N.Y.: Doubleday, Anchor Books, 1964), 265–75.

13. Kathleen M. Kenyon, "Palestine in the Time of the Eighteenth Dynasty," *The Cambridge Ancient History* (Cambridge: Cambridge University Press, 1973), vol. 2/1:555–56.

had made a union with some of the people of the land, a union that would plague them in days to come (2 Sam. 21:1–9).

The Southern Campaign (Joshua 10:28–43)

When the Amorites learned of the new alliance between Israel and Gibeon, five of their kings led their city-states, Jerusalem, Hebron, Jarmuth, Lachish, and Eglon, against Gibeon as a retaliatory move (10:1–5). Under the terms of the treaty, Israel was obligated to come to Gibeon's aid, which they did after a forced march overnight from Gilgal to the Valley of Aijalon, just west of Gibeon. The Amorites were no match for the hosts of the Lord, and they fled to the west down the valley. By way of direct supernatural assistance, the Lord cast down huge hail-stones from heaven on the fleeing hordes. Moreover, in answer to the prayer of Joshua, he permitted the day to lengthen in order that the grisly task might be completed by the light of day. The best explanation for the miracle seems to be that God simply arrested the universe in toto, thus permitting the heavenly bodies to maintain their proper interrelation-ships. There are traditions from other parts of the world that speak of a long day or long night (as the case would be on the opposite side of the globe from Canaan), but there is no evidence that the world has ever "gained" or "lost" a day or any part thereof.[14] Yet, to state that the story merely reflects Joshua's overactive imagination or a peculiar refracting of the sun's rays that produced the illusion of a longer day[15] is incongruous with the clear statement of the text that "the sun stopped in the middle of the sky and delayed going down about a full day" (Josh. 10:13).

The Amorite kings, thoroughly routed, fled to Makkedah in the Judaean Shephelah, where they hid themselves in one of the numerous caves in the region. When Joshua learned of their whereabouts, he left Gilgal once more, went to Makkedah, and found the cave of refuge. He summarily dragged forth its pitiful inhabitants and just as summarily hanged and buried them in their erstwhile hiding place. Israel then struck deep into the Negev and, in a series of brilliant campaigns in which they apparently met only token resistance, conquered all the towns of any importance. That this onslaught did not result in the final control of the populace but only in its temporary subjugation is clear from the fact that a

14. Theodor H. Gaster, *Myth, Legend, and Custom in the Old Testament*, 2 vols. (New York: Harper and Row, 1969), 2:414–15.

15. Bernard Ramm, *The Christian View of Science and Scripture* (Grand Rapids: Eerdmans, 1954), 156ff.

short time later these same towns continued to resist Israelite conquest and settlement (Judg. 1:1–21).

The Northern Campaign (Joshua 11:1–23)

With the northern and southern parts of the land cut asunder by Israelite control of the central hills and valleys, and with the further devastation of the south, there is little wonder that the northern Canaanite populations were becoming fearful for their wellbeing. With determined organization, they welded themselves into a vast federation consisting of city-states stretching from the valley of Jezreel in the south to the headwaters of the Jordan in the north and from the Mediterranean on the west to the slopes of Hermon on the east. Their leader, Jabin of Hazor, gathered them at the waters of Merom, just to the east of his great city. There, with all their chariots and other advanced weapons of war, they awaited the Israelite invasion. Having been assured of victory by God's promise, Joshua marched north, met the Canaanites on their own ground, and administered a crushing defeat. Hazor itself, a city of perhaps forty thousand people, was burned to the ground, while the remaining cities of the coalition were left "standing on their tells" (Josh. 11:13), a fact, incidentally, that has been thoroughly substantiated by archaeology.[16] All of Canaan now had felt the strength of Israelite conquest, and except for pockets here and there, especially in the plains and along the southern coast, everything theoretically was in Israelite hands. Just how theoretical this was is revealed in the subsequent chapters of Joshua and all through Judges, where the unmistakable impression is that any land seizure was only temporary at best and had to be repeated many, many times. Not until David, or perhaps Saul before him, did Israel come near occupying its promised territory. Almost without exception the tribes were unable to retain the areas that had without doubt fallen to Israel, at least during this initial conquest recorded in Joshua 1–11.

Subsequent Attempts to Settle (Joshua 12:1–22:34)

After a summary of the conquests (Josh. 12), the biblical account describes the attempts by the various tribes to occupy the lands to which, either by casting of the sacred lots or some other means, they had been assigned. An indisputable evidence of the failure of the original conquests is found in Joshua 13, where a complete catalogue of unconquered lands is given. When he had outlined to the people what their task was, Joshua

---

16. J. Alberto Soggin, *A History of Ancient Israel* (Philadelphia: Westminster, 1985), 162–64. Soggin, however, dates the destruction of Hazor at the end of the thirteenth century.

proceeded to instruct the eastern tribes, Reuben, Gad, and Manasseh, about their inheritance in Transjordan. To Reuben he gave the land synonymous with Moab, just to the east of the Dead Sea. North of the Arnon River, the original land of Gilead, Gad was established. Its territory was to be bounded on the west by the Jordan, the east by Ammon and the Jabbok River, and the north by a line stretching from the southeast corner of the Sea of Chinneroth (Galilee). The area to the north of this and east of Chinneroth, formerly known as the land of Bashan, was assigned to half the tribe of Manasseh. The other half had elected to settle on the west of Jordan with the remaining tribes.

In Canaan proper, the first matter in the disposition of the land concerned Caleb, who, because of his lifelong faithfulness to the Lord, had been promised an individual inheritance by Moses (Deut. 1:36). Joshua honored the agreement by assigning the area around and including Kirjath-arba (Hebron) to the old hero, who promptly, despite the weight of eighty-five years, drove out the Amorites who had resettled the area following the original conquest. He next allotted Judah the region south of a line extending west from the northern tip of the Dead Sea, bounded on the west by the Mediterranean, on the south by a line from the southern end of the Dead Sea to the River of Egypt (Wadi el-Arish), and on the east by the Dead Sea (Josh. 15). Included in Judah were the lands of Caleb and the Simeonites (19:1–9), the latter apparently having been so decimated by their slaughter in the Plains of Shittim (Num. 25:14) that they were unable to claim an independent allotment.

To the north of Judah was the tribe of Ephraim, whose borders were as follows: on the east, the Jordan; on the west, the Mediterranean; on the south, Judah; and on the north, the Qanah Valley and eastward. In other words, the southern part of the central hill country was the major part of Ephraim's holdings (Josh. 16). Just to the north was Manasseh. It bounded Ephraim on the south, the Mediterranean on the west, the Jordan on the east, and, apparently, the Valley of Jezreel on the north. At least it is clear that the inhabitants of this great plain could not be displaced by Manasseh and that Manasseh, therefore, was also restricted to the central hills, and even there had only limited control of the land (Josh. 17).

The allotment of Benjamin is described next. It, strangely enough, seemed to be carved out between the territories of Judah and Ephraim (18:11–28). At any rate, it extended from Jericho on the east to the Sorek Valley just west of Kirjath-jearim and north and south into parts of Ephraim and Judah. The principal point is that the city of Jerusalem now became Benjamite, for the new boundary of Judah looped to the south of the city along the Hinnom and Kidron valleys. Jerusalem was not inhabited by Benjamites, however, or indeed by any Israelites until the time of David, who made it his capital.

North of the Valley of Jezreel there were four more tribes. Zebulun was north of Mount Carmel, east of the Mediterranean, and south of the upper Galilean hills. It reached to the east almost to the Sea of Chinneroth (19:10–16). To the south of it and north of Manasseh was the tribe of Issachar. It extended to the Jordan on the east, to the foothills of Carmel on the west, and to the beginning of the lower Galilean hills on the northeast (19:17–23). Asher settled right on the Mediterranean, north of Zebulun and west of Naphtali. Its northern boundary was the Canaanite region known later as Phoenicia (19:24–31). Finally, just to the east of Asher and north of Zebulun and Issachar, was the tribe of Naphtali, whose eastern border was the Sea of Chinneroth and the Jordan. It reached in the north all the way to Dan (19:32–39).

The tribe of Dan was assigned a parcel of land cut from that of Ephraim. This unfortunate clan settled west of Ephraim and along the Mediterranean coast, where the native Philistines proved too much for them and restricted them to a tiny area in the hills (19:40–48). In a desperate search for extra land, the Danites moved from their assigned portion and migrated north of Naphtali to Laish, a sequestered territory of peace-loving peoples. They slaughtered the inhabitants, moved into their homes and fields, and renamed the place after their father, Dan. This event is described in more detail in Judges 17–18.

Joshua also received a portion, for he, like Caleb, had been promised a reward for his faithfulness. He requested and obtained a parcel of land in Ephraim, and there he built his city, Timnath-serah (19:49–51).

The Levites had been told by Moses that they would not inherit land, but that their inheritance was spiritual (Num. 18:20; cf. Num. 3:5–51; 18:1–32). Nonetheless, they lived in the flesh and needed a physical dwelling place, so the assignment of cities of the Levites was made (Num. 35:1–8; Josh. 21). These were forty-eight in number and were evenly distributed throughout the land on both sides of the river. It seems that others besides Levites could and did dwell in these cities, but Levites must dwell in none other than these. Evidently certain religious ceremonies and services that did not have to be performed at the tabernacle itself were carried out by the Levites in their various cities. The life of the Levite was not to be secular in any sense; he could not work with his hands in gainful employment. The only exception was that he might keep a few animals and raise a minimum of crops in the fields immediately surrounding the town, but only for his own use. Of these forty-eight Levitical cities, six were cities of refuge, three on the east of the Jordan (Bezer in

Reuben, Ramothgilead in Gad, and Golan in Manasseh) and three on the west (Kedesh in Naphtali, Shechem in Ephraim, and Hebron in Judah). The purpose of these cities has already been discussed.

Lest the settlement of the tribes seem too simple, it is important once more to emphasize that it was complex. More often than not, the boundaries and allocations just described were extremely idealistic; they were seldom realized by any of the tribes. Judah was plagued by pockets of resistance within its borders and never was able to push to the coastal plain or into the Negev to the south (Judg. 1). Ephraim, though in the comparative safety and emptiness of the central hills, was nevertheless beset by the Canaanites, especially in the area around Gezer (Josh. 16:10). Manasseh was so hard-pressed by the Canaanites because of its nearness to the Jezreel Plain that, although it brought many of them under tribute, it was completely unable to drive them from the land. The Canaanites' use of iron, particularly in chariots, gave them a great advantage over the Israelites. The Book of Judges gives ample testimony that the four tribes north of Jezreel were harassed throughout their early history by the Phoenician Canaanites and other peoples (Judg. 4–5). The undesirable location of Dan, which prompted its evacuation, has already been mentioned. The situation was discouraging on the whole, and as long as Israel maintained its loosely federated tribal society nothing better could be expected. Not until the monarchy three hundred years after the conquest was a measure of unity and stability brought to Israel in its Canaanite environment.

This tendency for Israel to become disparate after its settlement in the various parts of the land is understandable in light of the extremely fractured nature of its geography. There came to be actually four different communities of tribes, each with its own geographical, cultural, and linguistic peculiarities (Judg. 12:5–6), though, to be sure, these differences came about only gradually. First, the tribes east of the Jordan, because of both their isolation by the river and their tendencies to absorb the culture of the people surrounding them, became vastly different in their outlook from the majority of the tribes, those to the west. These tribes feared such a result even very early, for before the men of the eastern tribes were allowed to go home after the Canaanite conquest, they were solemnly warned to remain true to the Mosaic faith (Josh. 22:1–6). When they built an altar by the Jordan near Jericho, the western tribes questioned their motives, and it was only with difficulty that they could persuade Joshua's messengers that the altar served purely a commemorative function.

The four tribes north of the Jezreel Valley, known later as the Galilee region, also became quickly independent of the mainstream of Israel.

Though, as far as can be determined, they must have observed the annual feasts at the tabernacle, they nevertheless seemed so preoccupied with internal affairs and with defense from their ever-present Canaanite neighbors that they had little time for close contact with the south. The Valley of Jezreel, which lay between them and the tribes to the south, provided more of a barrier between them than a means of access.

Though Judah and the tribes of the central hills were much closer in their relationships with each other than with either of the other tribal groups, there was still a certain geographical separation between them, and from time to time they were kept apart by Canaanites and Philistines who moved into villages along their common border. There was always some rivalry between Judah and her northern neighbors, a rivalry that became full blown in the time of Saul and David and again following the death of Solomon. All of these factors tended to produce certain differences within Israel, though, to be sure, the similarities more than outweighed them. Most basic to Israel's continued sense of unity was the cult itself, for the people's recognition of a common God, a common law, and a common center of worship more than compensated for their lack of physical and geographical cohesion, though even that commonality of spirit seemed to be endangered more than once.

In the process of allocating to the tribes their inheritance, Joshua selected a place where the tabernacle and ark were to rest permanently. This had to be a place that was central and, if possible, at or near a spot already sacred to Israel's memory. Such a place was Shiloh (Josh. 18:1), which, though apparently never occupied before, was close to the famous cities of Bethel and Shechem and was also in the central and relatively secure tribal area of Ephraim. After having rested at Gilgal and possibly Shechem since the crossing of the Jordan, the ark finally found a home where it was to dwell for nearly three hundred years. To Shiloh all the tribes, both east and west of the Jordan, resorted for the annual pilgrimages and other special occasions; Shiloh they recognized as the earthly dwelling place of their God. More than any other factor this served to maintain their unity until a king should come and transform their entire national composition.

After the initial conquest had been completed, perhaps within seven or eight years after the crossing of Jordan, Joshua sent the two and one-half eastern tribes (Reuben, Gad, and Manasseh) back to their wives and children in Transjordan. He reminded them of their covenant with God and of their need to assemble at the stated times at the central sanctuary at Shiloh. They swore their allegiance, but they had no sooner done so and started for their homes than they decided to erect a memorial altar by the brink of the Jordan. This alarmed the western tribal leaders, for it seemed to be a breach of the law that stipulated only one place of worship (Deut. 12:5; Josh. 22:19). A delegation was sent from Shiloh to investigate, and only after much protestation were the eastern tribes able to convince their brethren that they were up to no mischief. They built their monument and named it ʿēd ("witness").

Covenant Renewal at Shechem (Joshua 23:1–24:33)

The closing years of Joshua's life witnessed the futile attempts of Israel to occupy its tribal allotments. By about the year 1360 B.C., sensing that the end was near, the indefatigable man of conquest gathered his nation about him and addressed them in sacred convocation (Josh. 23). He first encouraged them to continue in the will of God, but his encouragement was interspersed throughout with warnings of the judgment of God should they defect from that course. He next reminded them, as they stood in the sacred precincts of the ancient altar of Shechem, of their entire redemptive history from the call of Abram to the present moment. He went on to declare that Israel's responsibility as a result of God's past dealings was to commit itself once again to the covenant relationship and to choose God afresh over against the alternatives of false gods. To lead the way, Joshua declared his loyalty to God and vowed that he and his entire household would serve Yahweh regardless of the consequences. The people unanimously assented to the covenant terms. The words were written down and the event was commemorated by the setting up of a great stone at Shechem, a monument of witness that would thenceforth speak of their covenant renewal.

On his death, Joshua's body was entombed at Timnath-serah. In fulfillment of Joseph's desires, his bones, which had been carried up from Egypt, were also buried, after these many years, at his family home at Shechem. Finally, Eleazar, son of Aaron, passed away, and his remains were placed in Mount Ephraim. The record of these deaths and burials seems to speak of the passing of an age. The formation and settlement of the nation had become a fait accompli, at least in general terms, and a new generation must rise to perpetuate the glorious heritage of Israel.

Problems after Joshua (Judges 1:1–3:6)

Admittedly, there is a historical complexity at the beginning of the Book of Judges, for there are accounts of the conquest that duplicate those given in Joshua, and there are others of events that definitely follow that period. However, once it is understood that the first two chapters of

Judges are not in chronological order, most of the difficulties disappear. A possible reconstruction is as follows: Judges 1:1–7 discusses the events of Judah's conquest after the death of Joshua. Then, verse 8 relates Judah's taking of Jerusalem, presumably before the death of Joshua. This means that 1:9–2:7 speaks of times that follow the destruction of Jerusalem under Judah but precede the death of Joshua. His death is described in 2:8–9, as it had been in Joshua 24:29–30, and the passing of the elders contemporary with Joshua is also mentioned, as it had been before. Then, after all this, there is a recitation of the succeeding generations of Israel's history in a capsule form. Judges 2:11–23 presents in almost a cyclic manner a preview of the period under the judges, that entire era from Joshua to Saul. The people went after other gods, they were chastened by God through the instrumentality of foreign invaders, they repented, God raised up a deliverer (the judge), they enjoyed prosperity and freedom, they again went after other gods. Thus the period went on almost monotonously; as a whole it can be written off as an era of failure for God's people.

In the lifetime of Joshua, Israel had been unable to drive out its enemies and occupy the land. This was in spite of the presence of God and his stern rebuke through the mouth of the Angel of Yahweh, a rebuke that produced only momentary repentance. In clear language the Lord spoke, angrily denouncing Israel for its sin of breaking the covenant. The record states that "the Lord had allowed those nations to remain; he did not drive them out at once by giving them into the hands of Joshua" (Judg. 2:23). The list of these nations is found in Judges 3 and is followed by the account of the first of the enemies of Israel who invaded and subjugated them.

Canaanite Religion[17]

The first sin of Israel following Joshua was intermarriage with the native populace, a relationship strongly condemned in the law. This was associated with the worship of Baal and Asherim ("sacred trees" or "poles" or "groves"), a worship that was carried on in a framework of sexual immorality of the basest sort.[18] Fertility cults were a common feature in the ancient Near East, but they reached their culmination in Canaan. They were formulated on the idea that the gods themselves were originally created by an act of reproduction on the part of the pristine forces of

17. Helmer Ringgren, *Religions of the Ancient Near East* (Philadelphia: Westminster, 1973), 124–76.
18. For a discussion of the underlying ideas, see Mircea Eliade, *The Sacred and the Profane* (New York: Harper and Row, 1961), 125–28. On the Asherah, see Raphael Patai, "The Goddess Asherah," *Journal of Near Eastern Studies* 24 (1965): 37–52.

the universe and that everything living finds its origin in the same way. Its adherents believed that plants, animals, and men came about by the intercourse of the gods and that, to guarantee the continuance of life, the gods must be entreated by ritual and sacrifice. Perhaps to encourage the gods to procreate and produce plant and animal life, the priests and priestesses of the cult would practice "imitative magic." That is, they would engage in ritual prostitution in an effort to cause the gods to emulate their example. If the gods could be so induced, there was every prospect for a successful agricultural year. Crop failures and other agricultural calamities were attributed to divine disfavor. The Canaanite ritualistic orgies were carried out either in a temple or in the shelter of green trees or groves that spoke of fertility. The goddess associated with reproduction was commonly known, therefore, as Asherah ("grove") or, plural, Asherim.

It will be helpful also at this point to discuss briefly the Canaanite pantheon in general.[19] Over all there was a shadowy, nebulous figure known as El. He seems to have been most prominent in early Canaanite theology but to have been displaced gradually by his chief rival, Baal, though he did continue to exist as Father God. His wife was Asherah, the aforementioned goddess of fertility, who was also, strangely enough, thought to be the virgin goddess. Baal was actually the god who was most directly involved with mankind. The name means simply lord, and it is most likely that it was originally only a title. Later on it came to be a proper name, but even then it seemed to represent many deities or manifestations of the same god. For example, there was a Baal at Peor in Moab (Num. 25:3). There were also a Baal-berith (Judg. 9:4) and a Baal-perazim (2 Sam. 5:20) and a Baal-zebub (2 Kings 1:3), plus many others. Yet there was a personal Baal of whom these were local representations or later expressions. According to some scholars, this god died and was resurrected, achieving victory over the god of death, Mot.[20] The commemoration of this event was celebrated every fall at the new year's beginning, which coincided also with the former rains. It was thought that the resurrection of Baal heralded the end of the dry, hot, unproductive summer, during which Mot was in control, and the beginning of the life-giving season of planting and growth signalled by the first rainfall of the year. If rain did not come, it was assumed that Baal could not escape from the underworld and that Mot had the upper hand. Perhaps, in the drought of Ahab's time, Elijah makes reference to all this when he taunts the

19. Ulf Oldenburg, *The Conflict Between El and Ba'al in Canaanite Religion* (Leiden: Brill, 1969), 15–100.

20. Ringgren, *Religions of the Ancient Near East*, 146–50.

prophets of Baal about Baal's absence at Mount Carmel, an absence they would feel had caused the drought. When rain did come after Elijah's prayer, all the people could see that Yahweh and not Baal provided rain and all good things (1 Kings 18). The sexual union of Baal and his sister-consort, Anath or Astarte, was held responsible for the rain and the consequent fertility of the soil. Therefore, the New Year's festival was a special time of immorality, for the priests and priestesses, and perhaps the laity as well, were involved in their gross rituals of invocation.

This was the situation, then, when Israel went after other gods and "committed whoredom." This adultery was not solely spiritual but also physical, and it brought Israel into the most heinous of sins. This religious background explains the monstrous enormity of Israel's transgression in going after other gods and forsaking Yahweh.

The Judges (Judges 3:7–16:31)[21]

Othniel (3:7–11)

The first oppressor God raised up to bring Israel to its senses was Chushan-rishathaim, king of Mesopotamia (Aram). This conquest must be dated about 1360 B.C.; it lasted for eight years (3:8). In answer to Israel's cry for deliverance, God raised up Othniel, son-in-law of Caleb, to judge the people and save them from their enemy.

Because the term *judge* bears different connotations to modern readers, it is helpful to discuss the office and responsibilities of the judge. There were at least twelve judges in all, some of whom were contemporaries, and they ministered until the midst of the eleventh century. Their principal task seemed to be that of arbiter and governor, as the name implies, but they also had the responsibility of acting as military leader when the need arose. One essential prerequisite was that the judge, like the prophet, must be charismatic.[22] This means that he neither was elected by the people nor succeeded his predecessor by family inheritance or appointment. He had to be chosen by God, and the proof of divine selection was his being empowered by the Spirit to perform deeds otherwise impossible for mere men (3:10; 6:34; 11:29; 13:25). It seems fairly clear that few if any of the judges wielded control over all Israel at once. Rather, they must have been responsible for only limited areas, in some cases only a tribe or two. There were probably times during this era when there were no judges at all and

---

21. For proposed dates for this complex period, see Eugene H. Merrill, *Kingdom of Priests: A History of Old Testament Israel* (Grand Rapids: Baker, 1987), 146–51.

22. Max Weber, *Ancient Judaism*, trans. and ed. Hans H. Gerth and Don Martindale (Glencoe, Ill.: Free Press, 1952), 40.

other times when there were several at once. For example, it is certain that both Jephthah and Samson judged at the same time, the former over Transjordan during the oppression of the Ammonites and the latter over Judah and its surroundings during the oppression of the Philistines. When there were no enemies, there were probably no judges, or at least none mentioned in the Bible.

Ehud and Shamgar (3:12–31)

Under Othniel's inspired leadership, Israel regained its freedom from harassment and the land "had rest" for forty years. Then the cycle commenced again, and about 1300 B.C. Eglon, king of Moab, attacked Israel and set up a provincial capital at Jericho. This presupposes a defeat of the eastern tribes, at least the tribe of Reuben (which, incidentally, had nearly disappeared from history by now) and suggests the strength of Moab. Again Israel cried out, and again a judge was chosen, this time Ehud of Benjamin. By means of a clever ruse, Ehud was able personally to assassinate Eglon; in the resulting fray, Israel, after an eighteen-year servitude, overcame her Moabite foe. Then followed some eighty years of peace extending well to the end of the thirteenth century (ca. 1200 B.C.). Probably during this period there was some difficulty with the Philistines, but under the leadership of Shamgar ben Anath this was quickly stifled.

Deborah (4:1–5:31)

The next cycle involved the Canaanites, who had become active in the north. Under their leader, Jabin of Hazor (possibly a descendant of the Jabin of Joshua's time), they had accumulated a great host in and near the Valley of Jezreel, apparently under the command of a certain Sisera. Using their nine hundred chariots of iron and other awesome instruments of war, they kept northern Israel in bondage for twenty years. Finally, God spoke through his prophetess Deborah, a resident of Ephraim, and commanded her to select Barak of Kedesh-naphtali as the deliverer of his repentant people. When Barak refused to go to battle against the Canaanites without Deborah's presence, the courageous woman consented to go, but she reminded Barak that the glory for the victory would not be his but would belong to a woman. Lest history be too harsh with Barak, it is important to remember that Deborah was the one blessed with the charisma, and Barak wanted her to go with him only as a guarantor of the presence of God. Ten thousand men of Naphtali and Zebulun rallied to the call and, led by Deborah and Barak, marched down the slopes of Mount Tabor to battle Sisera's hosts in the Jezreel Valley. Against incredible odds, God's forces prevailed through personal heroism and an assist from the Almighty Hand, which caused a rain storm to come suddenly and fill the little River Kishon to overflowing. The chariots, the invincible weapons of the Canaanites, were bogged down in the mud, and their crews had to flee for their lives on foot (Judg. 5:21). Sisera himself ran to the tent of a certain Kenite whom he thought he could trust, but when he fell asleep in his hiding place from sheer exhaustion, the lady of the house, whose sympathies obviously were with Israel because of common ancestry or other reasons, drove a tent peg through his temples. Thus Jabin and his forces were devastated by most unlikely foes, women divinely empowered to achieve the victorious purposes of God. The event was celebrated by Deborah and Barak in one of the most beautiful and stirring songs in the history of literature (Judg. 5).

Gideon (6:1–9:56)

The next judge of Israel, Gideon, lived near the beginning of the twelfth century, the time of the Midianite peril. For seven years, these fierce desert tribesmen, the first to use camels as a common practice in warfare, overran the land, especially in the north.[23] The critical problem with these invaders was not so much military as economic, because their animals threatened to devour the entire produce of the land and strip the country bare. In the midst of this crisis, the Angel of Yahweh appeared to Gideon, son of Joash, a resident of the village of Ophrah in Manasseh (Judg. 6:11). He instructed Gideon to assume the leadership of God's people in their hour of need, but Gideon protested that he was ill equipped for the task, being nothing more than a poor peasant from a poor family. Yet, he recognized the presence of Deity and hastened to make an offering on a nearby altar. When the sacrifice was prepared, the Angel touched it with his staff and fire leaped forth from the crude stone altar, consuming the sacrifice. Gideon fell prostrate before the Angel, who in this case, as in others, is synonymous with Yahweh (see Gen. 18; Exod. 3:2; 14:19; 32:34; Josh. 5:13–15; Judg. 2:1; 13:6; 2 Sam. 14:17, 20; Isa. 63:9). The Angel assured him that he would not die for having seen the face of God. At this, Gideon built an altar at the spot and named it Yahweh-Shalom ("Yahweh is Peace").

That night God ordered Gideon to tear down the Baal altars of his father and to cut down the groves associated with them (6:25). With trusted accomplices, he carried out the command and built in place of his

23. W. F. Albright, *The Biblical Period from Abraham to Ezra* (New York: Harper and Row, 1963), 41.

father's altar a new altar to Yahweh. On this altar he sacrificed a bullock to God. His stealthy work was soon found out, however, and the devotees of Baal in the community went to Joash and demanded an accounting for his son's acts of desecration. Joash, probably not a very faithful Baalite (though he had named his son Jerub-baal originally), responded by asking the crowd why Baal did not vindicate himself if his honor had been so greatly violated. This averted further action against Gideon, who proceeded to summon the standing armies of Asher, Zebulun, and Naphtali in addition to his own Manassehites. After confirming through a series of signs involving dew and fleece that God was with him, Gideon took in his hand the standard of battle and rushed to meet the Midianites in the Valley of Jezreel south of Mount Moreh.

On the way, the Lord informed Gideon that his army of thirty-two thousand men was much too large, for in the event of victory Israel would claim success through its military strength and not through God's power. So Gideon permitted all who wished to do so to return to their homes, an invitation some twenty-two thousand accepted readily. Still the army must be pared down. Gideon led his army to a brook nearby and watched as they drank in preparation for the battle. Of the entire host, only three hundred were cautious enough to drink from their hands with upraised heads so that they could watch for a surprise attack. The rest immersed their faces in the water, demonstrating their unreliability in emergencies. The latter Gideon also released. Now, with a tiny contingent that was in turn divided into three companies, Gideon proceeded to the fray. He and his servant previously had overheard some of the Midianite soldiers discussing the impending Israelite invasion. From their place of hiding in the night, they were encouraged by a dream that one of the Midianites had had and was relating to his companion. The dream virtually guaranteed Gideon success by predicting that the Midianite camp would be overturned; so without further ado Gideon made his charge. Never was a stranger assault made! Bearing only torches concealed in pitchers in one hand, and trumpets in the other, the gallant three hundred sallied forth. Suddenly, in the thick of darkness, the trumpets blared, the pitchers were shattered, and the brilliant light of the torches stabbed the blackness in all directions! Thinking they had been set upon by untold thousands, the Midianites began to strike out in all directions, but they succeeded only in decimating their own ranks, until a comparative handful were left. The kings of Midian fled to the east over the Jordan, but two were caught and executed. The other two eluded immediate capture, thanks to the refusal of the citizens of Penuel and Succoth to divulge their whereabouts, but finally were apprehended; the reluctant informers were severely chastened by Gideon (8:13–17).

The victory was so glorious in the eyes of Israel that certain leaders appealed to Gideon to proclaim himself king. This is the first reference in the biblical narrative to a clear desire for a monarch, though there may have been such wishes in the past. Gideon refused the offer, acknowledging that God was their King, but he did make a richly decorated ephod, which, because of its association with Gideon, became an object of religious devotion and, hence, a "snare" to Israel. Apparently Israel was preserved from enemies all the rest of Gideon's life, but on the whole the spiritual situation was less than desirable. Gideon himself married many wives, who bore a multitude of children, a fact that was to prove grievous in Israel's national life.

After Gideon died (ca. 1150 B.C.), his illegitimate son, Abimelech, who hailed from Shechem, went to his native city, stirred the people up to make him king, and slew the seventy sons of Gideon, his half-brothers. One of the sons, Jotham, escaped, prophesying to Abimelech in a clever parable that he would not last long and that Shechem itself would turn on him and reject him (9:7–21). After three years, the people of Shechem did indeed become disaffected with Abimelech, and while he was out of town a band of Shechemites led by a certain Gaal declared their independence of him. Zebul, mayor of the city, notified Abimelech of the plot. He returned, a battle ensued outside the city, and Gaal and his revolutionaries were dispersed. Because he suspected that Shechem as a whole was involved in this affair, Abimelech ordered the city destroyed and its ruins sowed with salt. Some of the refugees fled from the Tower of Shechem to the sanctuary of Baal-berith but were unsuccessful in eluding Abimelech, for he burned the temple to the ground (9:49). He then turned to the nearby village of Thebez, where he also no doubt suspected a pocket of resistance to his rule, but when a woman cast a millstone from the top of the tower his career abruptly ended. Thus the first attempt at Israelite monarchy was aborted, ending in dismal failure.

Tola, Jair, Jephthah, Ibzan, Elon, and Abdon (10:1–12:15)

There next followed a period of stability under the judgeships of two otherwise unknown figures, Tola, of Issachar, and Jair, of Gilead, the territory across the Jordan. In the meantime, the Philistines had entered Canaan in great numbers from an unsuccessful Egyptian incursion (ca. 1200 B.C.) and had added to the smaller Philistine population already settled on the lower Palestinian coast. In their desire for expansion, they pushed east by 1100 B.C. and naturally came into conflict with the

Israelite tribes, especially Judah. To the east the Ammonites, long dor-
mant, also came to life and pressed hard on Gilead. It appears that the two
judges called by God to deliver Israel from these enemies, Samson in the
west and Jephthah in the east, were contemporary, or nearly so, and that
the Philistine and Ammonite oppressions also were (10:6).

The narrator draws attention to developments on the eastern front
first. After the usual apostasy and punishment, this time by Ammon,
Israel cried out to the Lord, and he raised up Jephthah. This unfortunate
man, who hailed from Gilead, was born of a harlot and therefore rejected
by his brethren and forced to dwell in exile near the eastern Galilean
wilderness. His valor was nonetheless recognized; when Israel found itself
in danger, he was invited to come back and assume leadership. He agreed,
but only on condition that he not be removed from his position once the
victory was achieved. With little option available, the Gileadites assented,
and Jephthah returned to take the initiative against the Ammonite
invaders. In an effort to avert bloodshed if possible, he wrote a letter to
the king of Ammon and reminded him of the peaceful relationships they
had had for the past three hundred years since the exodus (11:15–27). He
entreated the king to remember that God in the past had always cared for
and preserved his people and that he would do so in this conflict, a conflict not of Israel's making. The king of Ammon turned a deaf ear to the
communication, and preparations were made for war.

Before Jephthah entered into conflict, he made a vow that if God
granted him success he would offer up to God the first thing that met him
on his return home. This is often called Jephthah's "rash vow," and rightly
so, but in the opinion of this writer the passage often has been misunderstood. It is suggested that when Jephthah came home, his young daughter,
an only child, rushed out to meet him, and he, fulfilling the terms of the
vow, offered her up as a burnt offering to God.[24] This seems highly
improbable for the following reasons: (1) The story specifies that Jephthah
was filled with the Spirit of God. It is not likely that a Spirit-filled man
would even leave open the possibility of human sacrifice, a practice
strongly prohibited in the law. (2) Jephthah must have been very much
aware that the possibility of his daughter's meeting him at his return was
great. (3) In verse 31, the conjunction *waw*, translated "and," can just as
well be translated "or," the result meaning that Jephthah promises to present whatever meets him at the door to the Lord *or* to offer it up as a
burnt offering. In other words, Jephthah has made allowance for his

24. George F. Moore, *A Critical and Exegetical Commentary on Judges* (New York: Charles Scribner's
Sons, 1895), 301.

daughter by promising God to give her to him in a lifetime of service if she should be the first to greet him. (4) When the bereaved father realized that he had given his only child to the Lord, thus losing any possibility of perpetuating his family name, the rashness of his vow dawned on him. He had no sons, and his hope for a descendant rested in this daughter, who would now remain unmarried. (5) That the daughter begged permission to go into the wilderness to bewail her virginity seems to bear out the idea of her impending temple service, for if she were about to be sacrificed it hardly seems she would bewail her unmarried state or spend her last two months away from her father, whom she dearly loved. Rather, she would bemoan the brevity of her life. (6) Finally, the text says that she "knew no man," a meaningless statement if she was put to death. But it makes perfect sense if she entered a life of celibacy. In addition, the maidens of Israel made it a custom from that time to "lament" the daughter of Jephthah four days out of every year. A possible translation might be that these maidens went annually to "recount" the daughter of Jephthah.[25] The translation *lament* is perhaps based on the assumption that she died, an assumption, as just argued, that is unnecessary.

The tribal jealousy discussed earlier is manifest in the reaction of the tribe of Ephraim to the success of Jephthah and the Gileadites over Ammon (12:1–4). Because Jephthah allegedly did not invite them to participate in the campaign, a charge the judge denied, they decided to burn his house down in retaliation. Their efforts were not successful, however, and the intertribal war that developed resulted in the deaths of thousands of Ephraimites. In their haste to return west over the Jordan, the Ephraimites were intercepted at the fords of the river by Gileadites who demanded that they identify themselves by pronouncing the word *šibbōlet* ("stream"). Because of certain dialectical changes in the Hebrew language, these westerners could not pronounce the "sh" sound, but rather said "s" (12:6). This showed that they were Ephraimites and sealed their doom, but at least the land again knew respite from foreign adversity.

The peace gained under Jephthah in the east was unknown in the west, where the Philistines became the chastening rod of God to punish delinquent Judah. There was a judge in Judah at the time, a rather obscure figure named Ibzan, but he seems to have had little relationship to the Philistine scourge (12:8–10). There were also two other minor judges in other parts of Israel, Elon of Zebulun (12:11–12) and Abdon of Ephraim (12:13–15), but they, like Ibzan, seem to have been only local judges who

25. The idea would be that of recitation or commemoration, not necessarily of lament. See Ludwig Koehler and Walter Baumgartner, *Lexicon in Veteris Testamenti Libros* (Leiden: Brill, 1948–53), 1034.

were not involved in the weightier matters of warfare and national security from external forces. So by the first quarter of the eleventh century Israel looked for a savior once more.

Samson (13:1–16:31)

At the beginning of Philistine oppression, the Angel of Yahweh appeared to a barren woman, the wife of Manoah of the tribe of Dan, and promised her a son. This son would be unusual in that he would be a Nazirite from his mother's womb and would be used in a special way to bring deliverance to God's people. Manoah was not present at the first visit of the Angel, but when he learned of the exchange, he made sure he was included in the next heavenly visitation. At that time the Angel repeated his promise, and when Manoah made an offering, the Angel ascended in the flame from the altar. Awestruck, Manoah fell on his face with the realization that he had seen God and that God was about to use his yet unborn son for the salvation of Israel.

From the earliest years of the lad's life, it became apparent that God's hand was on Samson, for the Spirit of God began to manifest himself through him (13:24–25). Yet, it was equally obvious that Samson was not one who would submit willingly to the plan of God. Once he saw a lass from Timnath, a nearby Philistine city, and, smitten with love for this alien girl, requested his parents to arrange marriage with her. His parents' arguments availed nothing, so the wedding date was set. Earlier, on his way to Timnath, he had seen a lion by the way; with no effort at all he had slain the savage beast. Thus did the Spirit reveal himself in Samson, who evidently had no unusual physical prowess otherwise. When he returned to his fiancée to celebrate the wedding, he saw the carcass by the way and, in violation of his Nazirite vow, touched the dead body to obtain honey made there by a swarm of bees. At Timnath, Samson suggested to the wedding attendants a riddle concerning the lion and honey (14:14). If they could reveal the meaning by the end of the seven-day period before the wedding day, he would give them certain items of clothing; if they could not, they each must give him the same. All through the week they tried in vain to solve the puzzle, until finally they prevailed on the Philistine bride-to-be to exact the answer from Samson. When they told him, he knew they had threatened his fiancée, so in a rage he went to the Philistine city of Ashkelon, slew thirty men, and gave their clothing to the attendants in fulfillment of his vow. Then he stormed off to his own home, leaving his intended wife at the altar.

When he began to reflect on the incident, he realized that he might have acted rashly, so he went back to Timnath to get his bride; but, alas, she had been given to the best man in Samson's absence (14:20). This so enraged him that he caught three hundred foxes, tied their tails together, ignited the brands he had placed between them, and set them loose to burn the standing crops in the Philistine fields. They in turn burned the home of his erstwhile bride, killing her and her father in the flames. Samson, his wrath yet unsatisfied, fled to the summit of a hill named Etam and there was approached by some of his Judaean kinsmen. They demanded that he come down so that they might bind him and deliver him to the Philistines as a bounty. He agreed, but only under the condition that they themselves would not lay hands on him. To this they consented, but the moment Samson was among the Philistines he burst his bonds and, with a great demonstration of superhuman strength, slaughtered one thousand men with the jawbone of an ass (15:15).

Samson's life seemed strangely entwined with the lives of ungodly women; perhaps they were his greatest weakness. First he went to Gaza, one of the chief Philistine cities, and fell to the allurements of a harlot (16:1–3). When it appeared that the Philistines might slay him there, he arose in the night and, filled with the Spirit, carried off the huge gates of the city and left them at Hebron, many miles to the west. But another Philistine maiden, who lived in the valley of Sorek, proved his ultimate undoing. Delilah, heavily bribed by the Philistines, tried several times to learn from Samson the secret of his great strength, but to no avail. Finally, he yielded to her demands and revealed that if his hair were cut he would be like any other man. This suggests not that the hair itself possessed supernatural powers, but that the uncut hair represented the bond that tied him to God as a Nazirite. Cutting it would signify rupturing the bond and the departure of the Spirit from his life. Indeed, when the bond was broken, he did become like any other man.

In the last scenes of this tragic figure's life, Samson, blinded, was grinding the grain in a Philistine gristmill (16:21). But his day of final triumph came. The Philistines, in convention in the great temple of Dagon at Gaza and desiring entertainment, brought their former nemesis into their midst to make sport of him. His hair having grown back and, more important, his faith and power having been restored, he welcomed this moment as an opportunity to vindicate himself and his God among these pagans. At the climax of the merrymaking, he was led by a lad to the two central pillars of the massive building; exercising the last measure of strength in his possession, he pulled the posts together. The roof, covered with hundreds of the Philistines, collapsed and buried Samson and everyone within. When the dust had settled, it was learned that Samson had slain more of the enemy in his death than in his life. Thus, at about 1085 B.C.,

TABLE 5

The Judges of Israel

Oppressors	Judge	Reference
Mesopotamians (1360–1352)	Othniel (1352–1313)	Judges 3:8–11
Moabites (1300–1284)	Ehud (1284–1204)	Judges 3:12–30
Philistines (?)	Shamgar (?)	Judges 3:31
Canaanites (1260–1240)	Deborah (1240–1201)	Judges 4–5
Midianites (1201–1194)	Gideon (1194–1155)	Judges 6–8
?	Tola (1152–1131)	Judges 10:1–2
?	Jair (1131–1107)	Judges 10:3–5
Ammonites (1124–1106)	Jephthah (1106–1100)	Judges 10:6–12:7
?	Ibzan (1083–1076)	Judges 12:8–10
?	Elon (1076–1066)	Judges 12:11–12
?	Abdon (1066–1058)	Judges 12:13–15
Philistines (1124–1084)	Samson (1105–1085)	Judges 13–16

the threat from the west was at least temporarily held in abeyance, and a kind of shaky peace was sustained for a few years.

The Condition of the Times (Judges 17:1– 1 Samuel 7:17)

Two accounts of events of special importance during the period of the judges appear in Judges 17–21. They are vital not so much because they had political significance, though they did, but because they reveal the spiritual conditions that prevailed during the entire era, conditions summed up in the slogan that "everyone did as he saw fit" (17:6; 21:25). Though Israel was theoretically a theocracy bound to God by a covenant it had voluntarily accepted, the nation had disintegrated, not merely geo-graphically, but especially socially and spiritually. The people had lost interest in the heritage from which the nation had sprung and had permit-ted the outrages of anarchy to supplant a people governed by the law. One must not get the impression that all were evil or negligent of the divine will, however, for among the citizens of Israel there were notable excep-tions. The Book of Ruth, set in the time of the judges, exhibits the godly lives of the minority. Still, the two stories in this last part of the Book of Judges (the appendix, as it is sometimes called) describe scenes of almost unbelievable immorality and license.

Judges 17 and 18 recount that a man from Ephraim named Micah had stolen a certain sum of silver from his own mother. When he repented and confessed to her that he had done so, she rewarded his "honesty" by offering him the silver as a gift from which to make some images. He refused the gift, but his mother made the images anyway and had them placed in a specially constructed shrine. Micah then commissioned one of his own sons to be his priest, completing the requirements for his own independent religious system. Meanwhile, a young Levite from Beth-lehem, who apparently was looking for employment, ventured to Ephraim, where he came in contact with Micah. Micah, after some bargaining, hired the Levite and consecrated him to the priesthood, hoping that by employing a Levite he might lend some semblance of legitimacy to his maverick religion.

At this time, the tribe of Dan was having its difficulties along the Philistine coastal plain (18:1–2). Its people were unable to occupy their territory because of the superior Philistine armament and population, and they found that the area of the western hills left to them was unable to sustain them. So they sent a delegation to search out the land in hopes of finding a better location. In transit they passed through Mount Ephraim and by the home of Micah. They enquired of Micah's priest as to the prospects that awaited them in their search. Assured that all would be well, they proceeded to a far northern region inhabited by a people who dwelt in peace and security. There at Laish, just north of the waters of Merom, they decided to settle. When they returned to their people and told them of the land of Laish, it was decided to migrate en masse. The route of the Danites led them once again by Mount Ephraim, and when the leaders remembered that it was there that they had met the Levite of Micah, they stopped by. Enticed by the richly decorated shrine and the images of silver, they appropriated them, but not before they were discov-ered by the Levite. They quickly persuaded him, however, that the life of a tribal priest was far more prestigious and lucrative than a mere family chaplaincy, so with little reluctance he followed them. When Micah discovered the loss of his images and priest, he set out after the pilfering Danites, but even when he caught up with them he was unable to prevent their thievery. Downcast, he turned back while the Danites went on to Laish, where they cold-bloodedly slaughtered the helpless citizenry. More significantly, however, they set up Micah's silver images and established the Levite, Jonathan ben Gershom, as their priest.[26] Thus idolatry was formally inaugurated in Israel on a tribal basis. From that day to the time of Christ, Dan remained a center of idolatry.

The second incident is discussed in Judges 19–21. There another Levite from Ephraim is the focal character, but this one had married a concubine from Bethlehem. She had run away from him to her home, but because he loved her deeply he had followed her there and begged her to return. The father had insisted that the Levite remain in Bethlehem for several days no matter what, but finally the Levite had excused himself and departed with his wife. They had gotten such a late start that day that they had not nearly reached home before it began to get dark. They thought about spending the night in Jerusalem, but because this was not an Israelite city as yet they abandoned the idea. Then they decided to stay in Gibeah of Benjamin, even though it was too late to find accommodations. While they prepared to sleep on the street, a citizen who happened to be a native of Ephraim invited them to stay with him in the city. To this they willingly assented, but in the middle of the night some ruffians beset the house, demanding that the Levite be sent out to satisfy their depraved natures. The host protested this insult to his guest and offered instead to release his daughter and the Levite's concubine to them.

The next morning the Levite went to the door, where he found his ravished wife lying dead on the doorstep. He picked up her corpse, returned to his home, and then, in an act of unparalleled imagery, dissected her body into twelve pieces and sent them to the leaders of the twelve tribes (19:29–30). Sometimes a person or nation can be awakened to reality only by something so bizarre or shocking that it is impossible to overlook. This was the case in this dark hour. For generations, Israel had been lulled into a false sense of security. The people had forgotten the covenant made with God at Shechem under Joshua. They had gone after other gods time and time again; though punished every time by the nations God raised up for that purpose, they were saved by their judges, only to apostatize again. They had forgotten the very reason for their being. Now, with the gory,

26. This may have been Moses' grandson (18:3); if so, this places the event in the beginning of the period of the judges. See on the problem of "Manasseh" (Judg. 18:30) or "Moses," Robert G. Boling, *Judges*, Anchor Bible (Garden City, N.Y.: Doubleday, 1975), 266.

mutilated body of the concubine as a symbol of the state of their nation, the tribes awoke with one great national response to the critical issues of the day. How could Israel go so far that such a brutal deed could be countenanced? Surely the time had come to restore sanity if at all possible.

The tribal leaders assembled with their troops at Mizpah and issued a communique to Benjamin that that tribe should punish the infamous deed perpetrated within its borders (20:13). Benjamin refused, and an intertribal war began, a war hardly matched for bloodiness. After a series of unsuccessful maneuvers by the eleven tribes, occasioned by the unusual resourcefulness of the tiny tribe of Benjamin, the larger host finally won. They did their work so well that Benjamin was virtually annihilated; with the exception of six hundred men who had fled to the hills, all its men, women, and children were destroyed. Alarmed at the devastation they had wrought, the Israelites confronted the problem of an incomplete nation. Theirs had always been a twelve-tribe confederacy, and it was unthinkable that the number should decline. Now, in the heat of their anger, they had done what they would never have contemplated in a saner moment. They had wanted to punish, but surely it was not God's will that they do so this thoroughly.

The tribal leaders, confronting this new problem, met at the central sanctuary and sought a means whereby the remaining six hundred Benjamites could form the nucleus of a new tribe. This was not as simple as it might seem, for besides the fact that the Benjamite women had all been slaughtered, the Israelites had made an inviolable vow that they would not permit any of their women to marry a Benjamite (21:1). One sage finally suggested a way out of the dilemma. He asked that a survey be taken to determine if there were any peoples who had not sent troops to assist Israel's cause. After careful search it was learned that the city of Jabesh-gilead had not done so. The elder then suggested that the men of Jabesh-gilead be put to death and their unmarried women be obtained as wives for Benjamin. This was carried out, but unfortunately there were only four hundred such maidens, two hundred too few. Another man of wisdom proposed that the two hundred betake themselves to Shiloh, where the maidens of that city were wont to celebrate an annual festival by dancing near the vineyards.[27] When the girls came to dance, the two hundred men were to seize any whom they wished and make them their wives. Though this was unjustifiable, it was done, and the completeness of Israel was assured.

27. Evidently Shiloh had become a center of Baal worship by now, or at least the worship of Yahweh had deteriorated immensely (cf. 1 Sam. 2:12–22).

Ruth

Thus were the fortunes of Israel, a nation whose people did what was right in their own eyes. But for God's grace there is no doubt that the covenant community would have ceased to function because of the people's neglect of the divine precepts and their interest in the idolatry and immorality of the peoples among whom they had settled. Yet, as already suggested, one must not conclude that there were no righteous souls at all; occasionally, in the midst of the perversion already described, there were found those whose whole intent was to worship the Lord in truth. The outstanding example of this is described in the Book of Ruth, set early in the time of the judges. This entertaining and inspiring tale is an oasis of purity and wholesomeness in a desert of corruption and anarchy.

There had come a famine to the land of Judah so severe that many of the inhabitants, including Elimelech, Naomi, and their two sons, had fled for relief to Moab, east of the Dead Sea. While there, the boys matured and married Moabite women, Orpah and Ruth, but in due course Elimelech and his sons died. The three widows were uncertain of their future, but when Naomi learned that the famine in Judah had ended, she determined to return home. The bond of love between this godly woman and her daughters-in-law had become so strong that they begged her to take them with her. Orpah finally was convinced to remain among her own people, but Ruth was adamant. In as beautiful a passage as can be found in any literature she avowed, "Where you go I will go, and where you stay I will stay. Your people will be my people and your God my God. Where you die I will die and there I will be buried. May the Lord deal with me, be it ever so severely, if anything but death separates you and me" (Ruth 1:16–17).

On returning to Bethlehem, Naomi was greeted by her old friends. Saddened at the loss of her family, she requested that they no longer call her Naomi ("pleasant") but Marah ("bitter"). God had sent her away full and brought her back empty; little did she realize, nor could she, that the daughter-in-law who came with her, though a Moabite woman, was to become the great-grandmother of King David! She had not come back empty, but instead had brought the source of life's greatest blessing to herself. But she had come back with little material wealth. In fact, she had had to sell her late husband's property in Bethlehem to make ends meet. With no means to redeem it (buy it back), she and Ruth were destined to poverty, at least until the year of jubilee when, of course, the property would come back to them automatically.

In the meantime, Ruth would not presume on the good graces of her mother-in-law but decided to alleviate the financial burden by doing whatever work she could find. According to Mosaic law, the poor of the land had the privilege of gleaning the fields of the more fortunate. This meant they could follow the reapers and pick up any scraps left behind. In addition, they could reap the corners of the fields, for these were not to be cut by the owners but were reserved for the poor (Deut. 24:19–22). It just so happened that Ruth went to the field of Boaz, one of the wealthier and more prominent men of the city, and a near relative of Elimelech, though Ruth did not know this. When Boaz spied the beautiful foreign girl, he asked someone her identity and background and was told that she was the daughter-in-law of his deceased kinsman. One ought not to read into the story any romantic motifs, at least not at this point, for it seems that Boaz was interested in her because of the family tie. Besides, he no doubt was many years her senior, for he addressed her as "my daughter." He told her to remain in his fields if she wished, and to guarantee her success he commanded his reapers to deliberately leave scatterings where she might pick them up (2:16). He warned them to refrain from bothering her and even (and this was unthinkable in a country where the women drew the water) allowed her to drink of their water. The real reason for all of this kindness was the kinship that bound them together, but Boaz told Ruth that he was doing what he did because he had heard how kind she had been to her unfortunate mother-in-law.

When Ruth returned with a huge basket of barley at the end of that first day, Naomi asked where she had done her gleaning. On learning that it had been in the field of Boaz, she began to meditate on a plan both to find a husband for the young widow and to redeem her property from her creditor. Several weeks later she instructed Ruth to go to Boaz's threshing floor on a certain night and lie at his feet. In that time and place such an act carried no overtones of impropriety, for it was legal and customary for a woman to make known her matrimonial aspirations that way, especially under these circumstances regarding property redemption.[28] When Boaz inquired who she was and what her intentions were, she was to let it be known that she desired marriage. Naomi, in accordance with the law, wished to redeem her property. Because she was unable, the responsibility to do it rested on her next of kin, who she thought was Boaz. But if Boaz redeemed the property, he must at the same time take Ruth as wife and rear up children in the name of her deceased husband (Deut. 25:5–10).

---

28. See Robert L. Hubbard, Jr., *The Book of Ruth* (Grand Rapids: Eerdmans, 1988), 201–5.

The plan to make Boaz redeemer, then, involved his becoming Ruth's husband at the same time.

When Boaz discovered Ruth's intent, he was overjoyed, for no doubt by now he had been smitten with an overwhelming love for her. Yet, he said, he was not indeed the next of kin! Another in Bethlehem had this honor; the option to redeem or not redeem must be decided first by him. The next day Boaz met this man near the gate of the city and asked him what he wished to do (4:1). The kinsman agreed to redeem the property for Naomi, but when Boaz mentioned to him that he would have to marry Ruth also, he changed his mind because he was already married and had sons of his own. If he should marry Ruth also, and if they had sons, those sons would take possession of their deceased father's goods and would likely gain other rights as well. In any event, the man was afraid that such a marriage would not benefit himself and his family, so he turned down the offer. This, of course, left Boaz in the clear, but there must be a formal ceremony in which the next of kin relinquished all claim of redemption rights and bequeathed them to Boaz. Before the elders at the gate, the usual place for such a transaction, the two men enacted the usual procedure in such matters. The kinsman took off his shoe and handed it to Boaz, which signified that the property rights, including marriage to Ruth, were now in his hands. And Boaz testified to the assembled witnesses that he intended to redeem the property of his kinswoman Naomi and to marry Ruth and beget sons in the name of her late husband.

Boaz, who, incidentally, was a descendant of Rahab the harlot (Matt. 1:5), married Ruth, and in due time a son, Obed, was born. He was the father of Jesse, the father of David, showing once again how the hand of God guided the lives of individuals as well as the nation in achieving his desired ends. The simple Moabite woman who left such a beautiful impression in such dark days was destined to become another ancestress in the family of her greater Son, the Lord Jesus Christ. Not all was bleak in the days of the judges. A few did not do what was right in their own eyes but determined to follow their God no matter the cost.

Samuel (1 Samuel 1–7)

Near the end of the period of the judges lived one of the most important figures of the Old Testament. He was the bridge between the era of the judges and that of the monarchy, which he was instrumental in form-

---

29. Samuel, a direct descendant of Levi (cf. 1 Chron. 6:33–38), was thus qualified to serve in priestly ministry. See Eugene H. Merrill, "1 Samuel," *The Bible Knowledge Commentary: Old Testament*, ed. John F. Walvoord and Roy B. Zuck (Wheaton: Victor, 1985), 433.

ing. Samuel was considered a judge himself, certainly not in the sense of a man like Samson, but more importantly he was a priest[29] and prophet. Concomitant with the rise of the monarchy was that of the school of the prophets, of which Samuel apparently was the head. Though there had been individual prophets in Israel's history, there had not been any established order of prophets until this time.

The birth of Samuel is another example of the theme of the barren mother with which the Old Testament is so familiar. It seems that his father, Elkanah, lived at Ramathaim-zophim (Ramah) in Ephraim with his two wives, Hannah and Peninah. The latter had borne him several children, but Hannah was unfruitful despite her devotion to God. Peninah would harass the unfortunate Hannah because she was barren and because Elkanah, in compensation, showed Hannah greater affection. It was their custom to make annual pilgrimages to Shiloh to worship the Lord at the tabernacle, and every year Elkanah gave Hannah a double portion of offerings to make to the Lord.

One year Hannah knelt before the tabernacle and, in great heaviness of heart, began to pray that the Lord would grant her a son. She promised that if the prayer were answered she would dedicate the son to the Lord as a lifelong Nazirite. In the intensity of her supplication, she moved her lips, and when the high priest, Eli, noted this, he thought she must be drunk (1:10–13). She denied this and told him the burden of her heart. When the priest knew of her faith, he assured her that God would answer her prayer. Within a year the child was born and named Samuel ("heard of God") because he had come as an answer to special prayer. A few years later, when the child was weaned, he was returned to the tabernacle and entrusted to Eli's keeping to train him to minister to the Lord. First Samuel 2 records the wonderful poem in which Hannah expressed her thankfulness to God for making her fruitful and giving her victory over her adversaries. Hundreds of years later, Mary, the mother of Jesus, based her Magnificat on this ancient song of exultation.

Another glimpse of the wickedness of the times is seen in the behavior of Eli's sons, the priests at Shiloh. Whenever the people brought offerings to the Lord, these wicked men would appropriate them to their own use and, in effect, steal from God. They even turned the tabernacle of God into a brothel, where they engaged in sexual immorality with loose women who consorted there.[30] But, and perhaps even more astoundingly,

---

30. Of course, this may very likely refer to religious prostitution accompanying fertility rites. If so, the worship of Yahweh at Shiloh must have been little different from that of Baal elsewhere. See A. F. Kirkpatrick, *The First and Second Books of Samuel* (Cambridge: Cambridge University Press, 1930), 19–20.

all this was carried on under the very gaze of Eli, who did nothing more than register a mild protest. Naturally, such desecration in the priesthood was bound to incur the wrath of God, so it was not long before a prophet was sent to Eli to inform him that the priestly office would be taken from his family and given to another that would discharge it more faithfully. This was later fulfilled in the accession of the priest Zadok and his family to the office in the time of Solomon (1 Kings 2:35). But it was more fully realized in the perfect priesthood of Christ (Heb. 2:17).

While all this was going on, Samuel was growing up and gaining favor in the sight of God and men. His faithful mother, who had been blessed for her unselfishness by bearing five more children, came annually to worship God and to visit her son. The day came finally when God manifested himself to Samuel, a remarkable event in light of the fact that there had been no divine revelation as a general rule since the time of Moses (1 Sam. 3:1). The call of the Lord was so clear that Samuel mistook it for the voice of Eli, until Eli convinced him otherwise. The message of this first revelation was ominous, indeed, for in it God spoke of the overthrow of Eli's priesthood once again; so convinced were Eli and the people of Israel of the validity of the message that they recognized that Samuel was a prophet of God (3:20). In further fulfillment of this and other predictions, Samuel's authority was substantiated, for none of his prophecies failed in any respect.

The Philistines had been temporarily subdued by Samson. Now, toward the beginning of the eleventh century, they arose with greater unity and determination than ever, making a sweeping incursion into the western highlands of Judaea and Ephraim. The Israelite army quickly mobilized to meet the Philistine invaders near Aphek, at the western edge of Ephraimite territory in the Plain of Sharon (4:1). The Philistines apparently had little difficulty in this first encounter; when the Israelites assessed the reason for their defeat, they decided it was because of the absence of the ark of God, which was at Shiloh. Another effort was made to repel the invaders, but again Israel was routed, this time at the cost of the lives of Eli's two wicked sons, Hophni and Phinehas, who had brought the ark into battle. Furthermore, the ark itself, which by now appeared to be no more to Israel than a superstitious relic of a bygone age, was carried off by the enemy to Ashdod (5:1).

When news of the defeat of Israel, the death of his sons, and the capture of the ark reached Eli at Shiloh, the aged priest was so overcome that he fell from the seat on which he was resting and broke his neck. At the same time, as though prophetically, the wife of Eli's son Phinehas gave birth to a son, whom she named Ichabod. The meaning of the name ("where is the glory?") spoke eloquently of Israel's plight without God (4:21–22).

The ark was set up in the temple of the god Dagon at Ashdod. The very first morning after its arrival there, however, the "corn deity"[31] was found lying on its face before the ark. It was set up again, but the following day it not only lay prostrate before the ark but also was broken in pieces. This convinced the Philistines that their god was inferior to the God of Israel, who they imagined was confined within the chest, or at least represented by it. When they broke out with horrible diseases, they felt that surely Yahweh was wroth with them (5:6–7). They quickly sent the ark to Gath, hoping the change would appease Yahweh, but the results were just as disastrous there. After moving it once more, this time to Ekron, and experiencing similar calamities, they decided the only wise course was to return it to Israel. The problem was how to do it. They could not personally escort it there, for this would expose whoever carried it to Israelite vengeance. But it was unlikely that the Israelites would venture into Philistine territory to retrieve their sacred relic. Finally a solution was devised whereby the ark could be returned and the Philistines could learn whether it had been responsible for their misfortunes. They made a new cart, attached unbroken cattle to it, and placed the ark on it, together with objects of gold as a trespass offering to the Israelites' God. If the cattle returned directly to Israel, they would know that Yahweh indeed had occasioned their grief. If, however, the cattle meandered aimlessly, they would see that their troubles had been only coincidental (6:3–9).

As soon as the cattle were released, they set out directly for the Israelite border, convincingly demonstrating God's power over Israel's enemies. First they reached the Judaean town of Beth-shemesh, about twenty-five miles southwest of Jerusalem. The men of the city were so overjoyed to see the ark, the tangible expression of God's presence, that they offered the Philistine cattle as burnt offerings, which they kindled with the wood of the cart. With unrestrained enthusiasm some of them peered into the ark, an act forbidden in the law, and one that cost the lives of many (6:19). Frantically they called to the people of Kirjath-jearim, a village in the Valley of Sorek some miles to the east, who sent a delegation to get the ark and place it in the home of Abinadab, where it remained for at least the next one hundred years.

31. Donald B. Harden, *The Phoenicians*, 2d ed. (New York: Praeger, 1962), 86–87.
32. Merrill, *Kingdom of Priests*, 176.

Some years following the capture of the ark and the destruction of Shiloh (ca. 1100 B.C.),[32] Samuel gathered the fighting force of Israel at Mizpah. The Philistines learned of this and set out for further conquest. The Israelites knew, of course, that one more decisive defeat could eliminate them as a nation and deliver them into the Philistine orbit. In desperation they cried out to Samuel to pray for them, and the prophet responded in faith. Taking a young lamb as a burnt offering, he cried out to Yahweh, who answered in a mighty thunderstorm. This unnerved the Philistine troops, who broke formation and were soon beleaguered by Israel. The victory so impressed Samuel that he erected a monument at the site, a stone pillar that he named 'eben-'ezer ("stone of help"), as a tribute to the God of Israel (7:12). And well might Samuel be impressed, for from that day until the time of David, at least, Philistine aggression was curbed. The rest of Samuel's days could be lived in comparatively peaceful labor at Bethel, Gilgal, Mizpah, and his hometown of Ramah, cities he traveled in circuit as the last of Israel's judges (7:15–17).

So ends the period of conquest and judges, an era of frustration, defeat, and failure. Yet there shines forth from this time an occasional gleam of courage, faith, and dedication. A land had been entered, conquered in some measure, and at least partially settled in answer to the prophetic word of God. Israel had reached peaks of strength and unity interspersed with corruption and defeat, but it had become more and more clear that the loose tribal confederation of the past would not suffice for the present, especially in light of the fact that all the surrounding powers had well-organized and efficient central governments headed by kings. Israel had a King too, but he had been forgotten except by the few. The demand now was for an earthly hero who could give the nation a place in the world and cohesion within the body politic. God did give a king, but to safeguard his interests he also provided a corrective and shepherding influence, the prophet.

7

An Age of Greatness

Historical Background

The rise of the Philistine threat that culminated in the destruction of Shiloh in about 1100 B.C. signalled the end of any hope of Israel's maintaining itself as a loose federation of tribes with no central authority. Though the Egyptian Empire had for all practical purposes ceased to exercise any kind of direct influence on Israel, the dangers and undesirability of remaining unfederated nevertheless became obvious, because lesser powers all around were strongly organized and becoming increasingly militant. Israel's major problem was that she had forgotten God in any national sense, but the people overlooked this in favor of the view that her continued existence depended on a king like those of the surrounding nations.

The Philistines, or "Sea Peoples," had succeeded in finishing the task of removing the Hittite menace, a task the Assyrians had begun shortly before 1200 B.C.[1] They then swooped down into Canaan from the Aegean region, bringing with them Hittite arts and crafts, especially the use of iron, and established themselves on the south littoral. Content with this limited area at first, they began to push east and north by the turn of the eleventh century and were contained only by the exploits of Samson and

1. O. R. Gurney, *The Hittites* (Baltimore: Penguin, 1952), 39.

other defenders of Israel. However, as already noted, they did manage to penetrate into Ephraim far enough to destroy Shiloh, and they undoubtedly occupied many other sites within Israelite territory by the time of Samuel and Saul. This singular danger most prompted Israel to demand a king who would follow in the line of the judges but whose office would be more permanent and stable. Without such a leader, it was thought, the entire nation would be swallowed up by the Philistines.

Toward the north, a people known as the Aramaeans were settling. They organized into various states independent of each other but with certain cultural and linguistic affinities.[2] Also during this time of Philistine expansion, other peoples, including the Midianites, Ammonites, and Moabites, began to make their presence known, especially east of the Jordan. These have already been considered in relation to some of the judges of Israel. One other group, the Phoenicians, lived north of Carmel in strong, independent cities whose main interest was not in territorial expansion, at least in the Near East, but in maritime trade and colonizing. They achieved no prominence before the time of the Hebrew monarchy, but about that time they began to enlarge their horizons in many ways. Besides their skill in sailing and building, both of which are mentioned frequently in the Old Testament, they no doubt invented the first practical alphabet, the origins of which may come from as early as 1500 B.C. On the whole, Israel maintained peace with these northern neighbors, the kings of Tyre and Sidon especially being very friendly with David, Solomon, and Omri.[3]

The Assyrians, having overthrown the Hittites with Philistine help by 1200 B.C., went on to subjugate all the area around the northern Tigris and marched into Babylonia with great success. Until ca. 1100 under Tiglath-pileser I, Assyrian expansion was limited, but then it renewed with even greater intensity. But the Aramaean states were successful in preventing any Assyrian movement into Palestine for another two hundred years, thus permitting the united monarchy of Israel to enjoy security from that quarter. Into the seventh century, the Babylonians continued powerless in the wake of Assyrian conquest. This era from 1050–930 proved to be one in which the great nations exchanged power, the Egyptians, Mitanni, and Hittites having given way to the Sea Peoples, Aramaeans, and Assyrians. Taking full advantage of all this jousting for power, Israel under its kings reached unparalleled heights of strength, wealth, and security. The lesser nations, like the Edomites, Ammonites,

2. Merrill F. Unger, *Israel and the Aramaeans of Damascus* (Grand Rapids: Baker, 1980), 38–46.
3. H. Jacob Katzenstein, *The History of Tyre* (Jerusalem: Schocken, 1973), 77–166.

and Moabites, were brought under Israelite domination, friendly neighbors like the Phoenicians supplied badly needed skills and commodities, and even such enemies as the Philistines and Aramaeans were contained for the most part and eventually even conquered.

Saul (1 Samuel 8–31)

His Ascendancy (8–14)

When Samuel finally reached an advanced age and it appeared that his death was imminent, the elders of Israel approached him regarding a successor to take his place. His sons they ruled out, for unlike their father they were dishonest and greedy, but the people at least wished Samuel to appoint one who could assert the authority that had been his. This leader must be more than a judge, however; he must be a king like the kings of all the surrounding peoples. In distress Samuel turned to the Lord, who assured him that the nation had not rejected Samuel but had rejected him from ruling over them. He then instructed the prophet to permit a king but to carefully outline what results would accrue from such a decision. The new king would be autocratic and would reduce the young men and maidens of Israel to servitude to satisfy his own interests. In spite of the warnings, the people insisted on their way, so Samuel acted to find a likely candidate.

It must be categorically asserted that the idea of a king was not wrong, for provision for monarchy had been made in Deuteronomy 17:14–20, but the people's demand was premature. God had a king in mind, and had the nation but awaited his will, all would have turned out differently. But because they insisted on this hasty action, God allowed the people to have a king and selected the best possible person under the circumstances.

[handwritten margin note: Scary Personal Thoughts]

This was Saul, a native of Gibeah in Benjamin, a young man described as a physical giant who was choice and goodly (1 Sam. 9:2). While searching for some strayed asses that belonged to his father, he came to the city of Ramah, where the prophet Samuel made his home. The Lord had told Samuel that his candidate for king would appear in the city that day, and when Saul came to him to seek advice about the lost animals, Samuel immediately knew that this huge man was that choice. He entertained him at a religious festival that day, and on the following day he announced to him that God had selected him to rule Israel. Although the prophet followed this declaration by anointing Saul, the Benjamite argued that he was from the smallest of the tribes and was, therefore, an unlikely candidate. Samuel assured him that he would see certain signs by which God would manifest his favor, then requested him to meet him later at

Gilgal, where the man of God would offer sacrifices as a token of Saul's acceptance as king.

As Saul departed from Ramah, he met two men who informed him of the whereabouts of his asses. Next, he was confronted by three others headed for Bethel and carrying bread and wine. Finally he met a band of prophets coming down a hill, singing their prophetic messages. All these happenings transpired exactly as Samuel had said, and by this Saul knew that the prophet spoke truth. Furthermore, Saul proceeded to prophesy with the prophets; filled with the Spirit of God, he became another man. This need not mean that he was converted, for his later life seems to belie this; it means simply that the rude, unlettered country youth was now given the heart of a king and the wisdom requisite for the kingly office.[4]

It might be well to pause here briefly to discuss the prophetic institution.[5] The Old Testament shows that prophetism itself was very ancient, even Abraham being designated a prophet, but as an office its beginnings can be found no earlier than Samuel and probably under his guidance. In one sense, many godly persons in ancient times were prophets, because God spoke through them to their generations in the absence of any objective standard of truth. When the prophet Moses received the law at Sinai, however, there no longer was need for every individual to receive revelation, for final instruction had been given to all the nation in written form. As special needs arose in the future, though, God spoke to individuals from time to time, as in the time of the judges, but there was no organized prophetism of any kind. When Samuel was made a prophet in an age characterized by little revelation from God, he apparently went on to train others in the prophetic ministry. This is not to say that a prophet could be trained to prophesy, for most assuredly the prophetic ministry was the result of God's call and endowment, but once men were called of God they could be trained in certain prophetic functions and arts. The prophets whom Saul met coming down the hill were singing, for example, and Saul, filled with the Spirit, was enabled to join them (1 Sam. 10:9–12). The result of this unexpected behavior—unexpected because he had given no prior evidence of charismatic blessing—was that the people of the land asked whether Saul indeed was now one of the prophets.

There is little information about the ministry of these unnamed and relatively unimportant prophets, but one may suppose that they acted as correctives to abuses within both the priesthood and the monarchy. It is interesting that the spiritual nadir of the priesthood under Eli and his sons

4. C. F. Keil and Franz Delitzsch, *Biblical Commentary on the Old Testament: Samuel* (reprint ed.; Grand Rapids: Eerdmans, 1948), 100.

5. Willis J. Beecher, *The Prophets and the Promise* (Grand Rapids: Baker, 1963), esp. 21–172.

corresponds precisely with the rise of a strong prophetic movement. It is also coincident with the establishment of a monarchy, an office that could easily become secularized and would need continuous disciplining by prophetic spokesmen. Though the prophets are usually associated with prediction in the popular mind, it is clear that this was only one aspect of their ministry. Their principal task seemed to be to speak to their own day and to keep the theocracy in line as much as possible.[6]

After Samuel's death, there is little reference to the bands of the prophets until the time of Elijah and Elisha (ca. 875–800 B.C.), when they again appeared, but with the new designation *sons of the prophets*. It is safe to assume that the prophetic groups continued to exist after Samuel and until Elijah, but that without the dynamic leadership of such men they occupied a much less prominent place in national life.

Besides the common term *prophet* (*nābî'*), the names *seer* (*rō'eh* and *hōzeh*), *watchman, sentinel,* and many others also occur. The first of the terms is by far the most common, however. It basically means spokesman, both by etymology and by usage.[7] The classic biblical definition is found in Exodus 7:1 and 4:15–16, where Aaron is called the *nābî'* of Moses on the one hand, and the mouthpiece or spokesman on the other. In other words, the proper function of the *nābî'* was to speak on behalf of or for another person. This should be the task of the prophet of God, to speak for him to the people. The seer, moreover, was a prophet of God whose receptive ministry was stressed. That is, he saw revelation from God, whether with the eye in visions and dreams, by the ear in an audible voice, or by impressions of other kinds. It is obvious that a prophet could be both a *nābî'* and a seer; indeed, he had to be both, for he could hardly proclaim what he had not seen. Proof that both designations were applied to the same man may be seen in the case of Samuel (1 Sam. 3:20; 9:11).

Sometimes critics allege that the earlier prophets of Israel were nothing short of mad men who, in an ecstatic frame of mind, pronounced mere babblings incomprehensible even to themselves.[8] Such a view is based on the opinion that the Hebrew prophets were analogous to Canaanite and other Near Eastern prophets who did indeed act insane. But there is no way to support this contention, for nothing in or out of the Old Testament bears it out. Even when Saul hysterically "prophesied" (1 Sam. 18:10), all that is meant is that he acted like a prophet in the sense that

6. Ibid., 88–105.
7. Eugene H. Merrill, "Name Terms of the Old Testament Prophet of God," *Journal of the Evangelical Theological Society* 14 (1971): 240–42.
8. Theodore H. Robinson, *Prophecy and the Prophets* (London: Duckworth, 1950), 50.

he spoke things typical of a prophet, though in his case with no control over his message. Similarly, when Saul pursued David to Ramah later on, he was overwhelmed by the Spirit and began to "prophesy" (1 Sam. 19:23–24). This resulted in his lying prostrate on the ground day and night, making it possible for David to escape. But this should not suggest that prophesying and lying prostrate were one and the same or necessary to each other. The prophesying in this case, too, probably means nothing more than that Saul broke out into singing or speaking, perhaps in praise to God, but in this unusual circumstance such expostulations were beyond his control. To make the case of Saul, who was demented and irresponsible (see pp. 194–96), typical of the prophetic office is unfounded and unfair. Other examples commonly pointed out will be considered as they appear in the historical narrative.

The time came when Samuel gathered the people together at Mizpah to announce the new king publicly. But when Saul was introduced, he was nowhere to be found, for in his embarrassment and humility he had hidden among the goods of the people (1 Sam. 10:22). They shortly located him, and as he stood before them, the people were greatly impressed with their new leader in every way. He was physically imposing and had already demonstrated that he was Spirit-filled, yet he was very modest. Surely, from the human standpoint he was a logical choice for a hero who could deliver his people from the Philistine menace. Yet not everyone thought so, for certain renegades despised this great hulking fellow, perhaps because of his unassuming attitude, and refused to acknowledge him as their king. But Saul's graciousness appears in his refusal to be moved by their opposition; even when he later returned in glorious triumph from his first campaign, he granted them immunity from reprisal.

The new king was tested first against the Ammonites, who, following their king Nahash, surrounded the Gileadite city of Jabesh-gilead with the view of forcing it to capitulate. In desperation, the men of Jabesh-gilead begged the Ammonites to make a covenant with them, which they agreed to do, but only on condition that they thrust out their right eyes. In other words, they would make a league, but the terms of the arrangements would be so costly that the men of Jabesh-gilead would hardly be likely to comply. To this proposition the men of Jabesh-gilead answered that they would make such a league, and at such a price, but only if the Ammonites in turn would give them seven days' respite during which to try to get help from the Israelites. This strange request was granted, because the Ammonites knew that such help would be unlikely; furthermore, they would be much better off waiting for the city to surrender in seven days than undertaking a costly siege to starve it out.

When the appeal reached the ears of Saul, who was plowing in the fields near his primitive palace at Gibeah,[9] he rose up in fierce anger, seized the oxen with which he was tilling the ground, and slew them on the spot. He cut their bodies into twelve pieces, reminiscent of the Levite and his concubine (Judg. 19:27–30), and sent the pieces throughout the land with the warning that this would be done to any Israelite who refused to come to the aid of Jabesh-gilead. Israelites came eagerly from every part of the nation, the first real cooperative effort since the massacre of Benjamin, and completely overwhelmed the Ammonites. This successful effort by Saul was culminated by his official acceptance by the assembly at Gilgal.

While at Gilgal, and presumably in connection with the inauguration of the king, Samuel delivered his challenging discourse regarding the rejection of Yahweh in favor of an earthly king. He reminded the people of God's gracious dealings in the past and that without a human king they had done quite well. Nonetheless, he said, God would still be with them and their king if they both would abide by the law. To strengthen his admonition, Samuel called for divine sanction, a sanction that appeared in the form of tremendous thunder and rain (1 Sam. 12:17–18). This occurrence, in the midst of the summer when it almost never rains in that area, convinced the assembly that Samuel spoke the truth of God and that they could disobey only at the peril of their own lives.

After two years on the throne, Saul had his first engagement with the Philistines. He divided his small army, which was probably nothing more than his personal palace guard and militia, into two groups. One of these he himself commanded; the other he entrusted to his son Jonathan. At a given signal, the Israelites attacked a Philistine garrison at Geba, but the immensely superior numbers and armament of the Philistines repelled the attack, and Saul and his men fled for their lives to caves and other places of security across the Jordan. Saul remained in Gilgal, where he waited for Samuel according to an agreement made two years earlier. Realizing that the Philistines were about to destroy him, Saul knew that the only hope was in God. He therefore disregarded the command of the prophet to wait seven days until he could arrive and offer proper sacrifices, and proceeded to do so himself.[10] At precisely that moment Samuel appeared and, when he noted Saul's presumption, declared that Saul's reign would not be

9. This site has been excavated by W. F. Albright, who found it to be most rustic and primitive, just as the biblical evidence would suggest (1 Sam. 11:4–5). See a description in G. Ernest Wright, *Biblical Archaeology* (Philadelphia: Westminster, 1962), 122–24. See also Paul W. Lapp, "Tell el-Ful," *Biblical Archaeologist* 28 (1965): 2–10.

10. For the apparent chronological difficulty here, see Eugene H. Merrill, *Kingdom of Priests: A History of Old Testament Israel* (Grand Rapids: Baker, 1987), 202 n. 25.

hereditary because of his disobedience. Dejectedly, and yet with the buoyancy of spirit afforded by the presence of Samuel, Saul turned back to the west toward Michmash, where he drew up his lines of battle in preparation for the inevitable confrontation with the Philistines stationed there.

One of the most important advantages of the Philistines was their monopoly on the iron market of their day (13:19–22). Recent evidence indicates that they learned how to smelt iron and employ it for peacetime and military purposes from their close association with the Hittites, who apparently were the first to discover its secrets.[11] They recognized the value in maintaining the secret, and only by the payment of exorbitant rates could the Israelites purchase iron implements or have them sharpened by the Philistine smiths. In time of war, the Philistines would retain all iron for their own use, leaving other peoples with their weapons of bronze.

After a series of deft maneuvers, and against the superior weapons of the Philistines, Saul and Jonathan gained a significant victory at Michmash, one that seemed to avert the present threat of complete Philistine domination. But in the course of the battle Jonathan, ignorant of a decree his father had made that the army would fast until victory was won, took a bit of honey on the end of his staff to sustain himself. When the first phase of the encounter was over, the people seized the Philistine spoil of sheep, oxen, and calves, slaughtered them, and ate them with the blood. This infraction of the Mosaic law Saul tried to compensate for by building an altar at the scene of battle and offering a legal sacrifice. But when he shortly tried to ascertain the will of the Lord for the remainder of the engagement, the Lord did not answer him. This convinced Saul that someone in Israel had broken the fasting vow he had decreed, and he determined to kill the transgressor (14:39). Even when he knew that it was his son, he was adamant, and but for the intercession of the people he would have carried out his threat.

Saul's conquests are summarized at the end of chapter 14. He fought against the kings of all the surrounding nations, including Moab, Edom, Zobah (an Aramaean state), Philistia, and the Amalekites, evidently with some success. Yet there was war throughout his reign and into that of his successor, David. Only when Solomon ascended the throne was there a long period of real security and peace.

His Rejection (15)

The account of Saul's activities against the Amalekites is of special importance because of its relationship to his status as king. Since the time

11. W. F. Albright, *The Archaeology of Palestine*, rev. ed. (Baltimore: Penguin, 1971), 110.

the Amalekites had attacked Israel in the Sinai desert four hundred years earlier, God had resolved to destroy them (Exod. 17:14). Now, under Saul, the time had come. Samuel instructed the king to lead a force against Amalek down in the southern desert and to destroy its people completely, just as Jericho as an "accursed" city had been destroyed by Joshua. Saul complied, but when he returned he brought the king of Amalek back alive and some of the better animals as spoil. Samuel asked him why he had not obeyed God fully. After he unsuccessfully tried to blame his folly on the pressures of the people, who, he said, kept the animals against his better judgment, Saul finally admitted his guilt. In a remarkable statement, Samuel reproached Saul with the words that obedience is better than sacrifice, the alleged purpose for the animals (1 Sam. 15:22). He added that because Saul had rejected the word of the Lord, God had rejected him as king. This, coupled with the earlier declaration to the same effect, made final the impossibility of the house of Saul occupying the royal throne. Saul made at least a superficial protest of repentance, but apparently Samuel saw no genuine contrition, for after slaying the king of Amalek himself, he departed from Saul once and for all.

The critics usually feel that there was animosity between Samuel and Saul and that the crisis in kingship was as much a personality clash as anything else. True, there always seemed to be a conflict between them over something, but to ascribe petty feelings of vindictiveness to Samuel just because Saul had been made king over his objections is to belittle the great prophet. And when the entire "struggle-motif" is extended to include antagonism between the sympathizers with royalty and those with the pre-monarchial tribal federation, that criticism goes far beyond the evidence.[12] There is absolutely no proof that Samuel or anyone else was opposed to the principle of monarchy when the right man was on the throne. All the conflicts between Saul and Samuel came about because Saul as an individual refused to adhere to the clear precepts of the law. The only way one can possibly construe a fundamental antagonism between the early prophets and the monarchy is to believe either that the prophets were not familiar with the Deuteronomic law that made provision for a king, or that the Book of Deuteronomy was written much later, by an author of the seventh century. These options are equally impossible to substantiate. Samuel was not opposed to a king, as his subsequent anointing and support of David show beyond question, but he was, as a

12. Johannes Pedersen, *Israel, Its Life and Culture*, 4 vols. (London: Oxford University Press, 1926–40), 2:49ff.

true prophet, opposed to any violation of the will of God, whether by king or by peasant.

Saul and David (16–26)

With the utter rejection of Saul, the Lord spoke to Samuel about the appointment of a successor. The prophet was directed to the Judaean town of Bethlehem, where he was to offer a sacrifice at the home of Jesse. Following this, he asked for the sons of Jesse to pass before him, for one of them was to inherit the crown. When all had appeared and the divine will was still not revealed, Samuel asked if there were any other sons. Jesse responded that he had a young lad tending the family flocks. Samuel summoned him, and when he appeared the seer knew at once that the handsome young man was the future king. He took the anointing oil, poured it on David's head, and from that day the shepherd youth was filled with the Spirit of God.

Coincident with God's rejection of Saul and subsequent anointing of David, the Spirit left the king and an evil spirit began to trouble him incessantly. This evil spirit "from the Lord" was perhaps a demonic spirit of madness permitted by the Lord to have his way in Saul's life.[13] The only remedy for his fits of madness was soothing music, and for that purpose, David, who was skilled with the harp, was brought into the royal court at Gibeah. He not only had established a reputation for unusual musical skill but also, because he had slain wild animals barehandedly, was known even from his youth as a courageous hero. This so impressed the king, as did his pleasing demeanor, that Saul eventually made him his armor-bearer (16:19–23).

After some time David returned to Bethlehem for an indefinite period; in his absence, Saul experienced the most challenging threat of his career. The evenly matched Philistine and Israelite armies were lined up for battle on either side of the Elah Valley, southwest of Jerusalem. Rather than attack, it was decided by the Philistines, at least, to settle the matter through hand-to-hand combat by two representative heroes. Their challenger, a nine-foot giant named Goliath, stood in the valley cursing God and defying Israel to respond to his challenge. David came to the scene of battle in time to witness the Philistine's blasphemy against Yahweh; in anger he decided that if no other Israelite, including the king, thought enough of the national honor to meet the giant, he would do so. When he had finally convinced Saul to allow him to fight, he went forth with only

---

13. Walther Eichrodt, *Theology of the Old Testament*, 2 vols. (Philadelphia: Westminster, 1967), 2:55.

a sling and a few stones. With faith in his heart and a prayer on his lips to the God of Israel, he slung a stone and brought the giant hulk of a man crashing to the ground. Summarily, he decapitated the fallen hero and carried his head and sword back to the Israelite lines in triumph. In astonishment, Saul inquired who the father of this lad might be, for though he had known David in the past as his personal musician and armor-bearer, this feat of courage drew forth admiration for the father who could produce such a son.

David once again began to dwell in the palace at Gibeah, and in due time Saul's son Jonathan became his closest friend (18:1–4). David's estimation in the eyes of the people was so great that it was not long before the maidens would recite on the return of Israel from battle, "Saul has slain his thousands, and David his ten thousands" (18:7). At first this seemed to bother the king very little, but as it became more and more apparent that David was stealing the affection of the nation, Saul began to regard him with suspicion and eventual hatred. More than once in his demented state he tried to kill the young hero, but each time David eluded him. Finally Saul removed him from his position, but to no avail, for David's popularity increased despite all that Saul could do.

Saul at last hit on a way of putting David out of the way. He urged David to marry his daughter Merab, but when the wedding day came she was given to another. But a second daughter, Michal, loved David, and Saul decided he could use this situation to his advantage. He promised David her hand if he would go first and kill one hundred Philistines and bring him the proof that he had done so. In his zeal to please the king and to show his gratitude for the opportunity to marry into the royal family, David exceeded the demand and slew two hundred Philistines. Saul, who had hoped, of course, that David would perish in this unreasonable assignment, admitted defeat again and permitted the marriage. Having failed in all else, the king told his son and servants to take the necessary steps to assassinate David, but Jonathan not only was able to convince his father that this was a horrible wrong but also persuaded him to forgive David and reinstate him to his old position in the court (19:1–7).

Once again, however, Saul's wrath overcame him, and he struck out at David with his lance, narrowly missing him. David fled to his home in the city, bade farewell to Michal, who helped him escape, and set out for Samuel's home at Ramah, where he hoped for sanctuary. When Saul's henchmen reached David's residence, they found him gone, for, thanks to the clever ruse on the part of Michal, he had gotten a long head start on them. Saul immediately dispatched his servants to Ramah, suspecting that David might have gone to join his old enemy Samuel, but by the time they arrived there, the prophet and David had gone to Naioth, a place near or at Ramah associated with the schools of the prophets (19:18). Then the servants met a company of the prophets, over whom Samuel was head; beyond their own control, they began to prophesy with the prophets. This perhaps means that they were overcome by God's Spirit so that whereas they had come to apprehend David they now became his friends and aides. When Saul followed the matter up and came to Naioth, he too began to prophesy, much as he had at his first encounter with the prophets when he had become "another man." He became so over-whelmed by the divine presence and power that he fell on the ground and, with his outer garments cast aside, prophesied all day and night. This was so unusual an experience for Saul that witnesses asked the proverbial question once more, "Is Saul also among the prophets?" The purpose of the experience is clear: God had rendered Saul immobile in this fashion so that David could escape his evil designs and make his way to security in the wilderness far away.

On his way, David passed by Gibeah to confer with Jonathan, hoping desperately that he might find some way to make peace with Saul. Jonathan said he would try again to convince his father that David meant him no harm, then arranged to meet him in a field outside the city the next day to report the results. For fear of his father's knowledge of the tryst, Jonathan arranged to contact David through certain signals. He would take his bow and arrows and pretend to be practicing archery. If he shot an arrow and told the boy with him to go out beyond to bring it back, David, in hiding, would know that it was not safe to return to Gibeah. If Jonathan directed the lad to come in closer, David would know that all was well.

When Saul returned, he waited a day or two before inquiring about David; when he learned from his son that David had gone to Bethlehem without taking leave of him, the king became infuriated and vowed once more to kill David. Even Jonathan barely survived his father's temper tantrum. He returned with a heavy heart to the field to signal David that his efforts had failed. After one last farewell, they left each other, not to be reunited until their final encounter at Ziph (23:16–18). David first went down to Nob, where the tabernacle was, and, after begging the priest for some bread and the sword of Goliath, which was stored there, went on to the Philistine city of Gath. Presumably he went disguised, but never-theless this was a dangerous move, for this was the home of Goliath, whom he had recently slain. He was soon identified and reported to Achish, the Philistine lord. Only by pretending that he was mad was he able to escape and return into Israelite territory.

He next centered his activities in the Shephelah region of Judah, living in caves and wherever he could find shelter and hiding places. Before long he attracted a renegade band about him, men who were wanted by the law or who were just tired of the decadent society (22:1–2). His family evidently stayed with him for a time, but fearing Saul's retribution he sent them all to the land of Moab, the homeland of his great-grandmother Ruth (see Ruth 4:18–22). At the direction of the prophet Gad, he left the caves at Adullam and went farther into the Judaean wilderness to the forest of Hareth. Saul by now had learned of his whereabouts and recent activities from Doeg, an Edomite who had been at Nob when David had visited there earlier. Doeg informed Saul that the priest at Nob had assisted his enemy to escape, so Saul hastened to Nob and ruthlessly slaughtered all the priests there except Abiathar, who fled to David and became his personal chaplain. The extremes to which Saul's mental and spiritual condition had driven him became all too apparent in this bloody purge of the anointed priests of God.

David, meanwhile, had gone to Keilah to deliver the inhabitants of that unfortunate place from a Philistine attack. Such acts of deliverance naturally endeared David to the hearts of the Judaeans, so it is little wonder that they later made him their king so willingly. Saul also went to Keilah, but to seize David; only he was too late. David had gone to the wilderness of Ziph, where he met Jonathan and was encouraged by his continued friendship. Then he moved on to Maon and, passing on one side of a mountain while Saul passed on the other, managed to elude his pursuer once more. At that time an urgent notice came to Saul that the Philistines were attacking again, so he had to leave temporarily, a departure that afforded David some much needed rest.

David and his men found a new hiding place on the western shore of the Dead Sea at Engedi (1 Sam. 23:29). Saul, having returned from the latest Philistine campaign, soon learned of his whereabouts and followed him there. The area provided excellent protection for a fugitive because of the hundreds of caves in the steep hillsides, and in one of those David next encountered his tormentor. Saul had gone into a cave to rest, and by chance David was already inside. While Saul was deep within the grotto, David took the royal cloak that Saul left in the outer part of the cave and cut off its hem. Then, pressing close against the wall, David watched Saul pass by. As he did, David came close behind him and called out his name. Stunned, the king turned back, and before he could utter a word David related what he had done and hinted that he could as easily have taken the king's head as he had his garment. Chagrined, Saul could only confess his wickedness against his former friend and promise to discontinue his malice. Though Saul immediately returned home, David was not convinced of his sincerity and remained in his place of hiding.

Because David was a Judaean and believed he was suffering for a righteous cause, he felt that his fellow citizens should afford him some relief in his desperate plight. He therefore requested a farmer named Nabal to send him forthwith a plentiful supply of food and other provisions to sustain his band of men (25:8). Nabal flatly refused, whereupon David set out to take what he wanted by force and punish Nabal at the same time for his selfishness. Nabal's wife Abigail became aware of David's intentions and prepared the materials David had demanded. She met the outlaw on the road, offered him her goods, and begged him not to kill her husband, though, as she said, Nabal was nothing but a fool, as his name suggested (*nābāl* means "fool"). She had no sooner returned home than her husband died in a drunken stupor. David, whose heart had been won already by the beautiful Abigail, heard of Nabal's death and took the widow as his own wife. In addition, he married Ahinoam of Jezreel, having already wed Michal, daughter of Saul.

By now David had moved back to the wilderness of Ziph. Saul, who quickly forgot his pledge to leave David alone, went there after him. Exhausted from his swift pursuit, Saul went to sleep on the slopes of a steep valley while his chief captain, Abner, stood watch. After a time, even Abner could not stay awake, and the whole camp slumbered. With great daring, David and his right-hand man, Abishai, stole into Saul's camp, took the king's spear and water canteen, and silently made their way back across the gorge. Again David had had an opportunity to be rid of his adversary—indeed, it was all he could do to prevent Abishai from murdering Saul on the spot—but he could not help but realize that Saul, despite his wretchedness, was still the anointed king of Israel. Safely out of reach, David shouted across the ravine to Saul and Abner. He taunted the latter by asking him where he was when his master was robbed of his spear and canteen; had Saul not been so startled by the turn of events, Abner's own well-being might have been in jeopardy. Saul again begged David's forgiveness and seemed deeply repentant. But when David offered to return the king's spear, he indicated how much he trusted Saul's repentance by suggesting that someone from Saul's camp come to where he was to get it. Nevertheless, Saul returned to Gibeah once more and never again attempted to wreak vengeance on the unhappy David.

Saul's Last Days (27–31)

David felt that this latest withdrawal of Saul was only temporary and that eventually he would be caught. Throwing caution to the winds, he elected to go again to the Philistine Achish and volunteer his services to him. By now the Philistines had heard of the complete breach between David and Saul, so it is not especially surprising that Achish welcomed David. Any man who could slay such a warrior as Goliath would make a valuable ally. Achish, as the *seren* ("prince") of the region around Gath, held other towns within his jurisdiction, and one of these he selected as a dwelling place for his new friend. In keeping with what is now known about Philistine political organization, it seems likely that David was given the city of Ziklag as a feudal fief to administer in cooperation with Achish.[14] He would be responsible to support Achish in both peace and war and, in turn, could no doubt count on the assistance of the Philistines. From this base of operations David sallied forth from time to time to battle his enemies in the desert while Achish, oblivious to David's real objectives, esteemed his new Israelite ally most highly.

Back in the Valley of Jezreel, the forces of Saul were drawn up in preparation for battle with the Philistines. David himself was numbered among the enemy because of his Philistine associations and so found himself in a most compromising position. He could hardly refuse to fight for the Philistines, because he had pledged his support to Achish. Yet he knew he could never bring himself to draw sword against Saul and the Israelites, because his true sympathies were still with his people. Fortunately, he did not have to solve the dilemma, for the Philistine rulers, suspecting that David would prove disloyal in the heat of battle, discharged him and sent him back to Ziklag.

But Saul's predicament could not be solved so easily. He had attempted to ascertain the Lord's will and secure divine blessing in this important enterprise, but God would not reveal himself to the king. Nor could Saul refer to the priests, for he had had them slaughtered at Nob some time before. Even Samuel, the prophet on whom the king had leaned so heavily, was dead. The only recourse, then, was to enquire of an illegitimate prophet or seer, though Saul himself had decreed previously that such should be destroyed from the land. Finally he located a prophetess in a nearby village, the witch of Endor. Disguising himself as best he could, Saul visited the woman and asked her to bring up Samuel the prophet from the dead. The woman, fearful for the consequence of disobeying the edict concerning such matters, at first refused; but when Saul assured her that she need fear no harm, she conjured up the deceased Samuel. To her

14. Martin Noth, *The History of Israel* (New York: Harper, 1958), 180. For some interesting alternatives, see Hanna E. Kassis, "Gath and the Structure of the Philistine Society," *Journal of Biblical Literature* 84 (1965): 259–71.

utter amazement, the prophet appeared and predicted that Saul and his son would be with him the next day, for the Philistines would win the battle and slay the king and Jonathan (28:19).

A variety of opinions has been voiced regarding this transaction. Some say that the entire matter was an illusion,[15] others that Samuel appeared in the flesh,[16] and still others that the old woman merely deceived the king.[17] The most likely view is that Samuel did actually appear, for if the appearance was only a vision or trick of the woman, why was she so afraid when it occurred? There is every evidence that necromancers could and did speak to the dead, for there would be no prohibitions against such things otherwise, but whether this woman under her own power, or even with demonic power, could raise up a godly prophet against his wishes is debatable. It is obvious that God commanded Samuel to appear, even using the witch as a medium in this unusual circumstance, to give Saul a final revelation of his and his nation's destiny. One cannot learn much here about the Old Testament view of the condition of the dead except that the dead were thought of as being down in the earth (28:11). Apparently there was no distinction between the resting place of the righteous and that of the evil, for Samuel said that Saul and Jonathan would be with him, with him, that is, in death.

Saul, overcome by the import of the revelation, barely made it back to the battle lines. Meanwhile, David had made his way to Ziklag, where he found the city pillaged and the people, including his wives, carried off by Amalekites (30:1–2). After enquiring of the Lord, he set out for the Negev to rescue his loved ones and goods. Having marched rapidly from Jezreel to Ziklag, however, his little army was hardly able to continue to the Amalekite encampments. Some of the men dropped from sheer exhaustion, while the rest wearily followed their leader onward. They managed to surprise the enemy with the help of a guide whom they had met along the way, and, after a fierce encounter, dealt the Amalekites a stunning defeat, at the same time keeping all the captives alive. Upon their return they came to the famished troops they had left behind; after an argument concerning the division of the Amalekite spoil, David made a decree, from that day a custom of war, that those behind the lines or in

15. For a host of interpreters holding this position, see John Peter Lange, *Commentary on the Holy Scriptures: Samuel* (Grand Rapids: Zondervan, n.d.), 335.

16. Keil and Delitzsch, *Samuel*, 262. This means, of course, that it was really Samuel, though in a "spiritual body."

17. G. Henton Davies, Alan Richardson, and Charles L. Wallis, eds., *The Twentieth Century Bible Commentary* (New York: Harper and Brothers, 1955), 187.

reserve should share and share alike with those who actually participate in the fighting (30:24).

Back at Jezreel, the conflict had begun in earnest. Soundly defeated, the Israelites retreated, leaving their dead and wounded, including Saul and Jonathan, behind. Mortally stricken, Saul ordered his armor bearer to finish him off, but from dread of striking the Lord's anointed the faithful servant refused. At this, Saul took his own sword and, falling on it, quickly joined his dead son Jonathan and Samuel. The Philistines came on his body, gleefully decapitated it, and fastened it on the wall of Beth-shean. In a final gesture of homage and gratitude, however, the people of Jabesh-gilead, whom Saul had rescued from Ammon in his first act as king, came under cover of night, retrieved his body, and buried it in their own city, which was just across the Jordan in Gilead. A grateful people had remembered their king, though the king himself had fallen long since from the eminence that was his under the initial blessing of God.

The Reign of David (2 Samuel 1–1 Kings 2; 1 Chronicles 11–29)

Rule at Hebron (2 Samuel 1–4; 1 Chronicles 11:1–3)

David is by any standard one of the most striking figures of all history. Reared in the simple life of a Judaean village, he gave early evidence of unusual gifts. He was at once a warrior of courage and valor, a talented musician, and a man of letters who wrote the finest poetry of the Old Testament. Added to all this was the hand of God on his life, a divine infilling that made of David the first of the great kings of Israel at the same time that he was the last truly charismatic political figure after the order of the judges and Samuel. But perhaps his most outstanding characteristics were his patience and longsuffering in the face of undeserved persecution. Through no doing of his own he had been anointed by Samuel to be king long before Saul officially abdicated the throne, and through a series of reversals occasioned by Saul's bitter envy and hatred had spent many years of his life in hiding and loneliness. Yet, through all this he had constantly been serenely aware that he was in God's will and would be vindicated in God's own time.

Meanwhile, it is evident that David, consciously or not, had been slowly building up favor with his fellow citizens throughout the realm, especially in Judah. His early feats of prowess against the Philistines had made him an almost legendary figure; even his disputes with the popular King Saul must have been to many people a source of sympathy for David. Probably with the passing of time and through the advantage of his position as king, Saul was able to wean the people of the northern tribes, at least, away from his adversary, but the exploits David accomplished on behalf of Judah even while he was in flight from Saul succeeded in gaining the almost universal approval of the southern tribe. When the time came that he could rule, it was only a matter of formality for Judah to select him as their leader, even though the other tribes, because of their pro-Saul feeling, were a little slower in acknowledging him as sovereign.

Immediately after Saul's death at Gilboa, a runner came to David at Ziklag and gave him the sad news that both the king and his son were slain. The messenger, hoping to get a reward from David, told him that he had personally finished Saul off. But David, who had had many opportunities to do the same in the past but had refused to lift his hand against the Lord's anointed, ordered the lying messenger put to death for something he had only pretended to do. Then David burst out into one of the most heart-rending laments in the Bible, expressive at once of his great love for Saul and Jonathan and of his poetic genius (2 Sam. 1:19–27).

With no king at all in the land, the men of Judah at once took David to Hebron, the chief Judaean city, and made him king of their tribe. This was one of the first clear expressions of division in the kingdom since the time of the judges, and it bespoke greater division in the future. It was only with difficulty that either David or Solomon could keep the kingdom intact, and on the latter's death it became divided between south and north for the remainder of its history. In the north, while David was being anointed in Judah, Ish-bosheth,[18] a son of Saul, was proclaimed king. The capital was moved from Gibeah to Mahanaim of Gilead, perhaps because a great part of the northern tribes was in Philistine hands (2 Sam. 2:8–9).

From the start the real power in the northern tribes was in the possession of Abner, Saul's chief military officer, and he made every effort to both reunite the nation and procure more power for himself. He attempted to invade Judah, but David's troops, under Joab, met him at Gibeon; after a short skirmish involving the elite from either side, Abner was forced to retreat, the Judaeans in pursuit. Asahel, Joab's younger brother, singled out Abner as his victim, whereupon Abner, a seasoned veteran, turned on him and slew him. Joab never forgot this and, from that day forward, looked for an opportunity for revenge.

After this first clash, David grew stronger, while the northern tribes became weaker. During the seven years of his residence in Hebron,

18. The Book of Chronicles (1 Chron. 8:33) calls him Esh-baal ("Fire of Baal"), which indicates the pagan influences in Saul's own family.

David's family also began to grow. He had several wives by now, each of whom bore him many sons and daughters; when he later moved to Jerusalem other children, including Solomon, were born. But his first wife, Michal, was still not with him. One day, after a falling out with Ish-bosheth, Abner went to David to try to arrange peace between the two parts of the kingdom (2 Sam. 3:12). He promised to deliver Israel to David if David would make an alliance with him, but David insisted that no such league would be possible until Michal was brought to him at Hebron. Abner returned to get her, and the bargain was immediately consummated. When Joab, who had been off to war, learned that his arch-enemy Abner had been in Hebron and that David had entertained him there and bargained with him, he sent word to Abner that David wished to see him again. Abner returned to Hebron, where Joab met him and, feigning friendship, assassinated him. David reacted with great mourning for Abner, an act Joab could not comprehend and that created a rift between them.

Back in Mahanaim, the situation was ripe for revolution. Abner, the strength of the kingdom, was dead, and only the ineffective Ish-bosheth was in control. Hoping to take advantage of the situation for personal gain, two assassins murdered Ish-bosheth in his bed and immediately notified David that the throne in the north was now empty. Again David, unwilling to be advanced in such a bloody way, punished his would-be accomplices by cutting off their hands and feet and hanging them over the pool at Hebron. But the elders of Israel now knew that with Saul's house gone there was only one thing to be done—David must be king over the united nation. They came to Hebron and anointed him ruler over them as the tribe of Judah had done seven years earlier (2 Sam. 5:3).

David's Prosperity (2 Samuel 5–10; 1 Chronicles 11:4–19:19)

The first official matter was a delicate one, indeed. David had to locate the capital in a place suitable to all the citizens, especially when tribal feelings still ran so high. Hebron was not possible, because it was manifestly Judaean, a fact that the northern tribes would bitterly resent. Yet, he could not turn his back on his loyal countrymen in Judah, for they had stood by him when all else failed. The ideal location, naturally, would be in the center between the two. Such a place existed, Jerusalem, but it was still occupied by Jebusites, as it had been from ancient times. The only solution was a forcible takeover of the city, but this was no easy matter. The old Jebusite city was perched atop a steep, commanding hill surrounded on all but the north by almost perpendicular valleys, the Kidron to the east and southeast and the Hinnom to the west and southwest. In addition, the city was well fortified with massive walls, especially in the north, where it most lacked natural defenses. Moreover, there was an adequate water supply because of a tunnel leading from the city cistern to an underground spring in the Kidron Valley.[19] But this tunnel was to be the city's undoing. David, camped on a hill somewhere near the city, promised anyone who could get into the city through the tunnel a position of honor in the court. Joab did so and opened the gates from the inside, after which Jerusalem fell with little struggle (2 Sam. 5:6–8; 1 Chron. 11:4–6).

Now that he occupied the imposing city of Jerusalem, David's reputation began to cross international boundaries. Here was no ordinary tribal chieftain, but a full-fledged king who could match any in the surrounding nations. Hiram of Phoenicia, for example, later sent materials and men to build him a palace consonant with his new position of prestige (2 Sam. 5:11–12). But the Philistines recognized him in another sense. They saw the possibility of a crippling, if not fatal, blow to their ambitions to occupy all of Palestine. Most of the country was in their hands, thanks to their victory over Saul and Israel at Gilboa, but they had not reckoned on the meteoric rise of this former vassal of theirs from Judah. Now, before it was too late, they moved against David, even to the outskirts of Jerusalem in the Valley of Rephaim. More than equal to the challenge, and with the special promise of God, David moved forth against this foreign threat and thoroughly routed it (2 Sam. 5:25).

Once the solidarity of the kingdom was established within and without in a political sense, David realized that such solidarity could be maintained only by a strong moral and spiritual emphasis. The religious life of the nation had more or less fallen into desuetude since the destruction of Shiloh and the removal of the ark of the covenant from there to Philistia. Of course, the real core of Israel's faith had begun to deteriorate much earlier, even as early as the generation or so after Joshua. Now, however, even external religious trappings had disappeared from the national life. There had been efforts to restore worship at various sites like Gibeah and Nob, to be sure, but these were not wholly appropriate as far as the law was concerned, for the ark was not there. Even these places suffered under the hand of Saul, who not only purged the priesthood of Nob, as has been seen, but also tended toward religious syncretism, as evidenced by the names of some of his sons, like Esh-baal (1 Chron. 8:33).

19. For a description of the water shaft, see Kathleen M. Kenyon, *Jerusalem* (New York: McGraw-Hill, 1967), 22–23.

To rectify an obviously improper situation, David acted to bring the ark back into use from its resting place at Kirjath-jearim. He made no effort to relocate it at Shiloh, Shechem, or any other place made sacred by past associations, but determined to carry it to his political center, Jerusalem. This was not unlawful, as some have argued, for the law stated only that there should be a central place where the ark of the covenant could remain and where the principal festivals could be celebrated (Deut. 12:1–5). The selection of such a place was supposed to be in the will of God, and there is no evidence that David did not consult the Lord's will when he decided on Jerusalem. In addition, Jerusalem seemed to have some importance in the spiritual history of Israel, as attested by Abram's associations with it.

Perhaps through carelessness, or even ignorance, David set about getting the ark in the wrong way (2 Sam. 6:3–7; 1 Chron. 13:7–10). He had it placed on a cart for the journey from the house of Abinadab to his new tabernacle, which he had pitched in Jerusalem. Moses' law states quite clearly that the Levites were to carry the ark on staves on their shoulders, not on a cart or other vehicle (Exod. 25:14–15; Num. 4:5–8). When, therefore, David's servants were in the process of transporting it unlawfully, the ark began to slide off the cart in a rough place along the way. Uzzah, one of Abinadab's sons, reached out to steady the ark, an act of impiety that resulted in his death. This so terrified David that he left the ark at the house of one Obededom for three more months, and only then undertook to remove it, this time properly. Accompanied by appropriate sacrifices and ceremony, the sacred chest made its way up the mountains to the royal city. And when, with great pageantry and feeling, the Levites finally brought it within the walls, David was so overjoyed that he danced before the Lord with all his might. Michal, who had been watching from a palace window, ridiculed the happy king for shamelessly exposing himself before the peasantry. To David, this was the last barrier of many that had come between them throughout their tragic marriage, and he rebuked his wife by discontinuing any effort at normal relations with her the rest of her life (2 Sam. 6:23; 1 Chron. 15:29).

When complete security from outside interference had become a reality, David decided to house the ark in a far more impressive and durable setting than the tabernacle he had pitched on Mount Zion.[20] But Nathan the prophet, who seemed to be God's prophetic instrument in David's life, revealed to the king that God had not lived in a more substantial dwelling

20. The tabernacle of Moses had evidently been taken to Nob and later to Gibeon (2 Chron. 1:3). This tabernacle of David was only a temporary expediency.

in the past and was quite satisfied to continue to live among his people in a humble tabernacle. At least, Nathan pointed out, David was not the one to build a temple, for his function was war. Until the kingdom should be established even more firmly, no thought should be given to erecting a more permanent place of worship, though David could and did go ahead with the plans and collecting materials for a temple (1 Chron. 28). Nathan went on to outline what is known as the Davidic covenant, however, a covenant describing both the prospects of a temple to be built by David's son and successor and, even more importantly, the promise of an eternal kingdom over which David's descendants would reign (2 Sam. 7:12–16; 1 Chron. 17:11–14). It would culminate in the reign of the chief Son, the Lord Jesus Christ, who would reign forever (Isa. 9:1–7). This covenant was not in any sense a replacement of the earlier covenants, as though David dreamed it up for his own personal political advancement, but functioned as a continuation of God's great design to disclose himself progressively in salvation through Israel. At the same time, it is clear that this promise to David did eventuate in the founding of a royal family, a concept that originated only at this time in Israel's history. There had been abortive efforts in the past, such as Abimelech's attempt to succeed Gideon, his father, or Ish-bosheth's short-lived occupation of the throne of Saul, but only with David is there the beginning of true dynasticism.

The list of David's military accomplishments is most impressive. Before many years passed, and following his initial humbling of the Philistines at Rephaim, he overcame the Moabites, certain Aramaean states such as Zobah and Damascus,[21] and the Edomites east of the Dead Sea. This extended the borders of Israel from deep in the Negev in the south to the Euphrates River, with the exception of Phoenicia, with which he was allied, in the north. On the west he pushed as far as the Philistine pentapolis in the southern coast and all the way to the Mediterranean farther north, while to the east he occupied virtually everything as far as the Great Desert. Those lands that he did not actually possess were forced to pay heavy tribute, thus greatly enriching Israel's coffers and providing a standard of life she had never known before.

Encouraged by his great increase in material prosperity, David took steps to be as beneficent as possible to his friends, especially the survivors of Saul's family. One of the sons of Jonathan, a cripple named Mephi-bosheth, he took into the protection of the palace and sustained the remainder of his life as a token of his friendship for his dearest friend. In other ways David

21. For David's relationships with the Aramaeans, see Abraham Malamat, "The Kingdom of David and Solomon in Its Contact with Egypt and Aram Naharaim," *Biblical Archaeologist* 21 (1958): 96–102.

showed his great heart of compassion, though his treatment of enemies sometimes seems a little harsh even for holy war (2 Sam. 8:2).

The Ammonite wars seem to have given David the greatest difficulty of all as far as his international relations were concerned.[22] The Ammonites had been bitter enemies of Israel in Jephthah's time, but peace had at last been achieved between David and Nahash, king of Ammon. When Nahash died, David sent an envoy to bring solace and encouragement to Hanun, the crown prince and son of Nahash. Hanun misinterpreted David's intentions, however, and humiliated the Israelite embassage, thinking they had come to spy (2 Sam. 10:4; 1 Chron. 19:4). This provoked hostility between the two kingdoms, and when the Aramaeans joined the Ammonites against Israel matters only worsened. Joab managed to defeat the coalition, however, and the Aramaeans never again attempted to aid Ammon.

Most important in the long run were David's activities while Israel was in battle. According to custom, the king, if physically able, should be personally involved in military excursions. David, however, remained in Jerusalem for some reason, while Joab and the army sallied forth to Ammon to besiege the capital city, Rabbah (Rabbath-ammon). While at home he became infatuated with Bath-sheba, the wife of Uriah, one of his Hittite mercenary commanders, and committed adultery with her.[23] When she knew she was pregnant, David sent for Uriah and suggested that he go home to his wife for a few days on furlough. Too honorable a man to enjoy the pleasures of home while his men were on the front line, Uriah declined, remaining on the steps of David's palace for several nights. Thus, David could not attribute the conception of the child to Uriah. The only alternative was to remove Uriah so that Bath-sheba could be free to marry him. David therefore arranged for Uriah to carry a note back to Joab in which the king ordered his commander to place the unwitting Hittite on the front lines and then order a retreat without Uriah's knowledge. The dastardly command was carried out, and, with a man's blood on his hands, David took the widow to be his wife (2 Sam. 11:26–27).

David's Decline (2 Samuel 11–21; 1 Chronicles 20)

Naturally the whole sordid affair displeased the Lord, and he sent Nathan to David with a parable about a rich man who had stolen the lamb

22. On the Ammonite nation, see George Landes, "The Material Civilization of the Ammonites," *Biblical Archaeologist* 24 (1961): 68–86.

23. This great sin of David is not mentioned by the Chronicler, whose general tendency, under inspiration of course, was to minimize the sorrier aspects of David's life. For a discussion see Eugene H. Merrill, *1, 2 Chronicles*, Bible Study Commentary (Grand Rapids: Zondervan, Lamplighter Books, 1988), 13.

of his poor neighbor, though he had many to spare (2 Sam. 12:1–6). David was so incensed that he ordered the greedy man to pay the penalty, even with his life. When the prophet pointed out that the king himself was the culprit, the whole ugly truth reached David's heart for the first time. In abject contrition, he begged God's forgiveness for his heinous acts of murder and adultery, and though God did forgive, the illegitimate child died despite David's fervent prayer. Another child was born to the marriage later, however, and was named Solomon ("peace"), perhaps to indicate that peace had come again to the repentant king's heart and soul (12:24).

This seems to have been the turning point in David's life and, consequently, in the life of the nation. Up until then everything seemed to go well, but after this his personal and family life became a sequence of tragedies. First came the rape of David's daughter Tamar by her halfbrother Amnon (13:14). This brought on the revenge of her full brother, Absalom, who determined to punish Amnon with death. He arranged a festival two years later, to which Amnon was especially invited. When the unwary man arrived, Absalom's servants assassinated him, and Absalom himself fled to Geshur, the homeland of his mother. This internecine strife gave David such a heavy heart that he resolutely refused to allow Absalom to return home, even though he missed him sorely and may have seen some justification in what he had done. Finally, after three years, Joab, with great diplomacy, arranged for a reunion, but when Absalom returned to Jerusalem, David would not greet him. Two more years passed, unfortunate years for the stubborn king who, because of pride, refused to make peace with his son. Then the day came when Joab once again interceded, this time with success, and father and son reunited (14:33).

But Absalom's joy at reconciliation was only feigned. For five long years he had brooded over his father's rejection, a rejection he felt had been completely unwarranted under the circumstances. And he had had a long time to contemplate revenge for his father's callous treatment. Now that formal friendship had been achieved, he could enact the plot he had formulated. He began to frequent the main gate of the city, where he could contact hundreds of persons every day. They came there often to vent their grievances to the king, but the busy monarch had but little time for these comparatively petty matters. But Absalom, with sympathetic ear, listened to their complaints and subtly suggested that if only he were king they could get satisfaction. Gradually, he won the multitudes over (15:6); only when it was too late did David sense what was afoot. Gathering his faithful entourage, the king fled his own palace and city, abandoning them to his traitorous son. Some of his friends he left behind to serve as spies and saboteurs, including his priest Abiathar, another priest, Zadok, their two sons, and an old wise man, Hushai. David instructed Hushai to give misleading counsel to young Absalom so that David's escape and future return could be more assured.

The king and his loyal subjects crossed the Mount of Olives to the Jericho road and went on to the other side of the Jordan, where they mustered what troops they had. Back in Jerusalem, Absalom was in firm control and proceeded to demonstrate that he was in the shoes of his father by taking his father's concubines for himself (16:22). Meanwhile, Hushai had gained the prince's confidence and made every effort to use his office as counselor to David's advantage. Ahithophel, the official court sage, advised Absalom to go immediately in pursuit of David, lest David attempt to retake the throne. But Hushai countered that if Absalom attempted to fight David before he had secured his position as king a little more firmly, David, the more seasoned warrior, would surely prevail. This worked out to David's favor, giving him time to consolidate his forces and obtain the help of friendly Ammonites and others. When Ahithophel saw that his counsel was rejected, he hanged himself. Absalom bided his time and, when he thought all was ready, headed for Transjordan with his army under the command of Amasa.

A fierce battle ensued in the Forest of Ephraim, near the Jordan, and David's more experienced band of heroes held the day. Absalom himself caught his head in the boughs of a huge oak and, while suspended in the air, was thrust through the heart with darts hurled by Joab (18:14). Runners were dispatched to inform David of the victory, but the glad news was more than offset by his knowledge of Absalom's cruel death. With bitter tears he bemoaned his son's terrible end, though Absalom had given him so much grief. Joab, disgusted by his show of emotion, reproached David, reminding him that time after time he had mourned for his enemies when he should have rejoiced at their defeat and death. First it was Saul, then Abner, then Ish-bosheth, and now his own iniquitous son. If David possessed one overriding fault, in Joab's sight it was an irresponsible love for all men, including his enemies (19:6). That fault engendered ill feeling between the two that was to bear fruit in a complete breach.

David resented Joab's presumption and, on his return to Jerusalem, appointed Amasa, Absalom's general, commander in Joab's place. Everyone else he graciously forgave, even those who had been most instrumental in the coup that had sent him in ignominy from Jerusalem in the first place. But this forgiving spirit did not ingratiate the king with his people. There had always been a certain animosity against David because of Saul's great popularity, especially among the northern tribes, and Absalom had managed to capture the people's fancy as not even David had been able. No wonder, then, that when David returned to his capital, led primarily by men of his own tribe of Judah, seeds of fresh rebellion began to sprout. This time the usurper was Sheba, a Benjamite, who announced that the northern tribes had no real share in the king because of his obvious favoritism toward the Judaeans (20:1). David thereupon ordered Amasa to take whatever troops necessary to squelch this newest revolution and show the nation that he was still in control. On the way to battle, Joab called Amasa aside as though to confer with him, and instead stabbed him to death. Commander once more, Joab led the king's army north to Abel, in the northern part of Naphtali, where he located Sheba and his band in the shelter of the city walls. When he threatened to burn the city down with all its inhabitants, a wise old woman demanded the reason for the attack. Joab told her they were after only Sheba. Soon Sheba's head came over the wall as the price of the city's security (20:22).

These political emergencies in the realm were followed by agricultural calamities occasioned by a three-year drought. In reply to David's query concerning the reason for this judgment, the Lord informed David that Saul's family had mistreated the Gibeonites by breaking the ancient treaty made by Joshua (Josh. 9:15) and that the famine was punishment for this. So David asked the Gibeonites what they wished, but he was totally unprepared for their answer: Saul's remaining sons must be hanged. The king faced a serious dilemma. He must grant the Gibeonites their request, but he must try to preserve the family of Saul as much as possible. A compromise was reached in which seven of the sons were delivered to the Gibeonites, but Mephi-bosheth, son of Jonathan, was saved in Jonathan's memory. Then, as a sort of compensation, David sent for the bones of Saul and Jonathan, which still remained in Jabesh-gilead, and had them properly interred at Gibeah, Saul's royal city and real home.

David's Final Years (2 Samuel 22–1 Kings 2; 1 Chronicles 21–29)

One other impropriety recorded in 2 Samuel was David's census of the army. This book says that "he" moved David to number the people (2 Sam. 24:1), the antecedent to the pronoun apparently being the Lord, but Chronicles states that Satan tempted David to this sin (1 Chron. 21:1). No doubt "he" in 2 Samuel refers to the Lord, but only as the Lord used Satan, a fact that becomes clear in light of the well-established biblical truth that God himself does not entice men to commit evil. In any event, counting the army seems to suggest a reliance on the flesh rather than on the spiritual resources of God, and such lack of confidence in God must be punished. In due time David recognized the sin of pride that prompted the enumeration, but already Gad the prophet had come announcing divine judgment. This time David had the choice of seven years' famine, three months' flight from his enemies, or three days' plague. Fearing to fall into the hands of men, he rejected the second alternative and cast himself on the mercy of God to suffer what he must. A great epidemic broke out and took seventy thousand lives. In deepest repentance, David prayed for the Lord's grace and, under Gad's instruction, built an altar at the threshing floor of Araunah, on the site of ancient Mount Moriah, where he interceded by sacrifice before the Lord (2 Sam. 24:25). God heard and the pestilence ceased. Later Solomon chose this very spot, just north of the old Jebusite city of Jerusalem, as the site for his magnificent temple, and incorporated it within the city walls.

David's latter years were spent in comparative peace, at least as far as international affairs were concerned. The problems within his family precipitated by his adulterous affair with Bath-sheba continued to rise, however, and his dying days witnessed a struggle for the throne among his own sons. Adonijah, whom he had spoiled with fatherly attention, waited until his father was too senile to interfere and then persuaded Abiathar, David's longtime priest and friend, and Joab, the hero of many a military campaign, to side with him in an effort to take the throne on David's decease. Properly, though, the kingdom should have gone to Solomon by virtue of the divine promise (1 Chron. 22:9–10), so Nathan the prophet, Zadok the priest, and certain other notables aligned themselves with Solomon in opposition to Adonijah.

Nathan encouraged Bath-sheba, mother of Solomon, to go to the king and inform him that Adonijah was conniving against her son, the legitimate successor to the crown. While she was presenting her case, Nathan came into the royal chamber and seconded what Bath-sheba had said. The old monarch ordered Nathan and Zadok to anoint Solomon king without delay. The ceremony took place promptly, accompanied with such shouting of "God save the king!" that the whole city rang with the echo. Adonijah, in another part of the city, heard the commotion, and when Abiathar's son informed him that Solomon had taken the throne at his father's instigation, he fled for his life to the security of the great altar of the tabernacle. For a time no retributive action was taken by either David or Solomon, but when the final moment of the king's life came, he solemnly charged Solomon to punish the revolutionaries. Then the great man, seventy years old, slept with his fathers, resting at last from a lifetime of exacting labor and strife (ca. 971 B.C.).

Solomon quickly established his position with ruthlessness and utmost efficiency (1 Kings 2:12). His half-brother Adonijah foolishly asked for his late father's concubine, an acquisition calculated eventually to give him royal status, but Solomon wisely saw the implications. With unleashed vengeance he ordered his strong man, Benaiah, to murder Adonijah and thus remove any possible threat from that quarter (1 Kings 2:25). Next, the new king commanded Abiathar to leave Jerusalem and to surrender his priestly office, the only reason for his salvation being his holy position. Joab was then considered and, catching wind of a threat to his life, fled to the horns of the altar, but to no avail. Benaiah caught him there and, after dragging him from the holy precincts, summarily stabbed him to death. Finally, Shimei, a man who had mocked David when the unfortunate king had been run out of the capital by Absalom (2 Sam. 16:5–7), was warned by Solomon that if he ever attempted to leave the city, he too would die. Heedless of the warning, he left and, on his return, fell victim to the purge that had already taken a horrendous toll.

The Reign of Solomon (1 Kings 3–11; 2 Chronicles 19)

Solomon's Wisdom (1 Kings 3–4; 2 Chronicles 1:1–12)

It is almost impossible to describe the dramatic and far-reaching changes that occurred in David's forty-year reign over Israel. From a badly divided or at best loosely federated group of distantly spread tribes, the nation had become united, powerful, and comparatively very wealthy. Whereas the kingdom had been ruled by a man who was not much more than a powerful tribal chieftain in a crude palace located in an insignificant Benjamite city, a king in the real sense of the term now occupied the throne. Not only the tribes but surrounding kingdoms had been either welded together formally into the Davidic sphere of influence or at least reduced to the status of tributaries. The kingdom of Israel had become a power to be reckoned with, even rivaling, perhaps, the world's leading states. With its strategic location in the Fertile Crescent, the nation stood to wield considerable influence in all directions and to extract revenues from trading peoples who must pass through it. In addition, under David there appeared to develop genuine signs of spiritual renewal, if the monarchy itself is any gauge, for the great religious poetry of Israel's history was written then and in the succeeding generation (2 Sam. 22; 23:1–7; 1 Chron. 23–29). Moreover, there is almost no mention of idolatrous practices in Israel, so one may conclude that the pious king had pretty well purged such things from the realm. Now that he was dead, and his erstwhile enemies had also perished at the hand of his son, there can be little doubt as to the significance of the statement that "the kingdom was established in the hand of Solomon" (1 Kings 2:46).

Some idea of the new importance of the nation Israel might be seen in the fact that Solomon appeared almost on equal terms with Pharaoh of Egypt. At least, he married Pharaoh's daughter, an accomplishment almost without parallel, for Egyptian princesses were reserved for Egyptian royalty.[24] But that honor planted the seeds of the nation's demise, for the record states that a quasi-legal religious practice was being carried on outside of Jerusalem at various "high places" (*bāmôt*), probably to accommodate Solomon's heathen wives. Such shrines were located on the summits of hills, perhaps to indicate a closer relationship to God. In any event, the king himself frequented these places of worship, especially resorting to the great Bamah at Gibeon (1 Kings 3:4; 2 Chron. 1:3).[25] There the Lord approached him very early in his reign and offered him whatever gift he might choose. With unusual discernment, the young ruler acknowledged his immaturity and inabilities and requested above all else wisdom to govern his great nation. The Lord not only graciously bestowed this but also, because of Solomon's selflessness, promised him great wealth and honor among men. The new wisdom was quickly put to the test in Solomon's extraordinary judgment regarding two harlots and their babies, a story celebrated for its simple logic and fairness. Like wildfire the king's wisdom spread far and wide and became proverbial, so much so that people came from around the eastern world to catch his words.

His astuteness may be seen also in his political organization of the kingdom. He appointed certain court officials, perhaps after Egyptian models,[26] and also divided the kingdom into twelve administrative districts over which he placed officers. He did not follow the ancient tribal boundaries, thus preventing too much nationalism among the tribes, but he was conscious that he must retain the twelvefold division lest he entirely reject tradition. These districts were responsible for supplying a certain amount of provision to the court every month, a considerable task, and they no doubt also supplied manpower for public works as well as for war.[27]

24. John Bright, *A History of Israel*, 3d ed. (Philadelphia: Westminster, 1981), 212.

25. It seems that Moses' tabernacle was at Gibeon (2 Chron. 1:3) while the ark was in Jerusalem in the tent David had built there on Mount Zion (2 Chron. 1:4; cf. 2 Sam. 6:17). This suggests that the high place at Gibeon was not considered illegitimate as a place of the worship of Yahweh. If it were, Yahweh surely would not have revealed himself to Solomon there.

26. Wright, *Biblical Archaeology*, 70–72.

27. Martin Noth, *The Old Testament World* (Philadelphia: Fortress, 1966), 96–97; I. Mendelsohn, "On Corvée Labor in Ancient Canaan and Israel," *Bulletin of the American Schools of Oriental Research* 167 (1962): 31–35.

Solomon's Building (1 Kings 5–8; 2 Chronicles 2–7)

Solomon is not known primarily as a man of war; indeed, there is no record of conflict until the end of his reign. His fame lay in his literary and building accomplishments. The former will be addressed elsewhere, but the latter should receive some attention here. When Hiram, the friend of his father and king of Phoenicia, learned of David's death, he immediately offered his services to Solomon in any way he could use them (1 Kings 5:1). For this Solomon was grateful, for he had long since been commissioned by his father to build the temple in accordance with the Davidic covenant. Moreover, he had certain other projects in mind that he could accomplish only with the skills for which the Phoenicians were renowned.

In return for a certain quantity of wheat and oil year by year, Hiram would supply cedar and fir from Lebanon as well as skilled craftsmen. Solomon would also use labor from his own country, as many as 150,000 men under conscription, who would serve as hewers of timber, porters, and stone masons. When all arrangements had been made, the work commenced in Solomon's fourth year (ca. 966 B.C.), which, as previously noted, was the 480th year since the exodus. The temple, fashioned after the general pattern of the tabernacle of Moses but much larger, was ninety feet long, thirty feet wide, and forty-five feet high. On the front was a porch, and in front of that were two free-standing pillars named Boaz ("strength") and Jachin ("uprightness"). Along the two sides and the back were chambers and storage rooms. The interior was lined with richly decorated boards and beams of cedar. Within and without were lavish carvings and other decorative motifs that combined to make the temple one of the finest buildings in history. The seven-year period involved in its construction suggests something of the magnificence of the edifice.

Also in the temple area, located on Mount Moriah just north of the old Jebusite city, were several other great buildings, including the House of the Forest of Lebanon, the Judgment Hall, a Porch of Pillars, a palace for Pharaoh's daughter, and Solomon's own opulent palace. The fancy work in all these projects was under the execution of another Hiram (1 Kings 7:13), a native of Naphtali, whose gifts are reminiscent of those of Bezalel and Aholiab. The general construction was undoubtedly under Phoenician direction, for besides being great shipbuilders they also distinguished themselves for their work in stone, as is clear from many of their temples that have been excavated recently. To suggest that Solomon's buildings, especially the temple, were influenced to any great degree by Phoenician Baal temples, seems unwarranted, however.[28] We may say that there were certain common fea-

28. Contra Donald B. Harden, *The Phoenicians*, 2d ed. (New York: Praeger, 1962), 91.

tures among Near Eastern temples in general and that Solomon's temple adopted some of these within the framework of the earlier tabernacle arrangement, but even at this point we must use care, for anything that would detract from the originality of Israel's faith, even as expressed in the architecture of its temples, is risky.[29] Though there is no record of direct revelation to Solomon in building this place of worship (cf. 2 Chron. 3:3), his gift of wisdom obviously included knowledge of such matters.[30]

When the temple was finished, a tremendous ceremony of dedication was carried out. The ark was carried from its resting place at Mount Zion and placed with greatest reverence in the Oracle (Holy of Holies) of the new structure on Mount Moriah (2 Chron. 5:7). At that moment the glory of God filled the temple, as it had the tabernacle in days past, and the nation knew that God was at last pleased to dwell in this new, more permanent residence among them. Following this demonstration of God's presence, Solomon offered the longest prayer recorded in the Bible, a prayer laden with recognition of God's grace, Israel's responsibility, and the importance of the ancient covenant relationships between them. Nowhere else are found such clear statements concerning the transcendence of God, and yet such realization that he dwells among and within his faithful people. Solomon prayed urgently that if the nation ever sinned so grievously that it must be exiled from the land, it might repent and graciously be allowed to return, to the glory of God. After the prayer, the ready dedication of the people was expressed by an offering of the greatest magnitude in man's memory—22,000 oxen and 120,000 sheep.

Solomon's Covenant (1 Kings 9:1–9; 2 Chronicles 7:12–22)

Some time later, the Lord appeared to Solomon again as he had at Gibeon and reviewed with him the glorious covenant promises he had spelled out to David (1 Kings 9:1–9). He assured the king that as long as he faithfully executed his royal function in uprightness and obedience he would reign forever through his posterity. Should he deviate from this holy calling, however, his family and nation would be cast aside, at least for a season, and all the world would know that unfaithful Israel was the object of God's displeasure.

Solomon's Glory (1 Kings 9:10–10:29; 2 Chronicles 8–9)

The last years of Solomon's life, like those of David, were filled with a mixture of joy and sorrow, triumph and defeat, but for different reasons.

29. Merrill F. Unger, *Archaeology and the Old Testament* (Grand Rapids: Zondervan, 1954), 232.

30. It is clear, however, that David had been given heavenly plans and specifications for the temple and that he had handed these on to Solomon (see 1 Chron. 28:11–19).

His extensive building programs had oppressed the people with heavy taxation and hard physical labor that he extracted in lieu of taxes.[31] Some of
his friendly neighbors, notably Hiram of Phoenicia, became dissatisfied
with Solomon's business dealings with them. Hiram objected that
Solomon had not lived up to his agreements in that he had given him
poor villages in Galilee as compensation rather than the more munificent
payment he expected. To offset this, Solomon had to increase the burden
on his already overladen people. But he partially relieved their situation
by fitting out a navy under Phoenician direction, and these ships he sent
from his Red Sea port to lands throughout the known world. The ships
returned bearing all manner of exotic goods that Solomon presumably
sold, in some cases at a very handsome profit.[32]

His rapidly accumulating prestige and wealth were soon noticed by
even distant rulers. Some therefore began to travel to the court of
Solomon to feast their eyes on what he had done and to hear from his
own lips the words of wisdom for which he was even more celebrated.
Among these royal figures was the queen of Sheba, a fabulously wealthy
land in the southern tip of the Arabian Peninsula, which to this day is a
primary source of rich spices.[33] She came skeptically to test the king of
Israel with difficult questions, but she left convinced that the half had
never been told her of this amazing man. His buildings, his use of pure
gold for even common vessels, and his throne of ivory were her envy and
the envy of all the world.

Solomon's Sin and Death (1 Kings 11)

But his material prosperity was more than offset by his moral poverty
expressed in his love for many women. He took wives from many foreign
nations, including those with whom intermarriage was specifically forbidden
in the law, and this brought about the result anticipated in the law:
Solomon's heart was turned from God to the gods of these nations. This
need not imply that he forsook Yahweh entirely, for the text is clear that he
did not, but he probably instituted a rather syncretistic religion consisting of
elements from many different ones (1 Kings 11:4–8). The record states that
he built chapels for his wives in which they could worship their native
deities, and he may have associated with them there in their worship rituals.

31. For his extensive fortifications (1 Kings 9:15) and other building activity outside Jerusalem, see
Yigael Yadin, "New Light on Solomon's Megiddo," *Biblical Archaeologist* 23 (1960): 1–12; Nelson
Glueck, "Ezion-geber," *Biblical Archaeologist* 28 (1965): 70–87.
32. Cyrus Gordon, *The Ancient Near East*, 3d ed. (New York: Norton, 1965), 186–87; for the
explanation of Solomon's trade in horses (1 Kings 10:28–29), see Noth, *The Old Testament World*, 260.
33. Gus W. Van Beek, "Frankincense and Myrrh," *Biblical Archaeologist* 23 (1960): 69–95.

The result was as God had warned. The kingdom was to be wrested from Solomon's grasp, yet, for his father David's sake, not entirely. Only the tribe of Judah would be retained by the Davidic line (1 Kings 11:13). Revolution broke out soon in various parts of the empire. Hadad, an Edomite prince exiled to Egypt under David but now returned, broke away in the southeast (11:14). Then Rezon took over Damascus and from there revolted from Israel and reigned over all the Aramaean states (11:23). Even Solomon's own trusted servant Jeroboam, officer over the central part of the nation, declared his independence of the king. In this he was encouraged by the prophet Ahijah of Shiloh, who met him one day in a field and seized and tore his garment into a dozen pieces, explaining that the pieces symbolized the tribes. Ten of these he returned to Jeroboam, indicating that he would rule ten tribes, but two the prophet retained. One piece represented Judah, of course, and the other, as it turned out, stood for Benjamin, the tribe that eventually sided with its southern neighbor (11:26–36). This was only fitting, because Jerusalem, the city of David, by now had been incorporated into the area of Benjamin. After Solomon knew of the encounter between Ahijah and Jeroboam, he attempted to arrest the latter, but Jeroboam fled to Egypt, where he bided his time until opportunity came. It came quickly, for soon Solomon died, having completed an illustrious reign of forty years, but a reign that ended in dismal prospects for the future.

Hebrew Poetry

The most appropriate time and place to discuss the poetic sections of the Old Testament is in connection with the united monarchy, especially in the reigns of David and Solomon, for it was then that such literature reached its peak in finesse and abundance. Of all the books considered poetry by the Jews in ancient arrangements of the canon, Job, Psalms, and Proverbs, the greater part no doubt was written by either David or Solomon personally or by scribes in their courts. Certainly some of this is not poetry in the sense in which many modern westerners define the term, for it covered a much broader area then than is usual now. But if one means by it literature that cannot properly be called history or law or prophecy and that possesses certain formal literary characteristics, then the designation may be employed for lack of a better term. As suggested, the Hebrews designated one section of the canon "Writings," but even that is not entirely satisfactory as a description of poetry, for it includes materials like Chronicles and Ezra-Nehemiah, which can hardly be considered poetic at all.

Before discussing these three books of poetry, it may be helpful to examine Hebrew poetry as a whole to detect its outstanding genres and characteristics.[34] It places virtually no emphasis on rhyme and very little on meter compared with the poetry of other languages. The principal feature is parallelism, the idea that the second or following lines of a strophe somehow parallel the thought of the first. There are several kinds of parallelism, including synonymous, in which almost identical thoughts are expressed in both lines of a couplet (Ps. 49:1); antithetic, in which the second line contrasts with the first (Prov. 15:1); synthetic, in which the second line completes the thought of the first (Prov. 4:23); climactic, in which the lines proceed step-by-step to a climax in thought (Ps. 103:1); comparative, in which the second line forms a simile of the first (Ps. 103:12); and progressive, in which a new and related thought is introduced in the second line (Job 3:17). Almost without exception the poetic portions of the Old Testament, whether in the books listed or even in the historical and prophetic books, are represented by one of the foregoing types of parallelism.

The kinds of poetry are lyric, to be sung, found most commonly in the Psalms; didactic, or teaching literature, represented by Proverbs and Ecclesiastes; prophetic, found in lengthy sections of most of the prophetic books, notably Isaiah; elegiac, meant to convey grief and mourning, seen in the Lamentations of Jeremiah; and dramatic, meant to be acted, and expressed by Job and the Song of Solomon. All of these express the heartfelt feelings of their composers toward their fellowmen and especially toward God, whereas other kinds of scriptural literature reflect the attitude of God and his feelings toward men. It is unwarranted to make a hard and fast rule along this line, but in general this criterion can stand. It is furthermore essential to maintain that these books or portions, though they are human expressions, are at the same time the inspired Word of God. In some cases, especially in Job and Ecclesiastes, inspiration entails only the faithful, inerrant recording of what the poet said or wrote, but in other cases there is actual revelation from God to men through the poet. For example, the psalms that prophesy messianic activity cannot be merely the reasoning or reflection of a man about these things, no matter how godly he might be, but must be understood as a revelation somehow expressed by the poet in his voluntary utterances.[35]

34. G. B. Gray, *Forms of Hebrew Poetry, Considered with Special Reference to the Criticism and Interpretation of the Old Testament* (London: Hodder and Stoughton, 1915); M. O'Connor, *Hebrew Verse Structure* (Winona Lake, Ind.: Eisenbrauns, 1980), 29–166.

35. Franz Delitzsch, *Biblical Commentary on the Old Testament: Psalms*, vol. 1 (reprint ed.; Grand Rapids: Eerdmans, 1948), 64–71.

The Book of Job

Job undoubtedly was a historical figure (Ezek. 14:14; James 5:11), but there is no way to ascertain when or even where he lived except to say that it was probably in the desert east of Canaan during the patriarchal period. Most conservative scholars feel, however, that the book was not written that early, but probably comes from the time of Solomon.[36] Liberals for the most part assign it to a much later time, some even dating it in postexilic times.[37] The author is unnamed and thus unknown, but whoever wrote it has been considered one of the most gifted dramatists in the history of literature. His purpose was not, as some feel, to illustrate the patience of a godly man, though that surely is involved, but to attempt to answer the age-old problem of theodicy: why do the righteous suffer if there is a God of mercy and love? Or it might even be to teach that one must acknowledge the sovereignty of God, no matter what the circumstance, and that one's real problem might be the pride of one's own righteousness.

The drama begins with a prologue (Job 1–2) in which Job is singled out by God as an exemplary man whom not even Satan could defeat. Satan is allowed to do what he will to Job, except take his life, and he proceeds to subject Job to the greatest loss and punishment imaginable, but the patriarch stoutly maintains his faith in God. Then follows a series of speeches by three "comforters" who come to Job and try to account for his miserable condition (3–31). There are three cycles of dialogue in this series (chapters 3–14, 15–21, and 22–31), in each of which each friend speaks in turn and each time is answered by Job, who tries to defend his integrity. The main argument they advance is that Job must have sinned, either consciously or not, for otherwise he would not suffer as he did (8:3–6). But Job says he is innocent of any wrongdoing and is at a loss to explain his misfortune. A fifth figure, Elihu, then comes into the story, and his speeches appear next (32–37). He takes issue with the three preceding counselors, whom he considers ignorant (32:3), and then attempts to convince Job through a slightly different line of argument that he is somehow to blame. He especially emphasizes the instruction afforded by suffering (33:29–30), God's justice in all things (34:10–20), and the divine transcendence compared with Job's ignorance and limitations (35:5–6).

Through all this Job clings to his hope in God, but he eventually begins to question God on this basic issue: why should he, a righteous man, be afflicted (Job 31)? Yet, Job does not turn his back on God. Finally, God

36. Edward J. Young, *An Introduction to the Old Testament*, rev. ed. (Grand Rapids: Eerdmans, 1964), 340.
37. W. Baumgartner, "The Wisdom Literature," in *The Old Testament and Modern Study: A Generation of Discovery and Research*, ed. H. H. Rowley (Oxford: Clarendon, 1951), 219.

breaks his silence and explains that the gulf that separates Deity and humanity is so great that Job not only should not question his suffering but also should not even try to understand it (40:2). Some things are limited to God, and in these areas man is to be silent and let God work out his own wondrous will. In the epilogue (42:7–17), God restores Job, gives him even greater blessings than he had known before, and makes of him the intercessor necessary for the salvation of his recent critics. The story ends with the basic question unanswered, yet the message of God that he is absolute and does as he will without regard to man's comprehension of his mysteries must constitute the real theme and provide the fullest measure of hope.[38]

The Book of Psalms   (6 possible Authors)

The psalms constitute the hymn book of Israel. Many psalms were sung and recited on festal occasions and probably even in homes and at work. Approximately half of the 150 were written by David, who, it is evident, had great artistic abilities (1 Chron. 13:8); a few were by Solomon, whose reputation also is well established in these pursuits (1 Kings 4:29–34); by Asaph, one of David's court poets; and by the sons of Korah, another group of professional writers; and one was even written by Moses (Ps. 90). In addition, many are of anonymous authorship and were written over many years, some certainly as late as postexilic times. It is clear, then, that the majority of the psalms come from the united monarchy period (tenth century), and only a few from much later. This is in contrast to a view commonly espoused until recently that most of the psalms, if not all, were composed very late, some shortly before the time of Christ. The main theory was that the literature and theology they embodied were too elevated or advanced for the primitive period in which David was presumed to have lived.[39] With the discovery of Canaanite poetry of a similar nature and equally advanced from a literary standpoint at Ras Shamra in Syria, dating from four centuries before David, all arguments that David could not have written the psalms have been quietly laid to rest.[40] Now it is averred that David could have written them but did not, except maybe a few.[41]

Several themes appear in the psalms, which sometimes are grouped accordingly. For example, penitential psalms pertain to repentance and sorrow for sin. The best known of these is David's prayer of forgiveness uttered

38. Samuel Schultz, *The Old Testament Speaks*, 3d ed. (New York: Harper and Row, 1980), 285.

39. Robert Henry Pfeiffer, *Introduction to the Old Testament* (New York: Harper and Brothers, 1941), 627.

40. Gleason L. Archer, Jr., *A Survey of Old Testament Introduction* (Chicago: Moody, 1974), 441.

41. For a discussion of the uncertainties with regard to authorship in critical circles, see J. Alberto Soggin, *Introduction to the Old Testament*, rev. ed. (Philadelphia: Westminster, 1980), 366–69.

after his sin with Bath-sheba (Ps. 51). Others are Psalms 6, 32, 38, 102, 130, and 143. Imprecatory psalms invoke the wrath and judgment of God against ungodly men. Examples are Psalms 5:10 and 139:21–22. It is important to remember about these that the poet desires God's punishment of the wicked not to satisfy his own feelings but because he recognizes that the wicked have offended the honor of God.[42] Also, there is usually a strong eschatological sense involved in the imprecatory psalms. That is, the poet is not so much invoking and expecting the immediate judgment of God as he is looking forward to the day of the Lord when all unrepentant sinners must be dealt with according to their impiety toward God. Though many scholars attempt to demonstrate that the Old Testament is morally inferior to the New by referring to these "barbarous" imprecations, the true explanation of the ethical incongruity lies in the mistaken ideas some have concerning the biblical doctrine of sin and punishment. When one properly understands the nature of a holy and sinless God, he, with the psalmists, must cry out against the iniquity that so terribly offends him. This does not mean that the sinner himself is to be hated, but that sin is despicable and unrepentance unforgivable. To the Old Testament mind, the distinction between the two may not have been as clear as it is this side of the cross.

Some of the most important psalms are described as messianic because they prophetically describe the future Messiah of Israel and his work. Many of these depict him in the regal splendor in which he will come as King to reign over his dominion (2, 8, 45, 72, 89, 97, 110, 132) and therefore are sometimes called royal psalms. Others speak of him as the suffering One who must taste death before he can wear the crown. Among these are those referring to his betrayal into the hands of sinners (41, 109), his crucifixion (22, 69), and his bodily resurrection (16, 40, 66). Obviously the writers were not always completely aware of the significance of these writings, though surely at times they knew they spoke of the Anointed One. As the New Testament writers testify (Heb. 2:6–10; Matt. 27:34, 38, 46; John 19:24; 20:25), they speak of none other than the Lord. Because the higher critics refuse to believe in fulfilled prophecy, they must assume that these messianic psalms speak only in very general terms of some ideal figure of the future or even of the nation itself in some cases.[43] They avoid the implications of the New Testament writers' use of these portions of the psalms as prophecies that Messiah fulfilled, maintaining that the writers "read into" the life and death of Christ elements from the psalms. In other words, they say, many of the messianic psalms are used in reference to Christ where such use is his-

42. Archer, A Survey of Old Testament Introduction, 460.
43. Sigmund Mowinckel, The Psalms in Israel's Worship, 2 vols. (London: Blackwell, 1962), 1:75–76.

torically unjustified. Jesus did not really rise from the dead, but the Gospel writers said he did and supported their claims by referring to these messianic passages in the Old Testament. This seems to be an extremely frantic effort to deny any messianic character to the psalms except what was idealistic and hardly susceptible to literal fulfillment.

The Book of Proverbs

Proverbs claims to have been written largely by Solomon, and there is no convincing reason to argue otherwise.[44] The biblical account maintains that he was highly gifted in wisdom and literary talent (1 Kings 4:32) and wrote hundreds of proverbs and songs that have never been recovered. The main purpose of the book is to disclose human wisdom or observation in the light of that from God. It discusses the whole range of morals and ethics, providing wise insight into human behavior. Despite its seemingly earthly approach, there is clearly a recognition of divine revelation in the guidance of mankind's affairs (3:21–26). Solomon and the other wisdom writers did not merely express their own opinions here but regarded God as the fountainhead of all wisdom and, indeed, considered Wisdom (*hokmâ*) in almost a personified sense, perhaps as a manifestation of the Spirit of God. Wisdom to them was not, in a Gnostic sense, the means of salvation per se, but the gift of God available to all men whereby they might know him and their world as well.

In addition to the portions written by Solomon (1:12–22:16), there are also the "words of the wise" (22:17–24:34), perhaps by an unknown author; proverbs of Solomon copied out by Hezekiah's scribes and included in the final edition (25–29); the "words of Agur" (30), an unknown figure; the "words of Lemuel" (31:1–9), also otherwise unknown; and an anonymous acrostic poem written in honor of the virtuous woman (31:10–31). Most of the proverbs are dated much later by the critics because they seem to them to reflect wisdom concepts later than those of the time of Solomon. However, more and more evidence suggests that such wisdom was very ancient and that Solomon's proverbs were only a portion of the entire literature of this kind that circulated in the Near Eastern world.[45]

Hebrew Wisdom

Two other books, Ecclesiastes and the Song of Solomon, should receive attention here, since their traditional setting is also the period of the

44. R. K. Harrison, *Introduction to the Old Testament* (Grand Rapids: Eerdmans, 1969), 1010–18.
45. Charles T. Fritsch, "The Book of Proverbs," in *The Interpreter's Bible*, ed. George Buttrick et al., 12 vols. (New York: Abingdon-Cokesbury, 1951), 4:775.

united monarchy. The Hebrew canon lists them among the "Rolls," books designed for reading on festive occasions. By genre they are in the category of wisdom literature, their form, moreover, frequently showing a highly poetic flavor. That Job and Proverbs, both of which are clearly wisdom compositions, appear in the so-called Poetry section of the canon, and that Ecclesiastes and the Song of Solomon, though equally wisdom and poetic, do not, reveals the fluidity in ancient thought about literary categories. Thus, one may understand "wisdom" more as a term of content or perspective and "poetry" as the form in which the literature was cast.

The Book of Ecclesiastes

No book of the Old Testament has suffered more at the hands of the higher critics than Ecclesiastes. Because of its alleged secular and pessimistic tone, many feel it has no place in the canon at all, a rather presumptuous opinion, whereas others would date it so late that it could scarcely be called Old Testament. It was popular at one time, especially before the Dead Sea Scrolls and other ancient Jewish documents were found, to believe that Ecclesiastes was Hellenistic because it contained ideas allegedly Greek in character.[46] This idea is pretty well discredited now, because it is recognized widely that Jewish literature from a very early period contained ideas similar to Greek concepts, though unrelated.[47] But this has not discouraged the critics from dating the book very late on other, subjective grounds.

The book is essentially a record of the reasoning of "man under the sun," or the secular man who lives without recognition of God. The book's original name was *Koheleth*, or "The Preacher"; it was written by "the son of David, king in Jerusalem." It is tempting to identify this preacher and son of David with Solomon, and some scholars do just this,[48] but other evidence seems to call this into question. For example, the writer says that he "was king," perhaps indicating that he is not at the time of writing, which would hardly fit Solomon, who died in office (Eccles. 1:12). Furthermore, he states that his wealth and power exceeded that of any of the kings before him (2:7–9). This does not seem to refer to Solomon, because he would not be apt to speak of only Saul and his own father David as "all that were before me in Jerusalem." Yet, as Gleason L.

---

46. George A. Barton, *A Critical and Exegetical Commentary on the Book of Ecclesiastes* (Edinburgh: T. and T. Clark, 1908), 34.

47. W. F. Albright, "Canaanite-Phoenician Sources of Hebrew Wisdom," in *Wisdom in Israel and in the Ancient Near East*, ed. Martin Noth and D. Winton Thomas (Leiden: Brill, 1960), 3ff.

48. Robert Jamieson, A. R. Fausset, and David Brown, *Commentary on the Whole Bible* (Grand Rapids: Zondervan, n.d.), 403.

Archer suggests, the arguments can be explained in various ways reconcilable with Solomonic authorship.[49] Perhaps it is best after all to take the obvious meaning, that Solomon was the Preacher, but to recognize that there are difficulties in any view.

The authorship of the book is of little consequence, however, compared with the theme, which is vanity. The writer observes that the human condition is very pessimistic indeed, for time comes and goes, men are born and die, yet nothing basically changes (1:3–11). As he views this unending pattern, he remarks that there is nothing new under the sun and that everything man can do or become is mere emptiness. The central idea is beautifully expressed in the last chapter, where man is described as a house whose pillars and posts become weakened with age, whose windows (eyes) become darkened, whose grinders (teeth) become low and worn out, and whose daughters of music (the voice) are brought low. But this description of one who is old and about to expire is prefaced by the admonition to "remember your Creator in the days of your youth" (12:1–7). This, then, is the key to the book. The Preacher exhorts that a person should know God while he is young so that life will have a proper orientation and meaning. If he fails to do this, life will be nothing but emptiness, an experience devoid of purpose, direction, and satisfaction. Far from a pessimistic book, Ecclesiastes is a stirring, almost evangelistic sermon that shows the way out of the morass of a godless life into the brilliant radiance of God's presence.

The Song of Solomon

This short love story, ascribed to Solomon by both internal (Song of Sol. 1:1) and external evidence, has long been the focal point of vigorous discussion. Many reject it as unworthy of the Old Testament because of its allegedly sensuous and even erotic nature. They say that it speaks only of human love and in such terms that there can hardly be any spiritual edification to the reader.[50] Obviously, if the book was written by Solomon it must have some claim to canonicity for that reason alone, but the added fact that Jewish tradition and the consensus of the church support its authenticity constitutes a powerful argument.

The real theme of the book, apart from the interpretation forced on it by those who seem to delight in pointing out its bold descriptions, is the glorification of true love. One can hardly read it with an open mind without sensing the beautiful concepts related there. It seems that Solomon

49. Archer, A Survey of Old Testament Introduction, 486–96.
50. For views that suggest that the Song is a reflection of pagan cult-material, see Robert Gordis, The Song of Songs: A Study, Modern Translation, and Commentary (New York: Jewish Theological Seminary of America, 1954), 4–8.

(for surely he is the king in mind) fell in love with a beautiful maiden who, unfortunately, was beneath his class in life, being but a shepherd girl. The narrative relates the struggle of the king, who had everything he desired but the maiden, to win her affections, apparently successfully. Primarily there are dialogues in which he describes her and his love for her and she describes him. At last Solomon wins the maiden, and she enables him, by her beauty and character, to see that God's intention is for a man to have one wife and not the many who had come into his life to lead him from God.[51]

It has always seemed most unlikely that the whole episode, as personal as it is, was recorded only to give instruction in a love affair of the tenth century B.C. Hence, other interpretations have been suggested. The two most widely accepted among conservatives are that the relationship described is between God (Solomon) and Israel (the maiden), and that God is attempting in this type to show his love for his special people,[52] or that it is an allegory of the love of Christ for the church.[53] Both of these could be true, in which case the Song of Solomon would be a historical allegory showing both God's love for Israel and Christ's love for the church, both relationships frequently expressed in the motif of marital love. The main reason for the critics' rejecting the book is their failure to see the ideal love of God beneath the surface of this love affair of Solomon.

51. Franz Delitzsch, Biblical Commentary on the Old Testament: The Song of Songs (Grand Rapids: Eerdmans, 1948), 5.

52. Archer, A Survey of Old Testament Introduction, 500–502.

53. Ernst Hengstenberg, Commentary on Ecclesiastes, trans. D. W. Simon (Edinburgh: T. and T. Clark, 1876), 297–305.

A House Divided

Ancient Near Eastern Historical Background

The period embraced by the divided monarchy began ca. 931 B.C. and continued to the fall of Samaria in 722 under the Assyrians. After that time, the southern kingdom of Judah existed alone, but further remarks on this matter must be deferred until chapter 9. The era now under discussion was dominated by the meteoric rise of Assyria to dominance in the Near East, though other nations and peoples also were important to the overall story. Israel, of course, occupies chief importance in the following exposition, and, as the books of Kings and related matters in Chronicles receive attention, it will be possible to see how the people of God interacted with these other, greater nations. But before this is undertaken it is necessary to examine at least briefly the affairs of the more important of these surrounding kingdoms.[1]

1. For this period, except for the dates, see especially John Bright, *A History of Israel*, 3d ed. (Philadelphia: Westminster, 1981), 229–309. The extrabiblical dates earlier than the death of Solomon are based on the chronology of W. F. Albright as found in Edward F. Campbell, Jr., "The Ancient Near East: Chronological Bibliography and Charts," in *The Bible and the Ancient Near East*, ed. G. Ernest Wright (Garden City, N.Y.: Doubleday, 1961), 291–92. Those for the later Assyrian kings derive from A. K. Grayson, *Assyrian Royal Inscriptions*. (Wiesbaden: Harrassowitz, 1972, 1976), 1:157–58, 2:213, and William W. Hallo and William Kelly Simpson, *The Ancient Near East* (New York: Harcourt Brace Jovanovich, 1971), 131–41. The dates for the divided kingdom era are based on the chronology of Edwin R. Thiele, *The Mysterious Numbers of the Hebrew Kings*, 3d ed. (Chicago: University of Chicago Press, 1983).

227

Assyria

Until the beginning of the Early Iron Age (1200 B.C.), Assyria had remained fairly obscure since its days of greatness under Shamshi-Adad I (1748–1716). Occasional bright lights like Asshur-rabi I (1441–1425?) and Asshur-uballit (1365–1330) had come, both of whom seemed to raise hopes of Assyrian renascence, but Shalmaneser I (1274–1245) was the real genius of the nation's recovery. Among other feats, this brilliant monarch completed the conquest of the Mitanni that had begun in the preceding century. He was followed by Tukulti-ninurta I (1244–1208), who conquered Babylon and lay claim to a large area around Assyria. For about another century, however, Assyria was able to retain only what she had; little expansion occurred. Then one of the greatest imperialists in world history appeared, Tiglath-pileser I (1114–1076). He is properly considered the founder of the New Assyrian Empire, which extended in all directions except southwest. There the rising Aramaean states mentioned earlier held him in check.

Not until about 875 B.C., under Asshur-nasirpal II (883–859), were the Assyrians able to move beyond this stalemate and make serious incursions into Palestine. His successor, Shalmaneser III (859–825), made many contacts with biblical kings, some recorded on important monuments and in other inscriptions. But the real assault of Palestine, including Israel, was under the leadership of Tiglath-pileser III (744–727), otherwise known as Pulu or Pul. He was able to break up the Aramaean alliance completely and carry off many prisoners. In fact, some of the Israelites from Galilee are numbered among his captives, according to both his records and the Old Testament. The actual attack on Samaria, capital of Israel, was made by Shalmaneser V (726–722), who died shortly after the conquest of the city, though credit for its fall was claimed by a usurper, Sargon II (722–705).

Throughout this period, few attempted to challenge Assyria's supremacy, but by the end of the eighth century there were indications that that domination might soon end. Other nations, especially Media and Babylonia, were beginning to exert pressures on Assyria, and before another century passed, the kingdom of the Tigris had succumbed and passed from history. But Assyria's greatest importance lay in God's raising her up as a rod in his hand to chasten Israel (Isa. 10:5); this is why Assyria figures so prominently in the biblical narrative for this period.

Egypt

Egypt became an almost forgotten nation after its glorious Eighteenth and Nineteenth dynasties. The Twentieth and Twenty-first especially

were times of declension during which Egypt had little or no contact with
Palestine or, indeed, any place outside its own immediate borders except
the Sinai Peninsula. It was not until the Twenty-second Dynasty, founded
by Shishak I (940–919),[2] that the land of the Nile began to exercise influence on the Near East. This famous king penetrated into Palestine as far
north as Galilee, leaving behind steles and other markers in place after
place and a full account of his activities on the walls of the Temple of
Karnak in Thebes. The following king, Osorkon I (919–883), was not
quite so successful, however, for the Book of Chronicles relates that Asa
king of Judah defeated his general Zerah as he attempted to invade Judah
(2 Chron. 14:8–12). This defeat seemed to herald to Egypt the unmistakable impression that she was not yet ready for imperialistic ambitions.
Indeed, she never again was, except in the seventh century, when once
more she pushed up into Canaan. But even this movement was largely
with Assyrian permission and was brief and ineffectual.

Aramaea

It is impossible to consider the history of this period without a discussion
of the Aramaean states to the north of Israel.[3] These little kingdoms had
come into existence largely through a migration of northern peoples into
the region known as Aram or Mesopotamia (not to be confused with the
larger term describing everything between the Tigris and Euphrates rivers).
These immigrants blended with the peoples already there and, by 1200
B.C., became a formidable force. They remained generally independent of
each other until the need came for concerted defensive action. This was in
the time of Tiglath-pileser I, who was unable to annex the stubborn
Aramaeans. In fact, during the age just after Tiglath-pileser, when Assyria
receded somewhat, the Aramaeans took the initiative and founded several
settlements in the Tigris-Euphrates region to the east and as far as Cilicia
in Asia Minor on the west. They also pressed to the south, so that by the
time of Saul and David there were several important states just north and
east of Galilee, the chief being Hamath, Damascus, and Zobah.

With the revival of Assyrian power and the height of Israelite expansion under Solomon, these states were largely limited in scope, in many
cases brought under the control of their neighbors. But once again, after
the division of Israel, the Aramaeans became independent and, in the

---

2. The Egyptian dates are those of Hallo and Simpson, *The Ancient Near East*, 301.
3. See especially Benjamin Mazar, "The Aramaean Empire and Its Relations with Israel," *Biblical
Archaeologist* 25 (1962): 97–120; also Merrill F. Unger, *Israel and the Aramaeans of Damascus: A Study
in Archaeological Illumination of Bible History* (Grand Rapids: Zondervan, 1957).

tenth and ninth centuries waged almost incessant war, especially with the Northern Kingdom. These conflicts figure prominently in 1 Kings and will be considered in detail at the appropriate place. Suffice to say that the great Assyrian rampage of Tiglath-pileser III near the end of the eighth century removed Aramaea permanently from the world scene. It was not until the emergence of Syria hundreds of years later that the people there gained autonomy once again. The important contribution of Aramaea that cannot be overlooked even in this brief sketch is not political but cultural. The Aramaic language and manner of life pervaded the Near Eastern world, largely because of Aramaea's ideal location in the heart of the Fertile Crescent, so that by the time of Christ the lingua franca of that part of the world was Aramaic.

Babylonia

A final word should be said about Babylonia, for though this nation remained in the shrouds of her dark ages even through this period, there were faint glimmers of hope that the slumber might at last be broken. This hope was concentrated in a people known as the Sealands Dynasty, a rising threat located in the extreme south along the Persian Gulf. These people gradually extended their influence, though they lost almost everything along the way to the Assyrians, until there was an ultimate alliance with the Median kingdom to the north and east, which resulted, in the end of the seventh century, in the formation of the Neo-Babylonian Empire.

Israel and Judah to the Time of Jehu (1 Kings 12:1–2 Kings 9:6; 2 Chronicles 10:1–22:7)

Dynasty of Jeroboam I (1 Kings 12:1–15:26; 2 Chronicles 10:15)

After Solomon's death, the throne fell to his son Rehoboam (931–913), who continued to reign in Jerusalem, having been anointed previously at Shechem. This holy place in the north may have been selected to unite the nation, which had given evidence already of being seriously divided in opinion and loyalty. Proof of this may be seen in the appeal to the king by the northern tribes, led by Jeroboam, who had returned to Israel from Egypt (1 Kings 12:4). They demanded that the heavy tribute laid on them by Solomon be alleviated, but the demand went unheeded, for Rehoboam, counseled by his young friends, determined to tax them even more. At this, the representatives of the northern tribes declared their independence of Judah and set about to declare Jeroboam their new king. Rehoboam was not about to permit this revolu-

TABLE 6
Kings of Israel and Judah

Israel	Judah
Jeroboam I (931–910)	Rehoboam (931–913)
Nadab (910–909)	Abijam (913–911)
Baasha (909–886)	Asa (911–870)
Elah (886–885)	
Zimri (885)	
Omri (885–874)	
Ahab (874–853)	Jehoshaphat (873–848)
Ahaziah (853–852)	
Joram (852–841)	Jehoram (853–841)
Jehu (841–814)	Ahaziah (841)
	Athaliah (841–835)
Jehoahaz (814–798)	Joash (835–796)
Jehoash (798–782)	Amaziah (796–767)
Jeroboam II (793–753)	Uzziah (790–739)
Zachariah (753–752)	
Shallum (752)	
Menahem (752–742)	
Pekahiah (742-740)	Jotham (750–731)
Pekah (752–732)	Ahaz (735–715)
Hoshea (732–722)	
	Hezekiah (715–686)
	Manasseh (696–642)
	Amon (642–640)
	Josiah (640–609)
	Jehoahaz (609)
	Jehoiakim (609–597)
	Jehoiakin (597)
	Zedekiah (597–586)

tion without a fight, but when the prophet Shemaiah reminded him that the Lord had already decreed that this should happen, he desisted from an attack on the north (1 Kings 12:23–24).

Jeroboam (931–910) meanwhile had established the capital of the new kingdom of Israel at Shechem, hoping because of its sacred associations that this site would add legitimacy to the revolution. He also built the city of Penuel, east of the Jordan, as a sort of provincial capital. The most significant act of his early administration, however, was his selection of the cities of Dan and Bethel as centers of a new cult (1 Kings 12:29). He fully realized that if his people should return to Jerusalem annually for the stated feasts, they might soon become disenchanted with the division of the kingdom and might even desire to rejoin Judah. To prevent this, he must arrange for places of worship within his own realm, and yet this worship could not differ a great deal from that with which they were familiar. He therefore made calves of gold that he placed in the new shrines at Dan and Bethel, the extreme north and south respectively, instituting a new priesthood that could officiate at the cultus.

These calves were not images of Yahweh but only representations of the throne on which Yahweh stood. One can see in this, however, strong Canaanite influences, for some of the Canaanites too imagined their god, Baal, as seated or standing on a bull, the animal that signified strength and fertility.[4] Thus, Jeroboam exposed his people to the dangers of idolatry and nature worship, dangers that became more apparent as time passed. His selection of renegade and unqualified priests also constituted the gravest offense against the law. In this he was reproved by a man of God from Judah who was sent to him at Bethel by the Lord. As the king himself was celebrating a feast at the altar there, the altar was destroyed by the Lord at the prophet's word and the king became paralyzed (1 Kings 13:1–6). This blasphemous act of sacrifice at an improper altar and by an illegal priest was long remembered as the sin of Jeroboam whereby he made Israel sin. Tragically enough, Jeroboam was not dissuaded from a continuation of this evil practice, but enlarged the idolatrous worship he had instituted and filled the priestly office by bribery.

Soon after this encounter with the prophet from Judah, Jeroboam's son became deathly ill, and the king desperately sought out Ahijah, the prophet who had torn his garment and predicted his rise to power long before it happened. This man of God had no good words to say, however, and told the king's wife, who had come to him in an ineffective disguise, that their son would die because of the king's evil. Furthermore, the king's family would not continue to occupy the throne, but soon would be cut off completely. Shortly thereafter Jeroboam died, leaving his crown to his son Nadab (910–909), who was no less evil in following his father's pernicious ways (1 Kings 14:20).

The situation was hardly any better in Judah, for there Rehoboam permitted all kinds of idolatrous practices to come into the land, though undoubtedly without regal sanction. Such nefarious objects and persons as high places, *maṣṣēbôt* (religious pillars), *ăšērîm* (groves), and sacred prostitutes became prevalent, all of which were so obscene and illegal that Judah

---

4. W. F. Albright, *From the Stone Age to Christianity* (Garden City, N.Y.: Doubleday, 1957), 299–301.

indeed appeared little better than her northern neighbor (1 Kings 14:22–24; 2 Chron. 12:1). Perhaps at the instigation of Jeroboam, whom he had afforded protection, Shishak of Egypt invaded Judah at this time, carrying away many of the sacred temple objects from Jerusalem (1 Kings 14:26). His onslaught did not stop there, for Shishak turned on his old friend from Israel and advanced north to the Valley of Jezreel and beyond.[5] Throughout this period there was constant hostility between Israel and Judah, conflict that did not end with the death of the first two kings (2 Chron. 13).

Rehoboam was followed by his son Abijam, who reigned for only three years (913–911) and was, like his father, contemporary with Jeroboam (1 Kings 14:31). He too was evil, but because of Yahweh's love for David, the throne remained with the Davidic family. Whereas there are several dynasties in the relatively brief period of Israelite history, there is only the family of David in the south, though there were several kings of that line who were anything but godly. During Abijam's reign, the Canaanite religious influence that prevailed under Rehoboam continued and even increased. His mother was Maachah, a daughter of Absalom, an evil woman who seemed only to aggravate the apostasy during the early years of her young grandson, Asa, who followed Abijam as king, apparently when still a lad. When Asa became an independent king (911–870), one of the first things he accomplished was to remove his grandmother from her throne, along with the objects of worship she had set up (1 Kings 15:12–14; 2 Chron. 14:2–5). He failed to remove the Israelite high places (though evidently those of the Canaanites were destroyed), but on the whole he did what was right in the sight of the Lord.

The wars between Judah and Israel continued in the reign of Asa, but there were intermittent periods of peace in which he was able to build strong fortifications against the Northern Kingdom and Egypt (2 Chron. 14:6–7). When Zerah, the Ethiopian general under Osorkon I of Egypt, invaded in the beginning of Asa's reign, the latter defeated him in a great battle at Mareshah (2 Chron. 14:9–10).[6] Meanwhile, thousands of Israelites, recognizing that God was with Judah and her godly king, came to the south from their homes and made common cause with Judah (2 Chron. 15:9). Baasha (909–886) took the initiative against Judah by building a strong fortification at Ramah, mainly to prevent any crossing between the two nations either way (1 Kings 15:17; 2 Chron. 16:1). Asa therefore sent a handsome gift to Benhadad I (890?–841)[7] of Damascus and begged him to

5. Bright, A History of Israel, 233–34.
6. Ibid., 235.
7. This king is mentioned on the Milqart Stele found near Aleppo, Syria. For the text, see D. Winton Thomas, ed., Documents from Old Testament Times (London: Thomas Nelson, 1958), 239.

break his alliance with Israel and come to his assistance instead. This Benhadad did, and several cities in northern Israel fell to the Aramaeans (1 Kings 15:20). Furthermore, Baasha was forced to leave his building program at Ramah to divert his attention to this Aramaean threat, so Asa took the building stones from the unfinished Ramah and made fortresses of his own on the boundary at Geba and Mizpah. But because he had relied on the Aramaeans and not on God in his dispute with Baasha, the prophet Hanani predicted that he would thenceforth have war (2 Chron. 16:7–8). Presumably this occurred, though further war is not mentioned in the Old Testament. It is clear that Asa, because of a certain foot disease, was unable to complete his reign alone. In about 873 he was joined by his son Jehoshaphat (873–848), who became his co-regent.

Dynasty of Baasha (1 Kings 15:27–16:22)

Baasha, an unknown citizen of Issachar, successfully engineered a plot against Nadab, king of Israel, and founded the second dynasty of that kingdom. He evidently located the capital at Tirzah, though there is some evidence that Jeroboam had done that himself, and he followed closely the pattern of evil that Jeroboam had established. Consequently Baasha was embroiled in war continually. Furthermore, he was condemned by the prophet Jehu, son of Hanani, and told that his dynasty, like the one he had ended, would be transitory. After a reign of twenty-four years, he died, and the throne went to his son Elah (886–885), who, in turn, was assassinated by the captain of his charioteers, Zimri. Zimri managed to retain control for only one week, for the people, who were anything but sympathetic with what had happened, quickly appointed Omri to reign over them. As general of the Israelite army, Omri had the necessary resources to storm Tirzah and burn the royal palace with Zimri inside. Another man, Tibni, now appeared, also hoping to take the crown that Omri had won. But Omri was more than a match for this new challenger and, without further trouble, slew Tibni and proclaimed himself king of Israel (885–874). Thus, in two years Israel had four kings, a fact that helps explain the unstable condition of the kingdom at this time.

Dynasty of Omri (1 Kings 16:23–2 Kings 9:26; 2 Chronicles 17:1–22:9)

Only six verses are devoted to the reign of Omri, which makes his position seem rather unimportant, but contemporary historical records, especially from Assyria, place beyond question the fact that Omri was regarded as a king of great eminence both within Israel and in neighboring nations.

In fact, the Assyrians generally referred to Israel by the name Bit Humria ("House of Omri") from his time and onward.[8] He was able to bring order out of the chaos into which he had come and to extend Israelite influence farther than it had reached since the reign of Solomon. Among his more significant accomplishments, though certainly not good ones, were his alliance and friendly relations with the Phoenicians at Sidon. In fact, the daughter of Eth-baal, king of Sidon, became the wife of Ahab, son of Omri and heir apparent to the throne. This, as it turned out, contributed to the even more hasty demise of the Northern Kingdom and hastened its captivity. Omri also moved the capital once again, this time to Samaria (880 B.C.), where it remained until the Assyrian destruction in 722. The wisdom of such a choice for a capital may be seen by anyone who visits the mound there and sees its tremendously advantageous location. Evidence of Phoenician collaboration in the building of the palace of Omri, and that of Ahab as well, has been uncovered by archaeological research at Samaria.[9]

In 874 Ahab became king of Israel and inaugurated an age of transgression unparalleled thus far. His long reign (874–853) was contemporaneous with that of Jehoshaphat in Judah and Benhadad I in Damascus. It was also in his time that the Assyrians under Assur-nasirpal II (883–859) began to oppress the Aramaeans and tried to include even Israel in their maraudings. Because of Ahab's marriage to Jezebel, the Sidonian princess, he forsook God as not even Jeroboam had done and began to worship Baal.

This was the occasion for the ministry of the most important man in the entire period, Elijah the Tishbite. This strange figure came on the scene sometime in Ahab's reign with the declaration that Israel would have no rain until he should give the word. Then he disappeared into the wilderness, where he was sustained by God's miraculous use of a raven, which brought him meat from time to time. From there he went to the kingdom of Sidon, where he found a widow and her son starving because of the famine. He performed a miracle by creating an inexhaustible supply of meal and oil and was rewarded with shelter for a time under the roof of the grateful woman. His most astonishing act, perhaps, came when the child of the Sidonian woman became ill and died. As the Son of God was to do on several occasions in the future, Elijah, by God's power, raised the dead to life (1 Kings 17:21–23).

After three years, the prophet went to Samaria to inform Ahab that the famine would end. The king had sent his servants throughout the land in search of water and grazing land and had all but given up hope that the nation would survive. Elijah met one of these servants, Obadiah (not to be

8. Ibid., 49.
9. Donald B. Harden, *The Phoenicians*, 2d ed. (New York: Praeger, 1962), 52.

confused with the prophet by the same name), and told him to fetch the king. Reluctantly, Obadiah did so, and when Ahab and Elijah met face to face the king rebuked the prophet for having brought such misery on the nation. Elijah denied responsibility and said that it was the wicked king himself who had elicited God's judgment by his shameful worship of Baal. Thereupon Elijah challenged Ahab to meet him at Mount Carmel, a leading Baal shrine, and see for himself whether the true God was Baal or Yahweh.

Ahab appeared with 450 of his Baal prophets, though Jezebel's own 400 Sidonian prophets of Asherah, who had been invited, evidently failed to appear. A huge throng of Israelites was there to witness this showdown between the gods, and Elijah advised the people to make up their minds whom they would follow. When they failed to respond, he invited the Baal prophets to slay a sacrifice, place it on their altar, and pray to Baal to consume it in fire.[10] He would do the same to Yahweh after them. But in vain the Baalists called their god from morning until noon, until at last Elijah mocked them, asking if their god might not be asleep or away from home. Even when they cut themselves, a popular measure to procure the sympathy of the gods, no response came.[11] At last, in utter frustration, they abandoned their frenzied efforts and permitted Elijah his turn.

Finding some stones from the old abandoned altar of Yahweh, the prophet made a new one. On it he placed a sacrifice. But then he did a strange thing. He poured barrels of water over the altar, the wood, and the sacrifice, and even filled the surrounding trench with it. Over and over again he soaked the altar until there was no question that only a miracle could ignite it. Then he spoke a short but fervent prayer, in response to which fire descended from God and consumed sacrifice, wood, altar, and even the water in the trench. This empirical evidence compelled the assembled throng to acknowledge enthusiastically that only Yahweh was God. Taking advantage of their exuberance, Elijah ordered them to apprehend the prophets of Baal and slay them on the spot. In this dramatic manner, Baalism was seriously crippled in Israel, though it continued in one form or another for twenty years or more.

At the conclusion of this overwhelming experience, the rains came and the drought of three years ended.[12] Ahab, chagrined, rushed back to his

10. As the god of rain and lightning, Baal, if he really existed, should have had no difficulty in igniting the sacrifice. In fact, he should have been able to prevent the three-year drought. See Sabatino Moscati, *Ancient Semitic Civilizations* (New York: G. P. Putnam's Sons, 1960), 117.

11. For an example of this in the Ras Shamra literature, see J. C. L. Gibson, *Canaanite Myths and Legends* (Edinburgh: T. and T. Clark, 1977), 74.

12. This, of course, showed that Yahweh, not Baal, was God of rain, fire, and every other force of nature. Cf. Josh. 10:11; 1 Sam. 7:10; 12:18. See Frank E. Eakin, "Yahwism and Baalism Before the Exile," *Journal of Biblical Literature* 84 (1965): 413.

country home at Jezreel and related to Jezebel all that had happened. The wicked queen, enraged that her gods had been so treated, warned that if she could get her hands on Elijah the hapless prophet would meet the same fate as had the prophets of Baal. Terrified, Elijah ran from Jezreel, where he had gone ahead of Ahab, and headed for Judah. Down in the Negev near Beersheba he fell exhausted and wished to die rather than live in the face of such discouragements and dangers (1 Kings 19:4). The Lord sustained him there, however, and led him to Horeb in the plains of Sinai, where he appeared to him as he had to Moses nearly six hundred years earlier. God told him that he would redeem his people and that Elijah would be his instrument. The divine help would not come in a mighty, overt way, but quietly, as in a still, small voice. With renewed confidence, Elijah left those hallowed precincts and set out to discharge the specific tasks the Lord had assigned him. He must anoint Elisha ben Shaphat to succeed him as prophet (1 Kings 19:19), Jehu ben Nimshi to be king of Israel (2 Kings 9:6), and Hazael to be king of Damascus in the place of Benhadad (2 Kings 8:13). Only the first of these did Elijah accomplish personally, but through Elisha, who followed in his steps, the other two were also fulfilled.

On the international scene, Benhadad I had begun preparations for war with Israel. He had taken certain northern regions of Israel earlier, though these areas may have been retaken in the time of Omri and Ahab.[13] Now he felt confident enough actually to talk of subduing Samaria itself, so he sent an ultimatum to Ahab stipulating that Ahab must render a huge payment of gold or suffer the consequences. Ahab agreed, but Benhadad came the second time and threatened to take the city even if the ransom were paid. A prophet then came to Ahab and assured him of victory against his Aramaean foe. When the drunken Benhadad and his men entered the field of battle, they were ill equipped to tackle the courageous Israelite host. But their setback was only temporary, for Benhadad made a second attack. Again Israel won, this time cornering the Aramaean king in the city of Aphek. Failing to follow up on this opportunity to finish off his dreaded enemy, Ahab let Benhadad go free. A man of God told him that because of this his kingdom would soon be taken from him and bequeathed to the hands of another (1 Kings 20:42).

The setting for Ahab's final rejection involved the neighbor of the king, Naboth, who had a beautiful piece of land that the king wanted for himself. When she noticed how the king moped about, Jezebel asked him the reason for his dejection. When she found out, she ruthlessly hired wit-

---

13. Bright, *A History of Israel*, 242–43.

nesses who perjured themselves, swearing to the court that Naboth had blasphemed the king and God. Naboth therefore was stoned to death, and Ahab took his property. On this turn of events, Elijah came to the king and told him that what he had done would issue in violent death for both Ahab and Jezebel and that dogs would lick their blood where they had licked that of the murdered Naboth.

About this time a most significant event was taking shape in the north. Shalmaneser III of Assyria, who had already enjoyed considerable success in his efforts to annex northern Palestine, swooped down across the Euphrates with a great army in an effort to finish this conquest. At Qarqar he met a massive alliance of a large number of kings, including Ahab and Benhadad I.[14] According to his own records, Shalmaneser attributed over two thousand chariots to Ahab alone, a significant fact in support of the strength of the House of Omri at this period. It is difficult to know what happened at the Battle of Qarqar (853), but it is certain that Assyria was unable to advance farther south for the time being, and probably not for a number of years.

As soon as this united effort was over, Benhadad and Ahab renewed their own hostilities (ca. 853 B.C.). It seems that the Israelite city of Ramoth-gilead was still in Aramaean hands and Ahab would not be satisfied until he had taken it back. He urged Jehoshaphat of Judah to join in his efforts, and in a rather amazing display of friendship the king of Judah complied (1 Kings 22:4; 2 Chron. 18:1). This was unwise, because the prophet Micaiah had denounced the whole plan as foolhardy, declaring that God would dispossess Israel of its king as a result. But, more influenced by the false prophets of Ahab than by this stalwart man of God, Jehoshaphat joined in. In the thick of the fray, Ahab was mortally wounded, but he bravely fought on until he expired at the close of the day. Jehoshaphat himself was nearly slain, and only when he convinced the Aramaeans that he was not Ahab was he spared. Ahab's body was carried to Jezreel, where the chariot that bore it, covered with his blood, was licked by dogs in fulfillment of the prophetic word. Ahaziah, son of the king, immediately took the reigns of authority and did his best to keep the tottering kingdom together (1 Kings 22:40).

Jehoshaphat from the very beginning tried to fortify Judah against its enemy Israel (2 Chron. 17:1–2). Furthermore, like his father, he tried to rid the land of the idolatry that had become such a curse to Israel. Beyond this, he took extensive measures to instruct the people in the things of the Lord by sending teachers throughout Judah for this very purpose (2

14. For the text of the Kurkh Stele, which records this campaign, see Thomas, *Documents from Old Testament Times,* 47.

Chron. 17:3–4). In addition, he made great achievements in public works and commerce (2 Chron. 17:12–13). He outfitted a convoy of ships at Ezion-geber, as Solomon had done, but because Ahaziah of Israel was part-ner with him in the project, the ships were broken up before they ever got to sea (1 Kings 22:48; 2 Chron. 20:37). Perhaps a second effort was made, though this is not clear, but Jehoshaphat had learned the lesson of associ-ation with the ungodly and refused to make further such arrangements with Ahaziah.

Jehoshaphat also had his hands full with the Ammonites, Moabites, and certain other tribal peoples who combined to invade Judah from across the Dead Sea. The prophet Jahaziel assured him, however, that there was no need for alarm (2 Chron. 20:15). When Jehoshaphat went to the scene of the battle with his large host, he was amazed to see the Ammonites and Moabites engaged in battle with the Edomites. Why or how this came about is not clear, but when it was all over the people had almost totally decimated themselves. Of course, this was not the end of these peoples entirely, for very shortly after this (ca. 850 B.C.) they rebelled against Israel, who had theoretically controlled them since the time of Solomon, and declared their independence under Mesha king of Moab (2 Kings 3:4ff.).[15] This took place after the death of Ahab, so Joram, son of Ahab, attempted to recover the lost area. He requested and received aid from Jehoshaphat, and, through a miraculous intervention of God, the united forces of Israel and Judah achieved a great military vic-tory; however, they did not succeed in bringing Moab back under Israelite control. At length Jehoshaphat died and was followed by his son Jehoram (853–841).

In the north, Ahaziah (853–852) occupied the throne of Ahab, who had recently been killed by the Aramaeans. This evil son followed his father in all his wickedness and paid dearly for it in many ways. In his brief reign, Mesha rebelled against Israel. Ahaziah was unable to do anything about it, perhaps because of an accident he suffered when he fell through a second-story lattice in the palace and tumbled to the floor below (2 Kings 1:2). He sent servants to the city of Ekron to enquire of their god Baal-zebub ("Lord of the Flies") as to the prospects for his recovery. Along the way they met Elijah, who told them to save their time by returning to the king at once and informing him that he would not recover. Enraged, Ahaziah demanded Elijah's arrest, but Elijah was delivered twice from those who sought his life. Finally he went willingly to Samaria and told the king that there was no hope, because he, like his father, had repudiated

---

15. This is recorded on the Moabite Stone. For the text, see ibid., 196–97.

God. Shortly the king died, as the prophet said he would, and yielded the throne to his brother Joram (or Jehoram). This king reigned for twelve years (852–841), contemporary largely with Jehoram (or Joram) of Judah. (For purposes of ready identification, the northern king will henceforth be designated as Joram and the southern as Jehoram, though the spellings are used interchangeably in the Old Testament.)

At this point, the narratives of the prophets resume once again. The time had come for Elijah to pass from the scene. God disclosed to him that he would not die but be taken up bodily. Elisha, recently anointed to succeed his master, followed him closely in those days, hoping to witness his departure. The "sons of the prophets" were likewise curious and assembled one day near their headquarters at Jericho to view Elijah and Elisha, who had come recently and were preparing to cross the Jordan. Elijah took his prophetic mantle, swept it over the river, and together the men of God crossed over on dry ground. Sensing that the time of separation was near, Elisha asked his mentor to give him a double portion of his spirit before he left. Elijah replied that this would be possible if Elisha witnessed his disappearance. At that moment a chariot of fire appeared, and Elijah was taken up in a whirlwind, but not before he left his mantle behind in Elisha's keeping (2 Kings 2:11–12). Amazed by the phenomenon, Elisha was no less amazed, perhaps, that he could recross the Jordan as easily as Elijah and he had done at the first.

It is striking that Elisha performed about twice as many miracles as did Elijah, a fitting correspondence to his having received a double portion of Elijah's spirit. In fact, the miraculous makes up such a part of the prophet's ministry that it is possible here to do little more than enumerate the instances. There were, for examples, the healing of the water at the prophets' home at Jericho (2 Kings 2:21), the smiting of impudent young men on the road to Bethel (2:24), the multiplication of a widow's oil (4:6), the resurrection of the son of a Shunammite woman (4:34–35), the healing of a pot of deadly soup (4:41), the cleansing of Naaman's leprosy (5:14), the attachment of leprosy to his wicked servant Gehazi (5:27), the floating of an iron axe head (6:6), the blinding of the Aramaeans' eyes (6:18), and even the restoration of a man's life through contact with Elisha's dead bones (13:21)! As already pointed out, there were definite periods in biblical history in which the miraculous became more or less common. This time of great spiritual need in Israel and Judah provided the setting for the miracle-working prophets Elijah and Elisha. In addition, there were many more prophets in existence, though the others are not characterized by their miracles. Ahijah of Shiloh, Hanani, Jehu ben Hanani, Micaiah, and many others have already appeared in the sacred narrative to this point. Moreover, there were sons of prophets living in various communities throughout the land. These were no doubt the spiritual heirs of the schools of the prophets of Samuel's time who had remained more or less inactive until they had such leadership as Elijah and Elisha could afford. What their functions were is not readily apparent, but they presumably were trained in preaching and singing and certainly in the law.[16]

Some schools among the Canaanites and Phoenicians corresponded to these. Indeed, they were involved in the conflict with Elijah on Mount Carmel. From all the evidence available, it seems that these Baal prophets were modelled after the true prophets of God rather than that Hebrew prophetism derived from Canaanite religious practice.[17] Apart from a few references to seers and other practitioners of divination in ancient documents like the Egyptian story of Wen Amon and the Mari texts, there is little or no evidence of prophetism in the ancient Near East akin to that among the Hebrews. As noted, Hebrew prophetism is scarcely ecstatic in nature and cannot be considered parallel to other kinds in any respect.

One other matter should be mentioned in regard to the prophets of Ahab. The first group he had was definitely Canaanite and actually called on Baal in worship. When the prophets in this group were extirpated by Elijah, they were replaced by prophets who claimed to be spokesmen for Yahweh, but who had never received a divine call. In other words, there appear to have been two kinds of false prophets: prophets of false gods and false prophets of the true God. In either case, they were spurious and were equally to be shunned.

Relations between Damascus and Israel improved somewhat after the reign of Ahab, enough that Benhadad could send his chief captain, Naaman, a victim of leprosy, to Israel to see if he could obtain relief through the famous prophet Elisha (2 Kings 5:5). Joram, however, interpreted the request as an occasion for Benhadad to make war with him again. Nevertheless, Elisha learned of Naaman's coming and arranged to meet him. After much hesitation, the Aramaean soldier agreed to bathe in the river Jordan as the prophet suggested, a silly thing in his sight, seeing that the rivers of Damascus, the Abana and Pharpar, were much cleaner and apparently more conducive to healing. When his flesh was cleansed, he was so overjoyed that he wished to reward the prophet, an offer Elisha refused. Still, out of respect to the God of Israel, who had made the healing possible, Naaman carried a load of soil from Israel back

16. Willis J. Beecher, *The Prophets and the Promise* (Grand Rapids: Baker, 1963), 76–80.
17. Edward J. Young, *My Servants, the Prophets* (Grand Rapids: Eerdmans, 1952), 25ff.

to Damascus, intending to make with it an altar at the temple of Rimmon (5:17–18).[18]

Shortly thereafter, war broke out again between Damascus and Israel. Whenever Benhadad made plans to deploy his troops at strategic points, the Israelites always seemed to know in advance (2 Kings 6:10–11). Finally, he learned that Elisha the prophet, through the revelation of God, could know his every thought. His objective then was to seize Elisha and put him out of commission. The Aramaeans went to Dothan, where Elisha and his servant were staying, and surrounded the city. When the prophet awakened the next morning, he saw the huge enemy contingent, but with his spiritual vision he saw also an army of God on all the surrounding hills. He then prayed for the Aramaeans to be blinded, and when they were, he led them into the city of Samaria. There their eyes opened, but contrary to the wishes of Joram they were freed and sent back to Damascus. As a result, Benhadad sent no more small foraging parties into Israel, but decided to mass his troops for one grand siege of the capital city (6:24). The siege was so effective that the people of Samaria were reduced to cannibalism and were on the point of surrender or extinction.[19]

Elisha, who also was in the city, was the special object of Joram's wrath, for the king accused him of bringing this grief on the kingdom. Elisha then predicted that within twenty-four hours there would be food in plenty, a suggestion that brought him only ridicule from one of the king's officers, who overheard. Elisha replied that the unbelieving lord would not live to share in the promised bounty. The next day the Aramaeans, who were camped in the valley near the city, heard what they thought were the hoofbeats of a great army. Thinking that Joram had hired Hittite or Egyptian mercenaries (2 Kings 7:6), they fled their camps and dashed back toward Damascus. In their haste, they left their food and gear behind to be found and appropriated by the starving population of Samaria, thanks to some beggars who had come upon the deserted tents. The nobleman who would not believe the prophet was trampled by the rampaging mob as it streamed forth through the gates of the city.

At length Benhadad of Syria became ill, and Elisha, under divine orders, went to Damascus to see him and to anoint a successor, as Elijah had been commissioned to do at Horeb (2 Kings 8:7). Hazael, one of the king's aides, met him and asked how the king would fare. Elisha said that the king would not die of this present sickness but would nevertheless die

18. For the nature of this god, see Unger, *Israel and the Aramaeans of Damascus,* 142.
19. For the chronology, see John Gray, *I and II Kings, A Commentary,* 2d ed. (Philadelphia: Westminster, 1970), 466.

of something else, and that Hazael would rule in his place. This Hazael must have taken as a hint, for he went into the royal palace, put a thick wet cloth over the sleeping king's face, and smothered him to death. Hazael then took the throne and reigned for over forty years (841–801).

In the south, Jehoram, son of Jehoshaphat, had been reigning (2 Kings 8:16; 2 Chron. 21:1). He was extremely evil, unlike his father, but this is understandable in that his wife was Athaliah, daughter of Ahab and Jezebel. During his rule the Edomites revolted from Judah, although, as previously observed, they had evidently sided with Judah at the time the Moabites rebelled from Israel. Jehoram was never able to recover Edom, perhaps largely because of a terrible internal disease he suffered in the last two years of his life. Moreover, his territory was invaded by the Philistines, Arabians, and Ethiopians, who continually harassed his southern borders. Finally his tragic reign ended in death, and the suffering Jehoram was followed by his son, Ahaziah (841), who was named for his uncle Ahaziah, the former king of Israel.

Ahaziah's other uncle, Joram, was the present king of Israel, and was then at war with Hazael of Damascus over the disputed city of Ramoth-gilead, the place where his father Ahab had lost his life some twelve years earlier (2 Kings 8:28; 2 Chron. 22:5). Ahaziah decided to help him in the campaign, but in the thick of the fray Joram was wounded and had to be carried to Jezreel. Ahaziah decided to visit his uncle at the country palace and was there with him when a crucial series of events took place.

Elisha, led by God, had sent a young prophet to the battlefield at Ramoth-gilead to anoint a dashing military commander, Jehu ben Nimshi, to be king of Israel (2 Kings 9:6). The prophet instructed him that he was to cut off the house of Ahab, including the old queen Jezebel, and avenge the blood of all the prophets who had suffered at their hands. Jehu left the field to others and returned to Jezreel as quickly as possible, for he knew, of course, that his king was there recuperating. Without delay, Jehu encountered Joram, took his bow and arrows, and slew the wicked king (2 Kings 9:24). Ahaziah, king of Judah, was soon spotted, and Jehu, knowing that he too was related to Ahab's dynasty, assassinated him at the same time (9:27). Thus, both kingdoms were shorn of their kings at once (ca. 841). Jezebel heard all the commotion and looked out the window of her chamber. Jehu caught a glimpse of her and ordered her chamberlains to cast her bodily through the opening, which they did. The dogs came and ate her flesh, as Elijah had predicted, so that there were barely any remains of the vile woman to be buried.

Dynasty of Jehu (2 Kings 9:6–15:12)

Jehu did not stop here. He proceeded to slaughter the seventy sons of Ahab and even went so far as to annihilate the family of Ahaziah of Judah, whom he found along the way. Then he took measures to rid the land of Baalism. He invited all the priests and prophets of Baal to assemble at the great temple of Baal at Samaria under the pretense of holding an important religious observance. When they had all come and were securely locked inside the building, Jehu turned his soldiers loose on the defenseless crowd and soon finished them off. "Thus Jehu destroyed Baal out of Israel" (2 Kings 10:28). From that time Baalism was a matter of little concern. Yet, one gets the distinct impression that Jehu did more than the will of God in some ways in his haughty pride and utter ruthlessness. In addition, he failed to remove the golden images from the shrines at Dan and Bethel and apparently resorted there for worship, as the kings of Israel had done before him. All this shortened his dynasty, for after four generations another family took the throne. Furthermore, the kingdom began to suffer the encroachments of foreign powers early in his reign. An important extrabiblical inscription known as the Black Obelisk records that Shalmaneser III forced Jehu to pay tribute to Assyria, apparently in Jehu's first year, and it is clear that Hazael of Damascus also threatened from time to time (2 Kings 10:32–33).[20]

In Jerusalem, Athaliah, mother of the late Ahaziah, sat on the Davidic throne. Her brief reign (841–835) was marked by an effort to destroy all the rest of the royal family, including, naturally, her own children and grandchildren, so that she might hold undisputed sway in the kingdom (2 Kings 11:1; 2 Chron. 22:10). One grandchild, Joash, escaped, thanks to a God-fearing aunt and a faithful priest, Jehoiada. When the lad became about seven years old, Jehoiada secretly took him to the temple into the presence of the nobility assembled there. At a prearranged signal, the royal crown was placed on the boy's head and the shout "God save the king!" rang forth. The queen in her nearby palace heard the excitement and rushed into the temple to learn its meaning. The priest then ordered her to be dragged into the outer court and slain, removing once and for all any vestige of Ahab's family in Judah. Joash then began to reign (835–796), at first under the governorship of Jehoiada, then alone. He inaugurated many sweeping changes, including the removal of any remnants of Baal worship. Among his other projects in this direction was the restoration of the temple, a project so successful that he had to restrain

20. For the text of the Black Obelisk, see Thomas, *Documents from Old Testament Times*, 48.

the people from their giving. Unfortunately, he also had his failings, notably his lack of effort in removing the high places, though it may be assumed that only Yahweh was tolerated there at first. Still, he permitted the worship of Asherah, newly revived, and even sanctioned the stoning of the prophet Zechariah, son of Jehoiada, who had spoken out against this new apostasy (2 Chron. 24:18, 21). He had to take some of the temple treasure to buy off Hazael, who had threatened to take Jerusalem, having pressed as far south as Gath in the Shephelah (2 Kings 12:18). His death was the climax to a trend toward evil, for some of his trusted servants rose up against him and assassinated him in his bed.

Jehu died by the year 814 and was succeeded by his son Jehoahaz (814–798). This unrighteous king was plagued throughout his life by Hazael and his son Benhadad II (801–?) of Damascus and, despite divine deliverance on many occasions, continued to live in sinful ways. The prophets of Asherah continued to pervert the people unmolested by the king or his son Jehoash (798–782) who followed him. The same conditions prevailed into the reign of Jeroboam II (793–753), though this outstanding figure did regain all the territory lost to the Aramaeans and brought to Israel a measure of the glory she had enjoyed in more happy days gone by.

The prophet Elisha lived on into the reign of Jehoash of Israel, but at last the time of his death drew near. The stubborn king came to the aged seer and asked him if he had a message from the Lord. Elisha told the king to take an arrow and shoot it out the window of the chamber. This done, he predicted that Jehoash would be able to repel the Aramaeans at Aphek. He then told the king to strike the ground with his bundle of arrows, but, suspecting that the old man must be demented, the king only half-heartedly complied. The prophet, in response, told him that he would gain only partial victory over his foes and would eventually be unsuccessful against them. And Jehoash did barely manage to seize his lost lands from Benhadad II and pass them on to his son Jeroboam II (2 Kings 13:24–25).

Amaziah followed his murdered father, Joash, in the Southern Kingdom (796–767), and continued his basically good policies. He also avenged the death of his father by executing his assassins. He then set his sights on Edom in an effort to bring the former Judaean province back under his sway. But he made the mistake of hiring Israel to cooperate with him, and an unknown prophet told him as much. Heeding the prophet's advice, he sent the Israelite troops home, a matter that did not sit well with Jehoash. Amaziah went on into Edom, destroyed the capital city, and carried the nation's gods home with him as booty. Unfortunately, he set them up in Jerusalem and worshiped them along with Yahweh, for which the prophet predicted the downfall of the king (2 Chron. 25:15–16).

Meanwhile, the Israelite soldiers who had been sent back home vengefully pillaged many villages of Judah on their way, while Amaziah was away in Edom. When the king of Judah returned in victory, he challenged Israel to make war over the matter, a war that turned out very badly for Amaziah. Jehoash warned him not to attempt such a contest, but Amaziah, fresh from victory over Edom, paid no heed, much to his sorrow; Jehoash came into Jerusalem itself and plundered the treasuries of the temple and the royal palace. Eventually Amaziah, like his father, was assassinated by his own people and died in ignominy at Lachish. His young son Uzziah (Azariah) ascended to the throne in his place (790–739).

The reign of Uzziah is described in Kings, Chronicles, and Isaiah, though the last book merely mentions that the prophet began his ministry in the year that Uzziah died (Isa. 6:1). This king of Judah was righteous for the most part, but he failed to remove the high places and allowed the people to worship there (2 Kings 15:4). He undertook successful campaigns against the Arabians and Philistines and extended the kingdom as far to the southwest as the border of Egypt. In line with this, he built strong fortifications in Jerusalem and other strategic places, including several towers and wells in the desert, the remains of which have been uncovered (2 Chron. 26:6–10).[21] In time he gained a widespread reputation for his skill in inventing engines of war and for his military successes. "But when he was strong his heart was lifted up to his destruction" (2 Chron. 26:16), and he forgot the source of all his strength. The result was that he became a leper and was forced to dwell in a separate dwelling the rest of his life. His son Jotham (750–731) co-reigned with him, apparently, until his death in 739.[22]

In Israel, Jeroboam II retrieved much of the territory lost to the Aramaeans, particularly that lost during the reigns of Jehu and Jehoahaz. He probably pushed the borders all the way back to where they were under Ahab, if not farther. The Lord allowed this out of compassion for wicked Israel, though Jeroboam II, like his early namesake, continued the policy of idol worship and toleration of the Baal cults that still persisted in scattered locales. By 753 he was dead, and his son Zachariah (753–752) took his place in Samaria.

21. Nelson Glueck, "The Seventh Season of Archaeological Exploration in the Negeb," *Bulletin of the American Schools of Oriental Research* 152 (1958): 18–38.

22. A seal of Jotham was found at Elath, on the Red Sea, supporting the statement of 2 Kings 14:22 that Uzziah "restored Elath." See Thomas, *Documents from Old Testament Times*, 48–49.

The Collapse of Israel (2 Kings 15:13–17:41)

This ushered in a period of anarchy and regicide matched only by the overthrow of the Baasha dynasty 130 years earlier. Zachariah reigned only six months before he was assassinated by a commoner, Shallum, who held power for just a month. He was deposed then by Menahem (752–742), who initiated a barbarous purge of all those in Israel who had refused to support him in his grab for power. But he failed in the long run, for the Assyrians, under the mighty Tiglath-pileser III (744–727), had begun to swoop down unimpeded on Syria and even to the gates of Samaria. Menahem was spared only by paying a huge bribe and heavy tribute thereafter. This transaction is known from both the biblical record and the extensive annals that Tiglath-pileser (Pul) himself left for posterity (2 Kings 15:19–20).[23] The result of this tribute was an onerous taxation, a burden that no doubt hastened the end of the kingdom.

Menahem was succeeded by his son Pekahiah (742–740), who after a short time was removed by his captain, Pekah (752–732). The chronology at this point is confusing, for it appears that Pekah reigned throughout the period of both Menahem and Pekahiah. Thiele's solution, that Pekah actually exercised a measure of authority all through this time, enough even to be considered a co-regent, seems quite plausible.[24] In other words, he gained full control only after Pekahiah's death, though he had worked behind the scenes for many years leading up to this. Sometime in his reign, possibly about 734 B.C., Tiglath-pileser came down against Israel once more and carried away captives from the Galilee to Assyria (2 Kings 15:29). This first phase of the overthrow of the Northern Kingdom prompted Hoshea ben Elah to put Pekah to death and to reign in his stead. According to the Assyrian records, Hoshea was placed on the throne by Tiglath-pileser, and it is very likely that this is so.[25] One may postulate that after Hoshea assassinated Pekah, he was rewarded by the Assyrian king with the throne of Israel. In any event, Hoshea did not remain loyal to the Assyrians, and in the reign of Shalmaneser V (727–722) they came down on Samaria once more and put Hoshea in prison for a time (ca. 725 B.C.). On his release he foolishly rebelled against the Assyrians again and attempted to hold off the Assyrian armies.[26] For three years the siege failed, but in the year 722 the walls were broken down. Sargon II (722–705),

23. Ibid., 54–56. Several kings of Israel and Judah are mentioned by name in these texts.
24. Thiele, *Mysterious Numbers of the Hebrew Kings*, 114–15. For a more complete defense of this hypothesis (with corrections), see Eugene H. Merrill, *Kingdom of Priests: A History of Old Testament Israel* (Grand Rapids: Baker, 1987), 396–98.
25. See the Nimrud Tablet in Thomas, *Documents from Old Testament Times*, 55.
26. For the view that Hoshea was carried off before 722 and was not returned to Samaria, see Bright, *A History of Israel*, 275.

who was second in command under Shalmaneser, entered the city and carried away all but the peasantry of the land.[27] In line with Assyrian policy, the Israelites were settled in various parts of the Assyrian Empire, and other peoples were moved into Israel to take their places in the care of the soil. The intermarriage of these immigrants with the Israelites left behind produced a people known to this day as the Samaritans.

Second Kings 17 reveals in unmistakable terms the reasons for the captivity of the Northern Kingdom, reasons that have unfolded continually in this study of the history of this faithless people. From the time they had left Egypt until then, they had refused to obey Moses and the prophets and had habitually broken the gracious covenants of God. The Lord had pleaded with them over and over to repent and had sent his servants the prophets to admonish them for their evil, but to no avail. The only remedy was this final and harsh expediency: the nation must learn the meaning of obedience through captivity and punishment.

In Judah, Jotham and Ahaz occupied the throne of David throughout these tragic days of their northern neighbors (2 Kings 15:32; 2 Chron. 27). The former king, son of Uzziah, followed closely in his father's steps, both good and bad. He neglected to remove the high places and even failed to observe the temple ceremonies, but made a name for himself in domestic and foreign affairs. He built new fortifications in Judah and brought the Ammonites under tribute. However, he was troubled by Rezin (750–732), king of Damascus, though both he and Rezin stood in the shadow of still greater threats from Tiglath-pileser. In the reign of his son Ahaz (735–715), Pekah, king of Israel, combined with Rezin to invade Judah (2 Kings 16:5), a foolish move considering how important it was for these little kings to stand united against Assyria rather than to divide against one another. Ahaz, in desperation, sent for aid from Tiglath-pileser, a move that had been much discouraged by Isaiah the prophet (Isa. 7). The king of Assyria lent his assistance, even going so far as to slay Rezin and carry off the inhabitants of the Galilee, but at a dear price to Ahaz.

This king of Judah was the most evil in that nation's history up until then. He not only followed the example of his fathers but went beyond to an unbelievable degree. For example, he offered his own children as burnt offerings and worshiped in the high places and groves (2 Kings 16:3–4; 2 Chron. 28:2–4). He found it necessary, moreover, to rob the temple of its treasures to pay Tiglath-pileser for his services. As if this were not enough, he went to Damascus, where the Assyrian king was quartered, and, seeing the great altar of the Assyrian gods there, ordered one like it placed in the

---

27. Sargon has recorded this in his annals found at Khorsabad. For the text, see Thomas, *Documents from Old Testament Times*, 59.

temple at Jerusalem. These gods were powerless to help him, and Ahaz died, having been saved from Assyrian captivity only because he had sold his soul to Assyria and for the sake of David, whom God yet remembered.

With Israel in captivity, attention now falls almost exclusively on Judah. Under Ahaz this kingdom had almost perished because of the hostility of the Aramaeans, Israelites, Edomites, and Philistines, but Ahaz did survive seven years after Samaria's collapse (2 Chron. 28:18–19). He was followed by his son, the good king Hezekiah (715–686), who reversed as much as possible the iniquitous policies of his father. Besides the accounts in Kings and Chronicles, there is the full discussion of Isaiah for this period.

The Prophets of the Period

In addition to the prophets Elijah, Elisha, Micaiah, and others mentioned in this chapter, there were others whose names, except for one or

Table 7

The Writing Prophets

Name	Dates	Object
Obadiah	ca. 840–830	Edom
Joel	ca. 830–820	Judah
Jonah	785–775	Nineveh
Amos	765–755	Israel
Hosea	755–715	Israel
Isaiah	739–680	Israel and Judah
Micah	735–700	Israel and Judah
Nahum	ca. 650–620	Assyria
Zephaniah	635–625	Judah
Jeremiah	627–575	Judah
Habakkuk	620–610	Judah
Daniel	605–536	The nations
Ezekiel	593–560	Judah
Haggai	520	Jews
Zechariah	520–518	Jews
Malachi	470	Jews

two (Jonah and Isaiah), do not occur in the historical books. They lived in this time, however, and their own books of prophecy provide invaluable information regarding the historical background. It is impossible to discuss each prophet fully in a work devoted to a historical survey of the Old Testament, but it is important at least to list them and give very brief résumés of their historical importance and sketchy outlines of their books.

Obadiah

It is impossible to assign a certain date to this prophet and his book because of the lack of any clear historical references either internally or externally. Gleason L. Archer offers convincing reasons to date the book from about the latter part of the ninth century, which makes Obadiah contemporary with Elisha.[28] The reason for this is that Obadiah (and this is the theme of the book) predicts that Edom would be destroyed by the Lord for having failed to assist Judah, her brother, in a time of need. This mandates that one look for a time before the destruction of Edom and after such a period of danger for Judah. It was pointed out above that Amaziah demolished Edom ca. 790 B.C., so this is the latest possible date. Before that, in the reign of Rehoboam (931–913), Shishak of Egypt had invaded Judah and taken the temple treasures. There is no explicit information as to Edom's attitude, though it is not unreasonable to assume that the Edomites failed to assist Judah and even sided with Egypt. The time of Jehoram of Judah (853–841) may be best, however, for it is very likely that the Edomites assisted the Philistines and Arabians in sacking Jerusalem during his reign (2 Chron. 21:16–17).

Regardless of the time involved, the message is clear. The haughty and proud nation of Edom, secure in its mountains and valleys, would become an object of God's judgment. And the people of God would inherit Edom's territories and dwell in safety.

> OUTLINE OF OBADIAH
> I. Certainty of judgment (1–9)
> II. Cause of judgment (10–15)
> III. Conclusion of judgment (16–21)

Joel

It is possible that the next prophet in historical order was Joel, but again there is little evidence one way or another. The message of this

---

28. Gleason L. Archer, Jr., *A Survey of Old Testament Introduction*, rev. ed. (Chicago: Moody, 1974), 307–8.

prophet, who may have lived at the turn of the eighth century (ca. 800 B.C.),[29] is directed to Judah and has as its theme the Day of the Lord. This expression, which appears frequently in the prophetic books, speaks of the time of divine judgment and has many connotations. For example, it may speak of a historical day of judgment, or a period of judgment, or even an eschatological day or period of reckoning. At times, all of these may be in mind because the prophet, looking down through the years, may not distinguish in his mind exactly what fulfillment he sees. This "perspective" nature of prophecy allows many prophecies to have many fulfillments, though these fulfillments generally are somehow related.

So Joel sees the unfolding of Judah's sin and the punishment that must follow. He speaks of the Day of Yahweh when a great nation (Babylon) will come on the land to lay it waste (1:1–7). But he goes on to extend the promise of forgiveness if the nation will only turn to God (2:12–14). Then, in another aspect of the Day of the Lord, he indicates that the time will come when God will pour out his spirit on all flesh, with most amazing results (2:28–32; cf. Acts 2:16–21). Finally, he says that there will be a great day of wrath in which God will gather the nations of the world to battle (3:1–2), following which he will redeem his own forever (3:18–21). The outline indicates the order in which these events are recorded in his book.

OUTLINE OF JOEL
I. Plague of the locusts (1)
II. Prophecy of the Day of the Lord (2:1–27)
III. Promise of the Holy Spirit (2:28–32)
IV. Pronouncement of judgment (3)

Jonah

It is not difficult to locate Jonah in history, for he is mentioned in relation to Jeroboam II of Israel (2 Kings 14:25). This places him somewhere in the first quarter of the eighth century, in a time when Assyria was relatively quiet. His commission was to preach against Nineveh, the capital of Assyria, and to warn the great metropolis of its impending doom. He sought to evade the call (Jon. 1), was swallowed up by a great fish specially prepared for the occasion (Jon. 2), and arrived at Nineveh anyway. There he preached a message so convicting that mass repentance resulted, and God withheld what he had threatened to do to the city (3:10). Jonah, however, having expected God to visit the city with his wrath, was bitterly

29. A. F. Kirkpatrick, *The Doctrine of the Prophets: The Warburtonian Lectures for 1886–1890,* 3d ed. (London: Macmillan, 1901), 58–60.

disappointed when the fireworks failed to materialize (4:1). But God (and this is the real theme) asked the prophet if true repentance did not deserve divine mercy. To this the man of God could only give silent assent.

OUTLINE OF JONAH
    I. Jonah's perversity (1)
    II. Jonah's prayer (2)
    III. Jonah's preaching (3)
    IV. Jonah's pouting (4)

Amos

The prophet Amos lived and ministered in the luxuriant age of Jeroboam II. As noted, this king had regained the lands lost to Israel just prior to his time and had restored Israel to a position of great wealth and prosperity. This produced an atmosphere of materialism and carelessness in worship. To counteract this situation, God sent Amos (ca. 765–755), an untrained farmer and shepherd from Tekoa in Judah, to inveigh against the Israelite court. The message of this prophet of doom was anything but pleasant to Jeroboam and his nobility, and they made every effort to send the man of God home. But Amos fearlessly delivered the burden that God had given him.

It is possible to see from Amos, almost better than from any other book, the social and spiritual conditions of the eighth century. The rich were severely oppressing the poor and living in great opulence in their ivory houses (3:15; 4:1; 5:12). The people were worshiping unashamedly at the shrines of the golden calf at Bethel and Dan (3:14; 4:4; 8:14). The political leaders subsisted largely on bribes and put their confidence in their own military and strategic strength (2:14–15; 6:1; 9:2–3). As a result, Amos said, the kingdom of Israel would meet violent destruction at the hands of a great oppressor (6:14). This was understood to refer to Assyria, whose troops had already begun to mass for attack under Ashurdan III. In the end the Lord would save his people and "raise up the tabernacle of David that is fallen" (9:11). Then nobody would be able to pull them up out of the land that the Lord would give them forever.

Amos is particularly instructive in showing us that a man need not be a member of the "sons of the prophets" (the meaning of 7:14) in order to be called to do the prophet's task. It seems that he was engaged in agricultural pursuits when God issued the divine call to service, and, without further preparation except for the revelation from the Lord, he set forth to thunder out the message to the nation of the north. His was an ad hoc ministry, one made possible by a special call and filling by God's Spirit. In an earlier generation of scholarship it was popular to maintain that Amos was the first true prophet, as though Samuel, Elijah, and Elisha were something less, but this was usually thought because he was one of the first prophets to commit his message to writing.[30] It is not clear, however, how this makes Amos more of a prophet than others who preceded him, for they, like Amos, responded to a call from God and exercised a faithful ministry, though their written messages, if any, are not in canonical literature. Some also made a point of proving that Amos, unlike his predecessors, was not an ecstatic prophet and that he introduced a long line of prophets who were not after the order of the Canaanite dervish-type prophets.[31] The fallacy of classifying the early Hebrew prophets as ecstatics has already been addressed, and once again it must be stressed that there is not the slightest biblical evidence to support the charge. Just because Elijah lived among Canaanite prophets who became overpowered with uncontrollable fits of religious enthusiasm is no reason to say that he was of their ilk. This is an insupportable argument from silence.

Yet with Amos a new direction did seem to arise. Now there are individuals whose main function is not working miracles but serving as correctives to the unstable monarchy and priesthood that characterized this period. But the prophets cannot be accused of having political or cultic ambitions, as some scholars suggest. Neither Amos nor any other true prophet was interested in the monarchy for political reasons of his own; each wanted only to deliver to the kings the "thus saith the Lord." Likewise, Amos did not desire to involve himself in the responsibilities of the priesthood as though he himself desired to be a priest or wished to introduce a new way of worship.[32] He wanted only to rid the priesthood of the undesirables, of whom there were many, and bring the people back to the faith of their fathers as expressed in the ancient law codes. The prophets were reformers, then; not reformers in the sense that they had developed higher and more refined theological concepts than already existed under such "crude" prophets as Samuel and Elijah, or even Moses, but in the sense that the early revealed covenant faith had been forsaken in the present generation and needed to be regained. They did not develop a new "ethical monotheism,"[33] as some critics are wont to say, but only urged a return to the pure monotheism presupposed by the law.

30. John Bayne Ascham, *The Religion of Israel* (New York: Abingdon, 1918), 115.

31. Alfred Guillaume, *Prophecy and Divination Among the Hebrews and Other Semites* (New York: Harper and Brothers, 1938), 110.

32. Thus Aubrey Johnson, *The Cultic Prophet in Ancient Israel* (Cardiff: University of Wales, 1944), 52.

33. Edward W. Hopkins, *The History of Religions* (New York: Macmillan, 1918), 431.

Amos, as the first of these "new prophets," created by his inspired ministry a certain tension between prophet, on the one hand, and priest and king, on the other, that could be resolved only by repentance by priest and king alike and a national return to God. This was the burden of his message, together with declaring alternative fruits of obedience and disobedience. If the nation would come back to God, there would be salvation and healing; if not, there would be certain judgment, though the immutable covenant with Abraham, Moses, and David required an ultimate day of glory and triumph for the saints.

OUTLINE OF AMOS
I. Punishment of the nations (1:1–2:5)
II. Punishment of Israel (2:6–9:15)
    A. Nature of the sin (2:6–16)
    B. Promise of judgment (3–4)
    C. Plea for repentance (5)
    D. Prediction of captivity (6)
    E. Defense of Amos (7)
    F. Promise of restoration (8–9)

Hosea

The last of the prophets whose ministry ended in the eighth century was Hosea. It is likely that his prophetic activity stretched over a period of at least forty years (ca. 755–715), embracing the reigns of several kings of Israel and Judah. He was sent especially to Israel with his message of divine love in an effort to turn the nation once again to the God who had given its raison d'etre, but the nation would not respond. Like Amos, Hosea could see only captivity by Assyria if Israel persisted in sin, and, indeed, he lived to see that tragic day.

The life of the prophet reflected the relationship between God and his people in a most lucid way. The Lord told the man of God to go and marry a woman who would become a harlot (1:2). Without argument, the faithful prophet did as he was told. After three children were born, all of whose names suggested the evil about to come to Israel, the faithless wife, Gomer, departed. Some time passed, and one day the hapless Hosea saw Gomer in the employ of her masters (3:1). Rather than revolting at the sight of his wife turned prostitute, the heart of the good man reached out to her, and he bargained with her owners to buy her back to himself.

Though some dismiss this as mere legend or parable, it seems that the only realistic interpretation is to take it as a true account of the life of the

prophet.[34] Hosea, having suffered such an experience, could now understand well the broken heart of God who had loved his own bride, Israel,
so much that he had brought her out of the bondage of Egypt (11:1). Even
now, God stood with outstretched arms, ready to forgive and cleanse his
adulterous wife, but the nation would not hear (6:1–3; 11:8; 14:1). Like a
silly dove Israel had hired herself out to other lovers like Egypt and
Assyria, and God's great love had gone unrequited (7:11). At last God
had had to turn his people over to those who would chastise them
(9:1–6), until finally they would see the error of their way and return to
him (13:9–14). Someday they would acknowledge his love and he would
restore them freely (14:4).

OUTLINE OF HOSEA

    I. Illustration of divine love (1–3)
        A. Marriage of the prophet (1)
        B. Message of the prophet (2)
        C. Mercy of the prophet (3)
   II. Indication of divine love (4–14)
        A. Defection of the people (4–7)
           1. Their sinfulness (4–5)
           2. Their stubbornness (6)
           3. Their silliness (7)
        B. Destruction of the people (8–12)
           1. Weakness of their gods (8)
           2. Wasting of their goods (9)
           3. Wresting of their glory (10–12)
        C. Deliverance of the people (13–14)
           1. Sin of Israel (13:1–8)
           2. Salvation of Israel (13:9–14:9)

---

34. Keil thinks that the marriage was symbolic only. See C. F. Keil, *Biblical Commentary on the Old
Testament: Minor Prophets*, vol. 1 (reprint ed.; Grand Rapids: Eerdmans, 1948), 38. In contrast, see
Edward B. Pusey, *The Minor Prophets: A Commentary, Explanatory and Practical*, 2 vols. (Grand Rapids:
Baker, 1950), 1:21.

Catharsis Before Calamity

Historical Background

The history of this period (722–586) and shortly after is the history of three great empires in succession.[1] Assyria reached its zenith in the eighth century and continued to maintain it well into the seventh. But by 625 there was no question that her former glory was irrecoverable, and within two decades she passed from the world scene entirely. Babylonia, under the inspiration of the Sealands Dynasty, had shown signs of awakening as early as the end of the eighth century, but only at the founding of the Neo-Babylonian Empire under Nabopolassar (626), an event coincident with and contributory to the collapse of Assyria, did the lower Mesopotamian land resume the importance it had lost a thousand years earlier. But what it regained, it rapidly lost, for by 539 Cyrus of Persia had reduced the great head of gold (see Dan. 2:31–45) to dust, and the Persian Empire took its place. This massive empire, spread from Greece in the west to India in the east, continued throughout the rest of the Old Testament period; not until Alexander the Great destroyed its last stronghold at Arbela in 331 B.C. did it pass into oblivion, to be supplanted by the Macedonians.

1. For fuller historical detail, see John Bright, A *History of Israel*, 3d ed. (Philadelphia: Westminster, 1981), 310–39.

Other nations like Egypt, Aramaea, Elam, Media, and Urartu must be considered in their relationships to these three great powers, as, of course, must Judah, but it might be best to establish such relationships not independently but as they occur in the detailed exposition of the historical narrative. To this we turn.

Sargon II, the self-possessed conqueror of Samaria, found himself in difficulty from the beginning of his reign. The Sealands Dynasty, at the head of the Persian Gulf, fell into the hands of a Babylonian nobleman, Merodach-baladan (722–711), who, with assistance from the Elamites, a neighboring people, declared Babylonia independent. Because Sargon was busy in the west and south at the time, he had no recourse but to permit Merodach-baladan to remain in power for a few years. When he did manage to expel him, the persistent Babylonian came back again very shortly and was not successfully removed until Sennacherib of Assyria (705–681) did so shortly after 700 B.C. Sargon also had to contend with invaders from Asia Minor and, in the north, with Urartu (Ararat), a people whom he destroyed with the help of savage tribesmen from south Russia.

In Egypt, the Twenty-second and Twenty-third dynasties were competing in a divided land. They both soon collapsed and were followed by the Twenty-fourth (725–709), the dynasty in power at the time Israel was taken captive. This feeble government also ended in a short time because of the rise of Ethiopian invaders who now swept into Lower Egypt and established the Twenty-fifth Dynasty (715–656). Their first king, Piankhi, restored to Egypt comparative influence, enough so that Hezekiah would try to get her to assist Judah in its efforts against Assyria.

Reign of Hezekiah (2 Kings 18–20; 2 Chronicles 29–32)

Hezekiah ascended the throne of his father Ahaz in 715 B.C.,[2] just six years after Sargon destroyed Samaria. This good king set out immediately to rid the kingdom of everything that had contributed to Israel's downfall, including the bronze serpent of Moses that had been turned into an object of idolatry (2 Kings 18:4). The result was a religious reformation the like of which Judah had not seen in all her history and would never see again. Even the pious of Samaria were invited to come to Jerusalem to participate in the worship of Yahweh (2 Chron. 30:1), something they had not been able to do legitimately since the kingdom was divided two hundred years before. This action may suggest some effort to reunify the nation

2. The dates for the kings of Judah are those of Edwin R. Thiele, *The Mysterious Numbers of the Hebrew Kings*, 3d ed. (Chicago: University of Chicago Press, 1983).

politically as well; if so, this constituted a brazen act of rebellion against Assyria, for Samaria now was an Assyrian province.[3]

Ahaz had remained subservient to Assyria, but Hezekiah, in line with his desire to reverse his father's policies, decided to rid Judah of Assyrian domination. He apparently was too preoccupied throughout the reign of Sargon with his programs of domestic reform to think much about revolution, but when Sennacherib became king he no doubt thought the change in administration was propitious for his moves in that direction. Besides, Egypt once more was powerful under the leadership of Piankhi and could be relied on to help remove the Assyrian threat. Isaiah insisted, however, that Hezekiah have nothing to do with the Egyptians, for they could not be trusted (Isa. 31:1–3); instead the people should trust in God.

The first act of resistance to Assyria consisted of withholding the tribute that had been paid since the time of Ahaz (2 Kings 18:7).[4] This act evidently was timed to coincide with Sennacherib's difficulties in Babylonia with Merodach-baladan and with increased Egyptian boldness under Shabako (710–696). In fact, Merodach-baladan even came to Judah to gain Hezekiah's support in his campaign against Assyria. Other lesser states like Tyre and some of the Philistine cities also became involved and, with Judah, formed a coalition to withstand what they knew to be certain Assyrian retribution. At this time Hezekiah rebuilt the fortifications of Jerusalem and environs (2 Chron. 32:1–8), constructing a water tunnel from the spring Gihon outside the city to the Pool of Siloam within (2 Kings 20:20). With courage and faith he awaited the impending assault by Sennacherib, feeling that his God would prevail no matter the odds.

In 701 Sennacherib moved west and south, sweeping all resistance from his path, until he reached Judah and Philistia. He even defeated the Egyptian army at Eltekah, but did not venture into Egypt. He then turned on the Philistine cities, which he easily destroyed, and finally set out for Judah. After taking some forty-six Judaean cities, he approached Jerusalem itself. Hezekiah then offered to come to terms by paying an immense sum to protect the city from destruction (2 Kings 18:13–16).

Shortly before that time Hezekiah became so ill that he thought he was going to die (2 Kings 20:1; 2 Chron. 32:24; Isa. 38:1). In desperation he turned to the Lord, and the Lord sent Isaiah to him with a message that he would live after all because God had heard his prayer. As a sign that the healing was a certainty, the Lord caused the sundial to go backward ten degrees, thus lengthening the day by some forty minutes. After the miracle,

3. W. F. Albright, *The Biblical Period from Abraham to Ezra* (New York: Harper and Row, 1963), 77.
4. This is the interpretation of Bright, *A History of Israel*, 284.

Merodach-baladan of Babylonia came to visit Hezekiah, ostensibly to wish him speedy recovery, but actually to enlist his support against the Assyrians (2 Kings 20:12–13). This Hezekiah cheerfully volunteered, and in a most amicable spirit he took the Babylonian on a guided tour of the city and temple, showing him everything, sacred and profane. Isaiah condemned this bitterly, predicting to the king that the time would come when these same Babylonian people would come into Jerusalem on an errand of destruction and would carry off the same holy treasures they had now seen (Isa. 39:6–7).

Some scholars propose that there was a second campaign by Sennacherib against Hezekiah several years later, for the story of the destruction of Assyria's army by the Angel of Yahweh, an event that they say could not have occurred in the siege of 701, must have happened later.[5] This second campaign, according to the proponents of this view, is described in Isaiah 36:2–37:36, 2 Kings 18:17–19:36, and 2 Chronicles 32:9–21. This must be dated about 689 B.C., for Tirhakah of Egypt, mentioned in connection with the siege, began to reign at that time.[6] Those who reject the two campaign hypothesis, however, point out that the Egyptian text on which the date of Tirhakah's accession to the throne is based has been misinterpreted and that he was indeed of adult age in 701 B.C. and fully capable of leading Egypt's armies then.[7] Moreover, the Taylor Prism (see n. 9), which presents Assyria's version of the siege, is incompatible with the biblical rendition only because Sennacherib understandably did not document the massacre of his own army. On the whole, it is best to understand the scenario as consisting of one Assyrian campaign (in 701 B.C.) with different phases.[8]

In any case, Sennacherib sent some of his ambassadors to Jerusalem to persuade Hezekiah to submit voluntarily, but he refused. Yet the king knew that he was in the gravest peril, so he sent for Isaiah the prophet. Contrary to his earlier advice to yield to the Assyrians, the prophet now urged the king to stand firm, for God would trouble Sennacherib by a rumor that assistance was coming to Judah from another source (Isa. 37:7). But even when the Assyrian king heard that Tirhakah, the Ethiopian king of Egypt, was on his way, he refused to be deterred from his objective of destroying Jerusalem.[9]

5. See Bright's extensive excursus on the historical and chronological problems of this period in A History of Israel, 298–309.

6. Martin Noth, The Old Testament World (Philadelphia: Fortress, 1966), 249.

7. See especially K. A. Kitchen, The Third Intermediate Period in Egypt (1100–650 B.C.) (Warminster: Aris and Phillips, 1973), 157–61.

8. For full argument, see Eugene H. Merrill, Kingdom of Priests: A History of Old Testament Israel (Grand Rapids: Baker, 1987), 413–15.

9. Sennacherib states that he had shut Hezekiah up in Jerusalem "like a caged bird." See the text of the Taylor Prism in D. Winton Thomas, ed. Documents from Old Testament Times (London: Thomas Nelson, 1958), 66–67.

Again he issued an ultimatum to Hezekiah to surrender while he could. This time Isaiah responded that, because Sennacherib had blasphemed the God of Judah by comparing him to the impotent gods of the nations he had conquered, he would not enter Jerusalem but would be forced to retreat to his homeland in shame. That night the Angel of Yahweh swept over the Assyrian camp and slew 185,000 troops, a calamity that gave Sennacherib no choice but to return home.[10]

Twenty years after his return to Nineveh, Sennacherib was murdered in the temple of Nisroch by two of his sons and was succeeded by a third son, Esarhaddon (681–669).[11] This able ruler stabilized the unsettled condition of government in Babylon by recognizing the validity of Marduk, the chief Babylonian deity, thus obtaining popular support for Assyria. He later pressed on into Egypt, hoping to eliminate the harassment that had come from that source ever since the founding of the Ethiopian Twenty-fifth Dynasty. By 671 he had defeated Tirhakah and had gone all the way to Memphis, which he occupied and made the center of his Egyptian domains. When his army left, however, Tirhakah rebelled; when Esarhaddon returned to put down the insurrection, he took sick and died along the way. His son Ashurbanipal (669–633) carried on, successfully routing Tirhakah and eventually (ca. 663) going as far south as Thebes (No).

Hezekiah reigned with his son Manasseh for the last ten years of his life; when he died, the young prince was ready to take the authority immediately. He ruled for fifty-five years (695–642, including the co-regency). He immediately made it known that he would set a new record in Judah for wholesale apostasy by building altars to the Baals and planting groves to Asherah. Moreover, he served the hosts of heaven, the planets and stars, and even built altars in their honor within the temple (2 Kings 21:3–7; 2 Chron. 33:2–7). Like Ahaz, he offered his children as sacrifices in the Valley of Hinnom and consulted witches and other workers of evil. In fact, the biblical testimony is that no king of either Israel or Judah excelled him in the abundance and nature of his iniquity.

The Book of Kings is silent as to whether Manasseh ever repented of his sins, but Chronicles makes a point of underscoring that the Assyrians came and carried him off to Assyria in bonds (2 Chron. 33:11).[12] When

10. Herodotus described the defeat of an Assyrian army by a plague, but there is no evidence of a plague in the biblical account. There is no alternative but to accept a miracle. Cf. Merrill F. Unger, *Archaeology and the Old Testament* (Grand Rapids: Zondervan, 1954), 269.

11. The Prism of Esarhaddon found at Nineveh confirms this. See Thomas, *Documents from Old Testament Times*, 72.

12. In line with this, see ibid., 74.

this happened is impossible to tell, but apparently the experience humbled the king so that when he returned to Jerusalem he turned to Yahweh, destroyed all the pagan altars and images, and repaired the neglected altar of God. But all this reformation was insufficient to erase the prophets' declaration that Jerusalem would be dealt with in the same manner as was Samaria (2 Kings 21:10–16). The revival under the leadership of Hezekiah had only stopped the gap between Ahaz and Manasseh temporarily; Manasseh's long reign had completely reversed any trend toward righteousness, sounding the death knell for Judah.

The Prophets of the Period (725–675)

Isaiah

Even before the collapse and captivity of Samaria there had arisen in Judah a man whose prophetic ministry was to make of him one of the most illustrious figures in history. Isaiah ben Amoz became conscious of the call of God in the same year that king Uzziah of Judah died, ca. 739 B.C. (Isa. 6:1). All through the incredibly difficult days of Tiglath-pileser's conquests of Samaria and on into those of Ahaz and Hezekiah of Judah, the courageous seer spoke the counsel of God. Apart from Jeremiah, no prophet's life and ministry are better known, and none excels him in the strength and beauty of his prophetic declarations.

Isaiah apparently came from a high social stratum in Jerusalem. All through his life he associated with royalty and occupied a place of unrivaled opportunity as far as shaping policy was concerned. Jotham, Ahaz, and Hezekiah, especially, knew him intimately and depended on him to an immeasurable degree, though his counsel was as often flouted as not. But, though he had come from good material circumstances, his eyes were not closed to the needs of the poor and afflicted. With boldness and zeal he attacked the social ills of the day, not just because he was a social reformer, but because he recognized that these abuses were a graphic index to the terribly sick spiritual life of the nation (1:3–9). In ancient Israel, there was no distinction between secular and sacred; a weakness in any part of the theocratic body was a blight on the whole corpus.

The prophet first became involved politically, at least on any significant scale, at the time of the Pekah-Rezin coalition against Judah (735–732). As noted before, Ahaz decided that his only alternative was to appeal to Tiglath-pileser III for assistance. Isaiah realized, however, that if Ahaz would quietly trust the Lord, the Syrian-Israelite alliance would come to nought (7:4). But Ahaz would not believe even when a special sign was given, so Isaiah had to tell him that his request of Tiglath-pileser would result in Assyria's domination of Judah. The sign, now famous, was that a virgin would conceive, bear a son, and call his name Immanuel ("God with us"). This prophecy naturally had some reference to a young woman of Ahaz's day, but it found its ultimate fulfillment in Jesus Christ, God in the flesh (7:14; cf. Matt. 1:23).[13]

Another child was born, this time to the prophet and his wife, and the Lord told Isaiah that the Northern Kingdom would fall before the child came of age (8:3). In the midst of these dire predictions, Isaiah confidently believed that God ultimately would restore his people through a holy child who would become the "Prince of Peace" (9:6). At the same time, Assyria, the threat to Judah and the whole world, would be broken by the Lord, who had used the nation only as a rod to chasten his own nation (10:5). Babylon, Moab, Syria, Ethiopia, Egypt, Arabia, and Tyre also were embraced in the prophet's denunciation; all were doomed to destruction because of their pride and arrogance.

Israel and Judah must recognize that they were not exempt from God's wrath. Even reliance on Egypt would not help (30:1–17), for the Egyptians were men and not God, their horses were flesh and not spirit (31:1–3). Only when the two nations repented and returned to God could they be assured of continued existence and of a future bright with the promises of a new heaven and earth (Isa. 35).

When Samaria fell, Isaiah turned his full attention to Judah, warning that kingdom of the folly of repeating the sins of her northern neighbor. When Hezekiah became king, the prophet found a willing heart to which he could outline the divine will. The good king, whose activities already have been described, was assured by Isaiah in his very first year on the throne that the Assyrians would not be able to injure Jerusalem (14:3–23). When the invasion of Sargon in 715 took place, Isaiah warned Hezekiah against trusting the Egyptians or Philistines, maintaining that the latter themselves would become slaves of Assyria (20:4). Though the people of Judah must not seek help in resisting Assyria, they must themselves resist the oppressor through their faith in God (31:5).

In the invasion of Sennacherib in 701, Isaiah recommended that Hezekiah stand fast and watch the miraculous deliverance that the Lord would effect (37:33–35). The death of the 185,000 troops certified that

---

13. Because the word *almah* can mean "young woman" or "virgin," it seems that the passage must have a twofold application; otherwise, the virgin birth aspect would have been meaningless to Ahaz. Yet, the primary reference was to the virgin birth of Christ, as Matthew plainly states. For the view that only the birth of Christ is in mind here, see Edward J. Young, *The Book of Isaiah*, 3 vols. (Grand Rapids: Eerdmans, 1965–72), 1:289–91. For the view that both a woman in Ahaz's time and a future virgin (Mary) are intended, see John A. Martin, "Isaiah," *The Bible Knowledge Commentary, Old Testament,* ed. John F. Walvoord and Roy B. Zuck (Wheaton: Victor, 1985), 1047–48.

God answered prayer and had a further purpose for his people. Through all his trying relations with the Assyrians, Hezekiah found a comforting and capable support in the prophet. After the death of Hezekiah, nothing further is said of Isaiah, though Jewish tradition suggests that he was martyred by the ungodly Manasseh.[14]

The last twenty-seven chapters of Isaiah (40–66) express an entirely different approach to the prophet's ministry. Whereas the first part was largely historical, though interspersed heavily with various oracles, this latter section is wholly predictive, with special attention to the eschatological aspects of Israel's future. Higher critics for nearly two centuries have denied that Isaiah wrote this part of the book, but on the flimsiest of evidence. There is no question that the early Jewish and Christian writers believed in the unity of the book, and Jesus and the apostles invariably ascribed the last section to Isaiah (John 1:23; 12:38; Luke 4:17; Matt. 3:3; Rom. 10:16, 20). The internal evidences, too involved and lengthy to be considered here,[15] also point to the unavoidable conclusion that the prophet wrote the entire composition. The chief reason for rejecting Isaianic authorship for this part is that there are so many detailed and specific predictions that one must presuppose supernaturalism in order to believe that Isaiah wrote it. The only alternative for the critic is that this section is history, not prophecy.[16] But if one accepts the biblical doctrine of verbal inspiration, the difficulties along this line cease altogether.

It is clear that Isaiah's purpose in writing is to comfort the captives and those who still live under the shadow of impending captivity (40:1). The time will come when the glory of the Lord will be revealed and "the word of our God shall stand forever" (40:8). This will be accomplished through the Servant of Yahweh (Isa. 42), who will be filled with God's Spirit and will bring judgment on the Gentiles (42:1; cf. Matt. 12:18). The folly of idols will be seen (44:9), and indeed they will be destroyed. Among the instruments of the Lord in performing his will in the future will be Cyrus, a king who will contribute to the building of the house of the Lord in Jerusalem. He will also figure in the destruction of Babylon, from whence the chosen of the Lord will be delivered (44:28; 45:1).

The highlight of these glorious chapters is certainly the elaboration of the Servant concept in 52:13–53:12. The Servant will be humiliated, beaten, and put to death, all for the sins of his people. He will be the

14. John D. W. Watts, *Isaiah 1–33*, Word Biblical Commentary (Waco: Word, 1985), xxv–xxvi.

15. See O. T. Allis, *The Unity of Isaiah: A Study in Prophecy* (Philadelphia: Presbyterian and Reformed, 1950).

16. Bernhard W. Anderson, *Understanding the Old Testament*, 4th ed. (Englewood Cliffs, N. J.: Prentice-Hall, 1986), 472.

means of bringing forgiveness to mankind and eventually will triumph even over sin and death. That this refers primarily to the Messiah is agreed by most interpreters, though many say that the Servant is either idealistic or speaks only of the future nation of Israel that will be God's means of redeeming the world.[17] The inescapable individualism of the passage, coupled with the fulfillment in Christ, suggests without question that Isaiah is painting in starkly realistic lines and colors the real and vital function of the Son of God in the prophetic future.

The remaining chapters of the book outline the benefits to be derived from the Servant's vicarious work. Included are satisfaction for the thirsty (55:1), forgiveness to the penitent (57:13), salvation to the Gentiles (60:3), and the reconstitution of Jerusalem, Israel, and the whole earth as the dwelling place of God and his saints forevermore (65:17–66:24). Words of greater comfort to people uprooted from their homes and land can scarcely be imagined. The imagery and poetic genius in which the thoughts are couched add to the grandeur of the glorious promises.

> OUTLINE OF ISAIAH[18]
>   I. The retribution of God (1–39)
>   A. The Lord's indictment of the nation (1–6)
>   B. Prophecies of deliverance (7–12)
>   C. Judgment on the nations (13–23)
>   D. Punishment and kingdom blessing (24–27)
>   E. The woes (28–33)
>   F. Vengeance and blessing (34–35)
>   G. Historical interlude (36–39)
>   II. The restoration by God (40–66)
>   A. Deliverance of God's people (40–48)
>   B. Restoration by the Servant (49–57)
>   C. Restoration completed (58–66)

Micah

A contemporary of Isaiah in Jerusalem was Micah, a lesser figure whose life nearly paralleled that of his colleague. Like Isaiah, this prophet inveighed against the social and moral aberrations of the time, paying special heed to the corrupt rulers and priests and the false prophets who cried "Peace!" when there was none (3:5). The people were trusting in the ceremony of their reli-

17. Otto Eissfeldt, "The Prophetic Literature," in *The Old Testament and Modern Study: A Generation of Discovery and Research*, ed. H. H. Rowley (Oxford: Clarendon, 1951), 147–51.

18. The outline of Isaiah is adapted from Martin, "Isaiah," 1032–33.

gion but had completely forgotten the spirit behind it all; thus, the prophet struck out against their empty formality, telling them in scathing terms that the Lord had no use for their hypocritical sacrifices. What he did demand was that they "do justly, love mercy, and walk humbly with God" (6:8).

But despite the headlong plunge of Judah into disaster in the footsteps of Israel, someday God would remember his people for good (4:1–8). The temple mountain would be exalted above all the earth; the nations, forgetting their war and conflict, would all flow to Jerusalem; and the Lord would reign forever and ever (Mic. 4). His ruler, who would come and accomplish this, in addition to the overthrow of Assyria and the wicked nations, would originate in Bethlehem Ephrathah (in Judah). He would permit the ravaging of his people for a time in order to teach them his displeasure at their sin (5:2–3). Then, in a demonstration of his wondrous grace, he would have compassion on them and remember his eternal covenant with Abraham and Jacob (7:19–20).

> OUTLINE OF MICAH
> I. Condemnation of idolatry (1)
> II. Corruption of the people (2)
> III. Craftiness of the leaders (3)
> IV. Consummation of the kingdom (4)
> V. Conquest of the Messiah (5)
> VI. Controversy with the nation (6)
> VII. Consolation of the nation (7)

The Last Years of Judah

Ashurbanipal extended Assyria's might farther than any of his predecessors, but the end of his empire came soon because of certain national and international complications that began to set in. In Egypt, the Twenty-sixth Dynasty, under Psammeticus I (663–609), began. This able ruler carried on the independent policies that had harassed Assyria under Tirhakah, and because Ashurbanipal was preoccupied with the Babylonians (though his brother was king there), Elamites, and barbarian hordes from the north, he was unable to look to his interests in the south. Chief among these newcomers from the north were the Medes, who figured prominently in the eventual collapse of Assyria.

Ashurbanipal was able, however, to meet the emergencies and, in a series of lightning moves, regained at least a good measure of the old Assyrian solidarity. He took Babylon from his own brother, crushed the Elamites, and brought Manasseh of Judah back under his firm control despite resistance by Psammeticus (2 Chron. 33:11). He then devoted the remainder of his life to collecting antiquities and constructing libraries and archives. Thanks to his efforts, the famous Babylonian creation and flood epics[19] exist in well-preserved form, as do thousands of other tablets representing countless ancient historical and legendary sources.

Ashurbanipal's son, Ashur-etil-ilani (633–629), had a very obscure and apparently unsuccessful reign and was followed by his brother Sin-shar-ishkun (629–612), who lived to see the kingdom totter, fall, and almost pass into oblivion. The Median king Cyaxares (625–585) began to trouble Assyria as soon as he took his throne, and his ally Nabopolassar of Babylonia (626–605) actually declared his independence of Assyria and defeated Sin-shar-ishkun at Babylon. Egypt, meanwhile, became friendly with Assyria, probably realizing that a weak but alive Assyria was better than an insuperable Medo-Babylonian front in the north and east. At any rate, Psammeticus attacked the Babylonian armies in Mesopotamia in 616, thus preserving Assyria a little longer. Two years later, however, Cyaxares took the city of Asshur, and then after two years more the Babylonians and Medes together took the capital, Nineveh (612). Sin-shar-ishkun, who died in the battle for Nineveh, was replaced by Ashur-uballit II (612–609). This unfortunate heir of Assyria's death struggle soon lost Haran, and by 609 every vestige of Assyria's glory had passed from the world scene.[20]

After Manasseh died (642), the throne of Judah was temporarily occupied by his young son Amon (642–640). After filling the land with idolatry again, he was murdered by his servants in his palace (2 Chron. 33:24). His son and successor was Josiah (640–609), a boy of eight years who became as renowned for his piety and zeal for the Lord as his father and grandfather were for everything opposite. When he came of age, he set about repairing the temple, which had fallen into disgraceful disrepair, and in the process was introduced to a scroll found in an inner recess of the building (2 Kings 22:8). On examination, he found it to be a copy of the law of Moses, something that had not been in circulation since the time of Hezekiah at least. Whether this was the entire Torah or only a part, like Deuteronomy, cannot be known for certain, though it seems unlikely that only part of the law would have been suppressed by Manasseh or otherwise lost.[21]

When the king finished perusing the book for himself, he recognized the awful indictment it contained regarding himself as an individual and

19. For these texts, see J. B. Pritchard, ed., *Ancient Near Eastern Texts Relating to the Old Testament*, 3d ed. (Princeton: Princeton University Press, 1969), 60–99.

20. For the last years of Assyria, see William W. Hallo, "From Qarqar to Carchemish: Assyria and Israel in the Light of New Discoveries," *Biblical Archaeologist* 23 (1960): 33–61.

21. Gleason L. Archer, Jr., *A Survey of Old Testament Introduction* (Chicago: Moody, 1974), 104–5.

the nation as a whole. He therefore sent it to Hilkiah the priest for his reactions, and the priest took it to the prophetess Huldah. This godly woman, having seen the message of the scroll, predicted that the curses written within it would pass on Judah because Judah had wantonly broken the covenant that had bound the nation to God. Josiah himself, however, because he had repented and humbled himself before the Lord, would not have to witness Judah's tragic end with his own eyes. For his sake, the nation would last until he had finished his days (2 Chron. 34:24–28).

The king then took the scroll and, standing before the assembled nation, began to read it aloud. With one accord the people responded by reaffirming their faith in God and, at least superficially, experienced a revival as sweeping as that in the reign of King Hezekiah. Superficial it was, for it bore no lasting fruit, no sign that God should understand it as sufficient reason for his holding back the wrath promised by Isaiah and Micah. Yet the instruments of heathen worship were demolished, the hireling priests were cut off, and the groves and shrines in both the valleys and the high places were cut down and burned. Josiah even destroyed the worship center at Bethel as the man of God from Judah had predicted long centuries before (2 Kings 23:15; cf. 1 Kings 13:3). The climax to it all was a magnificent Passover feast, the greatest seen in the kingdom since Samuel. No king did so much for God and so zealously in so short a time; yet, the nation could not be saved. Its iniquities more than outweighed any possible benefits to be derived from the piety of its remarkable king.

When Ashur-uballit of Assyria went to Haran to retake his city from the Babylonians, he was assisted by Necho II of Egypt (609–594), who rushed up through Canaan for that purpose. Josiah, hoping to rid himself of Assyrian aggression once and for all, and also deeply committed to Babylonia, elected to meet Necho at Megiddo and thwart his attempts to come to Haran in time to be of any help to the Assyrians. The valiant king was mortally wounded in the battle and was carried back to Jerusalem dead (2 Kings 23:29). It does seem, however, that this tactic delayed Necho enough that when the Egyptians arrived near Haran, the site of the battle, the Babylonians and their allies had already overcome the Assyrians and so were able to drive the Egyptians to their last stronghold at Carchemish.[22]

The Egyptians took advantage of the situation to install themselves in Canaan and Aramaea while Babylonia was stabilizing itself to the east of the Euphrates. Having slain Josiah, they took on themselves the responsibility of appointing a king in his place, his own son Jehoahaz (2 Kings

22. Hallo, "From Qarqar to Carchemish," 61.

23:30). Very shortly, though, this appointee was removed for some sort of insubordination and carried off to the Egyptian provincial capital at Riblah in Aramaea and from there to Egypt, where he died (2 Kings 23:33; 2 Chron. 36:4). Necho then placed another son of Josiah, Eliakim (609–597), on the throne, and changed his name to Jehoiakim. In exchange for his advancement, Jehoiakim was required to send an exorbitant tax to Egypt, a tax that the people bitterly resented.

Under Jehoiakim, the recent reform under Josiah was all but forgotten, for the king was anything but a spiritual leader. The Book of Jeremiah graphically describes the religious conditions of the time as well as the weakness of the king in every respect. He was interested only in satisfying the wishes of his Egyptian overlords in order to retain his petty power. But his power was to be threatened, this time by the Babylonians, who now had time and resources to press south of the Euphrates and down into the territory that Egypt had held now for only four or five years.

Nebuchadnezzar, the young commander of the Babylonian armies, decided to turn his attention to Canaan in 605 and, with little effort, overran the Egyptians at Carchemish and pursued them deep into Canaan.[23] Back in Babylon, Nabopolassar had died, and the news of that death sent Nebuchadnezzar back to the capital so that he might safeguard his interests there. After he was crowned king (605–562), he returned to his campaign in Canaan and remained there for three years. It seems likely that Jehoiakim submitted to him in his first onslaught (605), rebelled for three years when Nebuchadnezzar had to retire (2 Kings 24:1), and then fell back in line when the Babylonian finished his second campaign. This submission in 605 must have included the deportation of many people from Judah to Babylon, including Daniel and his friends (Dan. 1:3). It would also mark the beginning of the seventy-year captivity of Judah predicted by Jeremiah (Jer. 25:11).

In 601 Nebuchadnezzar faced Necho again near the Egyptian border. Evidently Necho was so successful this time that the Babylonians had to retreat and leave Canaan unprotected for several years. Finally, they marched west again in 597, but before they could get to Jerusalem to punish the rebellious Jehoiakim, he died, perhaps the victim of assassination (Jer. 22:18). His son Jehoiachin could hold out only three months and finally he, with members of his family and other important persons, was deported to Babylon (2 Kings 24:10–12). One of these deportees seems to have been the prophet Ezekiel (Ezek. 1:2). As for Jehoiachin, he was kept under house arrest in Babylon all through the reign of Nebuchadnezzar,

---

23. D. J. Wiseman, *Chronicles of Chaldaean Kings (625–556 B.C.) in the British Museum* (London: Trustees of the British Museum, 1956), 26.

but when that king was followed by Evil-merodach (562–560), the latter removed Jehoiachin from his imprisonment, exalted him above other captive kings, and even gave him a lifelong allowance (2 Kings 25:27–30).[24]

Jehoiachin's uncle, Mattaniah (597–586), was placed on the powerless throne of Judah and received the new name Zedekiah (2 Kings 24:17). This worthless fellow, who seemed to lack conviction and strove only to be popular with his lords (Jer. 38:5), also had the problem of not being regarded as the true king of Judah, since Jehoiachin was still alive, though a captive in Babylon. But he was able to rebel successfully against Nebuchadnezzar, largely because of problems Nebuchadnezzar was having with Jewish captives in Babylonia and also because of certain false prophets in Jerusalem who encouraged the people there by predicting that the Babylonian yoke would be broken shortly. Jeremiah rejected such ideas, for he had clearly taught that the captivity would last seventy years. He suggested that there was no alternative but to submit peacefully to the Babylonian suzerainty, a position he upheld even when Jerusalem fell under siege in 588–586.

This final conquest of Judah by Nebuchadnezzar involved the destruction of Lachish, Azekah, and other surrounding posts first, as the Lachish letters attest.[25] When nothing was left but Jerusalem, it became the object of the major thrust (Jer. 34:7). Meanwhile, the Egyptians had marched north to engage the Babylonians, but they were completely unsuccessful in stopping the Babylonian takeover. Together with their new king Hophra or Apries (588–568), they were forced to withdraw, leaving Judah at the mercy of Nebuchadnezzar.[26] The king of Babylonia was not disposed to be merciful, and in short order he took the city, arrested Zedekiah, carried him to Riblah, and then blinded him after forcing him to witness the execution of his sons (2 Kings 25:6–7). The unfortunate king eventually died in Babylon.

A month later, Nebuzaradan, captain of the Babylonian guard, returned to Jerusalem and burned its buildings to the ground. Only the poor were left to care for the land; the rest, together with the objects of special value from the temple, were taken to Babylon. Others of the rulers were dragged off to Riblah, where they were executed, probably because they had been ringleaders in the stubborn resistance to Nebuchadnezzar. Some, like the prophet Jeremiah, were allowed to remain in the city because it was thought, mistakenly of course in his case, that they had been pro-Babylonian all along. With the king absent, the state formally ended, but

24. For the "Jehoiakin Tablets," see Thomas, *Documents from Old Testament Times*, 86.
25. Ibid., 213–16.
26. Martin Noth, *The History of Israel* (New York: Harper, 1958), 285.

Nebuchadnezzar decided to preserve the new province, to a limited degree at least, by appointing Gedaliah as ruler (2 Kings 25:22). His tenure was all too brief, because for his efforts to placate the survivors he was branded a traitor to the Jewish cause and assassinated by Ishmael, a member of the royal family who had fled to Ammon. The villains involved in the plot then fled to Ammon, while Gedaliah's friends carried Jeremiah with them to Egypt, fearing, of course, that Nebuchadnezzar would somehow hold them accountable for what had happened. What happened to Judah after this is unclear, though it is likely that the provincial status did not last long and that both Samaria and Judah were incorporated together as a province.

The Prophets of the Period (650–585)

Though the dominant figure by far for this entire time was Jeremiah, the ministries of several others must have made a tremendous impact on the nation in these critical years. The situation roughly paralleled that of the Northern Kingdom in the days of Amos, Hosea, Isaiah, and Micah, and so it is not surprising to find many of the elements of social and spiritual decay typical of the earlier period. These latter prophets were no less vociferous and courageous in their denunciations than their earlier brethren. At the same time, they contain no fewer messages of hope and restoration. God must punish Judah, they said, but his everlasting covenant demands that he remember them in their ruinous state and regather them to himself and their land. Most important of all, he would save them and, through them, save the world by that Anointed One of Israel known by all the prophets.

Nahum

It is impossible to date the Book of Nahum, except in general terms, because of a lack of internal or external evidence. It is apparent, though, that his message consisted of a prediction that Nineveh, the great Assyrian capital, would be laid low (3:1–5). The book must be earlier than 612, then, for that was the date of Nineveh's conflagration under Nabopolassar and the Medes. And it must be after the fall of Thebes (No), because Nahum compares the devastation of Nineveh with that of Thebes (3:8), which had already perished under the blows of Ashurbanipal (663 B.C.). Nahum must, therefore, have lived in the latter part of the seventh century, though one can know little else about him.

He first outlines the majesty of God as seen in his mercy to his own people and his judgment on the nations (1:2–7). Then he presents a dramatic description of the subjugation of Nineveh by a tremendous host of chariots and infantry that would completely overrun the city (2:4–13). Finally he states that there will be no possibility of recovery for Assyria, for the kingdom, though an instrument in the hands of the Lord, has become bloody and, like Jehu, has overreached itself in doing God's will.

OUTLINE OF NAHUM
I. Psalm of praise (1)
II. Prediction of defeat (2)
III. Panorama of ruin (3)

Zephaniah

The prophet plainly states that he lived in the reign of Josiah of Judah (1:1), presumably before the great revival of that king in 622, for there is no mention of such an event. His message, like Joel's, revolves around the theme of the Day of Yahweh, though in his case this refers to the judgment of Judah exclusively. It will be a day of wrath, of trouble and distress, of waste and desolation, of darkness and gloominess, of clouds and thick darkness, of the trumpet and alarm against the fenced cities and high towers (1:15–16). It will also include the Philistines, Moabites, Ammonites, Ethiopians, and Assyrians, for all these nations vaunted themselves in sinful pride against the Lord of all the earth.

The leaders of Jerusalem, Zephaniah says, have been corrupt and venal, and there is no recourse but punishment (3:1–7). But one day God will remember his dispersed people and will be in their midst to save them (3:17), making them a people noteworthy in all the world because of his blessing on them (3:20).

OUTLINE OF ZEPHANIAH
I. Retribution exhibited (1)
II. Repentance encouraged (2)
III. Restoration explained (3)

Habakkuk

This prophet gives no certain hint as to the date of composition of his little book, but his frequent reference to the Babylonian (Chaldean) uprising, an event he undoubtedly sees as imminent, suggests a date of about 630 B.C., just before the Neo-Babylonian Empire was established by Nabopolassar (1:6).

Habakkuk's message is that God will raise up the Babylonians to execute his will against the Assyrians and Judah, much as he had raised up the Assyrians to afflict Israel. But they, too, will go beyond the divine will and will have to be punished for their presumptuousness. Their bloodiness, their drunkenness, their idolatry all will undermine them and reduce them to eventual oblivion (2:12). The whole process will result in the praise of God and salvation for all who trust him. The interesting note at the end of the book that the composition was dedicated to his chief singer might indicate that Habakkuk was a musician as well as a prophet (3:19).

> OUTLINE OF HABAKKUK
> I. The prophet's protestation (1)
> II. The prophet's prediction (2)
> III. The prophet's prayer (3)

Jeremiah

Just as Isaiah towered over his contemporaries in Israel's last days of history, so Jeremiah one hundred years later loomed largest on the scene of Judah's final hours. While more is known about him than about any other prophet because of his extensive autobiographical notations, no book of Scripture is more difficult to follow because of the lack of any consistent chronological scheme. It might be best in the long run, therefore, to try to follow his life according to the periods in which it was divided, largely as it related to the reigns of Josiah, Jehoiakim, and Zedekiah, and to consider the prophecies relevant to each time.

Jeremiah was born in Anathoth, just north of Jerusalem, and may have come from a priestly lineage (1:1). At an early age he was called to the prophetic ministry; in fact, God told him he had selected him even before he had been born. His task was clear: he must "root out, pull down, destroy, throw down, build, and plant" (1:10). From the beginning (627 B.C.; cf. 1:2), he saw that Jerusalem would be stricken by a power from the north, God's instrument in punishing the unbridled evil of the nation. When this came about, Egypt would be unable to give them help (2:18); neither would their idols rise up to support them (2:28). Only repentance would suffice (4:1), but this must come quickly, for the noises of war were already resounding in the distance (4:19).

Like his contemporaries, Jeremiah read clearly the symptoms of a sick nation. The rich oppressed the poor, the prophets taught lies, and the priests served only for material gain. What was worse, the people loved it that way (5:31)! Their sacrifices, therefore, were hollow and meaningless (7:21–24), yet they believed that in spite of their iniquities they would enjoy peace (8:11). All of this brought no joy to Jeremiah's heart; indeed, the "weeping prophet" wished that he might have unending tears to express the full measure of his grief over Judah's plight (9:1–2).

No prophet ever used object lessons more than Jeremiah to teach visually what he found difficult to convey by words alone. For example, he illustrated the torn and battered condition of Judah by a linen sash he buried in a hole (13:1–11). Later, he broke a clay pot into tiny fragments to show the completeness of Judah's destruction (19:1–12). He eventually went so far as to make a yoke of wood that he wore on his neck as a symbol of the bondage under which the nation must serve because of its stubborn resistance to God (27:1–2).

The prophet's ministry seemed to intensify after the death of Josiah, when the captivity was not only more imminent but also more certain and essential because of the reversal of Josiah's reformation principles under Jehoiakim. This evil king would meet a violent death, according to Jeremiah, and would not be mourned by his own people (22:18–19). His son Jehoiachin (Coniah) would go to Babylon in chains and die without an heir on the throne of David (22:30). In his place, however, a righteous Branch would shoot up and be the means of saving God's people and keeping the covenant promise alive (23:5–8). This Branch, of course, was to be the Messiah, the same one predicted by Isaiah as the root out of a dry ground (Isa. 53:2).

Specifically, Jeremiah said, Judah would be led off by Nebuchadnezzar and serve Babylonia for seventy years (25:11), though Jeremiah had done his utmost for twenty-three years to warn the people of this very thing and to encourage them to repent. Other nations also would fall under the heel of the Chaldeans, so it would be fruitless to trust in them, even Egypt. Naturally, such a message was unwelcome to the proud king Jehoiakim and his visionless counselors, so the outspoken prophet was placed under arrest (26:8–24), narrowly escaping death. While in prison, Jeremiah wrote a scroll (presumably much of his present book) and sent his servant and scribe Baruch to read it at the temple. Baruch was apprehended by the authorities, however, and the scroll was confiscated and taken to Jehoiakim. As it was read to him, the king took the scroll, cut it in pieces, and threw it into a blazing fireplace. Thereupon the Lord commanded Jeremiah to write an identical scroll, which he did, and to which he added many other words. Besides showing the tenacity of the prophet in the face of the greatest adversity, this event is instructive in showing how Scripture came to be written.[27] Especially significant are the statements that emphasize the verbal aspects of the revealed message (36:17–18, 28, 32).

27. For an interesting discussion of this, see J. Philip Hyatt, "The Writing of an Old Testament Book," in *The Biblical Archaeologist Reader*, vol. 1, ed. G. Ernest Wright and David Noel Freedman (Garden City, N.Y.: Doubleday, Anchor Books, 1961), 22–31.

The third phase of his ministry concerned Jeremiah's relationship with Zedekiah. When Zedekiah took the throne of Judah by the permission or even the orders of Nebuchadnezzar, he immediately rebelled. When the Babylonians came south to chastise him, he and others thought that the Egyptians, who were advancing north, would be able to save Judah from the wrath of Nebuchadnezzar. But Jeremiah stoutly affirmed that the only sane policy was to submit to Babylonia and put no trust in Egypt (37:6–10). When the Babylonians left Jerusalem to meet the Egyptians, Jeremiah was placed under arrest as a Babylonian sympathizer (37:14–15). When Egyptian help eventually failed, the prophet was released, for the inadequate Zedekiah knew he was more valuable free than bound, though he dared not release him completely for fear of the Jews' reaction (38:19). Until the fall of the city, then, Jeremiah remained in the outer court of the prison.

During his incarceration, Jeremiah continued to sound forth the unwelcome message that captivity by Babylonia was unavoidable (21:3–10) and that even the king would die (21:7). Yet he proclaimed that a remnant would be saved, a few, like good figs, would be carried off but would return and form the nucleus of a new kingdom (Jer. 24). Other prophets disagreed, notably Hananiah, and argued that the Babylonian scourge would end soon, perhaps as early as two years (28:1–4), and Jehoiachin would return to his throne. Jeremiah contested this, of course, and accurately predicted instead the death of the false prophet, an event that strengthened Jeremiah's position (28:15–17).

In a more positive vein, Jeremiah also wrote letters to the captives in Babylonia in which he urged them to settle down where they were, for seventy years must pass before there was any hope of return (29:1–23). Any prophets and priests among them who prophesied otherwise and who were living iniquitous lives would suffer the judgment of the Lord (29:32). But they must not get the equally erroneous impression that there would be no return at all, for this was decidedly not true. Israel would be restored and would participate in a new covenant, one engraved not on stone but on the people's hearts (31:31–34), one accompanied by joy and prosperity (33:1–18). As a token of his own personal confidence in the return, Jeremiah redeemed a piece of land and hid the deed in an earthen jar, fully expecting his heirs to return to claim it. The price was high, evidence that to him the land was not worthless, even though it would soon fall to Babylonia, but rich in the use to which the returnees would put it (32:6–15).

Finally the city was broken up, and Zedekiah was led off to Riblah to be blinded. Jeremiah, thought by even the Babylonians to be their compatriot, was allowed to remain in Judah. As noted before, he remained but briefly, for after the assassination of Gedaliah he was spirited off to Egypt along with Gedaliah's other friends. There he remained for the rest of his life, perhaps living long enough to write all of the books of Kings (ca. 560 B.C.), though this is uncertain. In Egypt, the prophet continued his ministry, predicting such matters as the conquest of Egypt by Nebuchadnezzar (43:8–13) and the fall of the Philistines (Jer. 47), Moabites (Jer. 48), and many other nations (Jer. 49). Babylon especially would be destroyed by the Lord because of her obstinate refusal to recognize him as God (50–51). Marduk, their god, would be completely unable to stave off ruin at the hands of the Medes and Persians.

Thus the courageous man of God lived out the remainder of his days in a strange and distant land, never to return to the city he loved. Misunderstood by both friend and enemy, Jeremiah suffered as have few others in the proclamation of truth. But his stout heart was unbowed, and his faith in God remained constant. The prophet of tears knew of a day when God in triumph would wipe them all away.

OUTLINE OF JEREMIAH
    I. Judah before the fall of Jerusalem (1–38)
        A. Jeremiah's task (1)
        B. Judah's sin (2:1–3:5)
        C. Warnings of judgment (3:6–6:30)
        D. A call for repentance (7–10)
        E. The linen sash (11–13)
        F. Promise of captivity (14–17)
        G. Visit to the potter (18–19)
        H. Jeremiah's arrest by Pashur (20)
        I. Prophecy of Babylonian conquest (21–29)
        J. Promise of return (30–33)
        K. Captivity of Zedekiah (34–35)
        L. Writing of the scroll (36)
        M. Jeremiah's arrest under Zedekiah (37–38)
    II. Judah during the fall of Jerusalem (39–45)
        A. Jeremiah's protection (39)
        B. Death of Gedaliah (40–41)
        C. Jeremiah's advice (42)
        D. Jeremiah in Egypt (43–45)
    III. Oracles about the nations (46–51)
        A. Egypt (46)
        B. Philistia (47)
        C. Moab (48)

The Book of Lamentations

While in Egypt, or shortly before going there, Jeremiah wrote a poetic description of his beloved city as it lay in the flames of Nebuzaradan's torches. No elegy ever written is more profoundly moving than this, for no other is filled with such intensity of meaning and importance. This is not just the description of a beautiful, proud, ancient city—though it is that—but the picture of the Day of Yahweh as it related to the heart of the covenant people. Symbolically, Jerusalem spoke to Judah of crushed hopes, desires, and aspirations. It also spoke of her dismal failure to serve the Lord. The smoke and ashes suggested disintegration of the national goal. All that the people could do now was to mourn their condition and reach out to God in loving penitence and faith, hoping that in his mercy he might give them a ray of assurance that this was not all. Of course, there is no suggestion that the picture might be changed, at least not in this book, for that was not its intention; but to the reader familiar with the glowing promises of restoration in the writings of the prophets, even this bleak and desolate scene would one day be changed, and all men would turn for salvation to the City of David, made new by the glorious presence of the Lord.

10

Return and Renewal

The Babylonia-Persia Contest

While Nebuchadnezzar was employed in the conquest of Judah, Cyaxares of the Medes was making territorial acquisitions of his own.[1] He went as far west as Asia Minor and occupied everything in the east and north of Babylonia. His death occurred at about the time of the fall of Jerusalem (ca. 585), and he was followed by Astyages (585–550), who was able to stay on peaceful terms with Babylonia throughout the reign of Nebuchadnezzar. In the south, Egypt, under Hophra, continued to endanger Babylonia's holdings in Canaan. As long as that king remained in power, Egypt was not punished, but when Amasis (568–525) took the throne in a coup, Nebuchadnezzar swept down into Egypt and registered a decisive blow against the new king. This seems to have succeeded in humbling Egyptian ambitions, for until Egypt fell to the Persians in 525 B.C. she remained relatively quiet.

After the reign of Nebuchadnezzar, the Babylonian Empire began to disintegrate rapidly. His son Evil-Merodach, who released Jehoiachin from imprisonment, reigned for only two years (562–560). He was followed by Neri-glissar (560–556), Labashi-Marduk (a few weeks), and, finally,

---

1. For the historical background of this period, see John Bright, *A History of Israel*, 3d ed. (Philadelphia: Westminster, 1981), 343–402. The dates are primarily those of Edwin R. Thiele, *The Mysterious Numbers of the Hebrew Kings*, 3d ed. (Grand Rapids: Eerdmans, 1983), 153–66.

Nabonidus (556–539), a usurper. This native of Haran worshiped the moon god Sin and brought images of this god to Babylon, an act that irritated the Babylonians immensely. Moreover, he neglected the religious rites of the Babylonians while engaged in conquest and in an insatiable search for antiquities, which he placed in museums. Eventually he took up residence in Teima, a small land in the Arabian desert, installing his son Belshazzar as regent in Babylon in his place. Most galling of all to the Babylonian priests was Nabonidus's failure to observe the national religious festivals, especially New Year's Day. On that day the gods were led down the great processional way, and the people reaffirmed their allegiance to them. When the king neglected these ceremonies, the people felt their nation to be in jeopardy because of the natural wrath of the gods. In fact, when Cyrus of Persia took Babylon by storm in 539, he credited Marduk, the chief Babylonian god, with having given him victory because Nabonidus had forsaken the cultus![2]

The Median threat was increasing in the meantime, until the southern Median province of Anshan revolted from the empire under the leadership of Cyrus the Persian (550–530). In short order Cyrus took all the old Median empire and began to push westward into Asia Minor. By 546 B.C., he had gone as far as the Aegean Sea and even threatened Greece for a time. After further expansion in the east, Cyrus began to concentrate on the divided and tottering empire of the Babylonians. He appointed Gubaru, a former Gutian general, to take command and to march on his old capital. By 539 Gubaru surrounded it, having met little resistance along the way, and the city capitulated without a struggle. Nabonidus fled in panic but was later recaptured, and Belshazzar lost his life. Thus, a new era of history commenced, an era bound to influence the changing fortunes of God's people.

The Age of the Captivity

The Prophet Ezekiel

Not much is known of the lives of the Jewish captives following the destruction of Jerusalem in 586 B.C. It appears that there were very few Jews left in Judah at all (perhaps no more than twenty thousand, according to W. F. Albright) and that most of these were from the lower classes and had been left to care for the soil and crops.[3] Evidently other people were not sent to Judah from other parts of the empire, so that from the

2. This information is on the famous Cylinder of Cyrus. For the text, see D. Winton Thomas, ed., *Documents from Old Testament Times* (London: Thomas Nelson, 1958), 92–94.

3. W. F. Albright, *The Biblical Period from Abraham to Ezra* (New York: Harper, 1963), 87.

time the city was destroyed until the first wave of migration back occurred ca. 538 there was very little change in the land.

But this was not true in Babylonia, Egypt, and elsewhere, for to these areas the Jews had been taken in great numbers. The dispossessed Jews were not placed in large concentration camps or anything of the kind. Instead, they began to settle down in large colonies. They were allowed to have their own homes, engage in business, and practice their religion as best they could without a temple (Jer. 29:5–7; Ezek. 8:1). Indeed, the synagogue arose during this period to compensate for the loss of the temple and to provide a place where the pious could gather to study and hear the Word of God. There is even evidence that a temple was built at Elephantine in Upper Egypt, where the Jews had a large community on an island in the Nile.[4]

Some of the captives became prominent in government, business, and other phases of national life, so much so that when the time came seventy years later that they could return to Jerusalem, very few desired to do so. Far from being oppressive, the captivity was to many of them an opportunity to prosper materially as they had never done at home.[5] One of the great dangers was not that the people would be eliminated as a race while in captivity, but that not enough of them would want to return home to continue the occupation of the promised land. Only the persistent and continuous encouragement of men like Ezekiel, Daniel, Ezra, and Nehemiah assured a restoration at all, and even with their leadership Judaism as a Palestinian movement seemed at times to be in danger of failing.

According to Ezekiel's own testimony, he was among the captives taken in the siege of 597 B.C. (Ezek. 1:1–2), along with Jehoiachin. He and his wife evidently lived in a colony of Jews along the banks of the Chebar Canal, a few miles from Babylon. From the sparse evidence available, it seems that he spent his entire life there, preaching and writing from 592 B.C. until about 560. And a strange life he lived! No prophet writes in such symbolic imagery as does Ezekiel; to him must go the credit for the first extensive use of apocalyptic.[6] By this is meant the presentation of future events, both political and spiritual, in a "hidden" way, that is, a way not immediately clear. It has the added feature of viewing time cyclically,

4. The Elephantine Papyri, first found more than a hundred years ago, speak of the affairs of the Jewish colony in Egypt. Some of these go back as far as the beginning of the fifth century B.C. See Thomas, *Documents from Old Testament Times*, 258–68, and Emil G. Kraeling, "New Light on the Elephantine Colony," *Biblical Archaeologist* 15 (1952): 50–67.

5. Edwin M. Yamauchi, *Persia and the Bible* (Grand Rapids: Baker, 1990), 243–44.

6. This was not a later development from the third or second century B.C., as Rowley implies; see H. H. Rowley, *The Growth of the Old Testament* (New York: Harper and Row, 1963), 92. That apocalyptic developed early in postexilic times is shown persuasively by Horace D. Hummel, *The Word Becoming Flesh: An Introduction to the Origin, Purpose, and Meaning of the Old Testament* (St. Louis: Concordia, 1979), 553–57.

as a series of events more or less repetitious from one age to the next but culminating in the breaking through of God into history and the establishment of another, spiritual order. It differs from ordinary prophecy in its use of imagery and symbolism and in its emphasis on God's dramatic self-initiated visitation in the Last Day. Much apocalyptic literature defies rational interpretation in itself but, when viewed in terms of clearer passages and well-founded eschatological principles, becomes rich in its meaning.

After an initial vision of cherubim and wheels, the priest-prophet received his prophetic commission: he must speak a message demanding repentance to the captive people among whom he lived (2:3). Despite God's judgment in sending them there, they obstinately refused to open their hearts to him and acknowledge their many sins. As a watchman, Ezekiel had to speak forth the message of warning in order to deliver his own soul from guilt for the nation's blood. If the people responded, all would be well, but if not, at least the prophet could not be blamed for not trying to alert the people about God's judgment (3:17–21; 33:7–16). Then, in two symbolic actions, the model of a siege against Jerusalem and the cutting and dividing of his hair, Ezekiel demonstrated visually how the city would be attacked by Nebuchadnezzar and how some of the people would be burned, some would be slain with the sword, others would be scattered to the four winds, and a tiny remnant would be saved to form the nucleus of a new nation (5:3–4).

Ezekiel spoke directly to the needs and conditions of Judah by pointing out the idolatry that occasioned their removal from the land and produced the violence and devastation that their holy city suffered. He referred to the abominable practices of the Jews in their temple worship (8:10), the wicked counsel of the rulers (11:2), and the deceitfulness of the false prophets (13:2). The situation was so hopeless that even if Noah, Daniel, and Job were to intercede on their behalf (14:14), the people of Judah could not be spared. Judah was worse than her sister Samaria or any of her ancestors (16:46–47), and it was for her own sin, not that of her fathers, that she must be punished (18:4). Although the Lord had been gracious to Judah, she had not acknowledged him, but had turned her back. Still, the Lord would not forget but would cleanse the wicked nation and eventually bring it back to himself (20:33–44).

Judah was not the only nation to be struck with the rod of God's anger. The Ammonites, Moabites, Edomites, Philistines (Ezek. 25), Tyre (26–28), and Egypt (29–32) all would feel his reproach and come to realize that he is God of all the earth. They would be punished for their antagonism toward God's people, for though God had permitted it, he had not sanctioned its unrestrained expression. Besides, all these nations had failed to observe that the God of Israel was the true God; they had consciously rejected the light he had given them.

One of Ezekiel's major themes is the future covenant. Like Jeremiah especially, he had to reconcile the present state of affairs with the glorious promises of Israel's past. God had told Abraham that he would make of him a great nation, had confirmed this covenant with Isaac and Jacob, and had revealed through Moses the theocratic principles that gave the covenant relationship a greater tangibility and framework in the form of a nation miraculously delivered in the exodus and organized at Sinai. He had, moreover, spoken to David regarding the royal line that would reign forever in the kingdom of God, and had specifically stated that that kingdom would abide eternally. But the Assyrian rampage of 722 dealt a severe blow to Israel's hopes, for after that the nation became only a small part of what it was in the promise, though it was true that the Davidic tribe of Judah still existed, if only tenuously. Now, however, even Judah was gone, and the nation as a political entity no longer existed. Most of the people felt that God had broken his covenant with them and that there was now no possibility of its renewal.

The prophets, though they did not view these events in this light, still suffered the shock of an uprooted kingdom. Theirs was the dilemma of reconciling the exiled nation with the immutable covenant of God. And through the revelation of God, the solution became apparent. The nation Israel had disappeared for all practical purposes, but the covenant had not been forgotten. It would continue, but it would be expressed in a different way. The dispersed Jews would return to their homeland, but not to resume their old relationship; rather, a new covenant would be made with them, one that further expanded and interpreted the previous ones (34:20–31). In the future God would "sprinkle water upon them" and they would be given a "new heart" in which would abide the Spirit of God (36:25–38). This renewal of the nation and its inspiration by the Spirit are depicted by the prophet as a resurrection of a valley full of dry bones (Ezek. 37). Israel, like dry bones that could not live, would be reassembled and rejuvenated with God's Spirit, and David would reign over the nation, now united into one people.

But this final restoration of Israel would be preceded by great international movements directed against the Lord and his covenant people. Gog and Magog (symbolic of world powers) would swoop down on Palestine in the last days and seek to destroy the saints (Ezek. 38). God, however, would cause them to fall on the mountains north of Israel and would consume them so completely and universally that seven months would be necessary for the burial of the dead (39:12). This eschatological picture of God's vengeance on the nations and his protection and revival of his own small kingdom must have seemed remote to the tiny remnant to whom the prophets preached, for the great nations seemed to make a mockery of Yahweh and the promises. Yet the prophets maintained, in the face of all the odds, that the eternal covenant was a reality and that Israel, both physically and spiritually, would rise to take her place of world dominance.

Ezekiel, as a priest, naturally had a strong interest in the more cultic aspects of the covenant of the future, so a large section of his book (40–48) is devoted to a delineation of the future glorious temple, its altars and instruments, the new priesthood, the division of the land, the order of worship and liturgy, and other such matters. Some of this was fulfilled in the return of the exiles who rebuilt the temple under Zerubbabel, but by far the most spoke of an eschatological day in the end of time. Whether Ezekiel speaks in literal or figurative terms is much disputed, but there is no doubt that the theme here, like elsewhere, is a fulfillment of the wonderful promises of the Lord to his people of all ages. The present world order, though it apparently triumphs now over righteousness and truth, will be discarded by God's direct intervention in the affairs of nations, and a new order will be instituted to take its place, an order characterized by the eternal fellowship of God with his covenant people.

OUTLINE OF EZEKIEL
I. The prophet's call and commission (1–3)
II. Prophecies against Judah (4–24)
   A. Destruction predicted by sign and symbol (4–7)
   B. Vision of Jerusalem's sin and punishment (8–11)
   C. Necessity of punishment (12–19)
   D. Last warning before Jerusalem's fall (20–24)
III. Prophecies against surrounding nations (25–32)
   A. Ammon (25:1–7)
   B. Moab (25:8–11)
   C. Edom (25:12–14)
   D. Philistia (25:15–17)
   E. Tyre (26:1–28:19)
   F. Sidon (28:20–26)
   G. Egypt (29–32)
IV. Final restoration (33–48)
   A. Events preceding the establishment of the kingdom (33–39)
   B. Worship in the kingdom (40–48)

1. Temple (40–43)
2. Worship (44–46)
3. Land (47–48)

Daniel

In Nebuchadnezzar's first campaign, during the reign of Jehoiakim (605), certain choice young men of Judah were spirited off to Babylon, including Daniel, Hananiah (Shadrach), Mishael (Meshech), and Azariah (Abed-nego). All were trained to serve in the court of the pagan king, but at least these four refused to forsake the laws and customs of their fathers in order to conform to Babylonian conditions. For this God blessed them, making them especially adept in knowledge, learning, and wisdom. Daniel, moreover, became an authority in dreams and visions, even surpassing those wise men of the kingdom whose forté was in these areas (1:17–20).

Daniel evidently was only a lad when he went to Babylon in 605, for he continued to prophesy until at least 539 B.C. His ministry was, therefore, contemporary with the reigns of all the kings of Babylonia from Nebuchadnezzar to the end of the empire under Nabonidus and Belshazzar. He lived even under the rule of the Persian king Cyrus and his provincial ruler Darius the Mede. His book, written partly in Hebrew and partly in Aramaic, is divided into two sections: the first six chapters, which have to do with his own experiences, and the last six, which describe his visions concerning the future. He is not counted among the prophets, because he did not occupy the prophetic office, but his book is placed among the Major Prophets in the English canon because Daniel did possess the gift of prophecy. As a statesman he made his greatest impact on his times through the message he delivered and interpreted.

Daniel seemed to be both respected and feared by Nebuchadnezzar. Very shortly after the king succeeded his father on the Babylonian throne, he dreamed a disturbing dream that he not only could not interpret but also forgot by the time he awoke. The imperious king summoned his wisest counselors, but they protested that without knowing the contents of the dream they could hardly interpret it (2:8–9). Dissatisfied with this perfectly legitimate excuse, the king ordered the wise men executed. Daniel, however, gained an audience with Nebuchadnezzar in time to prevent the massacre and, after glorifying God as the source of his wisdom, revealed both the dream and its meaning to the monarch. This persuaded the king to advance the young counselor, and Daniel became the overseer of the wise men.

Some years after that, Nebuchadnezzar erected a ninety-foot golden image in a conspicuous place and decreed that all men should bow down to it at a given signal. The Babylonian concept of the king as a representative of Marduk is seen here clearly, and Daniel was not about to show any such deference to a foreign god.[7] How Daniel escaped the consequences is not clear, but his three friends were apprehended when they refused to show obeisance to the king's image. With incredible hardness, the king ordered these three put to death in a huge furnace heated to utmost capacity. But in the midst of the flames appeared one "like the Son of God" who so protected the faithful young men that they came forth unscathed. This could not help but raise the prestige of Yahweh in Nebuchadnezzar's eyes, so he decreed that from then on the God of the Hebrews must be given full recognition as an acceptable deity in the realm (3:29).

Sometime in his reign, Nebuchadnezzar had another dream. In it he saw a great tree stripped of its branches and leaves and reduced to a mere stump. This stump then became like a beast of the field for seven years, eating grass and being driven from place to place. Daniel predicted that the king himself, represented by the tree in his dream, would become demented and, like a wild beast, would roam about unable to control himself, let alone the kingdom. After seven years his sanity would return, and he would acknowledge the supremacy of Almighty God. This did happen, according to Daniel, though as yet no secular documents from this period have been found to recount a seven-year period of incapacity for Nebuchadnezzar.[8] We must question whether the king became a convert to Yahweh. Rather, as was the custom in the times, it appears that he merely recognized more clearly than ever that Yahweh was a great god and that, indeed, Yahweh of the Hebrews might actually be synonymous with Marduk or some chief Babylonian god.

In his later years, Daniel became involved especially with Belshazzar, son of Nabonidus and last regent of Babylon.[9] This impious prince, who ruled in the absence of his father, held a great banquet during which he desecrated the sacred vessels of Solomon's temple by drinking wine from them (5:2–3). This blasphemous act, apparently in the last night of Belshazzar's reign (539 B.C.), so angered the Lord God of Israel that he caused a strange writing to appear on the banquet room wall, a writing that predicted the overthrow of the mighty Babylonian Empire that very

7. Sabatino Moscati, *Ancient Semitic Civilizations* (New York: G. P. Putnam's Sons, 1957), 88.

8. This is not surprising, since very few records from this period were preserved at all. D. J. Wiseman, *Chronicles of Chaldaean Kings (626–556 B.C.) in the British Museum* (London: The Trustees of the British Museum, 1961), 37–39; John Goldingay, *Daniel*, Word Biblical Commentary (Waco: Word, 1989), 83–84.

9. For texts that mention Belshazzar, see Thomas, *Documents from Old Testament Times*, 90.

night. Daniel was called to interpret the unknown characters. After berating the prince for following in the proud and sacrilegious steps of his predecessor, Nebuchadnezzar, he pronounced the doom of the prince and his city. That very night the Persians and Medes, under Gubaru (possibly the same as Darius the Mede),[10] invaded the city and, without resistance, occupied it and slew the prince. Daniel, who had been promoted to third place in the kingdom (next to Nabonidus and Belshazzar), went uninjured because Darius saw in him a man who could be useful in the solidification of his new empire.

Daniel's experiences with the Persians, though brief, were fraught with dangers and marvelous deliverances by the Lord. He was appointed as a chief official in the city, but other dignitaries, jealous of his position, cajoled the king into making a decree that no one should worship his own god for a certain period under penalty of death. Daniel, of course, continued to pray daily to the Lord and so was brought before the king and sentenced to death. Though the king did all he could to find a means of exempting Daniel from the punishment, the irreversible Persian law, which even the king must observe, could not be circumvented. The aged seer therefore was cast into a den of lions, but he was protected from the ravenous beasts by the presence of the Lord. His salvation through such dire circumstances convinced the king that Daniel's God must surely be a first-rate deity, ranking on a level with those others whom he recognized (6:26–27).

The dreams and visions Daniel experienced personally or interpreted for the king are based on one main theme: the nations of the world and their relationship to the covenant people of God.[11] Nebuchadnezzar had seen a great image whose head was gold, whose breasts and arms were silver, whose belly and thighs were bronze, whose legs were iron, and whose feet were part iron and part clay. Daniel revealed that Nebuchadnezzar himself was the head of gold, and that the other parts were kingdoms that would rise successively after him. There would be a stone cut without hands that would demolish the image. This stone represented the kingdom of God, which would overthrow the governments of men and take their place forever (2:44–45). This is amplified in the vision concerning the four great beasts (Dan. 7). The first, like a lion, corresponded to the first kingdom, of

10. John C. Whitcomb, *Darius the Mede: A Study in Historical Identification* (Grand Rapids: Eerdmans, 1959). Whitcomb identifies Darius the Mede with Gobryas (or Gubaru) the governor of Babylon, but more likely he should be identified with Gobryas I, the general under Cyrus who actually conquered Babylon. See Yamauchi, *Persia and the Bible*, 58–59.

11. For the theological significance of the Book of Daniel, see Eugene H. Merrill, "Daniel as a Contribution to Kingdom Theology," in *Essays in Honor of J. Dwight Pentecost*, ed. Stanley D. Toussaint and Charles H. Dyer (Chicago: Moody, 1986), 211–25.

Nebuchadnezzar of Babylonia (or the head of gold). The second, like a bear, was Medo-Persia, and its being raised up on one side suggested the superiority of Persia over Media. This paralleled the breasts and arms of silver. The third beast, like a leopard, had four heads and four wings and represented Greece (or the belly and thighs of bronze). The fourth beast was indescribable, but its iron teeth suggest the correspondence with the part of Nebuchadnezzar's image made of iron. Its ten horns were reduced to seven and then increased by one to a total of eight (7:24). This last horn, a usurper, spoke against the "most High" until he was destroyed by the kingdom of God (the stone cut without hands).

Daniel also recorded a vision in which he saw two animals, a goat and a ram (Dan. 8). The latter (Medo-Persia) pushed out in all directions until it was finally overcome by the goat (Greece). The goat had a great horn (ruler) between its eyes, but its horn was broken off in its prime and replaced by four others. From one of these four, another ruler would rise, who would stand against the people of God, but who also would be broken off. This very likely refers to the Macedonian Empire, whose chief king, Alexander the Great, died in his prime (322 B.C.) and was followed by his four generals, who divided his empire. From Seleucia, one of these parts, came Antiochus Epiphanes (Antiochus IV), who reigned from 175–164 B.C. This wicked king despoiled the temple in Jerusalem, offered sacrifices of swine on its altars, and even erected a statue of Zeus within its confines. Jews under Judas Maccabaeus revolted and restored the temple to its proper use.[12] This whole remarkable prophecy (found both here and in greater detail in Dan. 11) is the major reason why critical scholarship has rejected the historicity of Daniel, or at least the notion that it was written as early as the sixth century. Because it so clearly outlines Greek and Seleucid history as they actually occurred, the popular solution is to say that an anonymous writer composed the book after 165 B.C.[13] Without going into the arguments here, the fundamental reason for the critics' rejecting Daniel's authorship is their assumption that verbal inspiration and predictive prophecy of the detailed nature found in Daniel are impossible. But those with a high view of Scripture have no difficulty believing that God revealed these amazing events hundreds of years before they happened.

Daniel also predicted that 70 weeks must pass before the climactic eschatological day would be completed (Dan. 9). It is generally agreed that the term *week* (*heptad* in Greek) refers not to 7 days but to 7 years, and that

12. Flavius Josephus *Antiquities of the Jews* 12.5–6, in *Josephus' Complete Works*, trans. William Whiston (London: Tallis, n.d.).

13. Otto Eissfeldt, *The Old Testament: An Introduction* (New York: Harper and Row, 1965), 520–22.

70 weeks are therefore 490 years. This period would begin with the decree to rebuild the temple, and it would be broken up into three eras. After 7 weeks (49 years), the city would be rebuilt; after 62 more weeks (434 years), the Anointed One (Messiah) would be cut off; and after 1 more week (7 years), everything else would be completed, including the anointing of the Most Holy. Besides the critical school, which refers to this passage as imaginative apocalyptic and makes little or no effort to give it prophetic significance, there are two main views. The amillennial view is that these periods are figurative but that there is here a picture of the final restoration as represented by the death and resurrection of the Lord and the establishment of God's eternal kingdom through the church.[14] The premillennial interpretation is that the time spans are literal, dating from the decree of Artaxerxes in 458 B.C., and that Christ died 483 years after that. Then there is disagreement as to whether the seventieth week was fulfilled immediately after the death of Christ or there has been a lapse of time since the death of the Lord. If the latter is true, the seventieth week remains to be fulfilled in the future great tribulation that, according to this view, the Scriptures imply will endure for seven years.[15] In any event, the detail is amazing and the purpose is clear: God will permit the kingdoms of men to go just so far, and then he will step in and, through his Son, introduce everlasting peace and righteousness.

OUTLINE OF DANIEL[16]

    I. Personal history of Daniel (1)
   II. Prophetic history of the Gentiles during the times
       of the Gentiles (2–7)
      A. The dream of Nebuchadnezzar (2)
      B. The image of Nebuchadnezzar (3)
      C. The second dream of Nebuchadnezzar (4)
      D. The feast of Belshazzar (5)
      E. The edict of Darius (6)
      F. The vision of the four beasts (7)
  III. The prophetic history of Israel during the times
       of the Gentiles (8–12)
      A. The vision of the ram and the goat (8)
      B. The vision of the seventy "sevens" (9)
      C. The final vision (10–12)

14. Herbert C. Leupold, *Exposition of Daniel* (Columbus: Wartburg, 1949).
15. Robert D. Culver, *Daniel and the Latter Days* (Chicago: Moody, 1954).
16. The outline here is adapted from J. Dwight Pentecost, "Daniel," *The Bible Knowledge Commentary*, ed. John F. Walvoord and Roy B. Zuck (Wheaton: Victor, 1985), 1327–28.

The Persian Empire

The Persian conquest of Babylon by Cyrus the Great inaugurated still another phase of Jewish national life. This energetic emperor, who exercised power over the greatest realm hitherto known, had the eastern world at his feet by 539 B.C.[17] In 538 Cyrus issued his famous decree that all captive peoples might return to their native lands, thus reversing the oppressive policies of the Assyrians and, to a lesser extent, of the Babylonians. The contents of this decree are found in the Cylinder of Cyrus, a large clay monument unearthed in the last century, and, of course, in the biblical books of 2 Chronicles (36:22–23) and Ezra (1:1–4). This wise leader felt it would serve his interests better for people to return to their homelands and resume their religious and cultural practices without outside interference. When a people could be internally independent and happy, they would be far less apt to promote unrest in the empire. Thus the setting was laid for Judah's return to Jerusalem.

Cyrus reigned until 530 B.C., when he was killed in battle. His son and successor, Cambyses (530–522), maintained his father's holdings and even added to them by subduing Egypt (525). Amasis, king of Egypt, died in the process of Persian conquest, and his son Psammeticus held out for only a few months. With his defeat, Egypt became a Persian province, which it remained for over a century. Cambyses had slain his own brother Bardiya when he first had become king, but in 522 an imposter named Smerdis (or Gautama) seized the Persian throne in Cambyses' absence and pretended to be the deceased Bardiya. Completely broken by the news, Cambyses committed suicide, and his officer, Darius Hystaspes, took command. Darius, in spite of almost overwhelming odds and beset by unrest throughout the empire, managed to liquidate Smerdis and proclaim himself king (522–486).

After a year or two, Darius was able to consolidate the empire, which had for several years seemed on the verge of collapse. He engaged not only in military operations but also in notable building enterprises, including the new capital at Persepolis, a canal from the Nile to the Red Sea in Egypt, and extensive highways throughout his vast realm. Toward the close of his life he tried to annex Greece to his territory but suffered a crushing defeat at the Battle of Marathon in Greece (490). His son Xerxes (486–465), known as Ahasuerus in the Book of Esther, attempted to follow up the Greek campaigns of his father, but was defeated at the naval battle of Salamis, though he had been successful in annihilating the Spartans at Thermopylae and actually reached the city of Athens. He also

17. Bright, *A History of Israel*, 360–65.

had troubles at Egypt and Babylon and eventually met violent death at the hands of an assassin.

One of Xerxes' sons, Artaxerxes (464–423), followed him, but his reign was largely unsuccessful. He had constant difficulty holding his Egyptian province and was completely unable to push westward against the Greeks. As a matter of fact, by this time Persia had begun to lose its grip on the world and to slide backward, a slide that would culminate in its destruction under Alexander the Great a century later. The only interruption to this pattern was the reign of Darius II (423–404), a gifted king who was able to establish Persian authority in Asia Minor once more and even to subjugate Athens for a time. He was followed by Artaxerxes II (404–358), who gradually lost his empire through rebellions all over the world. The details of this period and of those that followed are not relevant to the biblical account, however, so it is possible to bring the discussion of historical backgrounds to a close here. Suffice it to say that the Macedonians under Alexander finished the Persian Empire at the Battle of Arbela in 331. Their new empire was broken up in turn by 322 B.C. into at least four parts. Though a Hellenistic influence held on for over a hundred years, there was no more empire until Rome appeared late in the third century, incorporating nearly all of the Near East into its hegemony by 63 B.C. This was to lay the political foundation for New Testament times.

The First Return from Babylonia

After Cyrus made his decree authorizing the Jews to return to Jerusalem, he provided such assistance as they needed for the journey and to begin to rebuild their country. He placed Sheshbazzar, who may have been a son of Jehoiachin (1 Chron. 3:18), over the exiles and later made him governor over the Judaean section of the province. In all, over fifty thousand people returned, including more than seven thousand servants. Two of the chief figures, besides Sheshbazzar, were Joshua the priest and Zerubbabel, who came shortly after. These two godly men took the initiative in setting up the broken altars of Yahweh in the blackened ruins of the temple and actually inspired the people to lay the foundation for a new temple in its place (Ezra 3:9–10). The joy that accompanied the beginning of this work can well be imagined, since for fifty years there had been no sacrifice. This was the beginning of a new era for them, an era in which God would truly begin to fulfill the promises of the prophets concerning a glorious future occasioned by the return and restoration.

The chronology of the books of Ezra and Nehemiah is a little complicated, especially at this point (Ezra 4), but it seems likely that the next events of biblical history come from the period of Darius of Persia shortly after he became king.[18] The only sources of information we have concerning the beginning of this time are the prophets Haggai and Zechariah, so it will be well to refer to them now very briefly.

The Prophet Haggai

It was sixteen years from the time the temple was begun (ca. 536) until the commencement of the ministry of Haggai (520). During that time, the initial enthusiasm of the people wore off, and the unfinished foundations remained as an ugly reminder of an uncompleted task. The people began to build their own residences and, under the sanction of Cyrus and Cambyses and the blessing of God, made a good start to recovery, though the undertaking staggers the imagination. This is, however, the motivation that prompted Haggai to speak. The people had no right to care for their own selfish needs while the temple of the Lord lay in an unfinished state (1:4–6). His message was so well received that the people immediately resumed work and, within five years, completed the temple (by 516). Thus, as Jeremiah had said, the captivity lasted for seventy years, a captivity in which God could not be honored in sacrifice because of the lack of a temple.

True, some remembered the magnificent temple of Solomon and wept when they gazed at the comparatively meager new structure (2:3). But Haggai strengthened them by affirming that this house would be filled with the glory of the Lord in an even greater measure than was the temple of old. The people had come home, and God would remember his covenant with them (2:9).

OUTLINE OF HAGGAI
  I. Rebuilding encouraged (1:1–15)
     A. Excuses of the people (1–2)
     B. Exhortation of the prophet (3–11)
     C. Effect of the plea (12–15)
 II. Restoration explained (2:1–23)
     A. Comparison of temples (1–3)
     B. Covenant of the Lord (4–9)
     C. Condemnation of the people (10–19)
     D. Choosing of Judah (20–23)

18. For support of the biblical tradition that Ezra preceded Nehemiah, see Eugene H. Merrill, *Kingdom of Priests: A History of Old Testament Israel* (Grand Rapids: Baker, 1987), 502–6.

The Prophet Zechariah

Zechariah, a contemporary of Haggai, also had a burden to rebuild the temple, but his vision, expressed largely in apocalyptic terms, was much broader than just that. He saw a measurement and rebuilding not only of a physical Jerusalem but also of a spiritual city wherein salvation could be found for all mankind (2:11–12). This salvation would become possible through the Branch, the anointed one of God, who would build the temple of God (3:8). The city itself would be filled with the joyous people of God (8:8). In time men would seize the skirt of one Jew and beg him to reveal to them the way of salvation (8:23).

The King of the city would come to it in humility and justice, bringing salvation, and yet would accomplish the destruction of God's enemies (9:9). Jerusalem would be free from idolatry and false prophets, who made it their business to deceive (13:2). But, as Ezekiel taught, this future glory must be ushered in by tribulation. Jerusalem must experience the wrath of the nations in the last days and await the deliverance of the Lord (14:1–3). But that deliverance would surely come when the feet of the Lord stood on the Mount of Olives and divided it in two, proclaiming doom on the nations assembled against Jerusalem for battle (14:4–11). The wicked would be crushed, the feasts of the Lord would be resumed, and everything would be holy unto the Lord (14:20–21).

OUTLINE OF ZECHARIAH
    I. Series of visions (1:1–6:8)
        A. Call to repentance (1:1–6)
        B. The horses (1:7–17)
        C. The horns and carpenters (1:18–21)
        D. The measurer (2)
        E. Cleansing of the priest (3)
        F. Candlesticks (4)
        G. The flying scroll (5:1–4)
        H. The flying ephah (5:5–11)
        I. The flying chariots (6:1–8)
    II. Symbolic crowning of the priest (6:9–15)
    III. Problem concerning fasting (7)
    IV. Promise of restoration (8)
    V. Future of the kingdom (9–11)
        A. Rejoicing of Jerusalem (9)
        B. Restoration of Jerusalem (10)
        C. Revelation to Jerusalem (11)

VI. Future of the King (12–14)
   A. Punishment by Jerusalem (12)
   B. Purification of Jerusalem (13)
   C. Plague of Jerusalem's enemies (14)

For the completion of the temple, one must turn back to Ezra, where the project is discussed more fully. The citizens of the land, the Samaritans, asked to assist in the rebuilding, but their offer was declined on the grounds that this was a Jewish project (Ezra 4:1–6). The suggestion that the Samaritans were less than Jewish and therefore unqualified to participate in the formation of the new state produced a friction between the two peoples that increased with time and was at its height in the time of Jesus (John 4). The Samaritans and their Arabian and Ammonite allies then attempted to frustrate the work, which may be one of the reasons for its delay until the resumption under Haggai and Zechariah. When it was resumed, Tatnai, governor of the Persian lands west of the Euphrates, sent a letter to Darius informing him of the Jews' activity and asking him to search in the official archives to see if there were any legal basis to what they were doing (5:6–17). This Darius did, and, to the chagrin of the opposition, the original decree of Cyrus was found that not only entitled the Jews to rebuild but also offered them help. Darius therefore ordered the opposition to cease and told Tatnai to supply whatever the Jews might lack (6:8). Within six years the temple stood complete, though the city was still mostly a pile of rubble and the walls still lay shattered.

Esther

Events are very obscure throughout the rest of the reign of Darius and into that of Xerxes. Presumably the work of rebuilding the state of Judah continued, though harassed from many sides. The Jews in exile mostly prospered, but some anti-Jewish currents arose. This is the main gist of the Book of Esther, a strange composition that does not even mention the name of God but whose every page reflects intense awareness of God's presence and power on behalf of his exiled people.

The setting of the book is the reign of Ahasuerus (Xerxes), and the first events are in his third year (483). It seems that the king was celebrating a magnificent feast that had gone on for seven days. All the lords and ladies of the empire were there, and spirits were high indeed. Near the end of the week, the counselors urged the king, who was in a drunken stupor, to invite his queen Vashti to the feast so that her great beauty might be admired. The king unthinkingly complied, but the noble Vashti refused (Esther 1:12). The counselors then advised the king to rid himself of

Vashti because of her disobedience, for if word of this got out into the realm, all wives would take the cue to disobey their husbands. Reluctantly, Xerxes followed the advice and added a decree that any disobedient wife should be treated in the same fashion.

The king then sought another queen. All the beautiful and intelligent maidens of the realm were brought before him, and one in particular caught his eye—Esther, the young cousin of Mordecai the Jew. Shortly after the marriage, Mordecai overheard a plot against the life of the king. He conveyed the information to his cousin, and she relayed it to her husband in Mordecai's name. Meanwhile, a greedy man named Haman had risen to prominence in the empire. Everyone acknowledged his eminence by bowing before him when he appeared—everyone but Mordecai. This so infuriated Haman that he set out to devise a way to remove the irksome Jew. When all other plans failed, he decided that a nationwide purge of the Jewish people would be best, so he convinced the king to decree such a purge by telling him that the Jews were seditious (3:8–9). Xerxes, who seemed to act rashly in any event, did not know that his beloved Esther was a Jewess, or he never would have made this irreversible decree. When Mordecai learned that a date had been set for the annihilation of his race, he quickly reached Esther with the news and advised her that she might be the means of salvation for her people (4:1–14).

After much soul searching, Esther agreed to do what she could. She would go to her husband unannounced, although, according to Persian custom, this could result in her death, and would invite him and Haman to a series of banquets. Amazingly, the king was well disposed to the idea and agreed to attend. Haman, overjoyed at the prospect of removing the Jews and attending such an important function, went home, only to meet the hated Mordecai along the way. When the Jew would not prostrate himself, Haman went home in a rage and, while there, accepted his wife's suggestion to build a huge gallows on which to hang his enemy.

That night the king could not sleep. He called for the state records to be read to him. It came to his attention afresh that his life had been saved by one Mordecai. When he asked if Mordecai had ever been rewarded, the answer was no. The king asked Haman, who had come to the palace early in the morning, what he would do to bestow extraordinary honor on a man. The selfish Haman thought the king must have him in mind, so he advised the king to give the man a place of great authority and to bestow lavish gifts on him. At that, Xerxes told Haman to go to Mordecai and so honor him (6:10).

When the banquet day came, Haman was there with the king and queen when the queen requested that her people be spared. It now dawned on Xerxes that he had sentenced his own wife to death with her people. When he learned further that Haman had instigated the whole affair, he ordered the wretched man hanged on his own gallows. Then he issued another decree that, though the first could not be changed, the Jews now could defend themselves. This so encouraged the Jews and unnerved their enemies that, when the appointed day of purge arrived, the tables were turned, and the Jews thwarted the designs of their foes. In commemoration of the divine deliverance, they celebrated the Feast of Purim ("lots"). The lots that had been cast by their oppressors to determine the order in which they would die now fell favorably in their direction (9:26). Mordecai, the faithful servant of God, enjoyed the honor of the man who thought to do him harm.

It is clear, then, that God's people were remarkably protected even in exile and in many similarly dire circumstances. Though the Book of Esther is not regarded favorably by higher criticism,[19] usually because of its allegedly secular tone and incredible turn of events, there is no reason historical or otherwise to deny the authenticity of the events and persons it describes.

Back in Judah, the original settlers under Sheshbazzar and Zerubbabel had laid a good foundation in many respects, at least as far as the material progress of the state was concerned. The temple had been rebuilt, and some effort had been made to fortify the city of Jerusalem. The people were getting along comfortably enough, as the books of Haggai and Zechariah attest, and apparently enjoyed some measure of independence under the Persians, even though their neighbors all around persisted in their harassment. The government was that of a high priestly rule, though officials designated governors were appointed by the Persian king. Judaea itself was not an individual political entity, to be sure, but was part of the larger satrapy that consisted of the Persian lands west of the Euphrates.

Subsequent Returns from Babylonia

Ezra and Nehemiah

Sheshbazzar, Zerubbabel, and Joshua the priest had all passed from the scene by the close of the sixth century, and the leadership that followed them did not seem to measure up to their stature. Only sparse records remain of governors from Zerubbabel to the time of Nehemiah (444),[20]

19. For example, see the remarks of Bernhard W. Anderson, *Understanding the Old Testament*, 4th ed. (Englewood Cliffs, N.J.: Prentice-Hall, 1986), 607–10.

20. For a reconstruction of the list of Judaean governors based on jar impressions, bullae, and seals, see Carol L. Meyers and Eric M. Meyers, *Haggai, Zechariah 1–8*, Anchor Bible (Garden City, N.Y.: Doubleday, 1987), 14.

but the high priestly line continued under Joiakim (ca. 510–475) and Eliashib (475–425?). These men could not establish a necessary spiritual leadership; as a result, the cult fell into bad times indeed. Moreover, and relatedly, the people began to intermingle with the natives of the land, even going so far as to intermarry. This presumably was the state of affairs for over fifty years, until Ezra came to Jerusalem in the company of a great crowd of exiles (Ezra 7:6–10).

This godly man was a direct descendant of Aaron and was therefore qualified to occupy the priestly office. Furthermore, he was a scribe or scholar in the law and had authority to render interpretations of it and make legal copies of it. When the returned people were forgetting their past and the covenant promises of the future, Ezra came and transformed them into a nation with renewed direction and purpose. It is too much to say that Ezra was the founder of Judaism,[21] for Judaism is simply the post-exilic expression of the ancient Old Testament faith. But that it was a different expression and was greatly influenced by Ezra cannot be challenged. The reemphasis on law and ceremony, the rise of the synagogue movement with its careful attention to the study of Torah, and the final shaping of the Old Testament canon all were largely effected by Ezra and his spiritual heirs.

Ezra first appears in the biblical record in the seventh year of Artaxerxes I (458), when he came, under the authority and assistance of that king, from Babylon to Jerusalem. He came not only to lead a caravan of the pious back to the fatherland but also to seek the law of the Lord, to do it, and to teach it to the community (Ezra 7:10). The ecclesiastical character of Ezra's movement is seen in the extensive lists of priests (10:15–44) and other people who either accompanied him to Jerusalem or came under his direction when he arrived. He was especially concerned about the lack of separation among the priests and the Levites in the community, for though they had not forsaken the faith and adopted other gods, they had intermarried with foreign women (9:1–2). This so aroused him that he broke out into prayer immediately on his arrival and interceded for his wayward people. A great assembly of the population from throughout the little country followed, leading to national repentance. This in turn led to a proclamation that the whole nation must convene at Jerusalem, failing which the disobedient would lose their earthly goods. The purpose for the gathering was to act to remove the foreign wives of those who had married outside the covenant. The response was so univer-

21. Jacob M. Myers, *Ezra-Nehemiah*, Anchor Bible (Garden City, N.Y.: Doubleday, 1965), lxii.

sal and overwhelming that there is every reason to believe that a genuine revival occurred under Ezra's leadership (10:12).

This more favorable condition continued for ten years or more, but then difficulties crept in again. It seems that sometime near 446–445 B.C., work on the walls and buildings, which had been progressing slowly, was stopped by the interference of hostile neighbors, and even what had been rebuilt was destroyed somehow (Ezra 4:24; Neh. 1:3). The antagonists had written a letter to Artaxerxes informing him that under Ezra's leadership the Jews had not only reestablished the cult, a matter the king had permitted, but also had gone beyond the king's express command by fortifying Jerusalem. They charged that the Jews were a notoriously seditious people and that Artaxerxes would do well to look out for his interests lest they conspire against him and hide behind their new walls. The king discovered that the Jews indeed had gained such a reputation in the past, so he sent immediate word that the work must cease until further word should be given.

This discouraging setback was related to Nehemiah, the Jewish cupbearer of Artaxerxes, when certain travelers from Judah came to see him at Susa (ca. 444 B.C.). Nehemiah, though he apparently had never been to Jerusalem, had the well-being of his ancestral home deep in his heart. His anxiety over the ruined condition of the city showed so plainly in his countenance that the king asked what ailed him. With a prayer on his lips, Nehemiah told all that had happened among his countrymen and courageously begged permission of the king to go to the Holy City to see what he could do. Amazingly, Artaxerxes, who had only recently ordered construction of Jerusalem to cease, acquiesced and sent his trusted servant on leave of absence (Neh. 2:6). More than that, he sent letters of conveyance with him that guaranteed him not only a safe journey but also access to any materials he might need from the provincial governor to resume the work at Jerusalem. Sanballat, governor of Samaria, and Tobiah, governor of Ammon, were naturally upset by this reversal, but because of the king's sanction there was little they could hope to do by way of force to prevent the work under Nehemiah.

Nehemiah's first task was to assess the damage and the amount of labor and materials necessary to finish the great task. At once he aroused the people of Judah to action, assuring them of both divine and royal authorization. The opponents, who hoped they might join the project now that they could not prevent it, were forbidden any part (2:17–20). The workers were divided up into gangs according to their occupations, places of residence, and families, and each became responsible for a different section of the wall of the city. It is not possible here to trace the lines of the walls and locations of the many gates, but the information presented has been remarkably well verified by archaeological exploration of the ancient city walls.[22]

When Sanballat, Tobiah, and their allies saw that they could not dissuade Nehemiah from his project, they became increasingly violent. At first they mocked the effort of the Jews, branding it feeble. The walls, they said, were so inadequate that even a fox brushing against them could topple them (4:3). When ridicule failed and the work was nearing completion, it became clear that mere words could not prevent it. Heedless of Artaxerxes' decree that the work go unhindered, the Samaritans, Ammonites, Arabians, and others took up arms and began to physically impede construction. This only made Nehemiah more vigilant. In a remarkable display of perseverance and fortitude, he ordered his men to work in shifts day and night and to fight with one hand while they built with the other. No wonder the entire wall was erected in only fifty-two days!

Still the enemy persisted. With all possibility of preventing the fortification of Jerusalem gone, they hoped to induce Nehemiah to negotiate with them in a neutral place. But as far as the Jewish leader was concerned, there was nothing to negotiate, for he clearly had the upper hand. Undaunted, they composed an open letter that they read loudly outside the city to attract the attention of the populace. In the letter they maintained that the purpose for the walls was to allow the Jews to rebel against the Persians so that Nehemiah could be its king (6:6–7). This ridiculous accusation Nehemiah hotly denied, and the people quickly saw the subtlety behind it. Finally, the foes essayed to diminish Nehemiah's good reputation among the citizens by attempting to persuade him to take sanctuary in the temple, arguing that such a valuable man should not expose himself to danger. But Nehemiah saw through this scheme all too well and revealed to all that the one who had rendered the advice was a crony of the opposition who had tried to weaken his position by making him appear cowardly.

At last, the problems of material reconstruction were pretty well solved, and Nehemiah had time to direct his attention to matters of even greater importance. In the twenty-five years or so since the great revival of Ezra, social and religious relapses had taken place on every hand. This seems to be difficult to understand and, indeed, has led some, like John Bright, to date Ezra after Nehemiah, for it is argued that if Ezra's revival was the success he says it was in his book, there should be no need this soon for another one, especially if Ezra were still living there among the people.[23]

22. Kathleen M. Kenyon, *Jerusalem* (New York: McGraw-Hill, 1967), 107–12.
23. Bright, *A History of Israel*, 393.

There is merit to this argument, but it is not conclusive. For one thing, the problems do not seem to be the same ones Ezra had faced earlier, the main difficulty now being the oppressive usury that Jew was exacting from Jew. It is true that some of the same matters Ezra had handled had to be dealt with again, but the Jews historically had been prone to quick reversal after revival, even in as little time as twenty-five years. How it could happen in Ezra's lifetime may be explained by assuming that Ezra by this time was quite old and simply was not alert to what transpired. It is also true that Nehemiah himself had been back for ten years or so before he instituted his reforms, but building the walls and city and securing a solid position in the face of great opposition from without could easily have prevented his taking a more active role in domestic and spiritual matters.

Nehemiah first struck out against those who were exploiting their fellow citizens by charging unduly high rates of interest, contrary to the law (5:1–5). He argued that since the impoverished Jews had sold themselves to the surrounding heathen and had been redeemed by those who had returned from exile, it was especially serious that Jew should so oppress Jew by charging unpayable rates of interest on loans. He reminded them that as long as he had been governor (444–433) he had worked for no wages and had not burdened the people in any other way. The least they could do was emulate his example and ease their common yoke.

He also set about allocating dwelling places on the basis of people's genealogical records, such as they had been since Zerubbabel and Joshua. Following this, a great crowd gathered before the Water Gate to listen to Ezra the scribe reading the law (8:1–8). On a specially erected platform, Ezra opened the scrolls. When he began to read, the people stood reverently before him. With clarity and expression he expounded the ancient covenant truths while the assembly wept on hearing their convicting precepts. But Nehemiah exhorted them to rejoice, for this was a day of gladness, a day when they could celebrate the actuality of the return from exile and the reestablishment of their sacred community. The next day the covenant renewal was consummated by the observance of the Feast of Tabernacles, the principal feature of which was the daily reading of the law by Ezra. This was the first time the feast had been celebrated in that manner since the time of Joshua the son of Nun. Now, after eight hundred years, it signified the beginning of a new era in Israel. The faith of their fathers had become bound up in the law (which means here the entire Old Testament), and Judaism became primarily a religion of the Book.

Evidence of this new direction may be seen in the people's repentance for failing to follow faithfully the precepts of Moses. And so, at the same time, it is clear that Judaism, as their religion may now be called, was not unrelated to its earlier composition. It found its roots deep in the historical dealings of God with Israel, just as Christianity must find its source in Judaism and the Old Testament. In united recitation, the Levites recounted God's past blessings and leading and acknowledged that their disastrous afflictions had come about deservedly. But God had not discontinued his covenant with them. He had only temporarily withheld its blessing. Now they had returned, as God had predicted through the prophets. They had become conscious that though things would never be exactly as they were before the exile, God had not forsaken the covenant. He had caused them to pass through the fires of purgation so that they might return refined and ready to resume their obligations to him. To this end they solemnly rededicated themselves and all that they possessed on that momentous day (9:38).

Nehemiah returned to Susa shortly after the Feast of Tabernacles and the subsequent ceremony of covenant renewal (ca. 433). He remained there for an indefinite period, and then obtained leave again from the king (presumably Artaxerxes I) to return to Jerusalem. When he reached the city, he found deplorable conditions in every area of life, though he had been absent for but a short time. For one thing, not only had Eliashib the priest permitted Tobiah to make an alliance with him, but also the crafty Ammonite had been given an apartment within the sacred temple of the Lord, a clear violation of the law of Moses (13:4–5). Angrily, Nehemiah evicted Tobiah and ordered the polluted chambers cleaned thoroughly. He then observed that the Levites were not supported by the gifts of the people and that they had to work in the fields to maintain their families. He assailed the people for their stinginess and saw that they paid the Levites their due. The sabbath, too, was violated by both Jew and Gentile, who bought and sold in the city on the day of rest. Nehemiah quickly stopped this, but the caravan merchants continued to linger outside the city all through the sabbath awaiting the first day of the week so that they could resume business. Even this Nehemiah considered a breach of the spirit of the law, so he warned these Gentile traders to stay a comfortable distance from Jerusalem lest they fall into his hands. Finally, he had to deal with the oft-recurring problem of mixed marriages, though Ezra had settled this matter over thirty years before (13:23). With a burst of temper, the energetic reformer forced compliance with the law of marital purity, apparently with success.

With this, Nehemiah's career passes from history; in fact, the course of Old Testament history reaches its completion. The only other allusions to the period are found in the book of the last prophet of the Old Testament, Malachi.

The Prophet Malachi

In order to see that there were unhealthy trends in normative Judaism just before and perhaps early in the time of Ezra, it is necessary to examine briefly the Book of Malachi. This prophet, whose indictments seem to point to the same conditions as those later in Nehemiah's age, concerned himself largely with invectives against the terrible travesties of law and righteousness he saw on every hand. Though the Jews never were idolatrous after the exile, still they very seldom lived up to the Lord's requirements. Malachi could point out such things as their offering inferior animals to the Lord (1:8), the sinfulness of the priests, and their mixed marriages, but they would only reply, "Wherein have we offended the Lord?" They had come through the exile, they had rebuilt their country, they had become covenant-conscious once again. Yet, their very security had produced a callousness of spirit and heart and had bred indifference and coldness into their relationship to God and each other.

But Malachi stated in no uncertain terms that the Day of the Lord was still coming, a day when the Lord would appear among them to purify and judge (3:1–3). Then they would offer the good sacrifices they were so unwilling to offer now. They had robbed him by failing to bring proper offerings, but if they would test him they would find that he could bless them beyond their wildest expectations (3:10). Those who were unprepared for his coming would be consumed by his wrath, but those who obediently awaited and feared him would be blessed with healing and salvation. The sign of the appearance of the Lord would be the preaching of Elijah, which, as Isaiah had said, would be the voice of one crying in the wilderness a message of judgment, repentance, and hope. The covenant had been reaffirmed over and over, even as late as this time of the prophet, but the fulfillment and perfect realization must await that wilderness voice that would pronounce jubilantly and with authority, "Behold the Lamb of God, which taketh away the sin of the world."

OUTLINE OF MALACHI
    I. Reminder to the nation (1:1–5)
    II. Reproof to the profane (1:6–14)
    III. Rebuke of the priests (2)
    IV. Restoration of the nation (3)
    V. Reign of the Sun of Righteousness (4)

Intertestamental History

Apart from the uncertain references of Josephus and documents like the Elephantine Papyri, virtually nothing can be known of Jewish affairs to the end of the Persian period and on into the Hellenistic. It seems fairly clear, however, that the pattern seen in the last chapter of Nehemiah and in Malachi must have persisted more or less until the breakup of the Macedonian Empire (322 B.C.). After that, the successive dominations of the Ptolemies of Egypt and the Seleucids of Syria and Babylonia brought in modifications of the Judaistic faith, minor to be sure, that continued to manifest themselves until the time of Jesus Christ and even beyond. The struggle for Jewish independence under the Maccabees (167–135), followed by the Hasmonaean Dynasty of Jewish kings (135–63 B.C.), also made its contributions to the nation and people, notably in the rise of parties like the Pharisees, Sadducees, and Essenes.[24] The Judaism of the Roman period (after 63), therefore, had much in common with that of Ezra, but the accretions from the sources mentioned, embodied largely in Hellenistic philosophy, Persian religious concepts to a more limited degree, and the oral law (Mishnah), all combined to make later Judaism something also quite different.[25] The hostility of first-century Judaism to Christ and the gospel cannot be explained as a clash between historical Judaism and Christianity. It was, rather, a clash between the Judaism perverted through four centuries since Ezra, and the fulfillment of the Judaism of the Old Testament expressed by Christ and the apostles. "In the fullness of time God sent forth his Son," the crucial and culminating act of all history, toward which the Old Testament story constantly pressed.

24. For this period, see F. F. Bruce, *Israel and the Nations, from the Exodus to the Fall of the Second Temple* (Grand Rapids: Eerdmans, 1963); Werner Foerster, *From the Exile to Christ* (Philadelphia: Fortress, 1964).

25. W. F. Albright, *From the Stone Age to Christianity* (Garden City, N.Y.: Doubleday, 1957), 345–80.

Bibliography

The following bibliography, by no means exhaustive, is intended to introduce the interested reader to some of the more important literature on the history and culture of ancient Israel and on the background to the Old Testament.

Ackroyd, Peter R. *Exile and Restoration: A Study of Hebrew Thought of the Sixth Century* B.C. Philadelphia: Westminster, 1968.

———. *Israel Under Babylon and Persia.* London: Oxford University Press, 1970.

Aharoni, Yohanan. *The Land of the Bible.* Translated and edited by Anson F. Rainey. Rev. and enl. ed. Philadelphia: Westminster, 1979.

Aharoni, Yohanan, and Michael Avi-Yonah. *The Macmillan Bible Atlas.* New York: Macmillan, 1968.

Albright, W. F. *The Archaeology of Palestine.* Rev. ed. Baltimore: Penguin, 1971.

———. *The Biblical Period from Abraham to Ezra.* New York: Harper, 1949.

———. *From the Stone Age to Christianity.* Garden City, N.Y.: Doubleday, 1957.

———. *Yahweh and the Gods of Canaan.* Garden City, N.Y.: Doubleday, 1969.

Allis, O. T. *The Five Books of Moses.* Philadelphia: Presbyterian and Reformed, 1949.

———. *The Unity of Isaiah: A Study in Prophecy.* Philadelphia: Presbyterian and Reformed, 1950.

Anati, Emmanuel. *Palestine Before the Hebrews: A History, from the Earliest Arrival of Man to the Conquest of Canaan.* New York: Alfred A. Knopf, 1962.

Anderson, Bernhard W. *Understanding the Old Testament.* 4th ed. Englewood Cliffs: Prentice-Hall, 1986.

Archer, Gleason, L., Jr. *A Survey of Old Testament Introduction.* Rev. ed. Chicago: Moody, 1974.

Bailey, A. E. *Daily Life in Bible Times.* New York: Charles Scribner's Sons, 1943.

Baly, Denis. *A Geographical Companion to the Bible.* London: Lutterworth, 1963.

————. *The Geography of the Bible: A Study in Historical Geography.* Rev. ed. New York: Harper, 1974.

Ben-Sasson, H. H., ed. *A History of the Jewish People.* Cambridge: Harvard University Press, 1969.

Bimson, John J. *Redating the Exodus and Conquest.* Sheffield: JSOT, University of Sheffield, 1978.

Bright, John. *A History of Israel.* 3d ed. Philadelphia: Westminster, 1981.

Bruce, F. F. *Israel and the Nations, from the Exodus to the Fall of the Second Temple.* Grand Rapids: Eerdmans, 1963.

Budden, Charles W., and Edward Hastings. *The Local Colour of the Bible.* 3 vols. Edinburgh: T. and T. Clark, 1925.

Castel, Francois. *The History of Israel and Judah in Old Testament Times.* New York: Paulist, 1985.

Corswant, W., and Edouard Urech. *A Dictionary of Life in Bible Times.* London: Hodder and Stoughton, 1960.

Davis, John J., and John C. Whitcomb. *A History of Israel from Conquest to Exile.* Grand Rapids, Baker, 1980.

Deursen, Arie van, and J. De Vries. *Illustrated Dictionary of Bible Manners.* New York: Philosophical Library, 1967.

Drane, John W. *The Old Testament Story.* San Francisco: Harper and Row, 1983.

Duncan, J. Garrow. *The Accuracy of the Old Testament: The Historical Narratives in the Light of Recent Palestinian Archaeology.* London: Society for Promoting Christian Knowledge, 1930.

Everyday Life in Bible Times. Washington: National Geographic Society, 1967.

Farb, Peter, and Harry McNaught. *The Land, Wildlife, and Peoples of the Bible.* New York: Harper and Row, 1967.

Filson, Floyd. "Method in Studying Biblical History." *Journal of Biblical Literature* 69 (1950): 1–18.

Finegan, Jack. *Handbook of Biblical Chronology: Principles of Time Reckoning in the Ancient World and Problems of Chronology in the Bible.* Princeton: Princeton University Press, 1964.

Foerster, Werner. *From the Exile to Christ.* Philadelphia: Fortress, 1964.

Goldingay, John. "The Patriarchs in Scripture and History." In *Essays on the Patriarchal Narratives,* edited by A. R. Millard and D. J. Wiseman, 1–34. Winona Lake, Ind.: Eisenbrauns, 1983.

Gray, G. B. *Forms of Hebrew Poetry.* London: Hodder and Stoughton, 1915.

Gray, John. *Archaeology and the Old Testament World.* New York: Harper and Row, 1962.

———. *The Canaanites.* New York: Praeger, 1964.

Harden, Donald B. *The Phoenicians.* 2d ed. New York: Praeger, 1962.

Harris, R. Laird. *Inspiration and Canonicity of the Bible: An Historical and Exegetical Study.* Grand Rapids: Zondervan, 1957.

Hayes, John H., and J. Maxwell Miller, eds. *Israelite and Judaean History.* Philadelphia: Westminster, 1977.

Kallai, Zecharia. *Historical Geography of the Bible: The Tribal Territories of Israel.* Jerusalem: Magnes/Leiden: Brill, 1986.

Kellner, Esther. *The Background of the Old Testament.* Garden City, N.Y.: Doubleday, 1963.

Kenyon, Kathleen M. *Archaeology in the Holy Land.* 5th ed. New York: Praeger, 1979.

Kirkpatrick, A. F. *The Doctrine of the Prophets: The Warburtonian Lectures for 1886–1890.* 3d ed. London: Macmillan, 1901.

Kitchen, K. A. *Ancient Orient and Old Testament.* London: Tyndale, 1966.

———. *The Bible in Its World: The Bible and Archaeology Today.* Downers Grove: InterVarsity, 1978.

Malamat, A. "The Kingdom of David and Solomon in Its Contact with Egypt and Aram Naharaim." *Biblical Archaeologist* 21 (1958): 96–102.

Mattingly, Gerald L. "The Exodus-Conquest and the Archaeology of Transjordan: New Light on an Old Problem." *Grace Theological Journal* 4 (1983): 245–62.

May, Herbert G., ed. *Oxford Bible Atlas.* 3d ed. New York: Oxford University Press, 1984.

Mazar, Benjamin. "The Aramaean Empire and Its Relations with Israel." *Biblical Archaeologist* 25 (1962): 97–120.

Mazar, Benjamin, ed. *Views of the Biblical World*. Jerusalem: International, 1958.

Mendenhall, George E. *Law and Covenant in Israel and the Ancient Near East*. Pittsburgh: The Biblical Colloquium, 1955.

Merrill, Eugene H. "The 'Accession Year' and Davidic Chronology." *Journal of Ancient Near Eastern Studies* 19 (1989): 101–12.

———. "Ebla and Biblical Historical Inerrancy." *Bibliotheca Sacra* 140 (1983): 302–21.

———. "Fixed Dates in Patriarchal Chronology." *Bibliotheca Sacra* 137 (1980): 241–51.

———. *Kingdom of Priests. A History of Old Testament Israel*. Grand Rapids: Baker, 1987.

———. "Palestinian Archaeology and the Date of the Conquest: Do Tells Tell Tales?" *Grace Theological Journal* 3 (1982): 107–21.

———. "Paul's Use of 'About 450 Years' in Acts 13:20." *Bibliotheca Sacra* 138 (1981): 246–57.

Miller, J. Maxwell, and John H. Hayes. *A History of Ancient Israel and Judah*. Philadelphia: Westminster, 1986.

Miller, M. S., and J. L. Miller. *Encyclopedia of Bible Life*. New York: Harper and Row, 1944.

Morris, Henry M. *Studies in the Bible and Science*. Philadelphia: Presbyterian and Reformed, 1966.

Moscati, Sabatino. *Ancient Semitic Civilizations*. New York: G. P. Putnam's Sons, 1960.

Noth, Martin. *The History of Israel*. New York: Harper, 1958.

———. *The Old Testament World*. Philadelphia: Fortress, 1966.

Oehler, Gustave, *Theology of the Old Testament*. Grand Rapids: Zondervan, 1883.

Owens, G. Frederick. *Archaeology and the Bible*. Westwood, N.J.: Revell, 1961.

Pedersen, Johannes. *Israel, Its Life and Culture*. 4 vols. London: Oxford University Press, 1926–40.

Pfeiffer, Charles, ed. *The Biblical World: A Dictionary of Biblical Archaeology*. Grand Rapids: Baker, 1966.

Pritchard, J. B., ed. *Ancient Near Eastern Texts Relating to the Old Testament*. 3d ed. Princeton: Princeton University Press, 1969.

Radin, Max. *The Life of the People in Biblical Times*. New York: Jewish Publication Society of America, 1929.

Schultz, Samuel. *The Old Testament Speaks*. 3d ed. New York: Harper and Row, 1980.

Selman, M. J. "Comparative Methods and the Patriarchal Narratives." *Themelios* 3 (1977): 9–16.

Tadmor, Hayim, and Moshe Weinfeld, eds. *History, Historiography and Interpretation: Studies in Biblical and Cuneiform Literatures*. Jerusalem: Magnes, 1983.

Thiele, Edwin R. *The Mysterious Numbers of the Hebrew Kings*. 3d. ed. Grand Rapids: Eerdmans, 1983.

Thomas, D. Winton, ed. *Documents from Old Testament Times*. London: Thomas Nelson, 1958.

Thompson, J. A. *The Bible and Archaeology*. 3d ed. Grand Rapids: Eerdmans, 1982.

Unger, Merrill F. *Archaeology and the Old Testament*. Grand Rapids: Zondervan, 1954.

————. *Israel and the Aramaeans of Damascus*. London: James Clarke, 1957.

Van Der Woude, A. S., ed. *The World of the Bible*. Translated by Sierd Woudstra. Grand Rapids: Eerdmans, 1986.

————. *The World of the Old Testament*. Grand Rapids: Eerdmans, 1989.

Vos, Geerhardus. *Biblical Theology: Old and New Testaments*. Grand Rapids: Eerdmans, 1948.

Warfield, B. B. *The Inspiration and Authority of the Bible*. Philadelphia: Presbyterian and Reformed, 1948.

Whitcomb, John C. *Darius the Mede: A Study in Historical Identification*. Philadelphia: Presbyterian and Reformed, 1959.

Whitcomb, John C., and Henry M. Morris. *The Genesis Flood: The Biblical Record and Its Scientific Implications*. Philadelphia: Presbyterian and Reformed, 1963.

Wilson, Robert Dick. *Scientific Investigation of the Old Testament*. Chicago: Moody, 1965.

Wiseman, D. J. "Abraham Reassessed." In *Essays on the Patriarchal Narratives*, edited by A. R. Millard and D. J. Wiseman, 141–60. Winona Lake, Ind.: Eisenbrauns, 1983.

————. *Chronicles of Chaldean Kings (625–556 B.C.) in the British Museum*. London: Trustees of the British Museum, 1956.

Wood, Bryant G. "Did the Israelites Conquer Jericho? A New Look at the Archaeological Evidence." *Biblical Archaeology Review* 16 (1990): 44–58.

Wood, Leon. *Israel's United Monarchy*. Grand Rapids: Baker, 1979.

————. *A Survey of Israel's History*. Grand Rapids: Zondervan, 1970.

Wright, G. Ernest. *Biblical Archaeology*. Rev. ed. Philadelphia: Westminster, 1962.

Wright, G. Ernest, ed. *The Bible and the Ancient Near East*. Garden City, N.Y.: Doubleday, 1961.

Yamauchi, Edwin M. *Persia and the Bible*. Grand Rapids: Baker, 1990.

Young, Edward J. *An Introduction to the Old Testament*. Rev. ed. Grand Rapids: Eerdmans, 1964.

———. *My Servants, the Prophets*. Grand Rapids: Eerdmans, 1952.

Index of Subjects

Aaron, 111, 112, 119, 121–23,
    136, 144, 145, 189
  rod, 122–23
  sons, 120
Abdon, 170
Abel, 58, 59
Abel (city), 210
Abiathar, 197, 208, 211, 212
Abigail, 198
Abihu, 120
Abijam, 233
Abimelech, 83, 168, 206
Abinadab, 182, 205
Abiram, 122
Abishai, 198
Abner, 198, 202–3, 203, 209
Abraham, 70, 71, 76, 77, 79,
    81–84, 86, 154
  dates, 99
  faith, 77, 83
  migration into Egypt, 78,
    96, 101
  as prophet, 188
  tithe to Melchizedek, 80
Abrahamic covenant, 77,
    80–81, 84, 86, 118, 152,
    283
Absalom, 208–9, 212, 233
Achan, 153
Achish, 196, 199
Adam, 56, 58
Adamic covenant, 66
Adonijah, 211–12
Adullam, 197
Aegean Sea, 280
Ahab, 98–99, 235–38, 239,
    241, 243, 244, 246
Ahasuerus, 290, 294. *See also*
    Xerxes
Ahaz, 248–49, 258, 259, 261,
    262, 263

Ahaziah, 238–39, 243, 244
Ahijah, 217, 232, 240
Ahinoam, 198
Ahithophel, 209
Ahmose, 101, 102, 106, 110
Aholiab, 119, 214
Ai, 153, 154
Akhnaton, 103–4
Akkadian Empire, 47
Alalakh, 95
Alexander the Great, 257,
    288, 291
Allegory, 225
Alphabet, 186
Altar, 139, 140, 143, 145, 161,
    212, 236, 262
Altar of burnt offerings,
    143–44
Altar of incense, 143–44
Amalek, 193
Amalekites, 117, 192–93, 200
Amasa, 209, 210
Amasis, 279, 290
Amaziah, 245–46, 250
Amenemhet I, 74, 100
Amenemhet II, 101
Amenemhet III, 102
Amenhotep I, 102–3, 106, 110
Amenhotep II, 103, 106, 112
Amenhotep III, 103, 148, 149
Amenhotep IV, 103, 148
Amillenialism, 289
Ammon, 157, 170, 207, 271
Ammonites, 83, 150, 248, 299
  judgment, 272, 282
  threat against Israel, 165,
    169, 239
  wars, 190–91, 207, 209
Amnon, 208
Amon, 267

Amorites, 75, 81, 124, 147,
    154, 155, 157
Amos, 252–54
Amraphel, 78–79
Anathoth, 273
Angel of Yahweh, 82, 89, 124,
    162, 166, 171, 260, 261
Animal sacrifice, 138–40, 143
Anshan, 280
Antiochus Epiphanes, 288
Antithetic parallelism, 218
Aphek 181, 237, 245
'apiru, 104, 106–7, 148
Apocalyptic literature,
    281–82, 293
Apodictic law, 127
Apries, 270
Arabia, 263
Arabians, 243, 246, 250, 299
Aram, 229
Aramaea, 186, 187, 206, 207,
    228, 229–30, 242, 258
  defeat, 245, 246
  domination of northern
    tribes, 234, 238, 239
  hostility toward Judah, 249
Aramaic language, 22, 230
Araunah, 211
Arbela, 257
Archaeology, 29, 30–32, 98,
    105, 109, 154, 156, 235
Ark, 60–63
Ark of the Covenant, 117,
    142, 151, 160, 181, 182,
    204–5, 215
Artaxerxes I, 289, 291,
    297–99, 301
Artaxerxes II, 291
Asa, 233–34
Asahel, 202
Asaph, 220

311

Asenath, 93
Ashdod, 181, 182
Asher (son of Jacob), 87
Asher (tribe of Israel), 107,
    158, 167
Asherah, 236, 245, 261
Asherim, 162, 163
Ashur-etil–ilani, 267
Ashur-uballit, 268
Ashur-uballit II, 267
Ashurbanipal, 261, 266–67,
    271
Ashurdan III, 252
Asia Minor, 258, 279, 280
Asshur, 267
Asshur-nasirpal II, 228, 235
Asshur-rabi I, 228
Asshur-uballit, 228
Assyria, 228, 229, 230,
    234–35, 238, 244, 247,
    248, 251, 252, 255,
    268, 90
  captivity under, 249, 254
  capture of Manasseh, 261
  defeat by Hezekiah,
    259–61
  demise, 266–7, 272
  overthrow of Hittites, 185,
    186
  rise, 74, 149, 227
  zenith, 257
Assyrian eponym lists, 98, 100
Astronomy, 98
Astyages, 279
Athaliah, 243, 244
Athens, 290
Aton, 103
Atonement, 114, 139
Avaris, 102
Ay, 104
Azariah, 285
Azekah, 270

Baal, 162, 163–64, 166–67,
    176n, 214, 232, 235–36,
    237, 244, 246, 261
Baal of Peor, 125
Baal prophets, 241
Baal-zebub, 239
Baasha, 99, 233–34, 247
Babylonia, 68, 73, 74, 186,
    228, 230, 251, 258, 259,

260, 261, 263, 266, 269,
    275, 279, 288
awakening, 257, 272
captivity, 27, 39
dark ages, 150
fall, 264, 279–80, 286
judgment, 273
law, 128
war against Egypt, 269–70
Babylonian creation and flood
    epics, 267
Balaam, 124–25
Balak, 124–25
Bamah, 213
Barak, 165–66
Baran, 280
Bardiya, 290
Barren wife motif, 86, 180
Baruch, 274
Bashan, 124, 125, 157
Bath-sheba, 207, 211, 221
Battle of Kadesh, 104
Battle of Marathon, 290
Battle of Qarqar, 98
Beer-Sheba, 83
Bel, 276
Belshazzar, 30, 31, 280, 285,
    286–87
Ben-Ammi, 83
Benaiah, 212
Benhadad I, 233–34, 235, 237,
    238, 241, 242
Benhadad II, 245
Benjamin (son of Jacob), 94
Benjamin (tribe of Israel),
    157–58, 176, 187, 191, 217
Berossus, 100
Bethel, 86, 153, 160, 231–32,
    244, 252, 268
Bethlehem, 175, 196, 266
Bezaleel, 119
Bezalel, 214
Bezer, 158
Bilhah, 87, 91
Bit Humri, 235
Bitter Lakes, 116
Black Obelisk, 98, 244
Blood, 113–14, 118, 137, 139,
    141
  scientific significance, 36
Bloody offerings, 138
Boaz, 178–79

Book of the Covenant, 118,
    129
Bronze, 192
Bronze serpent of Moses, 258
Bubaru, 287
Bur-Sagale, 98
Burning bush, 111, 117
Burnt offerings, 139, 141, 182,
    183

Cain, 58
Cainites, 59, 60
Caleb, 122, 157, 158, 164
Cambyses, 290, 292
Camels, 166
Canaan, 67–68, 95, 102,
    147–48
  conquest, 106, 149–50,
    154–56, 160, 183
  date, 39, 105, 107, 109
  corruption, 91–92, 94
  invasion by Philistines,
    168, 175
  settlement, 157
Canaanites, 122, 147, 151,
    154, 159, 160, 165–56
  poetry, 220
  prophets, 189, 241, 253
  religion, 135, 162, 163,
    164, 232, 233, 241
Canon, 17–19, 223, 224
Canon of Ptolemy, 100
Canopy of vapor, 51, 59, 62,
    63, 65
Canyons, formation, 64–65
Captain of the Lord's Host,
    152
Captivity. See Judah (southern
    kingdom), captivity
Carbon 14 dating, 49
Carchemish, 268, 269
Carthaginians, 68
Casuistic law, 127–28
Catastrophism, 66
Ceremonial law, 130, 134–37
Chalcolithic Age, 46
Chariot of fire, 240
Chariots, 116, 159, 166
Chebar canal, 281
Cherubim, 142, 143, 282
Child sacrifice, 261
Chronicles, 217, 261
Chronicler, 28

Index of Authors

Aharoni, Yohanan, 115 n. 38
Albright, W. F., 32 n. 24; 47 n. 4; 75 nn. 3, 6; 81 n. 18; 101 n. 11; 106 n. 20; 107; 108 n. 27; 109 n. 31; 166 n. 23; 191 n. 9; 192 n. 11; 223 n. 47; 227 n. 1; 232 n. 4; 259 n. 3; 280; 303 n. 25
Allis, O. T., 28 n. 23; 70 n. 42; 134 n. 8; 264 n. 15
Alt, Albrecht, 127, 128 n. 5
Anderson, Bernhard W., 27 n. 18; 28 n. 21; 37 n. 30; 115 n. 40; 154 n. 12; 264 n. 16; 296 n. 19
Archer, Gleason L., Jr., 220 n. 40; 221 n. 42; 224; 225 n. 52; 250; 267 n. 21
Ascham, John Bayne, 253 n. 30
Astruc, Jean, 25

Baly, Denis, 40 n. 32; 108 n. 29; 123 n. 49
Barr, James, 32 n. 25
Barton, George A., 223 n. 46
Baumgartner, Walter, 170 n. 25; 219 n. 37
Beckwith, Roger T., 17 n. 3
Beecher, Willis J., 188 n. 5; 189 n. 6; 241 n. 16
Bimson, John J., 110 n. 33
Boling, Robert G., 175 n. 26
Briggs, Charles, 50 n. 13; 115 n. 39
Bright, John, 27 n. 19; 73 n. 1; 76 n. 9; 103 n. 13; 105 n. 18; 108 n. 26; 117 n. 43; 213 n. 24; 227 n. 1; 233 nn. 5, 6; 237 n. 13; 247 n. 26; 257 n. 1; 259 n. 4; 260 n. 5; 279 n. 1; 290 n. 17; 299 n. 23

Brown, Francis, 50 n. 13; 115 n. 39
Bruce, F. F., 24 n. 13; 80 nn. 15, 16; 303 n. 24
Buber, Martin, 79 n. 14; 113 n. 35; 119 n. 45

Calloway, Joseph A., 153 n. 11
Campbell, Edward F., Jr., 47 n. 4; 227
Clark, W. E. LeGros, 55 n. 20
Collier, Donald, 49 n. 8
Craigie, Peter C., 126 n. 51
Cross, Frank M., 120 n. 46
Culver, Robert D., 289 n. 15

de Vaux, Roland, 76 n. 10; 79 n. 13; 132 n. 7; 141 n. 14
Delitzsch, Franz, 60 n. 27; 124 n. 50; 188 n. 4; 200 n. 16; 218 n. 35; 225 n. 51
Driver, S. R., 50 n. 13; 115 n. 39
Driver, G. R., 128 n. 4
Drower, Margaret S., 148 n. 2

Eakin, Frank E., 236
Eichrodt, Walther, 56 n. 22; 194 n. 13
Eissfeldt, Otto, 265 n. 17; 288 n. 13
Eliade, Mircea, 162 n. 18
Enslin, Morton Scott, 36 n. 29

Falkenstein, Adam, 45 n. 1
Foerster, Werner, 303 n. 24
Freedman, David Noel, 100 n. 7
Fritsch, Charles T., 222 n. 45

Garstang, John, 107
Gaster, Theodor H., 155 n. 14

Gibson, J. C. L., 236 n. 11
Glueck, Nelson, 108; 109 n. 30; 216 n. 31; 246 n. 21
Goldingay, John, 286 n. 8
Gordis, Robert, 224 n. 50
Gordon, Cyrus, 85 nn. 20, 21; 86 n. 22; 216 n. 32
Gray, G. B., 218 n. 34
Gray, John, 242 n. 19
Grayson, A. K., 227 n. 1
Green, William Henry, 17 n. 3
Greenberg, Moshe, 106 n. 20
Guillaume, Alfred, 253 n. 31
Gurney, O. R., 104 n. 15; 149 nn. 4, 5; 185 n. 1

Hallo, William W., 46 n. 3; 74 n. 2; 227 n. 1; 229 n. 2; 267 n. 20; 268 n. 22
Harden, Donald B., 182 n. 31; 214 n. 28; 235 n. 9
Harel, Manasseh, 116 n. 42
Harrelson, Walter J., 26 n. 17
Harris, R. Laird, 18 nn. 4, 5
Harrison, R. K., 121 n. 48; 222 n. 44
Hay, Lewis, 116 n. 41
Heizer, Robert, 49 n. 9
Hengstenberg, Ernst, 225 n. 53
Hole, Frank, 49 n. 9
Hopkins, Edward W., 253 n. 33
Hubbard, Robert L., Jr., 178 n. 28
Hummel, Horace D., 281 n. 6
Huxley, Julian, 25
Hyatt, J. Philip, 274 n. 27

Jacobsen, Thorkild, 59 n. 26
Johnson, Aubrey, 253 n. 32
Josephus, Flavius, 15 n. 1; 101 n. 11; 288 n. 12

323

Index of Scripture

4:1—181
4:21–22—181
5:1—181
5:6–7—182
6:3–9—182
6:19—182
7:10—236
7:12—183
7:15–17—183
8–14—187
8–31—187
9:2—187
9:11—189
10:9–12—188
10:22—190
11:4–5—191
12:17–18—191
12:18—236
13:19–22—192
14:39—192
15—192
15:22—193
16–26—194
16:19–23—194
18:1–4—195
18:7—195
18:10—189
19:1–7—195
19:18—196
19:23–24—190
22:1–2—197
23:16–18—196
23:29—197
25:8—198
27–31—198
28:6—145
28:11—200
28:19—200
30:1–2—200
30:24—201

2 Samuel

1:1–24:25—201
1:18—17
1:19–27—202
1–4—201
2:8–9—202
3:12—203
5–10—203
5:3—203
5:6–8—204
5:11–12—204
5:20—163

5:25—204
6:3–7—205
6:12–15—80
6:17—213
6:23—205
7:12–16—206
8:2—207
10:4—207
11–21—207
11:26–27—207
12:1–6—208
12:24—208
13:14—208
14:17—166
14:20—166
14:33—208
15:6—208
16:5–7—212
16:22—209
18:14—209
19:6—209
20:1—210
20:22—210
21:1–9—155
22—212
22:1–24:25—210
23:1–7—212
24:1—210
24:25—211

1 Kings

1:1–2:46—201, 210
2:11—99
2:12—211
2:25—212
2:35—181
2:46—213
3–4—212
3:4—213
3–11—212
4:29–34—220
4:32—222
5–8—214
5:1—214
6:1—99, 105
7:13—214
9:1–9—215
9:10–10:29—215
9:15—216
10:28–29—216
11—216
11:4–8—216
11:13—217

11:14—217
11:23—217
11:26–36—217
11:41—17
11:42—99
12:1–15:26—230
12:1–22:53—230
12:4—230
12:23–24—231
12:29—231
13:1–6—232
13:3—268
14:20—99, 232
14:22–24—233
14:26—233
14:31—233
15:12–14—233
15:17—233
15:20—234
15:25—99
15:27–16:22—234
15:33—99
16:8—99
16:23—99
16:23–22:53—234
16:27—17
16:29—99
17:21–23—235
18—164
19:4—237
19:19—237
20:42—237
22:1—98
22:4—238
22:40—238
22:45—17
22:48—239

2 Kings

1:1–9:6—230
1:1–9:26—234
1:2—239
1:3—163
2:11–12—240
2:21—240
2:24—240
3:1—98
3:4ff.—239
4:34–35—240
4:41—240
4:6—240
5:5—241
5–8—214

5:14—240
5:17–18—242
5:27—240
6:6—240
6:10–11—242
6:18—240
7:6—242
8:7—242
8:13—237
8:16—243
8:28—243
9:6—237, 243
9:6–15:12—244
9:24—99, 243
9:27—243
10:28—244
10:32–33—244
11:1—244
12:18—245
13:21—240
13:24–25—245
14:25—251
15:4—246
15:13–17:41—247
15:19–20—247
15:29—247
15:32—248
16:3–4—248
16:5—248
17—248
18:4—258
18:7—259
18:13–16—259
18:17–19:36—260
18–20—258
20:1—259
20:12–13—260
20:20—259
21:3–7—261
21:8—29
21:10–16—262
22:8—267
23:3—130
23:15—268
23:29—268
23:30—269
23:33—269
24:1—269
24:10–12—269
24:17—270
25:6–7—270
25:22—271
25:27–30—270